COVID-19 and the Tourism Industry

This book offers international perspectives on the economic, social, geopolitical, and environmental implications of COVID-19 on tourism, an unprecedented situation for this sector.

It considers the challenge of making the tourism industry more resilient to such crises and the future sustainability of tourism. Contributions explore the changing dimensions of tourism marketing post-COVID-19; the rising challenges in tourism education and ways to handle the crisis; the impact of the pandemic on tourism governance; and the emerging ethical issues of stakeholders' responsibility.

The book will be useful for researchers, students, and practitioners in the fields of tourism, geography, and crisis management disciplines.

Anukrati Sharma is an Associate Professor and Head of the Department of Commerce and Management, University of Kota, Kota, Rajasthan, India.

Azizul Hassan is a member of the Tourism Consultants Network of the UK Tourism Society.

Priyakrushna Mohanty is an Assistant Professor at the Department of Tourism and Travel Management, Jyoti Nivas College, Bengaluru.

Routledge Insights in Tourism Series

This series provides a forum for cutting edge insights into the latest developments in tourism research. It offers high quality monographs and edited collections that develop tourism analysis at both theoretical and empirical levels.

Millennials, Spirituality and Tourism
Edited by Sandeep Kumar Walia and Aruditya Jasrotia

Tourism, Safety and COVID-19
Security, Digitization and Tourist Behaviour
Salvatore Monaco

COVID-19 and the Tourism Industry
Sustainability, Resilience and New Directions
Edited by Anukrati Sharma, Azizul Hassan, and Priyakrushna Mohanty

For more information about this series, please visit: www.routledge.com/Routledge-Insights-in-Tourism-Series/book-series/RITS

COVID-19 and the Tourism Industry

Sustainability, Resilience and New Directions

**Edited by
Anukrati Sharma, Azizul Hassan,
and Priyakrushna Mohanty**

LONDON AND NEW YORK

First published 2022
by Routledge
4 Park Square, Milton Park, Abingdon, Oxon OX14 4RN

and by Routledge
605 Third Avenue, New York, NY 10158

Routledge is an imprint of the Taylor & Francis Group, an informa business

© 2022 selection and editorial matter, Anukrati Sharma, Azizul Hassan, and Priyakrushna Mohanty; individual chapters, the contributors

The right of Anukrati Sharma, Azizul Hassan, and Priyakrushna Mohanty to be identified as the authors of the editorial material, and of the authors for their individual chapters, has been asserted in accordance with sections 77 and 78 of the Copyright, Designs and Patents Act 1988.

All rights reserved. No part of this book may be reprinted or reproduced or utilised in any form or by any electronic, mechanical, or other means, now known or hereafter invented, including photocopying and recording, or in any information storage or retrieval system, without permission in writing from the publishers.

Trademark notice: Product or corporate names may be trademarks or registered trademarks, and are used only for identification and explanation without intent to infringe.

British Library Cataloguing-in-Publication Data
A catalogue record for this book is available from the British Library

Library of Congress Cataloging-in-Publication Data
A catalog record has been requested for this book

ISBN: 978-1-032-07502-0 (hbk)
ISBN: 978-1-032-07512-9 (pbk)
ISBN: 978-1-003-20746-7 (ebk)

DOI: 10.4324/9781003207467

Typeset in Times New Roman
by codeMantra

Contents

List of figures   ix
List of tables   xi
List of contributors   xiii

Introduction   1
ANUKRATI SHARMA, AZIZUL HASSAN AND
PRIYAKRUSHNA MOHANTY

PART ONE
COVID-19 and Tourism: Introduction   5

1 **The Impact of COVID-19 on Tourism Demand and Supply**   7
ADEJUMOKE ABIOSE AND HOSEA OLAYIWOLA PATRICK

2 **Coronavirus through the Eyes of Hospitality Customers**   19
GÜRKAN ÇALIŞKAN, EMRAH YAŞARSOY, AND HÜSEYIN PAMUKÇU

3 **The Bright Side of COVID-19 in the Context of Tourism: Models of Wellness Tourism and Purposeful Travel Drive the Way Forward**   37
YUE WANG AND LAURA ELL

4 **The Effect of COVID-19 Pandemic on Tourism and Hospitality Industry – A Review**   58
ANUKRATI SHARMA AND SHRUTI ARORA

PART TWO
COVID-19 and Tourism Marketing Sustainability — 71

5 Marketing and Demarketing Strategies for Hotel Operation under Epidemics and Pandemics — 73
MARIA JOSÉ MAGALHÃES AND SUSANA MARQUES

6 Futurology of Ethical Tourism Digital & Social Media Marketing Post COVID-19 — 92
BRIGHTON NYAGADZA AND FARAI CHIGORA

7 Rebranding Destinations for Sustainable Tourism Recovery Post COVID-19 Crisis — 109
ZANETE GARANTI, JOHN VIOLARIS, GALINA BERJOZKINA AND IORDANIS KATEMLIADIS

PART THREE
Tourism Education and Research for Tourism Sustainability — 125

8 Why Do We Teach Tourism? — 127
JOHAN R. EDELHEIM

9 Students Shaping Their Future: Virtual Reality Interactive Exercise to Engage in for Learning — 145
NURIA RECUERO VIRTO

PART FOUR
Ethics and Responsibilities in Tourism Management Post COVID-19 Pandemic — 161

10 Ethics and Responsibility in Tourism – the Impact of COVID-19 — 163
HAROLD GOODWIN

11 The Importance of Tourism Security and Safety after COVID-19 — 179
ÖZGÜR YAYLA, ALI SOLUNOĞLU AND HÜSEYIN KELEŞ

12 Defining Responsibilities of Tourists in the Post-COVID-19 Period 190
ANILA THOMAS

13 Applied Ethics in Post-COVID-19 Destination Management 210
JORDI ARCOS-PUMAROLA, MARTA CONILL-TETUÀ AND
NÚRIA GUITART-CASALDERREY

PART FIVE
COVID-19 and Tourism Governance 223

14 Impact of COVID-19 Pandemic on the Tourism Industry in Sri Lanka: The Dilemmas of Industry Sustainability 225
R. S. S. W ARACHCHI AND W. K. A. C GNANAPALA

15 Managing Events Tourism Sustainability Post-COVID-19: Exploring the New Realities 239
PRIYAKRUSHNA MOHANTY, PINAZ TIWARI AND
NIMIT CHOWDHARY

16 The Impact of COVID-19 Pandemic on Small Tourism Enterprises in Pakistan 252
KALSOOM B. AND MEHTAB ALAM

17 Perspectives in the Strategic Management of Destinations in the Post-COVID Period 267
DÁLIA LIBERATO, BEATRIZ LIMBADO, BRUNO SOUSA AND
PEDRO LIBERATO

Index 289

Figures

1.1	Growth in the global tourism industry (2000–2020)	10
2.1	Change in monthly tourist rates compared to 2019 (2020)	20
2.2	Changes in monthly tourist numbers in 2019–2020	20
2.3	Change in tourist rates by the region compared to 2019 (2020)	20
2.4	Expanded scenarios of the WTO	21
2.5	Map of the number of cases according to the WHO (data on the date of March 20, 2021) (World Health Organization, 2021e)	23
2.6	Map of death number according to the WHO (data on the date of March 20, 2021) (World Health Organization, 2021e)	23
2.7	Number of COVID-19 cases in Turkey (URL 6) (data on the date of March 21, 2021)	24
2.8	Number of deaths caused by COVID-19 in Turkey (World Health Organization, 2021f) (data on the date of March 21, 2021)	25
2.9	Number of tourist arrivals to Turkey by the year (from January to November 2020) (URL-2)	26
2.10	Code system	29
2.11	Vacation decision – COVID-19 effect (code map)	29
2.12	Precautions are taken by the hotel (code map)	30
2.13	Sense of confidence (code map)	31
2.14	Activities (code map)	31
2.15	Precautions taken by the country (code map)	32
3.1	Ecotourism continuum comparted to a new wellness tourism continuum	40
3.2	Location map of Heilongjiang province	43
3.3	Location map of Wudalianchi UNESCO Global Geopark	45
3.4	Geopark attractions map	46
3.5	Open space thermal springs in Geopark	51
3.6	Semi-open space volcanic stone sunbathing	52
4.1	Characteristics of tourism and hospitality industry	60
4.2	Sustainable tourism and hospitality	66
5.1	Room revenue as a function of both the number of single rooms (x-axis) and of the maximum rate of guest occupancy (y-axis)	79

x *Figures*

5.2	Room revenue as a function of the number of single rooms (*x*-axis) at 10%, 25%, and 40% reductions in guest capacity	79
5.3	Summary of Marketing and Demarketing strategies	88
6.1	Ethical tourism digital and social media marketing decision making framework	95
9.1	Proposed model	149
15.1	A sustainable approach for managing events in the post-COVID-19 phase	246
16.1	Conceptual framework	254

Tables

2.1	Distribution of the number of cases by regions	23
2.2	Distribution of the number of cases by country	24
3.1	Visits to Heilongjiang province by foreign nationals (person-times)	48
3.2	Tourist source market for Heilongjiang province	49
4.1	New dimensions pre and post COVID-19	65
5.1	Room revenue as a function of both the number of single rooms (x-axis) and of the maximum rate of guest occupancy (y-axis)	79
8.1	Types of Nordic HEs	131
8.2	Number and type of Nordic THEs	137
8.3	Faculty belonging of Nordic THEs	137
8.4	Research intensive institutions offering THE programs, number and percentage of total	138
8.5	Languages Nordic THEs are offered in	139
9.1	Profile of respondents ($N = 21$)	150
9.2	Descriptive analysis	151
9.3	Reliability and convergent validity of the final measurement model	152
9.4	Measurement model discriminant validity	152
9.5	Evaluation of the estimated models	153
9.6	Hypotheses testing	153
12.1	Different codes and its identified themes	194
12.2	Peri-pandemic travel experiences/responsibilities	196
12.3	Various sectors affected by COVID-19 pandemic	198
12.4	Perception about growth of domestic tourism	199
12.5	Perception about sustainability and accountability in practices	202
12.6	Adopting practices for the sustainability of rural tourism	203
16.1	Qualitative Data Analysis	258
17.1	Theoretical background of the interview guide	275
17.2	Areas most affected by COVID-19	277
17.3	Tourism products and services with decreasing demand	279

xii *Tables*

17.4 Evidence on the impact on different phases of confinement   280
17.5 Summary of evidence on modification of the typology
       of demand   281
17.6 Evidence to the future perspectives for the tourism sector   282

Contributors

Editors

Dr Azizul Hassan is a member of the Tourism Consultants Network of the UK Tourism Society. Dr Hassan has been working for the tourism industry as a consultant, academic, and researcher for over 20 years. His research interest areas are technology-supported marketing for tourism and hospitality, immersive technology applications in the tourism and hospitality industry, and technology-influenced marketing suggestions for sustainable tourism and hospitality industry in developing countries. Dr Hassan has authored over 150 articles and book chapters in leading tourism outlets. He is also part of the editorial team of 25 book projects from Routledge, Springer, CAB International, and Emerald Group Publishing Limited. He is a regular reviewer of a number of international journals.

Priyakrushna Mohanty is an Assistant Professor at the Department of Tourism and Travel Management, Jyoti Nivas College, Bengaluru. He is a former U.G.C. Senior Research Fellow at the Department of Tourism Studies, Pondicherry University, India. Mr Mohanty is an awardee of the prestigious Travel Corporation (India) Gold Medal for his outstanding performance in Master's degree in Tourism Studies from Pondicherry University, India. He also holds a Master's degree in Commerce along with three PG Diploma Degrees in Rural Development, Research Methodology, and Teaching Skills. Mr Mohanty has served the Indian Railway Catering and Tourism Corporation Ltd. for two years following which he was recruited as a Guest Faculty in the Department of Tourism Studies, Pondicherry University. He has published more than 20 articles and chapters in both international and national journals and edited books. He has presented more than 25 papers in both international and national conferences to his name and has been invited by a number of national and international institutes as guest speaker. Mr Mohanty is passionate about academic areas of Research Methodology, Tourism Sustainability,

Sustainable Livelihood, Events Tourism, Technology, and Tourism along with Gender issues in Tourism Development.

Dr Anukrati Sharma is an Associate Professor and Head of the Department of Commerce and Management, University of Kota, Kota, Rajasthan, India. In 2015, she received a Research Award from the University Grants Commission(UGC), New Delhi, for her project "Analysis of the Status of Tourism in Hadoti and Shekhawati Region/Circuit (Rajasthan): Opportunities, Challenges, and Future Prospects." Her doctorate from the University of Rajasthan is in Tourism Marketing, and she completed her dissertation research on Tourism in Rajasthan – Progress & Prospects. She has two postgraduate degree specialties – one in International Business (Master of International Business) and the other in Business Administration (Master of Commerce). Her special interest areas are Tourism, Tourism Marketing, Strategic Management, and International Business Management. She has edited books such as *Maximizing Business Performance and Efficiency through Intelligent Systems*, under IGI Global, *Sustainable Tourism Development: Futuristic Approaches* under Apple Academic Press, USA under the series Advances in Hospitality and Tourism, *Tourism Events in Asia: Marketing and Development* under Routledge, USA, *Future of Tourism: An Asian Perspective*, under Springer, Singapore, *Overtourism as Destination Risk: Impacts and Solutions* under Emerald Publishing U.K., *Over-tourism, Technology Solutions and Decimated Destinations* under Springer, Singapore, *Event Tourism in Asian Countries: Challenges and Prospects* under Apple Academic Press, USA, *The Emerald Handbook of ICT in Tourism and Hospitality* under Emerald Publishing U.K., S*ustainable Destination Branding and Marketing: Strategies for Tourism Development* under CABI. She has an authored book on *Event Management and Marketing Theory, Practical Approaches and Planning*. Another book authored by her is titled *International Best Practice in Event Management* published by United Kingdom Event Industry Academy Ltd. and Prasetiya Mulya Publishing, Indonesia. She is at present editing books on *The Emerald Handbook of Destination Recovery in Tourism and Hospitality*, Emerald Publishing, UK, *Festivals and Event Tourism: Building Resilience and Promoting Sustainability* to be published under CABI, UK. *Event Tourism and Sustainable Community Development: Advances, Effects and Implications* to be published under Apple Academic Press, USA, and *Strategic Tourism Planning for Communities: Restructuring and Rebranding* under Nova Science Publishers, USA. A member of 17 professional bodies, she has attended a number of national and international conferences and presented 45 papers. She has been invited to talks/lectures/panel discussions by different countries such as Sri Lanka, Nepal, Uzbekistan, and Turkey.

Contributors

Adejumoke Abiose is currently enrolled as a doctoral candidate at the Department of Cultural and Heritage Tourism, University of KwaZulu-Natal, South Africa. Adejumoke is a doctoral student with research interests in Sustainable Development, Destination Branding and Tourism Marketing, Hospitality Management, Tourism Development, Research Methodology, and Community-Based Tourism.

Mehtab Alam is a PhD scholar, from University of Cyberjaya, Selangor Malaysia. As a core area of Management and Public Policy; Soft Image and Image Development of Pakistan through tourism development are the primary part of research completed for degree of Master of Philosophy (M. PHIL). He obtained degree in Master of Arts in English Language & Literature and also holds Bachelor of Education from Allama Iqbal Open University, Islamabad. In addition to this, he serves in various Public and Private Institutions those include the National Assembly, Parliament of Pakistan as Research Associate and Ministry of Foreign Affairs, Pakistan on assignments/tasks of image development. As a writing specialist he also served in Skyscrapers Pvt Ltd. Over the years, his interest in research is developed and allow him to keep in touch with the advancement in research on various topics and subjects of management. These incorporated the field of Social, Communication, & Management Sciences, or issues of international concerns like Public Diplomacy, Foreign Policy and key changes brought about trade and business forb climate. During the time Mehtab Alam has the opportunity to interact with highly qualified and experienced individuals from various backgrounds. Various articles/chapters are in process of publications.

R. S. S. W Arachchi is a Senior Lecturer in Tourism at the Department of Tourism Management, Faculty of Management Studies, Sabaragamuwa University of Sri Lanka. His research focuses on Eco-tourism, Cave Tourism and Sustainable Tourism. He has involved in various administrative activities in the University and contributed his service for various government and private sector projects in Tourism.

Jordi Arcos-Pumarola holds a PhD in Education and Society from the University of Lleida, a Master Degree in Innovation in Tourism Management, specialization in Cultural and Natural Heritage Management by Barcelona, School of Tourism, Hospitality and Gastronomy CETT – UB, and a Bachelor in Philosophy at the University of Barcelona. He is a member of the Research Group on Tourism, Culture, and Territory at CETT-UB, where he also works as a lecturer on cultural tourism and tourism research methods. His two main research lines are cultural and literary tourism, and ethics in tourism.

Shruti Arora, PhD, is currently working as a guest faculty in the Department of Commerce and Management, University of Kota, Kota, Rajasthan, India. She has over 10 years of experience in education. Her core subjects are marketing, general management, international business management, and customer relationship management. She has published several research papers in international refereed journals and one chapter in edited book in the Routledge Advances in Event Research Series in 2018. She has also authored the book *Event Management and Marketing: Theory, Practical Approaches and Planning*.

Galina Berjozkina is a Senior Lecturer at City Unity College Nicosia. She is a PhD student at the University of Strathclyde, Department of Work Employment and Organization, engaged in research on seasonal employees' work performance in the tourism industry. She is lecturing courses on Tourism Planning and Development, Hospitality Animation, and Introduction to Hospitality amongst others. Her academic interests include tourism, hospitality, and management. She has attended several academic conferences and has published a book on Destination Management.

Gürkan Çalışkan started his master education in the Department of Tourism Management at Gazi University in 2016 and graduated in 2019. He began his academic career in 2019 as a research assistant in the Department of Tourism Management at Kastamonu University. In the same year, he started his doctorate education in the Department of Tourism Management at Kastamonu University. His academic studies are focused on virtual, augmented reality, and technology in tourism. He is improving himself on quantitative and qualitative analysis methods. He mainly conducts his research with qualitative analysis methods. He generally uses Maxqda and VOSviewer analysis tools for qualitative research. He has completed some courses on qualitative analysis methods and quantitative analysis methods.

Farai Chigora has a Doctorate in Business Administration from University of KwaZulu-Natal (South Africa), a Senior Lecturer in the Faculty of Commerce and a Dean of Postgraduate Studies at the Catholic University of Zimbabwe. He is a tourism branding specialist with interest in destination branding, strategic marketing, business research and related business areas which he has authored in various refereed international journals.

Nimit Chowdhary is an engineer and holds MBA and PhD degrees in Management. He has more than 26 years of postgraduate teaching and research experience. He has been a Full Professor close to 14 years serving at Mizoram University, IITTM (Gwalior, Noida and Nellore) and currently serving as the Head of Department of Tourism and Hospitality Management at Jamia Millia Islamia, New Delhi. Recently, Arizona State University accorded him the honor of Adjunct Professorship. He is a recipient of AICTE Career Award for Young Teachers; SIDA Fellowship, Sweden; Guest Scholarship, Sweden; Linnaeus Palme Exchange Programme Grants, Sweden; PIMG Research Excellence Award, Gwalior; Scholars' Grant (EMTM), Erasmus Mundus, Europe among others. Recently, he was chosen for prestigious LEAP Programme at Oxford University. His research has focused on tourism, travel, service experiences, and now transformation. He is a referred researcher in many international journals. He has researched for UGC, ICSSR, AICTE, and Ministry of Tourism, Government of India worth around US$ 5 million. He has supervised 15 PhDs, authored eight books, edited two books, and contributed more than 116 papers.

Marta Conill-Tetuà holds a PhD in Didactics of Heritage, Arts and Cultural Tourism from the University of Barcelona. She is currently working for the Vallès Occidental county council on the tourist management of the territory, and is particularly involved in the gastronomy tourism project "Xarxa de Productes de la Terra". Her main research interests are cultural tourism and cultural heritage.

Johan R. Edelheim worked for more than a decade globally in the hospitality and tourism industries before becoming a secondary and tertiary educator in the same fields. He now teaches at the Graduate School of International Media, Communication, and Tourism Studies at Hokkaido University. Prof. Edelheim has diplomas and degrees from education, philosophy, cultural studies, hospitality, and business. Behind most of his research lies a deeply rooted aim for humanism and equality. His studies focus in different ways on tourism, hospitality, leisure, education, and society. Prof. Edelheim chairs the Tourism Education Futures Initiative (TEFI) network.

Laura Ell is a spa and wellness tourism consultant with a two-decade track record of successfully advancing tourism enterprises and destinations. Her assignments have been through agencies such as UNWTO, WWF, World Bank, USAID, and UNDP as well as the private sector. Her work has yielded award-winning resorts and destinations as they appeal to the new market of visitors seeking authentic, healthful travel. Laura's research on Indigenous-inspired spa travel was nominated for the Governor General of Canada's Gold Academic Award and she helps spas respectfully integrate ritual into spa for more immersive experiences. Laura has been featured on CNN Travel and lectures for numerous institutions and is a faculty member at Mount Royal University in Calgary, Canada. Laura is also a certified EDGE Expert which is a green building program through the IFC, an initiative endorsed by the World Bank.

Zanete Garanti is a PhD holder and Associate Professor in City Unity College Nicosia, Cyprus. She is lecturing Marketing and Management courses and is actively researching marketing topics on branding, social media marketing, and influencer marketing. Her recent studies are on travel and tourism influencers, brand personality, loyalty and equity on social media networks, e-referral, brand image, and personality of Iran as a destination amongst others. Her work is published in internationally recognized books and journals.

Harold Goodwin has worked on four continents with local communities, their governments, and the inbound and outbound tourism industry. He is a Professor Emeritus and Responsible Tourism Director at the Institute of Place Management at Manchester Metropolitan University, Managing Director of the Responsible Tourism Partnership and adviser to the World Travel Market on its Responsible Tourism Programme at WTM London, which attracts 2,000 participants each year, and WTM Africa and Latin America and Arabian Travel Market. He chairs the panels of judges for the World Responsible Tourism Awards and the other Awards in the family, Africa, India, and Latin America.

W. K. A. C Gnanapala is a Professor in Tourism Management attached to the Dept. of Tourism Management, Sabaragamuwa University of Sri Lanka. Currently, he is working as the Vice Chancellor (Acting) of the University and the Dean of the Faculty of Management Studies. Further, he is the predecessor Head, Department of Tourism Management, Programme Coordinator of the MSc. in Ayurvedic Hospital Management degree programme. He obtained his first degree, B.Sc. Tourism Management, form the Sabaragamuwa University of Sri Lanka and the M.Sc. in Management from the University of Sri Jayewardenepura. He completed his Doctoral degree in Tourism Management at the School of Business, Xiamen University, P.R. China. His research interests include consumer behavior in tourism, travel motivation & satisfaction, wildlife tourism, sustainable tourism planning & development, destination management and marketing etc. He has published his research works as nearly 20 books and book chapters, more than 30 research articles in refereed and indexed journals, more than 50 international conference presentations.

Núria Guitart-Casalderrey graduated in Tourism and Official Master Degree in Innovation in Tourism Management, specialization in Tourism Management of Urban Destinations by Barcelona, School of Tourism, Hospitality and Gastronomy CETT – UB. PhD Student in Geography. Territorial Planning and Environmental Management from the University of Barcelona. She is a researcher of the Research Group on Tourism, Culture, and Territory at CETT-UB. Her main research lines are urban tourism management and tourism governance.

Iordanis Katemliadis is a Senior Lecturer at City Unity College Nicosia with more than ten years of teaching and industry experience. He is actively researching destination management organizations, destination branding, and destination marketing. He is a PhD candidate at the University of the Aegean and he is lecturing Destination Management, Hospitality Marketing, and Events Management among others.

Hüseyin Keleş is a Lecturer at Manavgat Tourism Faculty in Akdeniz University, Turkey. He received his Master's degree at Travel Management and Tourism Guidance from Selcuk University in 2017. Currently, he is a PhD candidate in field of Tourism Management at Necmettin Erbakan University, Turkey. His primary research interest involves tourism security, festival management, destination management, and the interactions between tourist and local people.

Dália Liberato, PhD Tourism, Tourism Professor at Polytechnic Institute of Porto, School of Hospitality and Tourism, Portugal. Coordinator of Tourism Activities Management Degree. Researcher in CiTUR, IELT | Nova FCSH and CEI – ISCAP (Portugal).

Pedro Liberato, PhD Tourism, Tourism Professor at Polytechnic Institute of Porto, School of Hospitality and Tourism, Portugal. Coordinator of Master Program – Tourism Management, and Head of Tourism and Leisure Department. Researcher in CiTUR, IELT | Nova FCSH and CEI – ISCAP (Portugal).

Beatriz Limbado, Master in Hotel Management – Sales and Marketing, Researcher in Polytechnic Institute of Porto, School of Hospitality and Tourism, Portugal.

Maria José Magalhães is pursuing her PhD in tourism in the University of Aveiro, after obtaining a PhD in Textile Engineering, a MSc in Environmental Sciences (Specialization in Environmental Quality) and a degree in Textile Engineering, having graduated as top of her class, all from the University of Minho. She started her academic career at University of Minho (1996) and later served as Assistant Professor at the Faculty of Philosophy and Social Sciences of the Catholic University of Portugal, where she lectured undergraduate and graduate courses in the fields of Quality and Organization Development, Mathematics and Tourism. She is an Associate Researcher at GOVCOPP (Governance, Competitiveness and Public Policies) research center at University of Aveiro amd was a member of 2C2T (Centre for Textile Science and Technology), at University of Minho, where she was involved in national and international research projects. Her current research topics focus on personal and organizational safety and security materials and processes; and regional sustainable development through Tourism.

Susana Marques completed her Ph.D. in Marketing at the University of Stirling (Scotland) with a scholarship from the Foundation for Science and Technology. She has a Master in Business Administration, with a specialization in Marketing, from University of Minho (Portugal) and a Graduate Certificate in Research Methodologies from the University of

Strathclyde (Scotland). She initiated her academic career at University of Minho (1997) and is, since 2014, a faculty member and Program Director of the Marketing undergraduate degree at the Higher Institute for Accountancy and Administration – University of Aveiro. Her research focus on the fields of Relational Marketing, Tourism, Social Marketing, and Critical Marketing.

Priyakrushna Mohanty is an Assistant Professor at the Department of Tourism and Travel Management, Jyoti Nivas College, Bengaluru, India. He is also a U.G.C. Senior Research Fellow at the Department of Tourism Studies, Pondicherry University, India. He is an awardee of the prestigious Travel Corporation (India) Gold Medal for his outstanding performance in Master's degree in Tourism Studies from Pondicherry University, India. He also holds a Master's degree in Commerce along with three PG Diploma Degrees in Rural Development, Research Methodology, and Teaching Skills. Mr Mohanty has served the Indian Railway Catering and Tourism Corporation Ltd. for two years following which he was recruited as a Guest Faculty in the Department of Tourism Studies, Pondicherry University. He has published more than 15 articles and chapters in both international and national journals and edited books. Mr Mohanty is passionate about academic areas of Tourism Sustainability, Sustainable Livelihood, Technology, and Tourism along with Gender issues in Tourism Development.

Brighton Nyagadza is a full time digital marketing lecturer at Marondera University of Agricultural Sciences and Technology (MUAST), Zimbabwe, an Associate of The Chartered Institute of Marketing (CIM), United Kingdom, Power Member of the Digital Marketing Institute (DMI), Ireland, Dublin, and Member of the Marketers Association of Zimbabwe (MAZ). His research expertise revolves on corporate storytelling for branding, public relations, marketing metrics, financial services marketing, digital marketing, and educational marketing. He has published in several reputable referred journals such as *Cogent Business & Management, Cogent Social Sciences, Taylor & Francis* (United Kingdom), *The Marketing Review (TMR)* (Scotland), *Journal of Digital & Media Policy (JDMP)* (Bristol), *Journal of Global Economics, Management and Business Research (JGEMBR)* (United Kingdom), *Retail and Marketing Review (RMR) (UNISA)* (South Africa), *European Journal of Business and Management Research (EJMBR)*, and *Africanus Journal of Development Studies (AJDS)* (UNISA Press).

Hosea Olayiwola Patrick holds a PhD in Political Science from the University of KwaZulu Natal, South Africa. He is at this time a Postdoctoral fellow and lecturer in the School of Built Environment and Development Studies of the same institution. Patrick is a transdisciplinary research scholar with research interest in Public Policy, Security, Peace and

Conflict, Environmental Politics, Political Economy, International Relations, Area Studies, Research Methodology, and Sustainability Research.

Hüseyin Pamukçu received a Master's degree from the Department of Business Administration of the Institute of Social Sciences at Afyon Kocatepe University. In 2017, he received his PhD from the Department of Business Administration of the Institute of Social Sciences at Sakarya University. He started to work as Research Assistant in 2013; Faculty Member as Assistant Professor in 2018 at Tourism and Hotel Management Department of Tourism Faculty in Kastamonu University. Currently a member of Kastamonu University Faculty of Tourism, Pamukçu has contributed numerous international and national research papers (articles, papers, book chapters, chapters in newspapers and magazines, etc.) to the literature. Pamukçu is invited to some international organizations as a speaker. He is married with one child.

Ali Solunoğlu is an Assistant Professor at Balıkesir University in Turkey. He graduated from Gazi University in 2010. He completed his Master's degree in Tourism Management Education in 2013 from Gazi University and his PhD degree in Gastronomy and Culinary Arts from the same university in 2018. He works as a project manager and project staff in various projects supported TUBİTAK and other public institutions. Basic fields of study include tourism marketing, gastronomy and culinary arts, street food, and entrepreneurship trainings.

Bruno Sousa, PhD Marketing and Strategy, is a Professor in Polytechnic Institute of Cavado and Ave (IPCA, Portugal), Head of Master Program – Tourism Management. Researcher at CiTUR and Applied Management Research Unit (UNIAG), Portugal.

Kalsoom B. is Assistant Professor at Centre for Policy Studies, COMSATS University Pakistan. Key Competent Areas in Research are evidence based opportunity of Public services, inequality, explicit planning of public facilities at regional and local level – Big data, Urban Sustainability, Foresight & Public Policy – Public Sector Governance, Public Management & Reforms – Governance, inter-provincial & Local Government – Public Services Ethics, Social Equity, Crowdsourcing, Social Innovation in Public Sector – behavioral insights in Public Sector, Outsourcing, Collaborative Management. She has more than 15 years of extensive experience in teaching and research. Her recent research findings appear in various International, National Journals and conference proceedings on issues of public sector reforms, public Policy, governance, sustainable Management and foreign affairs of China in higher education.

Pinaz Tiwari is a research scholar in the Department of Tourism and Hospitality in Jamia Millia Islamia, India. She has worked in the tourism sector for two years. She has expertise in customer management and has been involved in travel agents' capacity development projects in the organization. She has done her graduation in Commerce from Delhi University and completed her MBA in Tourism with specialization in International Tourism Business. She looks forward to making a career in teaching and creating a difference in the tourism industry with her research works. Her interest areas are in tourism marketing, destination management, tourism education, stakeholders' capacity development, and responsible tourism. She has contributed different chapters related to overtourism and tourism education in different books under well-known publications.

Anila Thomas is an Associate Professor and Head in the Department of Tourism and Travel Management at Jyoti Nivas College Autonomous, Bangalore, Karnataka. A very passionate researcher and an academician, Dr Thomas has a long teaching experience of almost 21 years. She has presented many research-based papers at both International and national conferences and widely published in both journals and books. She completed her PhD thesis in Tourism Management in 2012 from Mother Teresa Women's University, Kodaikanal, Tamil Nadu. Her research interests include Historicity of various Tourism destinations, Destination Planning and Policy-making, Women's contributions in the field of Ayurvedic Medical Tourism, and Community involvement for Sustaining Tourism Resources.

John Violaris is a Professor of Economics and Management at the Department of Business Administration at the City Unity College Nicosia and acts as the Director of Academic Programs of the College. He also lectures distance learning courses at the Frederick, Neapolis and European Universities. He has earned a BA in Economics from the American University of Beirut and an MSc in International Management and a PhD in Economics from Kensington University. He has been lecturing modules in Economics and Management since 1978 at a number of Colleges and Universities, among others: the Frederick Institute of Technology, the Frederick University (where he has also served as its first Dean of the School of Economic Sciences and Administration), the Intercollege, the Ledra College, the Alexander College, the University of Nicosia, the Neapolis and the European University, as well as the Mediterranean Institute of Management (MIM). He is the author, among other publications, of a unique, bilingual textbook in Economics and the co-author of chapters in three books. He has also published and/or presented his research work at international conferences and scientific journals.

Nuria Recuero Virto is currently employed as Assistant Professor at Universidad Complutense de Madrid. She is now in the Deanship of the Faculty of Commerce and Tourism, as Delegate for the Dean for Institutional Communication and Digital Transformation. She was awarded a Post Doctoral (2014–2018) and Predoctoral Scholarship (2010-2014). Due to this background, her specific areas of interest are: tourism marketing, employer branding and neuromarketing. She was finalist of FITUR's awards for best doctoral thesis (2013). Her research has been published in journals such as Journal of Destination Marketing & Management, Journal of Hospitality and Tourism Management, Tourism Review, among others.

Yue Wang is deputy-director of Technology Innovation Research Center on National Territory of Heilongjiang Provincial Institute of Urban Planning, Survey and Design. The main research direction includes healing gardens, wellness tourism, cultural heritage conservation, and hollowing phenomenon of rural areas. The number of published papers is nearly ten. She has given lectures on healing garden through web meetings and the awards include the 1st prize of the Provincial Excellent Urban and Rural Planning Award, 2018 World Golden Award of FIABCI World Prix d'Excellence Awards on Heritage (restoration/conservation) category, and Honorable Award of 2018 UNESCO Asia-Pacific Awards for Cultural Heritage Conservation. In 2019, she worked with UNWTO as the leader of translation team for Heilongjiang Inclusive Tourism Development Plan and Ice and Snow Tourism Plan.

Emrah Yaşarsoy is a research assistant of tourism faculty at Kastamonu University/Turkey. His research interests include tourism marketing, destination branding, and destination management. He has more than ten published articles, papers and books. He has been teaching International Hospitality Management, Meeting and Congress Management, Tourism Management and Effective Communication Technics for two years. He is currently working on some new articles and book chapters regarding tourism. Emrah received his Master's degree from Bournemouth University in 2014, where he studied as a government scholar and then he has graduated his philosophy of doctorate at Kastamonu University in 2019.

Özgür Yayla is an Assistant Professor at Manavgat Tourism Faculty in Akdeniz University, Turkey. He received his Master's degree in Tourism Management and PhD degree in Recreation Management from Gazi University. His primary research interests involve recreational activities, service quality, and the interaction between residents and tourists in destinations.

Introduction

Anukrati Sharma, Azizul Hassan and Priyakrushna Mohanty

COVID-19 has become an unprecedented threat to the global tourism industry, and exceptional problems like these require extraordinary responses. The aim of this book is to be one of the solutions, i.e. it will try to assess the impacts of COVID-19 on different spheres of tourism and suggest solutions that can put the sector back on track. The book provides a comprehensive analysis of the interrelated topics regarding COVID-19 and the global tourism industry. In this book, readers will gain insight into the economic, social, and environmental implications of COVID-19 for the travel and tourism industry. Further, issues about ethics and the responsibility of stakeholders in the Post COVID-19 scenario have been discussed at length. This book is essential from many aspects, especially about the varied positive outcomes of the COVID-19 pandemic. The focus of this book is on how the tourism and hospitality industry can recover from the negative impacts of COVID-19. In order to speed up the recovery and redesign of the tourism industry, there is a need to push many new and innovative marketing ideas. In the book, the suggestions for recovery from the COVID-19 pandemic are discussed exclusively.

The book contains five sections: the first section contains an introduction, effects, and impacts of the COVID-19. The second part of the book discusses the tourism marketing strategies aimed at sustaining the tourism business during and after COVID-19. This section of the book discusses marketing, de-marketing strategies, ethical issues in social media marketing, and rebranding strategies for sustainable tourism. A central focus of the third part of the book is how education and research play a vital role in educating the community about the scope of tourism studies, why tourism studies are important and how the study of tourism can promote learning and shape the future of students while preparing them for managing crisis situations. The fourth part of the book discusses an important aspect of tourism, namely ethics and responsibilities in tourism management during a crisis situation like COVID-19. This section of the book contains wonderful chapters emphasizing the importance of tourist safety post-COVID and clearly defining the responsibilities of tourists. The fifth and last part of the book provides a detailed analysis of COVID-19 and Tourism Governance.

DOI: 10.4324/9781003207467-1

A plethora of topics are included in the fifth part, including how small tourism businesses will survive in a post-COPID-19 era, how to manage local events, and what role destinations will play in strategic management of the destinations. In total, there are 17 chapters in the book. The book highlights contributions from all corners of the world and hence, provides the readers with a holistic view.

In the first chapter of the book, the authors Adejumoke Abiose and Hosea Patrick outline tourism supply and demand. COVID-19 has a severe impact on demand and supply as well as a rapid decline in jobs, according to the authors. In the chapter, the authors suggest policies and planning for protecting Small and Medium Enterprises (SMEs).

Chapter 2 by Hüseyin Pamukçu, Gürkan Çalışkan, and Emrah Yaşarsoy titled "Impact of COVID-19 on Hotel Industry: Emerging Issues and Challenges" provides a positive insight towards the decrease of the adverse effects of COVID-19 on the hospitality industry. The authors used the MAXQDA program and thematic analysis method to draw the conclusion.

"The Bright side of COVID-19 in the Context of Tourism" is the chapter number three authored by Yue Wang and Laura Ell who show hopes for the tourism sector. The authors discussed the current and ongoing management along with theoretical and applied tourism planning and execution. The chapter is quite aligned with SDGs.

Chapter 4 by Anukrati Sharma and Shruti Arora which is titled "The Effect of COVID-19 Pandemic on Tourism and Hospitality Industry – A Review" is all about the suggestions for a speedy revival and recovery of the economy. The chapter analyzes the impacts of COVID-19 on the tourism and hospitality industries and offers recommendations for the speedy recovery and sustainability of both industries.

Maria José Magalhães and Susana Marques authored a chapter entitled "Marketing/Demarketing Strategies for Sustainability of Hotel Operations" that introduced innovative management tools for stratifying marketing so that revenues could be maximized and risk was minimized.

Brighton Nyagadza and Farai Chigora discuss ethical digital marketing strategies in their Chapter 6, titled "Futurology of Ethical Tourism: Digital and Social Media Marketing for Sustainable Tourism Post COVID". A critical analysis was provided on the ethics of influence, privacy ethics, and representation ethics. They also discussed Accelerated Mobile Pages (AMP), Micro Vlogging, Voice Search, Blogging, and Social Media Marketing.

"Rebranding of Tourist Destinations to Drive Tourism Recovery and Sustainability – Post COVID-19 Period" is Chapter 7 by Zanete Garanti, John Violaris, Galina Berjozkina, and Iordanis Katemliadis explained how rebranding and repositioning destinations are crucial for sustainable tourism recovery after COVID-19, as tourism has to pursue all tourism models to gain competitive advantage. There is no doubt that travel after COVID-19 will and should be more responsible, and destinations that rebuild their image and rebrand themselves towards safe, sustainable and transformed tourism experiences will regain travelers' trust and activity levels.

Chapter 8 by Johan R. Edelheim focused on one of the most important aspects of tourism education. The chapter titled "Why do We Teach Tourism" analyzes why tourism has been taught in higher education institutions. The author presented the newness of tourism education by drawing attention to the critical matter dealing with tourism courses that are no longer of benefit to students.

Chapter 9 titled "Students Shaping Their Future: Virtual Reality Interactive Exercises to Engage in for Learning" presents a case study by Nuria Recuero Virto that deals with the students' attitudes towards Virtual Reality and their e-learning performance.

Chapter 10 titled "Ethics and Responsibility in Tourism – The Impact of COVID-19" by Harold Goodwin provides a comprehensive discussion of the relationship between ethics and responsibility, the similarities and differences, and the imperative to act that is at the core of the concept of responsibility. The chapter concludes with some suggestions for future living with COVID-19.

As COVID-19 approaches, the issue of tourist safety is gaining momentum discussed in Chapter 11 by Özgür Yayla, Ali Solunoğlu, and Hüseyin Keleş.

The Responsibilities of Tourists in the Post-COVID-19 Period are outlined in Chapter 12. Anila Thomas authored this chapter, which focuses on conceptual research techniques relating to revising the responsibilities of tourists in an emergency situation.

Chapter 13 titled "Applied Ethics in Post-COVID-19 Destination Management" by Jordi Arcos-Pumarola, Marta Conill-Tetuà and Núria Guitart Casalderrey focused on the different cases where PCR (polymerase chain reaction) tests and other health resources have been made available for visitors in order to revitalize the tourism industry. According to the author, there are various ethical arguments both in favor and against this approach.

Chapter 14 is titled "Impact of COVID-19 Pandemic on the Tourism Industry in Sri Lanka: The Dilemmas of Industry Sustainability" by RSSW Arachchi and WKAC Gnanapala. The chapter discussed the impact of the COVID-19 pandemic on tourism across the world and the sustainable tourism challenges the Sri Lankan industry faces. Furthermore, the study discusses the resilience strategies required by the industry to succeed during and after a pandemic. The purpose of this review is to help policymakers and planners, as well as industry operators, plan their future business operations. The authors of the article shared success stories of the Sri Lankan tourism sector, which can be applied by other countries in their context while avoiding the negative impacts caused by COVID-19.

Chapter 15 titled "Managing Global and Local Events in the Post COVID-19 Period" by Priyakrushna Mohanty, Pinaz Tiwari and Nimit Chowdhary presents a systematic review of the literature in order to examine recent developments in various global events related to COVID-19 and its implications for event management. The chapter describes a framework to manage events tourism with a focus on sustainability. In particular, the framework may serve as a guide for administrators (DMOs), practitioners and academics in the post-COVID-19 period.

The Impact of COVID-19 Pandemic on Small Tourism Enterprises in Pakistan by Kalsoom B, Sumra, and Mehtab Alam, which is Chapter 16, highlights the problems that tourism-related organizations and communities faced. According to the authors, a swift response could be used as a recovery initiative for sustainable tourist business.

Chapter 17 is Perspectives in the Strategic Management of Destinations in the Post-COVID Period by Dália Liberato, Beatriz Limbado, Bruno Sousa, and Pedro Liberato examines the history, the present, and the future of tourism and hospitality in Portugal, keeping in mind the pandemic period. The authors used a qualitative methodological approach consisting of a semi-structured interview study conducted with entrepreneurs and stakeholders from tourism and hospitality entities in the North of Portugal. This study aims to understand the impact of COVID-19 on the tourism and hospitality industries as a whole.

The book is one of its kind as it highlights the visions of the world of tourism in the post-crisis situations and highlights the value of ethics and responsibilities while providing the inadequately discussed silver linings of the crisis. It is hoped that the readers will find the contents of the book intriguing and exciting.

Happy Reading to all.

Part One
COVID-19 and Tourism
Introduction

1 The Impact of COVID-19 on Tourism Demand and Supply

Adejumoke Abiose and Hosea Olayiwola Patrick

Introduction

An outbreak of severe respiratory illness was first detected in the city of Wuhan, Hubei province of China, in late December 2019 (Chen *et al.*, 2020; Kaplan *et al.*, 2020; Yang *et al.*, 2020). The World Health Organization (WHO) and health care workers in China announced a rise in the number of patients with cases of pneumonia of unknown cause. It was subsequently identified that a novel virus named Coronavirus Disease 2019 (COVID-19), a highly communicable disease was responsible for the viral outbreak (WHO, 2021). This new strain of SARS also referred to as SARS-CoV-2 has since grown, spreading across many countries, and has been declared a global pandemic by the World Health Organization (WHO) (Gössling *et al.*, 2020). This novel virus is assumed to have originated from bats and wild birds and then spread down to non-mammals and hence to mammals, possibly by contamination of meat from wild animals as sold in China meat markets (Chen *et al.*, 2020; Cohen, 2020; Li *et al.*, 2020). A highly communicable respiratory disease, COVID-19, is mainly spread through droplets produced when an infected individual sneezes, coughs, or exhales. The virus spans through contact with other infected individuals with symptoms such as fever, cough, loss of taste and smell, and, in more severe cases, difficulty in breathing (Bakar and Rosbi, 2020).

Owing to the drastic spread of the virus, several suggestions were recommended to suppress and contain the further spread of the virus. Most countries responded with various forms of non-pharmaceutical interventions such as frequent hand washing, adoption of nose masks, total lockdown, travel controls, isolation/quarantine, and social distancing, i.e., maintaining physical distance from others (Chu et al., 2020; Gössling *et al.*, 2020; Moloney and Moloney, 2020; Patrick *et al.*, 2021: Shah et al., 2020). Imposing travel restrictions immediately affected national economies as the majority of the world's population became grounded. These travel restrictions led to airlines suspending flights, the closure of tourism sites and attractions, hotels, cafes, and restaurants closed, cancellation, or postponement of major events and festivals such as the Olympics, leaving the tourism industry virtually standstill (Mohanty *et al.*, 2020).

DOI: 10.4324/9781003207467-3

Within over 14 months of first reporting a pneumonia outbreak in Wuhan, China, there are over 111 million COVID-19 cases and over 2.46 million deaths across 219 countries as of February 23, 2021. As of March 10, 2021, the World Health Organization (WHO, 2021) reported that about 117 million people globally have been confirmed to have the virus, with approximately 2.6 million deaths (WHO, 2021). For instance, South Africa reported its first COVID-19 case on the 5th of March 2020 (NICD, 2020). Subsequently, widespread community transmission began to occur, and the number of cases continued to grow each day. With the highest number of SARS-COV-2 infections in Africa, South Africa has recorded about 1.52 million confirmed cases with approximately 60,000 deaths (WHO, 2020). The country is currently experiencing a second wave of SARS-CoV-2 with an increase in new infections and deaths. Quite a substantial number of these new infections are fueled by a new highly local contagious variant of the SARS CoV-2 and a series of super spreader events. The 501Y.V2 variant, first identified in South Africa, has spread quickly beyond South Africa and its sub-region.

It is pertinent to assert that while the tourism industry has withstood pressures from a wide range of pandemics and attendant crises in the past, the swiftness and implication of the COVID-19 pandemic have been unprecedented. The industry was hard hit by the measures taken to subvert the spread of the virus (Uğur and Akbıyık, 2020). Analysis for the present immediate COVID-19 impact for the tourism industry indicates that the international tourism industry would continue to experience a decline in tourism supply and demand with a slight hope of recovery until the fourth quarter of 2021 (UNWTO, 2020a). This would put approximately 100 to 120 million direct jobs at threat. Some nations are expected to be severely hit compared to others due to their high dependence on the tourism industry (Paola, 2020; Statista, 2020). The implication for the local tourism industry, especially in economies highly dependent on tourism, is better imagined than felt. In South Africa, the impact of the pandemic has been unprecedented, especially for the rural poor dependent on tourism-centered livelihood options (Mabuza, 2020; Makhaye and Mkhize, 2020). Owing to this assumption, this chapter explores the impact of COVID-19 on the demand and supply of tourism.

Impacts of Pandemics on Travel and Tourism

Going down history lane, the outbreak of diseases and pandemics has long had a transmuting effect on societies and environments. The principal reason for this sprawl emerges from the processes of globalization and urbanization (Hall *et al.*, 2020; Watts and Parks, 2018). In our current urbanized settings, unrestricted human movements towards urban environments have increased as half of the world population currently resides in urban centers. The prospect for infection and spread in these settings has also increased alongside the increasing population due to closer proximity and contact. Additionally, these urban centers are now more interconnected than ever before due to transport integration and development through plane, train, ship, and road. This goes without saying that while curtailing the spread of the disease by breaking its transmission chain is a necessity, the movement of people aided by easier and faster transportation networks serves to spread the disease faster than normal. In this sense, tourism becomes both an agent for proliferating the disease and also a casualty of the virus spread at the same time (Ishmael, 2020). In other words, a passenger plays a vital role in the transfer of diseases and epidemics from one urban center to another side of the world in a day (Connolly *et al.*, 2021). To this effect, the tourism industry is particularly affected as it is often a target for breaking the chain of disease transmission.

It is imperative to establish that the global travel and tourism industry has withstood the pressures of a wide range of pandemics and crises in the past (Mensah, 2020). Notable examples are the Ebola virus (2014–2016), the H1N1 swine flu (2009–2010), Severe Acute Respiratory Syndrome (SARS) (2002–2004), Spanish flu (1918–1920), and the Black Death pandemic (1346–1353), among others. Having a similar pattern with the recent COVID-19 pandemic, the Spanish flu led to the restriction on travels for about 4 months and led to about 21 million deaths within a short timeframe (CDC, 2020a, b, c; Mensah, 2020). SARS and the H1N1 virus caused an economic loss of over 21 billion and 8 billion US dollars for the America's Asian Pacific regions, respectively (Škare *et al.*, 2020). In the same vein, the Mexican tourism industry had economic loss amounting to approximately 2.8 billion dollars courtesy of the H1N1 epidemic (Glaesser, 2011; Mensah, 2020).

The sprawl and emergence of the COVID-19 pandemic have echoed through all facets of the globe, having an unprecedented impact on societies around the world, causing the loss of livelihoods, the loss of lives, and a major collapse in general economic activity to many individuals and organizations (Ishmael, 2020; Jaipuria, 2020). While demand for specific segments of the economy such as grocery stores saw growth during the pandemic, other areas of the economy such as the transportation and tourism industries experienced drastic decline (and in some instance, total disappearance) in the demand for their services (Del Rio-Chanona *et al.*, 2020). The travel and tourism industry are considered one of the hardest hits and worst affected of all major economic sectors by the COVID-19 outbreak. This is largely due to the heavily reliant nature of the industry on an intact environment (Jaipuria, 2020; UNWTO, 2020a, b). Despite the historical resilient nature of the tourism industry as depicted in its response to previous crisis, the COVID-19 pandemic present unprecedented challenge leading to immediate and immense shock to the sector.

As a result of governments' restrictions as a measure to curtail the spread of the virus, traveling from one country to another was restricted, resulting in a drop in international tourist arrivals and receipts in 2020 compared with

2019. The travel and tourism industry prior to the COVID-19 pandemic provided over 320 million jobs and account for approximately 10% of the global GDP (Behsudi, 2020). The sector experienced a 59% growth from 880 million to 1.5 billion US dollars between 2009 and 2019 and contributed about 8.9 trillion to global GDP in 2019 (Alaae Sbai, 2020). The World Travel & Tourism Council (WTTC, 2020a), however, projects a loss of roughly 75 million jobs and up to US$ 2.1 trillion dollars in relation to tourism due to the effect of COVID-19 pandemic on the industry. Richter (2020) argued that about 120 million jobs considered to be at risk, with approximately 1 trillion dollars in economic loss. It is speculated that depending on the length of the crisis and when travel bans are completely lifted, international tourism receipts are expected to plunge downward between the range of 910 billion and 1.2 trillion dollars from the year 2020, which would set the global tourism industry back by 20 years (Felix, 2020). As Figure 1.1 depicts, the steady growth recorded in the past 20 years (2000–2020) is at the risk of reversal as a result of the COVID-19 pandemic (UNWTO, 2020b). The figure shows UNWTO report on tourism growth from 2000 to 2019 and the possible scenarios from 2020 in a COVID-19 new world order. The steady rise from less than $500 billion recorded in 2000 to approximately $1.5 billion in revenue face the risk of decline to pre-2000 global average.

The Organisation for Economic Co-operation and Development (OECD) (2020) posited that the current pandemic would have long-lasting global impact on the supply and demand of tourism both internationally and locally. While the international tourism demand has the propensity of recovery in the fourth quarter of 2021, the domestic sector is projected to have a faster recovery. While a 60%–80% decline is generally projected for international

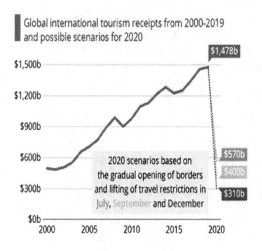

Figure 1.1 Growth in the global tourism industry (2000–2020).

tourism, Africa and the Middle East are expected to have begun recovery by the fourth quarter of 2020. Asia and Europe are, however, expected to begin recovery in 2021 despite the mixed outlet presented in these regions (UNWTO, 2020b, c).

The tourism industry is currently experiencing a swift and sudden drop in demand and supply, and a rise in job losses at global levels, thereby pushing many Small Medium Enterprises (SMEs) at risk. Small Medium Enterprises owners are enormously concerned about the severe impact of COVID-19 on their liquidity position and the survival of their businesses, particularly because of increase in the levels of vulnerability, resilience, and capacity to deal with the costs and weights that these shockwaves entail (OECD, 2020). With the scenarios being painted above, the pandemic would lead to the threat of direct job loss amounting to approximately 100 to 120 million, with more than half of the workers being women. This is because there has been an increase in women owning and managing SME businesses. Some nations are expected to be severely hit compared to others due to their high dependence on the industry (Paola, 2020; Statista, 2020). This is because tourism is a foremost employment source and job creation for many and provides a high number of jobs and businesses for both skilled and unskilled workers. The industry generates foreign exchange earnings, contributing to gross domestic product (GDP) with the potential to stimulate global, regional, and local economic development (OECD, 2020).

According to Statista (2020) latest evaluations of the pandemic's impact, Asia will encounter mostly a high plunge in travel and tourism revenues for the year 2020, with China accounting for the more significant percentage of lost revenues. On the other hand, the continent of Europe, where about 13 million jobs are in the tourism industry, is also expected to lose some revenues. Spain and Italy are the most affected countries. Not forgetting to mention the most vulnerable, the Small Island Developing States (SIDs), almost 30% of their economy relies on the share of total exports of goods and services from international tourism for foreign exchange earnings, job creation, and investments. Sub-Sahara Africa estimates that direct and indirect jobs would be affected with damaging impacts for countries such as Cape Verde, Seychelles, the Gambia, and Mauritius, among others.

Tourism Demand and Supply Chain

Tourism demand is a wide-ranging term that encompasses all the components governing the level of demand, demand types, and motives as well as the spatial characteristics of demand. It is pertinent to note that tourism demands are created by individuals (referenced to as the "Tourists"). These demands occur in a particular geographical space referred to as the "tourism destination." The enormity of demand fluctuates with times and from time to time with seasons conditioned by internal and external influences (Nelwamondo, 2010).

On the other hand, tourism supply has to do with providing the tourism industry's critical elements needed for the smooth operation of the industry. It captures all the dynamics involved in the entering of contractual relationships in the supply of goods, services, and products by different businesses. It also explains how services are accumulated into tourism product offerings at different points in the tourism supply chain. These services are also extended to the promotion, management, and maintenance of the tourism facilities and resources. The tourism resources essential for the supply of tourism products range from natural to human-made, while essential infrastructures needed include accommodation, telecommunication, and transportation (Nelwamondo, 2010).

The tourism industry characterized as an open system is in a unique situation (Uğur and Akbıyık, 2020). The disjointed, cross-cutting, and codependent characteristics of tourism products compels tourism organizations to initiate relations with several stakeholders such as tour operators, reselling travel agencies, tourism service suppliers, competitors, and government parastatals (González-Torres et al., 2020). The interrelatedness of societies around the world impacts on the tourism system as well as its environment. Holistically, the environment can be separated into various components comprising of the natural and technological environments, socio-cultural as well as political (Uğur and Akbıyık, 2020; Watts and Parks, 2018). A collapse from one section quickly spreads to others, thereby resulting in a plunging effect. Consequently, the high level of dependence of tourism with all its components makes the industry a very delicate and vulnerable sector to any risk or crises situation caused by external influences (González-Torres et al., 2020).

In the discourse on pandemic impacts, the infectious power of disease, geographical distance to the infection epicenter ("Ground Zero"), and the media attention and associated public hysteria determine the impact of a pandemic on tourism demand (Škare et al., 2021). This, by inference, implies that the combination of these factors impacts on tourism supply and demand. As Škare et al. (2021) argued, the level of epidemic outbreaks with less infectious potency has lower impacts on tourism and associated economic loss. While the world had experienced several disease outbreaks, the level of infections, mortality rate, and distance to the source country of each outbreak influence its impact on tourism supply and demand. The authors further argued that between 1950 and 2018, there have been regional disparities in the tourism supply and demand trends due to the epidemic outbreaks. For instance, while tourism loss between 1980 and 2019 amounted to 95 billion US dollars worldwide, the European region had less impact due to their geographical distance from the virus sources.

The distinct travel patterns of prospective tourists constitute one of the pivotal components in the decision for travel choice and destination. Nevertheless, due to the nearly boundless possibilities of potential destinations for travels, the safety and security of travelers constitute a fundamental influence in their decision making. The emergence of COVID-19 as a global pandemic takes away the sense of safety needed in making the decision for possible travel destination(s), thereby rendering tourism destinations unattractive. This situation now has a significant bearing on the individual travelers' travel decision as well as travel behavior. Travelers began to decide whether to rescind or postpone or cancel their trips, and discussions around travel assurance issues became more prominent.

The fear of COVID-19 pandemic and its impact have led to substantial ambiguity and chaotic circumstances for the tourism industry (Uğur and Akbıyık, 2020). Airlines companies have had to lessen their operations considerably and, in some cases, even stop them (González-Torres et al., 2020; ICAO, 2020). Tour Operators have also declined or ceased their operations (González-Torres et al., 2020; OECD, 2020). For the hospitality industry, due to the immense cancellations of hotel bookings and reservations, flights, tours, and other scheduled public and private events, the rates of hotel occupancy and the prices of the regular room plunged sharply, causing an unprecedented decline in profit margins and creating liquidity issues for all operators (Behsudi, 2020; Mensah, 2020). In addition, hotels are experiencing substantial revenue losses, utilities, and wages as well as other recurrent expenditure and statutory payments that need to be made (González-Torres et al., 2020).

The pandemic's threat and effect interact rapidly with the system of tourism, thus affecting tourism demand and supply. The recent spread of the novel virus has created panic attacks amongst the public led to a noticeable decline in the social consumption of tourism demand and supply. The demands for both domestic and international tourism in most countries have dropped sharply, making rise to demands for food and medical assistance. On the supply side, there has been a shortage of imported raw materials supporting the packaging and promotion of tourism products, which facilitates and contributes to slowing down economic activities for major developing countries that are heavily reliant on the proceeds of the tourism industry (Khan et al., 2020). Hardly is there any industry reliant on the growth of subtle products and services as the tourism industry. Revenues from tourism are based on provision, short- or long-time plans, and sometimes travelers' dreams and fantasies. This reality, therefore, demonstrates the vulnerable nature of the industry to crises, adversative scenarios, and pandemics.

It is no gainsaying that the COVID-19 pandemic has had a devastating and negative impact on the tourism economy in South Africa. In 2018 alone, about R273.2 billion was injected into the South Africa economy via tourism demand and supply (Manale, 2020). In 2019, the World Travel & Tourism Council estimated that about R425.8 billion, amounting to 8.6% of economic activities, was recorded by the tourism industry making South African the biggest tourism economy in Africa (SADT, 2020). The implication of the COVID-19 pandemic on tourism supply and demand has been enormous, with devastating scars for decades to come for South Africa

(Hlengwa, 2020). The statistics indicated that while a decline in tourism businesses would adversely impact only 39 municipalities owing to the COVID-19 pandemic, about 116 municipalities would be negatively affected by a decline in tourism supply and demand (Rogerson and Rogerson, 2020). The Department of Tourism (2020) survey in partnership with the Tourism Business Council of South Africa (TBCSA) and the World Bank's International Finance Corporation (IFC) indicated that over 160,000 employees in SA tourism had been affected by the pandemic due to the measures taken by the government in curtailing the virus spread (Manale, 2020). The SA Department of Tourism also estimated that over R149 billion and an estimated 438,000 jobs were lost in the second half of 2020 due to government lockdown policies (SADT, 2020; Shah et al., 2020). These continuous lockdown measures impacted tourism recovery hopes for 2020 (Hlengwa, 2020; Mabuza, 2020;). For instance, the KwaZulu-Natal province lost approximately R30 billion due to the COVID-19 lockdowns (Majola, 2020). Mphahlele (2020) asserts that the Comrades marathon alone, a yearly event in the KwaZulu-Natal province, led to a loss of about R700 million and over 1,000 jobs due to its cancellation. The implication for SMEs in the tourism industry is even more devastating as a decline in tourism demand affected the survival of many households and firms directly dependent on tourism demand and supply (Mabuza, 2020; Makhaye and Mkhiz, 2020).

Conclusion

The travel and tourism industry is considered one of the hardest hits by the COVID-19 outbreak. The sector is undergoing a swift and sudden decline in demand as well as a rise in job losses at the global, regional, and local levels, thereby putting at risk many SMEs especially in the developing world. In comparison to other industries, the tourism sector degree of vulnerability is heightened due to the unprecedented nature and complexities of the COVID-19 pandemic. Despite the industry historical resilience and recovery from other crisis in the past, the impact of this pandemic is projected to be long lasting for the industry. As evident everywhere globally, the impact of COVID-19 on tourism demand and supply has been devastating, leading to a decline in tourism returns across South Africa, with an impact felt more among the most tourism-dependent localities. This is also due to the potential long-term effects the pandemic has on travelers' behaviors and the degree of traveler's confidence to return to their old mobility. It is, therefore, no gainsaying that the COVID-19 pandemic has reconfigured tourism and traveling from 2020 and not only beyond but also significantly affected tourism supply and demand. This is because the fear of traveling and enforcement of social distance protocols will not go away soon after the pandemic subsides. According to experts, due to the uncertainty that constitute the COVID-19 pandemic, it is practically impossible to ascertain the magnitude of the economic and sociocultural/political impact of the pandemic as its duration cannot be accurately projected. Nevertheless, the economic decline this pandemic is causing is much more substantial. Hence, there is a need for a crisis readiness mechanism set in place by policymakers and tourism practitioners to serve as a shock absorber in the light of this pandemic and futures ones. There is also a need for policy and practice that will protect SMEs in the tourism industries from large shocks to reduce the impact on households solely dependent on tourism for livelihood support.

References

Alaae Sbai, A. (2020). How COVID-19 Impacted Travel & Tourism Industry Globally. Available at https://infomineo.com/covid-19-impacted-travel-tourism-industry/. Accessed March 23, 2020.

Bakar, N.A. and Rosbi, S. (2020). Effect of coronavirus disease (COVID-19) to tourism industry. *International Journal of Advanced Engineering Research and Science*, 7(4), pp. 189–193.

Behsudi, A. (2020). Tourism-dependent economies are among those harmed the most by the pandemic. *International Monetary Fund*. Available at https://www.imf.org/external/pubs/ft/fandd/2020/12/impact-of-the-pandemic-on-tourism-behsudi.htm. Accessed March 23, 2021.

Centers for Disease Control and Prevention (CDC) (2020a). Ebola (Ebola Virus Disease). Available at https://www.cdc.gov/vhf/ebola/history/2014-2016-outbreak/index.html. Accessed July 22, 2020.

Centers for Disease Control and Prevention (CDC). (2020b). Influenza Flu. Available at https://www.cdc.gov/flu/pandemic-resources/2009-h1n1-pandemic.html. Accessed July 22, 2020.

Centers for Disease Control and Prevention (CDC). (2020c). Severe Acute Respiratory Syndrome (SARS). Available at https://www.cdc.gov/sars/about/faq.html. Accessed July 22, 2020.

Chen, L., Liu, W., Zhang, Q., Xu, K., Ye, G., Wu, W., Sun, Z., Liu, F., Wu, K., Zhong, B. and Mei, Y. (2020). RNA-based mNGS approach identifies a novel human coronavirus from two individual pneumonia cases in 2019 Wuhan outbreak. *Emerging Microbes & Infections*, 9(1), pp. 313–319.

Chu, I.Y.H., Alam, P., Larson, H.J. and Lin, L. (2020). Social consequences of mass quarantine during epidemics: a systematic review with implications for the COVID-19 response. *Journal of Travel Medicine*, 27(7), p. taaa192.

Cohen, J. (2020). Wuhan coronavirus hunter Shi Zhengli speaks out. *Science*, 369(6503), pp. 487–488.

Connolly, C., Keil, R. and Ali, S.H. (2021). Extended urbanization and the spatialities of infectious disease: demographic change, infrastructure, and governance. *Urban Studies*, 58(2), pp. 245–263.

Del Rio-Chanona, R.M., Mealy, P., Pichler, A., Lafond, F. and Farmer, J.D. (2020). Supply and demand shocks in the COVID-19 pandemic: an industry and occupation perspective. *Oxford Review of Economic Policy*, 36(Supplement_1), pp. S94–S137.

Felix, R. (2020). Covid-19 Impact on Tourism Pandemic Could Set Tourism Sector Back by $1 Trillion. Available at https://www.statista.com/chart/22689/global-international-tourism-receipts/.

Glaesser, D. (2011). Toward a Safer World: The Travel, Tourism and Aviation Sector. Available at http://webunwto.s3.amazonaws.com/imported_images/41552/unwtotowardasaferworld.pdf. Accessed July 30, 2020.

González-Torres, T., Rodríguez-Sánchez, J.L. and Pelechano-Barahona, E. (2020). Managing relationships in the tourism supply chain to overcome epidemic outbreaks: the case of COVID-19 and the hospitality industry in Spain. *International Journal of Hospitality Management*, 92, p. 102733.

Gössling, S., Scott, D. and Hall, C.M. (2020). Pandemics, tourism, and global change: a rapid assessment of COVID-19. *Journal of Sustainable Tourism*, 29(1), pp. 1–20.

Hall, C.M., Scott, D. and Gössling, S. (2020). Pandemics, transformations, and tourism: be careful what you wish for. *Tourism Geographies*, 22(3), pp. 577–598.

Hlengwa, D.C. (2020). Systems' view of the economic impact of Covid-19 on event tourism in KwaZulu Natal, South Africa. *Journal of Critical Reviews*, 7(19), pp. 2432–2440.

International Civil Aviation Organization (ICAO) (2020). Effects of Novel Coronavirus (COVID-19) on Civil Aviation: Economic Impact Analysis. Available at https://www.icao.int/sustainability/Documents/COVID-19/ICAO%20Coronavirus%202020%2005%2004%20Economic%20Impact.pdf. Accessed on March 10, 2021.

Ishmael, M. (2020). Unpacking the Impacts of COVID-19 on Tourism and Repackaging the Hotel Service. Available at https://www.hospitalitynet.org/opinion/4098657.html. Accessed March 10, 2021.

Jaipuria, S., Parida, R. and Ray, P. (2020). The impact of COVID-19 on tourism sector in India. *Tourism Recreation Research*, 46(2), pp. 1–16.

Kaplan, E.H. (2020). Containing 2019-ncov (Wuhan) coronavirus. *Health Care Management Science*, 23(3), pp. 311–314.

Khan, A., Bibi, S., Lorenzo, A., Lyu, J. and Babar, Z.U. (2020). Tourism and development in developing economies: a policy implication perspective. *Sustainability*, 12(4), p. 1618.

Li, X., Song, Y., Wong, G. and Cui, J. (2020). Bat origin of a new human coronavirus: there and back again. *Science China Life Sciences*, 63(3), pp. 461–462.

Mabuza, E. (2020). We will continue to shed jobs: how lockdown ravaged SA's tourism industry. Timeslive. Available at https://www.timeslive.co.za/news/south-africa/2021-02-24-we-will-continue-to-shed-jobs-how-lockdown-ravaged-sas-tourism-industry/. Accessed March 22, 2021.

Majola, G. (2020). KZN Economy Contracts by R30 Billion Covid-19 Lockdown Takes Its Toll. Available at https://www.iol.co.za/business-report/economy/kzn-economy-contracts-by-r30-billion-covid-19-lockdown-takes-it-toll-50546250. Accessed March 22, 2021.

Makhaye, C. and Mkhize, N. (2020). All the rooms are empty': KwaZulu-Natal tourism reels from Covid-19 effects. Nation. Available at https://www.businesslive.co.za/bd/national/2020-03-18-all-the-rooms-are-empty-kwazulu-natal-tourism-reels-from-covid-19-effects/. Accessed March 23, 2021.

Manale, B. (Eds.). (2020). Covid-19 tourism sector response measures. South African Department of Tourism. Available at https://www.tourism.gov.za/AboutNDT/Publications/Bojanala%20-%20June%202020.pdf. Accessed March 23, 2021.

Mensah, I. (2020). Unpacking the Impacts of COVID-19 on Tourism and Repackaging the Hotel Service. Available at https://www.hospitalitynet.org/opinion/4098657.html. Accessed March 23, 2021.

Mohanty, P., Dhoundiyal, H. and Choudhury, R. (2020). Events tourism in the eye of the COVID-19 storm: impacts and implications. In S. Arora and A. Sharma (Eds.), *Event Tourism in Asian Countries: Challenges and Prospects* (1st ed.). Florida: Apple Academic Press, pp 1–14.

Moloney, K. and Moloney, S. (2020). Australian quarantine policy: from centralization to coordination with mid-pandemic COVID-19 shifts. *Public Administration Review*, 80(4), pp. 671–682.

Mphahlele, M. (2021). KZN Facing Staggering R700m in Lost Tourism Revenue after Comrades Marathon Cancellation. Available at https://www.sowetanlive.co.za/sport/2021-02-23-kzn-facing-staggering-r700m-in-lost-tourism-revenue-after-comrades-marathon-cancellation/. Accessed March 22, 2021.

National Institute of Communicable Disease. (2020). First Case of Covid-19 Coronavirus Reported in SA. Available at https://www.nicd.ac.za/first-case-of-covid-19-coronavirus-reported-in-sa/. Accessed March 10, 2021.

Nelwamondo, T. (2010). Tourism development through strategic planning for non-metropolitan small to medium size accommodation facilities in Limpopo Province, South Africa. *Doctoral dissertation*. University of Pretoria.

OECD. (2020). Tourism Policy Responses to the Coronavirus (COVID-19); OECD Policy Responses to Coronavirus (COVID-19) 2020 June. Available at https://www.oecd.org/coronavirus/policy-responses/tourism-policy-responses-to-the-coronavirus-covid-19-6466aa20/#. Accessed August 05, 2020.

Paola, M. (2020). April 29. The Impact of COVID-19 on Tourism. Available at https://www.policycenter.ma/opinion/impact-covid-19-tourism#.XwNdzKEzbDc. Accessed July 30, 2020.

Patrick, H.O., Abiolu, R.T.I. and Abiolu, O.A. (2021). Covid-19 and the viability of curriculum adjustment and delivery options in the South African educational space. *Journal of Transformation in Higher Education*, 6, p. 101. https://doi.org/10.4102/the.v6i0.101.

Richter F. (2020). Pandemic Could Set Tourism Sector Back by $1 Trillion. Statista. Available at https://www.statista.com/chart/22689/global-international-tourism-receipts/. Accessed August 2021

Rogerson, C.M. and Rogerson, J.M. (2020). COVID-19 and tourism spaces of vulnerability in South Africa. *African Journal of Hospitality, Tourism and Leisure*, 9(4), pp. 382–401.

Shah, J.N., Shah, J. and Shah, J. (2020). Quarantine, isolation, and lockdown: in context of COVID-19. *Journal of Patan Academy of Health Sciences*, 7(1), pp. 48–57.

Škare, M., Soriano, D.R. and Porada-Rochoń, M. (2021). Impact of COVID-19 on the travel and tourism industry. *Technological Forecasting and Social Change*, 163, p. 120469.

South Africa Department of Tourism. (2020). Tourism Sector Recovery Plan Covid-19 Response. Available at https://www.tralac.org/documents/resources/covid-19/countries/3992-south-africa-tourism-sector-recovery-plan-covid-19-response-august-2020-request-for-comments/file.html. Accessed March 23, 2021.

Statista. (2020). Travel and Tourism Industry Revenue in Selected Countries in 2019 and Projected Impact of the Coronavirus (COVID-19) Pandemic in 2020 (in Million US Dollars). Available at https://www.statista.com/forecasts/1103432/covid-19-revenue-travel-tourism-industry-country-forecast. Accessed August 05, 2020.

Uğur, N.G. and Akbıyık, A. (2020). Impacts of COVID-19 on global tourism industry: a cross-regional comparison. *Tourism Management Perspectives*, 36, p. 100744.

United Nations World Tourism Organization (UNWTO). (2020a). International Tourist Numbers Could Fall 60–80% in 2020, May 07 20 UNWTO Reports. Available at https://www.unwto.org/news/covid-19-international-tourist-numbers-could-fall-60-80-in-2020. Accessed July 22, 2020.

United Nations World Tourism Organization (UNWTO). (2020b). Impact Assessment of the Covid-19 Outbreak on International Tourism, 2020 May. Availableathttps://www.unwto.org/impact-assessment-of-the-covid-19-outbreak-on-international-tourism. Accessed July 31, 2020.

United Nations World Tourism Organization (UNWTO). (2020c). COVID-19: Putting People First. Available at https://www.unwto.org/tourism-covid-19. Accessed July 30, 2020.

Watts, R. and Parks, Z. (2018). Development of Tourism and Travel Industry. Scientific e-Resources.

World Health Organisation. (2020). New COVID-19 Variants Fuelling Africa's Second Wave. Available at https://www.afro.who.int/news/new-covid-19-variants-fuelling-africas-second-wave. Accessed March 20, 2021.

World Health Organization. (2021). Global research on coronavirus disease (COVID-19. World Health Organization. Available at https://www.who.int/emergencies/diseases/novel-coronavirus-2019/global-research-on-novel-coronavirus-2019-ncov. Accessed October 2021

Yang, J., Zheng, Y., Gou, X., Pu, K., Chen, Z., Guo, Q., Ji, R., Wang, H., Wang, Y. and Zhou, Y. (2020). Prevalence of comorbidities in the novel Wuhan coronavirus (COVID-19) infection: a systematic review and meta-analysis. *International Journal of Infectious Diseases*, 10, pp. 1–13

2 Coronavirus through the Eyes of Hospitality Customers

Gürkan Çalışkan, Emrah Yaşarsoy, and Hüseyin Pamukçu

Introduction

COVID-19, which is located close to the seafood market in Wuhan, the Hubei province of China, on December 31, 2019, has rapidly spread and turned into a global pandemic. This disease, a severe acute respiratory syndrome, has caused a global crisis worldwide due to insufficient recognition and lack of vaccine (Qiu, Chen & Shi, 2020; Tsou et al., 2020). On February 11, 2020, the rapidly spreading virus, named COVID-19 (World Health Organization, 2021a)), was declared a global pandemic by the World Health Organization (WHO) and caused thousands of deaths (World Health Organization, 2021d).

The pandemic has adversely affected many industries. Several precautions have been taken to prevent the pandemic transmitted by air and contact and prevent the spread, and countries have begun to stop international movements. International and national flights were stopped, many workplaces and venues, including restaurants, airlines, beauty centers, cafes, hairdressers, parks, and beaches, were closed, and the risk of contamination was tried to be minimized (Higgins-Desbiolles, 2020; Ruiz Estrada, Park & Lee, 2020).

The tourism sector is one of the sectors most affected by the restrictions. Due to restrictions, tourism movements have almost stopped. The bans have brought travel barriers, reservations, and holiday postponements, and there has been a severe decline in tourism demand. While some businesses decided to stop their operations, some businesses continued their activities even if the demand was low (Ioannides & Gyimóthy, 2020; Pham et al., 2021; Rio-Chanona et al., 2020) (Figure 2.1).

According to the World Tourism Organization (WTO) data, there was a 74% decrease in international tourism movements compared to the January–December period of 2019. This figure represents 1 billion tourists. There is a loss of more than USD 1.3 trillion in export revenues from tourism (World Health Organization, 2021b)) (Figure 2.2).

The region that lost the most tourists in 2020 in the world was the Asia and Pacific region, with a loss of 84%. Middle East follows Asia and Pacific region with 76% (World Health Organization, 2021b)) (Figure 2.3).

DOI: 10.4324/9781003207467-4

20 *Gürkan Çalışkan et al.*

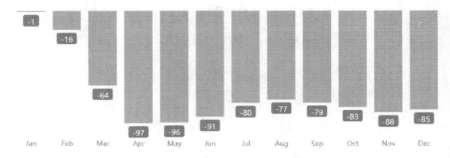

Figure 2.1 Change in monthly tourist rates compared to 2019 (2020).
Source: World Health Organization, 2021b.

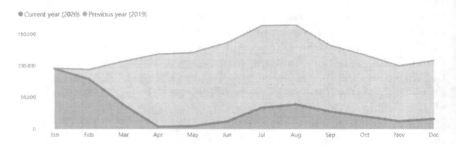

Figure 2.2 Changes in monthly tourist numbers in 2019–2020.
Source: World Health Organization, 2021b.

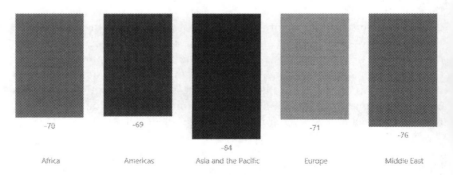

Figure 2.3 Change in tourist rates by the region compared to 2019 (2020).
Source: World Health Organization, 2021b.

When the expanded scenarios of the WTO for the years 2021–2024 are examined, it is understood that recovery is expected from the third half of 2021. The return to 2019 data is predicted to take between 2 and 4 years (World Health Organization, 2021c) (Figure 2.4).

The pandemic's influence on the tourism industry and the changes experienced have also affected the tourism paradigm, and many studies have been conducted to examine the COVID-19 pandemic-tourism relationship.

Acar (2020) aimed to identify the current and possible effects of the COVID-19 pandemic on the tourism industry. According to the results, it has been argued that the virus may have long-term economic impacts, and at this point, tourism will be one of the most affected sectors. Nicola et al. (2020) examined the socio-economic effects of the COVID-19 pandemic. The tourism industry has also been examined within the scope of the study. Their study emphasized that the sharp drop in hospitality services has caused a severe decrease in income and occupancy and caused some services to be temporarily terminated. Karim et al. (2020) studied the impact of the COVID-19 pandemic on the Malaysian tourism industry. In the conceptual-based study, the Malaysian tourism industry's disastrous consequences as a result of the pandemic were highlighted, and sectoral changes experienced during and after the pandemic were discussed. From this perspective,

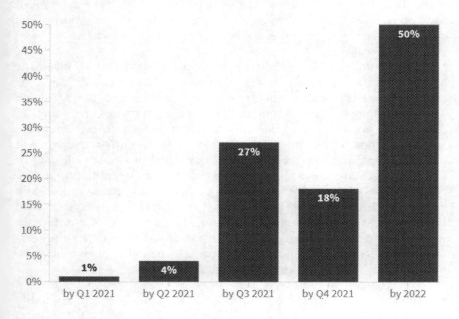

Figure 2.4 Expanded scenarios of the WTO.
Source: World Health Organization, 2021c.

avoiding possible long travels, the importance of hygiene, and the need to take local and administrative precautions to eliminate this adverse situation in the tourism sector have been determined as superior results.

Bahar and Çelik İlal (2020) studied the economic effects of the COVID-19 pandemic on the tourism sector conceptually. According to the results obtained, it was predicted that the pandemic would bring losses of employment and income. Jamal and Budke (2020) and Sánchez (2020) developed recommendations for the COVID-19 pandemic based on past pandemics. In the study, it was stated that the communication between tourism stakeholders and health officials should be more assertive, service providers should be well-informed and ready about the virus, and international tourism organizations such as the World Tourism Organization and the World Tourism and Travel Council might be needed in this process. Gössling, Scott, and Hall (2020) evaluated the possibilities of economy and tourism by comparing the COVID-19 pandemic with past pandemics and global crises. The study results reveal that the global growth models of tourism and the way of production related to the decrease in demand and change in tourism should be re-evaluated. Wanjala (2020) examined the impact of the COVID-19 pandemic on tourism and trade based on past pandemics. The study results show that demand and supply shocks will affect Kenya's economy, tourism, and trade sectors; the Kenyan government has taken various precautions to combat the virus's spread and protect the country from a possible economic downturn. The policies implemented are primarily focused on demand shock management.

Tourism studies are investigating the COVID-19 pandemic. When the relevant literature is examined, it is seen that there are studies that are conceptually focused, using secondary data and created with the document analysis technique. There are limitations in empirical studies examining the relationship between pandemic and tourism. In particular, examining the accommodation businesses, which are one of the sector's dynamic legs, will provide a more precise reflection of the pandemic process. In this study, a five-star accommodation business that continues its operations in the recent months that the pandemic emerged in Turkey has been examined as a case study. Within the scope of the study, interviews were conducted with the customers of the accommodation business. The purpose of this study, in which the interview technique is used, is to reveal how the pandemic process is perceived from the accommodation business customers' eyes. The questions that create the research problem are as follows:

- What are the effects of the COVID-19 pandemic on hospitality customers?
- Is there a change in the quality of accommodation experience of the customers?
- What are the customers' service expectations regarding the pandemic process?

Statistics of Coronavirus Pandemic in the World and Turkey

When the WHO's data are examined, the total number of patients worldwide as of March 20, 2021, is stated as 121,969,223 people, while the number of deaths is 2,694,094 people. Turkey ranks 9th in the world in terms of 2,971,633 cases. The death toll was 29,864 people (World Health Organization, 2021e; World Health Organization, 2021f) (Figures 2.5 and 2.6).

America stands out in the distribution of the cases according to the regions. Europe follows America (Table 2.1).

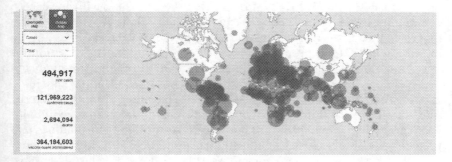

Figure 2.5 Map of the number of cases according to the WHO (data on the date of March 20, 2021) (World Health Organization, 2021e).

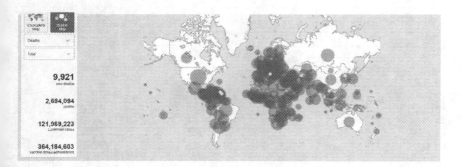

Figure 2.6 Map of death number according to the WHO (data on the date of March 20, 2021) (World Health Organization, 2021e).

Table 2.1 Distribution of the number of cases by regions

Region	Cases
America	53,731,830
Europe	42,260,060
Asia	14,130,838
East Mediterranean	7,091,557
Africa	1,763,132

Source: World Health Organization (2021b) (data on the date of March 20, 2021).

While the most diagnosed cases in the world belong to the United States of America, Brazil is the country with the second-highest number of coronavirus infections. India is currently in the third place. The top ten countries with the highest number of cases and the number of cases are as follows (World Health Organization, 2021e) (Table 2.2):

When Turkey's number of cases and deaths is examined, it is seen that there has been an increase in recent days (Figures 2.7 and 2.8).

Apart from health problems, the COVID-19 pandemic affects countries and individuals economically, psychologically, and socially. The International Monetary Fund (IMF) estimates that the pandemic will cause a 3% contraction in the global economy. Besides, more than 90 countries have requested debt. The World Bank estimates foresee a decrease of 2% to 3% in the countries' total production level. According to the Organisation for Economic Co-operation and Development (OECD) estimates, it is predicted that it is likely to cause a decrease of 33% in consumer spending and 20%–25% in production levels of many economies. The report also notes that the tourism industry will find it challenging to overcome the crisis, mainly involving small- and medium-sized businesses. According to the findings and predictions of London-based global information provider IHS Markit consultants Chris Williamson, Kenneth Wattret, and Rajiv Biswas, the most significant economic decline has been experienced since February 2009, and a 2% decrease is expected in the global gross domestic product. Additionally,

Table 2.2 Distribution of the number of cases by country

Country	Number of Cases	Number of Deaths
United States of America	29,437,770	536,008
Brazil	11,871,390	290,314
India	11,599,130	159,755
Russia	4,447,570	94,659
United Kingdom	4,285,688	126,026
France	4,111,105	91,162
Italy	3,332,418	104,241
Spain	3,206,116	72,793
Turkey	2,971,633	29,864
Germany	2,645,783	74,565

Source: World Health Organization (2021) (data on the date of March 21, 2021).

Figure 2.7 Number of COVID-19 cases in Turkey (URL 6) (data on the date of March 21, 2021).

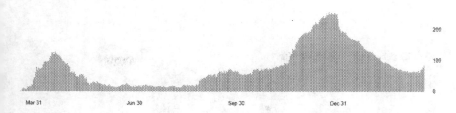

Figure 2.8 Number of deaths caused by COVID-19 in Turkey (World Health Organization, 2021f) (data on the date of March 21, 2021).

in particular, the economies of countries such as Croatia, Greek Cyprus, and Greece, where the tourism sector has a high share in the gross domestic product, will be the most affected in this process (URL-1).

One of the most critical factors in the adverse economic picture that emerged from the COVID-19 pandemic is the cessation of consumption, production, and tourism movements. According to the United Nations World Tourism Organization data, travel restrictions were imposed in all tourism destinations as of April 20, 2020, to reduce tourism movements. While 45% of the tourism destinations completely closed the country's borders, 30% stopped their flights wholly or partially. Hotel businesses are among the businesses that lost the most in this process. A survey of hotel operators conducted by the Greek Chamber of Hotel Management found that 46% of the facilities predicted the possibility of bankruptcy, while 18% seriously considered bankruptcy (URL-7).

January–November 2020 in Turkey has a 72% decrease in the number of visitors compared to 2019, according to the "Turkey Tourism Statistics" report of the Association of Travel Agencies of Turkey. The number of visitors decreased from 42.9 million to 12 million. The most visitors came from Russia, followed by Bulgaria and Germany. In Istanbul, where the study was conducted, there was a 66.6% decrease compared to 2019, and the number of visitors decreased from 13.7 million to 4.5 million (URL-2) (Figure 2.9).

Tourism demand has also been affected due to the pandemic. According to the "COVID-19 during domestic tourism demand in Turkey" report prepared in cooperation with The Association of Independent Industrialists and Businessmen (MUSIAD), New Tourism Resources Development Committee, and International Halal Tourism Association (IHATO), people were found to be indecisive about going on holiday, with only 28% of respondents intending to go on holiday. Although 27.1% of the participants believe that the pandemic will end in October and after, the pandemic has not yet ended. Another question posed to participants in the study is the holiday decision threshold based on the number of cases. 43.8% of the participants stated that they would consider going on vacation if it falls below ten people. 72.4% of participants have a fear of transmission of the virus. The findings of the study also show the disadvantages in economic terms. Accordingly, 80.5% of participants suffered economic damage during the pandemic (URL-3).

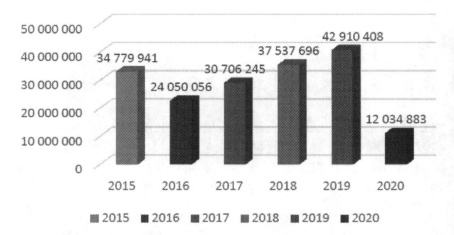

Figure 2.9 Number of tourist arrivals to Turkey by the year (from January to November 2020) (URL-2).

Coronavirus Precautions in Turkey

As of March, when the pandemic emerged in Turkey, the country has started to take some restrictions and precautions. The first COVID-19 case in Turkey occurred on March 10, 2020. The first meeting was held on March 12 after the virus appeared. After the meeting, primary, secondary, and high school schools were suspended for one week as of March 16, and later on, it was decided to switch to distance education as of March 23. Universities have been on holiday for three weeks as of March 16. Later, the distance education decision was taken. It was decided that sports competitions will be played without spectators first until the end of April. The competitions will be postponed after the development of the number of cases. Flight restrictions have been imposed. Public employees have started to work flexibly. It has been decided to temporarily close places such as bars, casinos, nightclubs, museums, libraries, coffee houses, cinemas, theaters, gyms, children's playgrounds, internet cafes, and Turkish baths. Most of the workplaces in the private sector have started to work from home. Economic-aid packages have been offered for citizens who have had difficulty during the pandemic days. It is aimed to reduce movements by imposing restrictions on inter-city transport. Curfew restrictions have been imposed at certain times on weekends and weekdays. Decisions made according to the number of cases were increased and stretched (URL-4).

The new world order has also emerged due to the pandemic. "COVID-19 Pandemic Management and Study Guide" has been prepared by the Republic of Turkey Ministry of Health. In this layout, where distance, mask, and hygiene are at the forefront, there are specific rules that accommodation businesses must follow. In the precaution reports prepared by the Ministry of Health for institutions and businesses, the rules that accommodation businesses must comply with are discussed under three headings. These are general cleaning rules, complaints about the disease, and staff training (URL-5).

- General cleaning rules are (URL-5) are as follows:
- The windows in the facility should be open during cleaning and ventilated for at least 1 hour afterward.
- Before and after cleaning, hands should be washed, and gloves should be worn.
- Cleaning should be done with water and detergent.
- Care should be taken to clean used places frequently, and those places should be cleaned with bleach or chlorine.
- Commonly used food and beverage equipment should be washed using detergents after each use.
- The products used by the guests should be collected without shaking and whisking.
- Textile products should be washed at 60–90 degrees in the washing machine using detergent.
- Common areas such as massage, sports, sauna, and children's playgrounds should not be used as much as possible and should be available for limited use by reservation.
- Toys that are difficult to clean should not be kept in children's playgrounds.
- Air conditioners should be regularly maintained and repaired.

In case of complaints about COVID-19 (URL-5):

- The suspect person should be separated from other guests and notified to the health units.
- Those who share the same room with the suspect should wear masks.
- The room of the person diagnosed with the patient should be ventilated for 24 hours after the person is delivered to the health units, and then detailed cleaning should be done.

Training should be given to hotel staff (URL-5):

- Care should be taken to hand cleanliness, and hands should be washed with soap for at least 20 seconds.
- If there is a staff with a respiratory tract infection, they should wear a mask and not enter crowded places,
- Hand disinfection should be provided after contact with guests' personal belongings.

Method

The interview form technique, one of the qualitative research methods, was used in the study. Within the study's scope, a 5-star accommodation business near the Istanbul Airport was selected as a case study. The structured Interview form, which was created by literature review and provided appearance validity by taking expert opinions, was applied to the accommodation business's customers. In the structured interview form, predetermined questions are asked to the participants in a particular order (Kozak, 2018: 82). The data were collected between December 20, 2020, and March 20, 2021. Support was received from the personnel of the accommodation business while obtaining the data. Due to the decrease in the number of residents and the customers' unwillingness to participate in the study, the study was carried out on 13 customers. Participants were given coding as "P1, P2, P3.....P13," and the participants' names were not evaluated within the scope of the study based on the privacy policy. Since foreign customers stay at the facility, the form has also been prepared in English and Arabic. The data obtained from the participants were encoded in the MAXQDA analysis program, and the encoded data were mapped using "MAXMaps" in the "Visual tools" section of the program.

The questions directed to the customers within the scope of the study are as follows:

- To what extent did the emergence of the coronavirus affect your holiday decision?
- What are the precautions taken by your accommodation business to protect against coronavirus? Do you think these precautions are sufficient?
- Do you feel safe in the hotel you are staying in? If you feel safe, which practices and behaviors of the hotel you are staying in, this feeling of confidence?
- What activities can you perform during your holiday due to the coronavirus? Is there an activity you cannot perform?
- How would you assess precautions taken by Turkey within the scope of the coronavirus protection?

Research Findings

The data obtained in the study were subjected to the thematic analysis process, and the data obtained were coded with the MAXQDA program. The data obtained from the interview form were encoded 204 times in total. The code system visual is presented in Figure 2.10.

The first question addressed to hospitality customers in the study is to determine the extent to which the COVID-19 pandemic affects their holiday decisions. Ten of the participants stated that the pandemic was influential in their holiday decisions (Figure 2.11).

Coronavirus – Eyes of Hospitality Customer 29

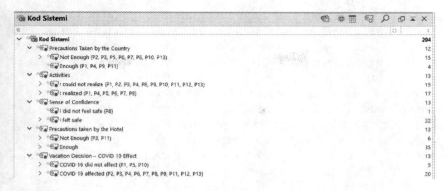

Figure 2.10 Code system.

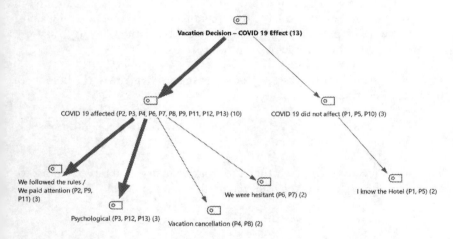

Figure 2.11 Vacation decision – COVID-19 effect (code map).

Participants were affected by the process negatively. Some participants stated that they obeyed the rules and had their holidays within specific processes (P2, P9, P11), while others changed and canceled their vacation plans (P4, P8). When the psychology dimension is examined, the response of the P3-coded participant reveals how much the effect dimension of the process can be:

> I am someone who travels to a different country every year for cultural purposes. When I talk about the beginning of the virus, prohibitions, economy, I feel isolated from society and trapped. Therefore, the virus left bad memories as well as bad psychology.

The second question asked to the study participants is the adequacy of the precautions taken by the enterprise within the scope of COVID-19 and what the precautions are. At this point, it is seen that only two of the participants found the precautions insufficient. It was determined that ten of the participants were particularly satisfied with the hygiene precautions (Figure 2.12).

P1 coded participants emphasized the importance of restricting the private pool's use to the family and giving disposable products. In contrast, P4 coded participants emphasized that they acted by the Ministry of Health guidelines. P3 coded participant, who found the precautions insufficient, expressed the points that accommodation businesses should pay particular attention to with the following statements:

> I stayed an estimated seven times during the pandemic process. I have been in 4 different hotels: five stars, four stars, and boutique hotels during these stays. Unfortunately, I haven't seen enough precautions in any of them. Except for hand disinfectants and distance warning signs, there were no precautions I thought should be in any hotel. (ventilation, mask, number of people in the dining area, contacts)

P9 coded participant expressed the importance of hygiene in the hotel with the following statements:

> The precautions were very successful. Our room and outdoor areas were constantly disinfected.

The third question asked to the study participants is about the sense of confidence they felt during the accommodation process. Twelve of the

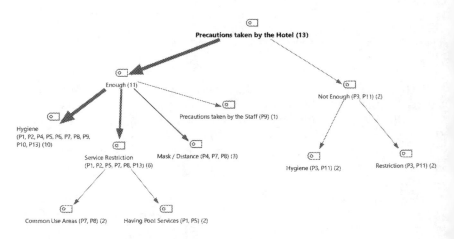

Figure 2.12 Precautions are taken by the hotel (code map).

participants emphasized that they felt safe while at the facility. This is because the operating personnel is sensitive, warnings are given about obeying the rules continuously, and hygiene rules are followed. It is seen that the only customer who has problems with the feeling of confidence is the P8 coded participant. The P8 coded participant stated that he did not feel safe and therefore did not enjoy his holiday (Figure 2.13).

The fourth question posed to the participants in the activities they could and could not experience during the holiday. At this point, the participants expressed their reservations. P3, P9, P10, P11, and P12 coded participants stated that they could not perform almost any activity they planned due to reservations and restrictions (Figure 2.14).

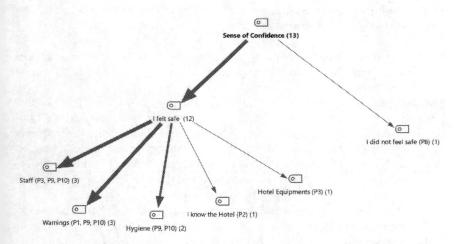

Figure 2.13 Sense of confidence (code map).

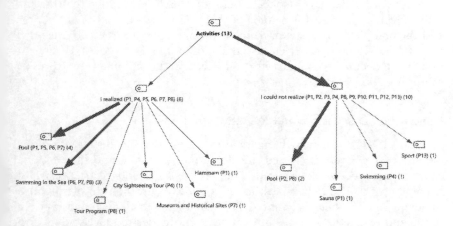

Figure 2.14 Activities (code map).

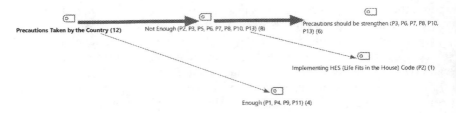

Figure 2.15 Precautions taken by the country (code map).

Although P7 coded participant carried out the activities s/he wanted, s/he reflected that s/he had reservations.

> I carried out museum-ruins trips, sea-pool activities. I tried not to prefer it, especially when it was very crowded.

The last question of the study is to evaluate the precautions taken by Turkey towards the COVID-19 pandemic. At this point, it is observed that two-thirds of participants find the precautions taken insufficient. Participants expressed the need to increase precautions and improve the implementation of the HES code (P2). While P1 and P9 coded participants find the precautions as sufficient, they stated that the spread of the pandemic in the country was the unconscious behavior of people (Figure 2.15).

The study's findings show that customers staying in accommodation establishments during the pandemic period have been affected by the process and can change some of their decisions while making holiday decisions. Despite the pandemic process, customers who find the business's precautions generally adequate also feel safe. It has been determined that the customers who cannot perform some of their activities due to the restrictions and the complex process experienced can partially add the activities they want to their holiday experiences. On the other hand, the country's precautions were deemed to be partially sufficient, and opinions were expressed as improvable.

Conclusion, Discussion, and Recommendations

The COVID-19 virus, which emerged in China and was declared a global pandemic, has deeply affected life. Regional, national, and international changes have been experienced, and prohibitions and restrictions have become a part of our lives. Although a decrease in the rate of spread of the pandemic has been attempted by mask, distance, bans, temporary closures, and restrictions, it has not yet reached the desired levels. This difficulty and change experienced negatively affected all sectors and employees.

International travel has come to a halt, and tourism has been one of the most affected sectors at this point.

Despite the negative change in the tourism sector, accommodation businesses continue to provide services. Although life is negatively affected, there will always be people who have to stay for work and experience a holiday. Although the movement has decreased, travel for tourism purposes will continue to occur during the pandemic. Considering that the transition period to regular life order and old dynamism is predicted to be between two and four years, it is inevitable that tourism dynamism will continue with the necessary precautions.

In this study, a five-star accommodation business, which continues its activities during the pandemic period, was selected as a case study. Within the study's scope, interviews were conducted with customers who carried out accommodation activities during the pandemic period. In the study, which was started with how the pandemic affected the customers, the data obtained were passed through the thematic analysis process. Themes are reflected in the code system and maps. When the data are analyzed, customers' holiday experiences are inevitably affected, and their movements are restricted. It is observed that some customers canceled their previously planned holiday and changed their decisions. Considering the tourists' decision change, findings obtained to support the research done by Karim et al. (2020) and Nicola et al. (2020).

Customers who were able to perform the desired activities, even partially, could feel safe despite the pandemic. The main reason for this is seen as business personnel's behavior, compliance with hygiene rules, and making the necessary warnings. Customers were found to be satisfied with the precautions taken by the accommodation business. For this reason, it has been determined that there is not much change in the experience quality of the customers except for the activities that could not be carried out during the stay due to pandemic concerns. At this point, our study's findings support the research done by Gössling et al. (2020) and Wanjala (2020). In tourism, the way of service production and delivery has changed. From this point of view, it can be predicted that the tourism movement can be revived with certain precautions and changes.

Accommodation companies that want to keep up with the new order after the pandemic and increase their demands should closely follow the change process. It is essential to impress tourists who do not want to travel with certain reservations and to be able to prove that tourism can be a reliable relocation movement. At this point, a small number of customers can be an essential advertising and incentive tool. Positive reflections of the customers who feel safe and find the precautions sufficient can increase tourism movement.

Accommodation businesses that aim to meet their customers' service expectations regarding the pandemic process and continue their activities with little demand should bring hygiene-oriented services to the forefront to survive in this challenging period and turn to more boutique and more personal points in their service understanding. It is observed that the customers are satisfied with the restrictions of the pools specifically for the families and the shared space restrictions. At this point, restrictions can be an opportunity to offer personalized holiday experiences. Despite the difficulties and limitations of the pandemic process, the situation can be turned into an opportunity.

As the COVID-19 pandemic is not over yet, there is an increase in virus mutations and cases. When the relevant literature is examined, it is seen that studies related to the ongoing pandemic period are carried out and that secondary data are usually used. It is beneficial to increase empirical and experimental studies. Our study was carried out in a five-star accommodation business in Istanbul. There is a severe decrease in tourist demand due to restrictions and reservations. Therefore, a limited number of accommodation business customers participated in our study. Researchers who will study the current state of the COVID-19 pandemic in accommodation businesses turn to comprehensive and empirical studies that can identify the current and possible situation.

References

Acar, Y. (2020). Yeni Koronavirüs (COVID-19) Salgını ve Turizm Faaliyetlerine Etkisi. *Güncel Turizm Araştırmaları Dergisi, 4*(1), 7–21. doi:10.32572/guntad.703410.

Bahar, O. & Çelik İlal, N. (2020). Coronavirüsün (Covid-19) turizm sektörü üzerindeki ekonomik etkileri. *International Journal of Social Sciences and Education Research, 6*(1), 125–139.

Gössling, S., Scott, D. & Hall, C. M. (2020). Pandemics, tourism and global change: a rapid assessment of COVID-19. *Journal of Sustainable Tourism.* doi:10.1080/09669582.2020.1758708.

Higgins-Desbiolles, F. (2020). Socialising tourism for social and ecological justice after COVID-19. *Tourism Geographies.* doi:10.1080/14616688.2020.1757748.

Ioannides, D. & Gyimothy, S. (2020). The COVID-19 crisis as an opportunity for escaping the unsustainable global tourism path. *Tourism Geographies.* doi:10.1080/14616688.2020.1763445.

Jamal, T. & Budke, C. (2020). Tourism in a world with pandemics: local-global responsibility and action. *Journal of Tourism Futures.* doi:10.1108/JTF-02-2020-0014.

Karim, W., Haque, A., Anis, Z. & Ulfy, M. (2020). The movement control order (MCO) for COVID-19 crisis and its impact on tourism and hospitality sector in Malaysia. *International Tourism and Hospitality Journal, 3*(2), 1–7.

Kozak, M. (2018). *Bilimsel Araştırma: Tasarım, Yazım ve Yayım Teknikleri.* Ankara: Detay Yayıncılık.

Nicola, M., Alsafi, Z., Sohrabi, C., Kerwan, A., Al-Jabir, A., Iosifidis, C., Agha, M. & Agha, R. (2020). The socio-economic implications of the coronavirus and COVID-19 pandemic: a review. *International Journal of Surgery,* 185–193. doi:10.1016/j.ijsu.2020.04.018.

Qiu, Y. C., Chen, X. & Shi, W. (2020). Impacts of social and economic factors on the transmission of coronavirus disease 2019 (COVID-19) in China. *Journal of Population Economics*. doi:10.1007/s00148-020-00778-2.

Pham, T. D., Dwyer, L., Su, J.-J. & Ngo, T. (2021). COVID-19 impacts of inbound tourism on Australian economy. *Annals of Tourism Research, 88*, 1–14.

Rio-Chanona, R. M., Mealy, P., Picher, A., Lafond, F. & Farmer, J. D. (2020). Supply and demand shocks in the COVID-19 pandemic: an industry and occupation perspective. *Covid Economics, 6*, 65–103.

Ruiz Estrada, M. A., Park, D. & Lee, M. (2020). How a massive contagious infectious diseases can affect tourism, international trade, air transportation, and electricity consumption? The case of 2019 novel coronavirus (2019-nCoV) in China. Available at SSRN: https://ssrn.com/abstract=3540667 or doi:10.2139/ssrn.3540667.

Sánchez, M. M. (2020). Flujos turísticos, geopolítica y COVID-19: cuando los turistas internacionales son vectores de transmisión. *Geopolítica(s). Revista de estudios sobre espacio y poder, 11*, 105–114. doi:10.5209/geop.69249.

Tsou, T.-P., Chen, W.-C., Huang, A. S.-E., Chang, S.-C. & The Taiwan COVID-19 Pandemic Investigation Team. (2020). Epidemiology of the first 100 cases of-COVID-19 in Taiwan and its implications onpandemic control. *Journal of the Formosan Medical Association, 119*, 1601–1607.

Wanjala, K. (2020). Economic impact assessment of the novel coronavirus on tourism and trade in Kenya: lessons from preceding pandemics. *Finance & Economics Review, 2*(1), 1–10. doi:10.38157/finance-economics-review.v2i1.57.

World Health Organization (2021a). *Rolling updates on coronavirus disease (COVID-19)*. Retrieved from: https://www.who.int/emergencies/diseases/novel-coronavirus-2019/events-as-they-happen (accessed: the 17th March, 2021).

World Tourism Organization (2021b). *International Tourism and Covid-19*. Retrieved from: https://www.unwto.org/international-tourism-and-covid-19 (accessed: the 20th March, 2021).

World Tourism Organization (2021c). *Impact Assessment of Covid 19 Pandemic on International Tourism*. Retrieved from: https://www.unwto.org/impact-assessment-of-the-covid-19-pandemic-on-international-tourism (accessed: the 20th March, 2021).

World Health Organization (2021d). *Coronavirus disease (COVID-19): Vaccines*. Retrieved from: https://www.who.int/news-room/q-a-detail/coronavirus-disease-(covid-19)-vaccines?adgroupsurvey={adgroupsurvey}&gclid=Cj0KCQjwutaCBhDfARIsAJHWnHsR4zp6fnPne0JGQhJI5IQnK_DxRi5HGDLgo-3Piy2uP0Ji35jg2PsaAjDtEALw_wcB (accessed: the 20th March, 2021).

World Health Organization (2021e). *WHO Coronavirus (COVID-19) Dashboard*. Retrieved from: https://covid19.who.int/ (accessed: the 20th March, 2021).

World Health Organization (2021f). *Data Table of Turkey*. Retrieved from: https://covid19.who.int/region/euro/country/tr (accessed: the 20th March, 2021).

Internet Sources

URL-1: https://tursab.org.tr/apps//Files/Content/8b368379-712e-4ca3-8425-69ae28b9f113.pdf, Accessed: 31.05.2020.

URL-2: https://www.tursab.org.tr/e-dergi?pdf=/assets/assets/uploads/istatislik/kasim-2020-tursab-istatistik-rapor.pdf, Accessed: 21.03.2020.

URL-3: https://www.musiad.org.tr/uploads/haberler/2020/mayis/covid19raporturizm.pdf, Accessed: 31.05.2020.
URL-4: https://www.tccb.gov.tr/haberler/?&page=1, Accessed: 21.03.2021.
URL-5: https://covid19.saglik.gov.tr/Eklenti/39265/0/covid-19salginyonetimivecalismarehberipdf.pdf, Accessed: 21.03.2021.

3 The Bright Side of COVID-19 in the Context of Tourism

Models of Wellness Tourism and Purposeful Travel Drive the Way Forward

Yue Wang and Laura Ell

Introduction

As many of our co-authors from other chapters in this book have demonstrated, the negative impacts on tourism are grander than we have seen in our lifetime. However, while there has been loss and severe economic downturn due to COVID-19, the pandemic has brought many opportunities to re-think tourism. This chapter provides hope to the sector as it presents new insights for both theoretical and applied tourism planning, implementation, and ongoing management. The timely concepts and case studies provide a frameworks and lessons learned from which enterprises, destinations, and other tourism stakeholders can forge a new path forward. A component of the resiliency has come from interdisciplinary partnerships, blending tourism with health as well as other sectors of government and industry that have traditionally not collaborated so closely. In a short time after the COVID era started, tourism stakeholders that have been liaising with such new partners have often been able to pivot to target more appropriate paths forward for destination planning, product development, visitor satisfaction, and triple bottom line benefits for community residents as well as investors. The models we will present are aligned with the United Nations (UN) Sustainable Tourism Development Goals (SDGs) and indeed may even support meeting the SDG goals faster than if COVID-19 had not provided us with the preverbal wake-up call that it gave us. This global journey will then take us around the globe to share successes that indicate the industry as a whole appears to be significantly away from mass tourism towards more purposeful travel. From China to the Americas, Caribbean and Mediterranean, we will learn much from those pioneering successful approaches.

The authors also examine the swift growth in demand and subsequent product shift to incorporate more wellness tourism elements to a broader range of visitors than niche market alone (Edelheim 2020). Navarrete and Shaw indicate that spas and thermal springs are seen as health agents in the COVID era and beyond (2020) while healing arts such as yoga, meditation, local cuisine, forest bathing, and other nature-based experiences also

DOI: 10.4324/9781003207467-5

provide wellness tourism experiences increasing in demand (Martin et al. 2020). The concept of healing gardens has been shown for several years to provide a benefit to hospitals and some medical tourism yet now is an ideal opportunity to introduce the framework more purposefully to the tourism industry as appropriate. Our case study dive deep into a case of healing gardens and thermal hydrotherapy in Northern China's Heilongjiang providing a successful replicable model and lessons learned for other destinations.

Our journey closes with highlighting how leaders in education train and prepare the workforce are evolving their curriculum and delivery methongs to such that the emerging tourism workforce is better prepared (Edelheim 2020).

Situational Analysis

The COVID-19 pandemic brought tourism, one of the world's biggest economic drivers to its knees and by May 11, 2020, UNWTO website reported that, for an albeit short time, 100% of all countries had some sort of travel restriction imposed. Notwithstanding, positive news was also being reported with accounts of collaboration to collectively begin recovery. The closing of tourism brought creative solutions and opportunity to pause and re-start with a focus more relevant to the future of tourism. Sharma et al., after conducting a literature review of 35 COVID tourism publications, proposed a resiliency-based framework focused on prioritization of sustainable tourism, society's wellbeing, mitigation of negative impacts to the climate, and the involvement of local communities for a more sustainable more sustainable way forward post-pandemic (2021).

UN SDGs as a Guiding Compass

Prior to the pandemic, select tourism players were starting to embrace the UN's SDGs, which are goals to be met by all industry sectors, not only tourism, by 2030. Commonly, the tourism sector was addressing Goals 8 Decent work and economic growth, Goal 12 Responsible Consumption and productions, and Goal 17 Partnerships for the goals (Spenceley and Rylance edited by McCool 2019, 107). With COVID-19, an opportunity opened up to more non-traditional partnerships (Goal 17). Climate Action Goal 13 is being addressed more purposefully as well, for example, Banff National Park, Canada, is launching *Banff Net Zero 2035* (https://banffnationalpark-netzero2035.ca/). Local Communities Goal 11 is also a growing priority (Sharma et al. 2021). Perhaps most notably of all is Goal 3, Good health and wellbeing as will become more evident as we explore the case studies and ideas throughout the rest of the chapter. Tourism has potential to address all goals according to the UNWTO (2015), which is a target that the industry as a whole should aspire to. Tools and education must be expanded to support this in order to avoid SDG-washing, an evolution of the term greenwashing (McCarton et al. 2021).

Emerging Traveller Aspirations

A survey in April 2020 of 1,800 global respondents who were asked about their fears and aspirations after travel the COVID-19 quarantine revealed that 11% are turning to ecotourism more than they did prior to COVID-19, while all other categories of travel were declining in popularity, especially mass gatherings, festival, and amusement parks (Pavelka et al. 2020). Comments pointed to opportunity for more meaningful, sustainable, nature-based experiences. Return to travel was a priority to get over stress of self-isolation, regain social connection, and overall improve wellness. This is aligned with results found in a 2020 study by Morse et al.

Forbes.com reported on June 11, 2020, that the Tourism Minister of Jamaica named the generation of travelers emerging after the pandemic who are more health and safety conscious as Gen-C.

A much greater priority for mainstream tourism now versus years past when it only got attention in niche segments of spa and medical tourism. Visitors do this not only to avoid health issues but to heal the mental, physical, social, and spiritual dimensions that have become depleted during their pandemic experience due to self-isolation and uncertainty (Ell and Pavelka 2020). Staycations also increased as a result of many air travel and government restrictions which as an upside reduced carbon footprint (SDG Goal 13). This surge in rubber-tire-traffic travel is introducing residents to meaningful experiences near to their homes that they previously had not encountered.

Wellness Tourism: an Opportunity to Re-set

This wide-spread demand by visitors to have more wellness centric experiences is projected to continue, thus presenting significant opportunity to revisit then re-set all typologies of tourism moving forward. The Global Wellness Institute (GWI) website defines wellness tourism as travel associated with the pursuit of maintaining or enhancing one's personal well-being (2020). Prior to the pandemic, the GWI forecasts were for wellness tourism to annual growth of 7.5% from 2020 to 2022 and the updated figures are in development but expected to be higher. As the use of the term wellness grows, tourism providers are rapidly positioning themselves as wellness travel to the post COVID-19 traveler. The majority of spend in wellness tourism according to GWI is by secondary travelers who have other primary goals of their trips but still seek wellness components.

Within the realm of wellness tourism, experiences include spa, health therapies, meditation, mindfulness training, yoga, spirituality retreats, balneotherapy, forest bathing, adventure, and more. Healthy cuisine and activity fresh air experiences are also in growing demands. While more research is needed and caution must be used in claiming curative benefits, many techniques used in wellness tourism are being sought out by travelers. One such example includes geothermal soaking which Navarrete and Shaw note "has a health dimension that may complement the mitigation of the effects of the pandemic at least in the recovery stage" (2020, 2). Some spas are getting permission from Indigenous knowledge keepers to share wisdom through Indigenous-inspired spa tourism (Ell and Pavelka, 2020). Once such example is Nawalakw, a language revitalization and healing center that supports and employs the community of Kwakwa̲ ka̲'wakw and be funded by an adjoining wellness eco-tourism lodge (https://nawalakw.com). Adventure travel is also growing in demand due to the fresh air and opportunity for safe distancing. Janowski, Gardiner, and Kwek present 22 dimensions of adventure tourism, many of which directly support health including physical activity, wellbeing, socializing exploration, flow, play, and escapism (2021).

Daniel Poulin of Accor Hotels coined the concept of *well-doing* as the achievement of a state of wellbeing by the active participation in physical activities, including adventure travel, all with a strong social element (Spa Business Handbook 2019, 78). Accor and many other hotel brands globally are increasing their programming and promotion of wellness components.

Wellness Tourism Continuum

Donohoe and Needham introduced the ecotourism continuum in 2008, demonstrating the range of tourism offers from least congruent with the tenets of ecotourism, often known as mass tourism (see top right of Figure 3.1) and then moving towards the left to tourism that is most congruent with ecotourism.

Ecotourism continuum		
Most congruent with ecotourism	more sustainable ecotourism lite	**Least congruent with ecotourism**
Tenets of ecotourism fully applied	Tenets of ecotourism partially applied	Tenets of ecotourism rarely applied / greenwashing

(adapted from Donohoe and Needham 2008 and modified by the authors)

Wellness tourism contiuum		
Most congruent with **Wellness Travel**	Healthier travel	Least congruent with Wellness Travel
Tenets of wellness fully applied	Tenets of wellness partially applied	Tenets of wellness rarely applied / wellness washing

Developed by the authors, inspired by the model by Donohoe and Needham 2008

Figure 3.1 Ecotourism continuum comparted to a new wellness tourism continuum.

There is a parallel to wellness tourism. The authors propose that a similar continuum can be developed with wellness tourism. Least congruent to wellness tourism may include such activities hedonistic travel, excess eating at unhealthy buffets, sitting on long bus trips without physical activity and stressful crowded experiences by operators with unsustainable and unhealthy environmental practices.

Visitors are more likely to be attracted to a wellness tourism product based on the effectiveness of the marketing images and copy, so with this comes responsibility to ensure the product is congruent with the marketing promise (Wang et al. 2021).

A cautionary tale we can learn from the ecotourism history of development is that tourism suppliers and operators have the responsibility to be true to their brand promise. It is key that they do not wellness wash or claim they are offering a healthful experience to travelers when they do no more than lip service, as has and continues to happen with the unethical practice of greenwashing when mass tourism falsely uses the term ecotourism in marketing.

Value of Nature

Buckley revealed the impactful benefits with a study of nature-based and adventure tourists in Queensland, Australia. Following of park visitation, 82% reported more happiness, 87.5% gained short-term emotional benefit, and 60% recovered from stress over the medium-term (2020). The Japanese art of Shinrin-yoku, also known as forest bathing, also has verified health benefits (Payne and Delphinus 2019). "Increasing both contact with, and connection to nature, are likely to be needed in order to achieve synergistic improvements to human and planetary health." Said Martin et al. (2020, 1). Banff Centre in Canada reported that the most popular conference add-on for their Meetings Conferences and Incentive Travel groups is the forest bathing experience (personal communication with Michael Code, January 2021)

Healing Gardens

Development and Definitions

An experience that has great potential within wellness in tourism is the healing garden. Healing gardens have witnessed a long history of use in health facilities and residential developments but until recent years were not broadly integrated into tourism planning (Pouya and Demirel 2015). The concept has garnered global attention (Xu et al. 2020). The target planning and design could realize the transfer from external morphology to the function of the physical elements. It emphasizes the micro-stimulation to visitors five senses and awakening of positive attitude. The physical and intangible elements can be applied to realize the maximum benefits from physical, psychological and social aspects (Xue et al. 2020).

Conceptualization of the garden not only considers aesthetics, but also strives to restore health and emotions using landscape elements. Physical planning and design, the space construction and zoning tend to satisfy the requirements from different users and there are connections among different spaces with the application of healing gardens. For different spaces, design of landscape elements have different characteristics, such as morphology, color, smell of the foliage, water flowing, sculptures, etc. so the concept of healing gardens realize the calls for people orientation, especially in space design (Wang 2019).

The Necessities of Combination of Healing Gardens and Tourism

During and after COVID-19, the concept of healing garden can be a breakthrough point for to use more often in various disciplines, especially tourism, to realize the true intonation of people orientation.

The Concept of Healing Gardens: Putting Wellness Tourism into Practice

Majeed and Ramkissoon's systematic review revealed that visitors seek therapeutic landscapes to promote wellbeing (2020). Wellness tourism may include elements from food, sport, accommodation, to most touchpoints of the visitor experience. The concept of healing gardens can provide a target and guidance for how to do and what to do in certain environment, more broadly from special planning, choice of plants, water features, sculptures down to the level of placement of where a chair is placed to optimize visitor experience. These are but a sample of considerations that would be adjusted based on the requirements from types of users.

The Concept of Healing Gardens: Considering Requirements for Various Users, Especially during and Post COVID-19

Interventions for ridding individuals of physical ailments as a result of COVID-19 were a priority in 2020 however even those who did not suffer physically will likely have the memories imprinted in their mind for life. Interventions for mental health challenges including stress are increasingly sought-out as a result of the pandemic (Kar et al. 2021). How can wellness tourism support the varying needs of individuals? While the solution is not simple, the concept of healing gardens can guide us to explore opportunities of the users from seniors to adults to children. Through careful planning, wellness tourism can become a restorative experience in contrast to more consumptive behaviors that mass tourism offers.

Success Case Studies

Heilongjiang, China: Healing Gardens, Medical and Wellness Tourism

HEILONGJIANG PROVINCE

Heilongjiang province is located in the northeast of China (see Figure 3.2). The north and east are adjacent to Russia, and the border is 3,045 kilometers long. It is an important land route from Asia and the Pacific to the Russian Far East and the European continent. The west and the south are adjacent to Inner Mongolia and Jilin provinces, covering an area of 473,000 square kilometers (Heilongjiang. Chinese People's Government. [2016-1-17]).

There are a wide range of tourism attractions in Heilongjiang. However, due to its climate, the province is most known for its winter sport and

Figure 3.2 Location map of Heilongjiang province.
Source: Heilongjiang Inclusive Tourism Development Master Plan (2020–2030), compiled by World Tourism Organization (2019).

festival events. Tourist numbers and revenues are increasing yet still below national average when compared to other provinces. In 2018, the number of domestic tourists increased to 143 million (+11.2%), with tourism receipts of RMB157.3 billion (+17.7%). The number of overseas tourists stood at 0.96 million (+14.7%), with a foreign exchange revenue of US$458 million (+15.9%).

WUDALIANCHI UNESCO GLOBAL GEOPARK

Location and Introduction Wudalianchi UNESCO Global Geopark (hereinafter referred to as Geopark) is located in the north central region of Heilongjiang province with a total area of 1,060 square kilometers.

Between 1719 and 1721, volcanoes erupted and lava blocked the Baihe River, forming five interconnected lakes; hence, it is named Wudalianchi. Heihe City, as one of the port cities along Sino-Russian border line, is one of the first open border cities, famous as Sino-Russian Window and the door between Europe and Asia. Geopark is just located within Wudalianchi City, which affiliates to Heihe City (see Figure 3.3), and therefore, it is featured as abundant natural resources and excellent geographical location, which greatly attracts a large amount of Chinese and foreign tourists, especially that many Russian tourists are attracted for medical and wellness tourism. In addition, it was designated as a global geopark in 2004 (by the National Geopark Network) and was included on the IUCN Green List of Protected Areas in 2014.

Tourist Resources Introduction Geopark's scenic volcanic formations, mountains and rivers, constitute a biodiverse ecological environment with distinctive landscape characteristics. The tourism resources are abundant and complete with strong theme, well-trained interpretive guides and diversity (see Figure 3.4). Volcanic resources have a prominent position in the resource system, so tourism activities are mainly focused on volcanic resources. This world-famous volcanic landscape combination of existing resource types is diverse, forms an extremely integrated destination of mountains, water, geothermal springs, rocks formations as well as cultural heritage assets, and culinary offerings which collectively is a rare combination to find.

VOLCANIC RESOURCES

Volcanic resources are diverse and present as the basis for the tourism development in Wudalianchi. They primarily include volcanic cones, lava, barrier lakes, and mineral springs.

The lakes inside Geopark have varying characteristics. Medical Lake has been refurbished and is an optimal site for visitors to relax and boat.

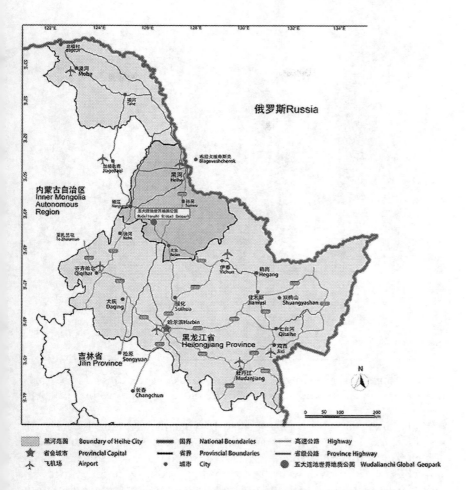

Figure 3.3 Location map of Wudalianchi UNESCO Global Geopark.
http://www.wdlcggp.org.cn/introductiontothepark/index.aspx.

Geopark is a tectonic activity and geothermal anomaly area, with a wide distribution and large number of mineral springs. The tourism resources can meet the needs of basic tourism, relaxing as well as scientific investigation, and sightseeing.

HEALTH BENEFITS OF WARM AND COLD MINERAL SPRINGS

Globally and in China, there is a long history of using mineral springs for medical recuperation (Gao et al. 2019; Gianfaldoni et al. 2017). Geopark including its springs is rich in physical and chemical properties offering

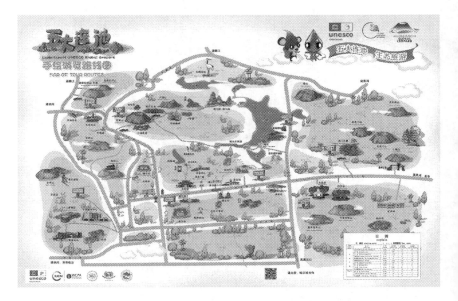

Figure 3.4 Geopark attractions map.
Wudalianchi Scenic Area Official Website, http://www.chinawdlc.gov.cn/pages/5a6e7d31f6e9fa189cd2ba86.

various functions of medical recuperation. A large number of Chinese and foreign patients and tourists come and enjoy the wellness benefits annually.

Wudalianchi mineral spring formed by volcanic eruption is one of the world's three largest low-temperature cold springs, comparable to the French Vichy mineral spring and Russian North Caucasus mineral spring. It is characterized by low temperature, high salinity, unique taste, and strong regeneration ability. Its mineral content is therapeutic containing iron, strontium, siliceous bicarbonate, carbonate, and more than 20 trace elements beneficial to human health (Gao et al. 2019; Navarrete and Shaw 2020). Some of the mineral water sources around Geopark can be drunk directly, and visiting researchers to the sites assessing patient have observed relief of such ailments as pain, insomnia, neurological alopecia, psoriasis, urinary tract diseases, ulcers, and gastritis.

The fertile volcanic soil in combination with natural mineral spring water provide nourishment to nearby agricultural operations resulting in delicacies including mineral fish, mineral tofu, mineral eggs, mineral beans, mineral fruits and vegetables, mineral rice, mineral wine, and more. The ingredients are integrated into the culinary offerings around Wudalianchi to further enhance the wellness tourism experience.

VOLCANIC FOLK CULTURAL RESOURCES WITH GREAT POTENTIALITY

History has endowed the region with the rich volcanic cultural resources. The many legends, such as the discovery of mineral springs, the rescue of Ameqige girl at mineral springs, the myth of five ponds, fairy and fairy palace, etc. Additionally, there are many traditional and interesting festivals related to spring water, such as the unique sacrificial activities of Zhongling Temple in the crater of Yaoquan Mountain. The Holy Water Festival is held on the fourth to the fifth day of May in the lunar calendar every year, which is also known as the Drinking Water Festival. During the recent years, the event has grown to contribute to building culture and prosperity for the local economy. Meditation and cultural sites are also strong cultural assets in the area.

Geopark is exploring the concept of becoming branded as a Wellness Town whereby the destination can be further developed into a comprehensive region integrating more sightseeing, eco-tourism, science tourism, leisure vacation tourism and recuperation tourism. World-class spa resort investors are assessing opportunity for sustainable development in the region which would further raise the appeal to wellness seekers. An opportunity exists to plan the upcoming built architectural designs of infrastructure to be much more in keeping with the local sense of place.

The Existing Problems of Tourism Resource and Destination

The Development of Tourism Resources Still Relatively Basic

At present, the main activities in the scenic area are visiting volcanic landform and drinking mineral water for recuperation. However, the water resources are not optimized. Surface water resources are insufficiently utilized, and the waterfront space is not fully utilized. At present, the development of waterfront space is only in the area of medical, not considering a wider tourism development scale and use.

Single Tourism Products and Obsolete Items

At present, the tourist activity is mainly sight-viewing of volcanic landforms and mineral springs but a lack of other participatory activities. The development of recuperation vacation and fitness activities need to be vigorously strengthened. In recent years, the innovation is only made in ice caves and there have been no breakthroughs in volcanic sightseeing and spa treatments. Spa products are limited to therapeutic pools and mud treatments, but there lies an opportunity to add massages and other spa treatments as well as expand merchandising.

The Tourist Service Facilities Are Underdeveloped

The development of tourism reception and service is slow, and the majority of the facility investments and development were completed in 1980s; thus, the facilities are notably outdated. The hotels and sanatoriums (institutes) in Wudalianchi Scenic Area are of low grade, and supporting services are in need of improvement. In addition, the traffic in the scenic area is inconvenient, and the development of tourism, entertainment, and shopping is limited.

Wellness Tourism Improvement and Strategies with the Application of Healing Garden

Analysis of the Tourist Source and Their Demands and Rules of Behaviors

Behaviors is the feedback to the environment stimulation from the people. Environment is the place for behavior. The mutual interaction between the environment and people will improve the environment.

In 2018, over 1 million foreign tourist visits were recorded in Heilongjiang, with Europeans (863,841), predominantly Russians, accounting for the majority (see Table 3.1). For Geopark, the main tourists mainly come

Table 3.1 Visits to Heilongjiang province by foreign nationals (person-times)

Region and Main markets	2018	2017	% Increase Or Decrease	% of Foreign Tourists
Europe	863,841	835,076	3.44	82.96
Russia	854,447	824,367	3.65	82.05
Germany	2,264	2,258	0.27	0.22
United Kingdom	1,894	1,669	13.48	0.18
France	1,667	1,811	−7.40	0.16
Asia	158,018	135,692	16.45	15.17
Korea	92,093	82,424	11.73	8.84
Japan	26,792	28,427	−5.75	2.57
Singapore	11,452	6,531	75.35	1.10
Malaysia	11,375	6,149	84.99	1.09
Indonesia	3,288	2,096	56.87	0.32
Thailand	3,124	2,679	16.61	0.30
Americas	10,310	8,906	15.76	0.99
United States	7,308	6,454	13.23	0.70
Canada	2,230	1,789	24.65	0.21
Oceania	3,652	3,251	12.33	0.35
Australia	2,974	2,738	8.62	0.29
Africa	1,170	333	251.35	0.11
Others	4,324	1,385	212.20	0.42
TOTAL	1,041,315	984,643	5.76	100.00

Source: Heilongjiang Provincial Tourism Bureau policy and regulation division.

from Russia for its international market because of its unique access for them and especially the appeal of wellness tourism. In sight of healing gardens, the demands of the tourists should be analyzed. Therefore, the prerequisite strategy for wellness tourism improvement should be the analysis of the tourist market and their requirements and rules of behaviors within the Geopark. As seen from Table 3.2, above 66% of Russian tourists travel

Table 3.2 Tourist source market for Heilongjiang province

Market	Key Points
Russians	• Largest market to Heilongjiang accounting for 82% of all foreign visits (nearly 600,000 visits measured in person-times) • For some visitors, Heilongjiang is also the first destination on the way to other destinations in China • A recent survey in 2018 identified them as mainly middle-aged and elderly, largely women interested in wellness and relaxation (especially in Wudalianchi and Daqing) as well as shopping *Market Analysis and Research Report on Heilongjiang Province Inbound Tourism commissioned by Heilongjiang Provincial Culture and Tourism Office* • Low-income and middle-income group in general but 10% are considered high-income/high-end tourists • Loyal market: 80% repeat visitors • Interests: hot and cold springs, history and culture • Less interested in wetlands, forests and volcanoes • Length of stay: mostly a week but up to 14 days (4–7: 58%; 8–14: 32%) • A third travel with family and a third with friends
South Koreans	• Account for 9% of total international visits to Heilongjiang • Middle-aged to elderly • Luxury tourists with high expectations of services and facilities • Interested in the history of Heilongjiang, particularly linked to Korean war of independence against the Japanese • Interested in the cool weather in summer, the hot and cold springs and the medical treatments (including traditional Chinese medicine) as well as the Ice and Snow festivals in winter
Japanese	• Third largest market to Heilongjiang but declining • The survey carried out in Heilongjiang suggested that the market is mainly middle-aged to elderly (nearly 75% over 36 years of age) • Relatively high disposable income and high purchasing power • Expectations of high service and quality infrastructure • Interest in Ice and Snow festivals but also military sites; they also like the food of Heilongjiang and the characteristic buildings • Short breaks in Heilongjiang of 2 to 7 nights with 60% coming with a group, half with their family and a quarter with their colleagues • Other surveys show that in the last decade there has been a marked reluctance by the Japanese to travel overseas, mostly due to economic downturns and unfavorable exchange rates as well as global insecurity • Disproportionate decline in travel to China is a result of incidents such as food poisoning in 2008 and tourist conflict in 2012

(*Continued*)

Market	Key Points
Hong Kong, Macao and Taiwan	• Two markets, middle-aged and elderly interested by the Ice and Snow experience but also by history and culture as well as architecture, and a young market interested in enjoying Ice and Snow activities and sports • Research by VisitBritain indicate that for Hong Kong residents, relaxation on a spa holiday, a cruise, or even learning new skills in cooking, photography or other interests are common motivations to travel https://www.visitbritain.org/markets/hong-kong • Well-being and health are also important motivators • More research needs to be carried out on these markets
Expatriates living in China	2010 census indicates 600,000+ expatriates living in China. More recent figures suggest it is closer to 1 million https://www.relocatemagazine.com/news/international-assignments-changing-times-for-expat-positions-in-china-dsapsted-0419 • Whereas they used to be dominated by language teachers, today there are more expats working in the service sector, IT and media industries • 2010 census: largest population live in Guangdong, Shanghai and Beijing • South Koreans account for 21%, the US 12%, Japan 11% (https://sampi.co/china-expat-population-statistics/) • Represent a captive market for winter and summer

with families or friends and stay for longer, usually between 1 and 2 weeks. Therefore, for the Geopark, the Russian tourist market should be explored further, such as their body conditions. For instance, it is cold in Russia, the whether the tourists suffer from cardiovascular and cerebrovascular diseases? If the young people account for the majority, whether they are faced with multiple pressure from work, families and society? What is the differences between demands amongst family members, such as the true demand of the children and how to make them satisfied? The most fundamental step for wellness tourism improvement is to analyze the visitor source and their demands in detail, which is also the core to drive sustainable development in the future.

Tourists-Oriented Spatial Planning and Design

Behavior-Guided Spatial Structure and Layout

The spatial planning and design of Geopark should benefit all types of visitors, especially those seeking wellness or remedies for their skin conditions. Types of spaces should be improved to vary with characteristics, to offer choices. The focuses of the space include morphology, color, vision, etc. The types of the space should include open, semi-open, and closed spaces.

Open space. It can accommodate group activities for informal communication, and visitors can feel the power from others even without communication. Due to the small market since wellness is still in its infancy, this space is not yet the primary type in demand.

Semi-closed space. It can accommodate 3–5 people, a suitable space for families or small groups. People inside can feel the sense of control. It is easier for visitors to watch others while immersing in their own world. Plants, paths, or structures can be used to define the boundary, especially the layout of the seats are very important to facilitate communication. In post-epidemic era, people who has suffered in the hospital or home isolation need this type of space to share with their families or friends to improve their mental health and relax.

Closed space. This type of space is urgently needed for the wellness tourism in Geopark. It caters for 1–2 people with strong privacy and isolation sense. Tourists for wellness purpose in Geopark have their own uniqueness, such as skin issues, they surely need their own space to enjoy the benefits from the nature. In the future, it is projected to be the most popular space for visitors who has suffered from COVID-19 to calm and relax themselves.

As shown in Figures 3.5 and 3.6, the types of existing spaces are mainly open without privacy, which shows consideration to tourists. Closed spaces (Figure 3.6) are simple hidden sites.

Figure 3.5 Open space thermal springs in Geopark.
Source: Photo by author.

Figure 3.6 Semi-open space volcanic stone sunbathing.
Source: Photo by author.

Healing-Based Integration of the Environmental Elements

The theme of wellness tourism is healing, and although plants, water, sculptures and structures tend to realize each function, these elements are not separated and they should be connected together as a whole to constitute the harmony, which will offer tourists senses of safety, positive guidance and comfortableness in physics, psychology and society through the stimulation of five senses. The tourists can stay longer and enjoy more experiences in one space only if all the elements are harmonious and unified. The length of stay is one of the most important indicators to mark whether the construction of the space is successful. A further benefit of satisfied client in a therapeutic environment is a likelihood of repeat visitation (Majeed and Ramkissoon 2020).

Plants selection and optimization. Plant life is the most important element. In addition to satisfy the traditional function and aesthetics, the selection and collocation should serve as a stimulus, which provide a carrier for tourists to release, memory recalling and participate activities. The uniqueness of wellness tourists within the Geopark calls for more attention to the selection and collocation of the plants. For the elderly, the plants should emphasize the flowering plants, or the leaf color is saturated, such as red, yellow or orange. Because the elderly, such as those with cataracts, tend to think that blue or lavender-like flowers are gray. Plants with longer life, even the whole year round, should be considered to symbol the meaning of longevity.

Integration of multiple elements. Space is dominated by the plants, but there are other elements, such as water, pathways, and even seating, which needs to consider as a whole based on the healing concept. For instance, in a small semi-open space, the plants should avoid excessive dazzling colors and aromatic plants, the set-up and arrangements of the seats should consider the number of communication ways of the users and the scale of the sculptures and structures should be small. The integration of all these elements will provide the users with a space for walking or resting and make them comfort and safety with a sense of control. Only under this context, they can obtain the connection to nature or even the opportunity to communicate with others to further realize the physical, psychological and social recovery. Also, the different ways of selection and combination among elements can offer people totally different sensory experiences, closed or control, happy or sad, relaxing or anxious.

The Multidisciplinary Wellness Team and Dynamic Assessment of Wellness Function

Wellness tourism is not a single subject, in comparison, it is a multidisciplinary event which needs the input from various aspects. Therefore, the development of wellness tourism actually is not only referring to the tourist planners, designers, consultants, it also should include doctors, psychologist, engineers, tourists, staff of the destinations, and more. All individuals along the touchpoint of the customer journey should be involved in the process holistically from planning, design, construction, consultation marketing, and then the subsequent product delivery, management and maintenance. Especially under COVID-19, the calls for wellness tourism is higher and more complex, from traditional health to the attention to the deep psychology, from obvious promotion to unconsciously influence and from short experiences to long-term immersion (Majeed and Ramkissoon 2020).

As a result of the COVID-19 pandemic, tourism providers are informed that that the pursuit of the visitor is changing rapidly and will continue to do so post-pandemic period. The traditional awareness for wellness tourism can't catch up with the wellness market forever. We are now tasked with assessing the effect of the wellness product offering periodically through various ways, such as questionnaires, site interview and online note to make the wellness tourism sustainable development. The assessment elements can include the space utilization, accessibility within and outside the destinations, social behaviors of the tourists, plant function, utilization of certain space, etc. The assessment results can be compared with the original design intention to generate the gap and differences, which can be the direction of efforts in the future.

Training, Education, and Research

Educators in the COVID-era are in an important leadership position to prepare the precarious tourism workforce for serving these changing needs in the industry. Edelheim recommends that reforming both tourism higher education curriculum as well as philosophies in research will support the success of tourism moving forward (2020). Similarly, Higgins-Desbiolle cautions that a rapid return for the tourism sector to pre-pandemic ways without serious modifications to the new realities, both operationally as well as the academic system, has a risk to the future of tourism leaving practitioners ill-prepared to deal with the challenges at hand (2020).

Post-secondary education offering international fields school programs are continuing in upward demand, and when done right they result in more culturally aware, experienced tourism professionals (Pavelka and Minions 2020). As a result of the pandemic, Mount Royal University's Ecotourism and Outdoor Leadership undergraduate degree it likely to begin offering a new degree minor in Wellness Tourism to its students.

In January 2021 the University of Iowa College of Pharmacy partnered with wellness tourism resort Jungle Bay Dominica to provide a rotation for their students which provided. Among many outcomes was the establishment of an innovative clinic in one of the spa treatment rooms to provide telehealth a blend of allopathic and local remedies with years of historic use. The experiential two-way learning provided capacity building for the local staff in Dominica better preparing them to deal with COVID and health in general while transferring local knowledge to future pharmacists in the USA (personal Communication Dr. Abrons, February 2021).

Local Resident Health

With measurable social impacts of residents occurring during tourism that operated during COVID, such as higher risk of community transmission, a way forward must include meaningful resident input (Qiu et al. 2020). Since residents differ depending on demographic and geographic influences Qui et al. suggest that a one-size-fits all approach will not work for instance younger generations are more connected to the Internet more generally and as such they may be informed in that way (2020). Holistic tourism planning processes are being encourage to place greater emphasis on health benefits not only for the visitor but also tourism providers as well as other residents and stakeholders in host communities (Martin et al. 2020; Sonuç 2020). Putting well-being indicators for the community like Gross National Happiness ahead of measuring traditional tourism metrics of revenue and tourism arrivals is a core philosophy in the Planet Happiness methodology (Musikanski et al. 2021).

Destinations Shifting Target Markets

According to Sanjay Nepal post-COVID, "the adventure travel sector has the opportunity for turning its attention away from haphazard development to one that repositions itself as a major partner in contributing to sustainable and mindful travel" (2020, 647). The Mediterranean is one of the world's most popular tourism regions. The destinations of Tunisia, Lebanon, Jordan, Catalonia Spain, and Puglia Italy recognized that they were too heavily reliant on sun, sand and sea tourism, which was proving to be increasingly economically, socio-culturally and environmentally un-sustainable. Through the MEDUSA project, a partnership of the World Wildlife Fund, European Union and others, the new vision of these five destinations was to shift towards adventure tourism 2019 through 2022 towards a comprehensive sustainable destination management strategy with grassroots input that prioritizes local benefits. The timing of this was ideal as COVID struck because the diverse tourism experiences that are being planned will emerge to increase competitiveness. The tourism system as a whole will be better prepared to serve the new post-COVID visitor demands while keeping an increase in the earnings within the local economies.

http://www.enicbcmed.eu/medusa-whats-adventure-tourism-and-why-it-more-sustainable.

Conclusion

What does this bright side of tourism mean moving forward? COVID-19 has indeed altered the way tourism is both operated and experienced. While more research and sharing of successes amongst the industry are still necessary, indications are strong that more emphasis on wellness, collaboration and spatial planning for infrastructure, such as healing gardens and balenothareap as is showcased in Heilongjiang, China. These models will be key to bringing growth and success via a new tourism paradigm. The tourism sector should celebrate these silver lining of the COVID-19 pandemic as a means of approaching tourism in a more healthful way for long-term sustainability for the climate and other aspects of the environment, host communities, the tourism workforce and the visitors themselves. They may indeed be helping the industry become more sustainable embracing of the UN's SGDs', enhancing host community quality of life, reduction of economic leakage and improving stakeholder health all along the tourism value chain.

References

Buckley, Ralf. "Nature tourism and mental health: parks, happiness, and causation." *Journal of Sustainable Tourism* 28, no. 9 (2020): 1409–1424.

Donohoe, Holly, and Needham, Roger. (2008). "Internet-based ecotourism marketing: evaluating Canadian sensitivity to ecotourism tenets." *Journal of Ecotourism* 7: 15–43. https://doi.org/10.2167/joe185.0.

Edelheim, Johan. "How should tourism education values be transformed after 2020?" *Tourism Geographies* 22, no. 3 (May 26, 2020): 547–554. https://doi.org/10.1080/14616688.2020.1760927.

Ell, Laura, and Joe Pavelka. "A code of conduct to guide indigenous-inspired spas." *International Journal of Spa and Wellness* 3, no. 1 (2020): 1–23.

Gao, Si Meng, Yu Juan Wen, Wen Qing Zhang, D. Z. Zhang, and Y. S. Yang. "Microbial characteristics and eco-health implication of mineral spring water in Wudalianchi, Northeast China." Ying yong sheng tai xue bao = *The Journal of Applied Ecology* 30, no. 8 (2019): 2865–2874.

Gianfaldoni, Serena, Georgi Tchernev, Uwe Wollina, Maria Grazia Roccia, Massimo Fioranelli, Roberto Gianfaldoni, and Torello Lotti. "History of the baths and thermal medicine." *Open Access Macedonian Journal of Medical Sciences* 5, no. 4 (2017): 566.

Global Wellness Institute. (2020). "Fact Sheet: Wellness Tourism Initiative 2020 global survey results." https://globalwellnessinstitute.org/wp-content/uploads/2020/05/GWI_FACT_SHEET_LEISURE-TRAVEL_2020.pdf.

Janowski, Ingo, Sarah Gardiner, and Anna Kwek. "Dimensions of adventure tourism." *Tourism Management Perspectives* 37 (2021): 100776.

Kar, Nilamadhab, Brajaballav Kar, and Shreyan Kar. "Stress and coping during COVID-19 pandemic: result of an online survey." *Psychiatry research* 295 (2021): 113598.

Majeed, Salman, and Haywantee Ramkissoon. "Health, wellness, and place attachment during and post health pandemics." *Frontiers in Psychology* 11 (2020): 573220.

Martin, Leanne, Mathew P. White, Anne Hunt, Miles Richardson, Sabine Pahl, and Jim Burt. "Nature contact, nature connectedness and associations with health, wellbeing and pro-environmental behaviours." *Journal of Environmental Psychology* 68 (2020): 101389.

McCarton, Liam, Sean O'Hogain, and Anna Reid. "The worth of water." In *The Worth of Water: Designing Climate Resilient Rainwater Harvesting Systems*, pp. 1–12. Cham: Springer International Publishing, 2021.

Morse, Joshua W., Tatiana M. Gladkikh, Diana M. Hackenburg, and Rachelle K. Gould. "COVID-19 and human-nature relationships: Vermonters' activities in nature and associated nonmaterial values during the pandemic." *PloS One* 15, no. 12 (2020): e0243697.

Musikanski, Laura, Rhonda Phillips, and Paul Rogers. "Well-being data gathering during COVID-19: exploring the feasibility of a contact tracing and community well-being safeguarding framework." *International Journal of Community Well-Being* 1–9(7 January 2021). doi:10.1007/s42413-020-00108-0 .

Nepal, Sanjay K. "Travel and tourism after COVID-19–business as usual or opportunity to reset?." *Tourism Geographies* 22, no. 3 (2020): 1–5.

Pavelka, Joe, and Carmanah Minions. "Defining the field school within study abroad." *Frontiers: The Interdisciplinary Journal of Study Abroad* 32, no. 2 (2020): 145–162.

Pavelka, Joe, Laura Ell, and Karly Upshaw. (September 14, 2020). "Traveler fears and aspirations during COVID-19 isolation in anticipation of a return to travel." Accessed, September 14, 2020 https://www.lauraell.com/travel-fears-and-aspirations/.

Payne, Mark D., and Elias Delphinus. "A review of the current evidence for the health benefits derived from forest bathing." *International Journal of Health, Wellness & Society* 9, no. 1 (2019): 19–30.

Pinos Navarrete, Aida, and Gareth Shaw. "Spa Tourism Opportunities as Strategic Sector in Aiding Recovery from Covid-19: The Spanish Model." *Tourism and Hospitality Research* 21, no. 2(April 2021): 245–250.

Pouya, Sima, and Öner Demirel. "What is a healing garden?" *Akdeniz Üniversitesi Ziraat Fakültesi Dergisi* 28, no. 1 (2016): 1–10.

Qiu, Richard T. R., Jinah Park, ShiNa Li, and Haiyan Song. "Social costs of tourism during the COVID-19 pandemic." *Annals of Tourism Research* 84 (2020): 102994.

Sharma, Gagan Deep, Asha Thomas, and Justin Paul. "Reviving tourism industry post-COVID-19: a resilience-based framework." *Tourism management perspectives* 37 (2021): 100786.

Spa Business Handbook. *Spa Business Handbook 2019-2020*. Herfordshire UK, The Leisure Media Company, 2019. https://www.spahandbook.com/digital/index1.cfm?mag=&issue=2019%20issue%201.

Sonuç, Nil. "Wellness Tourism Management: well-being as a sustainability concern for Wellness Tourism Management." In *Industrial and Managerial Solutions for Tourism Enterprises*, pp. 110–127. IGI Global, 2020.

United Nations World Tourism Organization (UNWTO). *Tourism and Sustainable Development Goals*. UNWTO, 2015.

Wang, Tsai-Chiao, Ming-Lang Tseng, Huei-Wen Pan, Chiou-Chi Hsiau, Ta-Wei Tang, and Chia-Liang Tsai. "The development of a sustainable wellness service marketing strategy in Taiwan based on consumer eye movements and preferences." *Journal of Cleaner Production* 282 (2021): 124382.

Wang, Yue. *Study on the Application Strategies of Healing Garden in Landscape Design of City Residential Community*. Harbin Institute of Technology, 2019.

Xu, Lina, Wei Xuying, Huang Weihao, Cai Junhuo. "Visual analysis of rehabilitation landscape research based on CiteSpace." *Landscape* 12 (2020): 78–84.

Xue, Binxia, Li Tongyu, Tang Haoming, Qu Jiping, Guo Jiayi. "The application of the concept of rehabilitation landscape in the planning and design of green space in urban residential areas." *Architectural Techniques* 05 (2020): 54–58.

4 The Effect of COVID-19 Pandemic on Tourism and Hospitality Industry – A Review

Anukrati Sharma and Shruti Arora

Introduction

The tourism industry, known as the travel industry, means public travelling to various locations, whichever domestically or internationally, for leisure or business trips. Hotel industry, the hospitality industry and the transport industry are closely connected to the tourism industry and try to keep tourists happy, engaged and prepared with the things they need away from home. Therefore, it is a wide-ranging industry. And the *hospitality industry is typically known as a more extensive service industry, through a focus on relaxation and customer satisfaction, rather than more basic needs.* The hospitality industry focuses more on lavishness, enjoyment, enjoyment and experiences. There are four sectors of the hospitality industry: Accommodation (Hotels, Bed & Breakfast, Resorts), Food and beverages (Catering, Bars, Drinks, Cafes), Travel and Tourism (Travel Agents, Online Travel Agencies, Car rentals) and Recreation (Museums, Casinos, Any participatory events, Theme park). The constant demand for tourism let the hospitality industry to predict demand and discover opportunities to increase consumer spending, creating a sign of secondary monetary impacts (Robinson, Lück and Smith, 2013). Modern tourism and hospitality is more business-oriented set of activities, gradually more intensive and commercially structured. It is an essential business sector for the economies of both developing and developed countries. A favorable country's image is critical to the accomplishment of these two sector marketing. The ever mounting global tourism industry is one of the major factors motivating the growth of the hospitality industry. These both industries go hand in hand. The factors that were stimulating the industries include increasing disposable income, new travel trends, increasing online travelling business due to enhanced internet connectivity and internet banking, web-presence of hotels & tourism directory. The expansion in the hospitality industry has resulted in the enlargement of restaurants, hotels and bars, which is anticipated to hotels market growth. Even the development in the tourism industry has played a primary role in the development of the hospitality industry and the hotels market. The hospitality business is based on the customs and traditions of serving guests with affection and care so that

DOI: 10.4324/9781003207467-6

they feel comfortable and secure being away from home. Both the industries bring valuable foreign exchange, as people who travel to other countries spend currency on hotel stay, transport, shopping, sightseeing, etc.

But as the effects of COVID-19 (Coronavirus) spread across the entire world in the starting of the year 2020, it has brought incalculable pain and hardships to many organizations from all corners of the globe especially tourism and hospitality. This virus is having an enormous effect on the tourism industry as the most crowded tourist destinations in the world are deserted due to shut borders, no domestic or international flights or transport system and mix up to deal with the biggest impact in the history of the world – Covid-19. The corona virus has arrived and altered the way we live and travel. And after COVID-19 people's expectations about vacation destinations will become more and more classy and the people will surely become choosier and will take more time while deciding for a particular destination. Selecting a destination that is suitable for compacted vacation time, family, income, hygiene factor, social value, that also satisfies the emotional needs and wishes, is a difficult undertaking. Morgan and Pritchard (2004, p. 61) indicate that indicate that the fight for buyers in tomorrow's destination marketplace will be battled not over price but over hearts and psyches and this is how places have motivated into territories formerly set aside for consumer brands. Post COVID-19, all three industries i.e. the travel, tourism and hospitality can easily be never same again as before. This means that business cannot go as usual, the industry both at national and international level will have to rethink a lot of practices from now. As Sheller (2020) expresses so clearly, "all human mobilities have been brought to a fast stop." Infact for the first time in the history, world's economy was close down almost overnight because of the Covid-19 pandemic.

Review of Literature

Tourism has developed as a significant monetary division and source of social and environmental change since the 1950s but initially, hospitality was not seen as a commercial industry. Nowadays, "hospitality has become a commercialized occurrence, where the visitor gives for the services/goods they consume by means of a bill" (Page, 2009). And tourism simply means the development of individuals to nations or spots outside their typical condition for individual or business/proficient purposes. Hospitality is a subsection of tourism. For an enhanced understanding of the terms, its characteristics should be defined as (Figure 4.1).

Traveling is a significant component of many of our lives. Though traveling either through flight or train to reach to a destination, spending time at restaurants and stay in a hotel is not the only part of our travel process but also involves the hospitality industry. All are essential pieces of the hospitality industry. Certainly the most imperative feature of the industry is service and the satisfaction that a guest has after rendering the services.

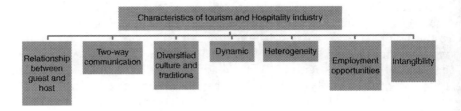

Figure 4.1 Characteristics of tourism and hospitality industry.

Basically, tourism and hospitality act as a promoter of generating employment, building image and friendship among the nations. The more pleased the guests are, the more liable they are to return. Like the Oberoi Group of Hotels or the Taj Group or *Marriot* International India Pvt Ltd maintained high standards of services and qualities, and extended their business overseas. Even the Ministry of Tourism in India has taken the several initiatives to identify and promote niche products in the country like endorsement of Golf Tourism and Medical & Wellness Tourism, Eco-tourism, Film Tourism, Adventure Tourism, Meetings Incentives Conferences & Exhibitions (MICE) and Sustainable Tourism.

On the other hand, the hospitality segment is one of the most profoundly taxed industries with several layers of tax, such as VAT, service tax, luxury tax, etc. from 20%–30% (Malhotra, 2017). The expansion in the hospitality segment and its assistance to the GDP will go on to be significantly fortunate than other sectors of the economy on the back of vast tourism potential. Through constantly civilizing the atmosphere for promoting the hospitality and tourism sector in India, many international hotel chains were lining up in India as there is plentiful opportunities accessible in this sector for foreign investors (Sufi, 2015). This sector magnetizes the most FDI (Foreign Direct Investment) inflow and is the most vital net foreign exchange earners for the nation. But hotel and hospitality industry has turned down harshly in the first quarter of 2020, because of COVID-19 eruption impacts different segments of the sector because of suppression measures introduced by the Government have resulted in a harsh fall in foreign and domestic travel, across both the tourism and business traveler segments (T3 News Network, 2020).

Most customers (over 50%) are not prepared to travel to a destination and stay at a hotel in the coming time. Approximately a quarter of the customers have now dined in a restaurant and only around one-third are willing to move to a destination and stay at a hotel in the next few months (Gursoy et al., 2020). At present, COVID-19 is rocking worldwide with more dangerous situation, more worries and increasing consequences.

Mensah I. (2020) says that hotels are among one of the hardest hit industries by COVID-19 due to which there is a huge cessation of flights, events, tours, travel, hotel reservations and ensuing rejection in inbound travel, hotel rates and average room rates have dropped harshly causing exceptional declines in revenue margins. In Italy, 90% and 80% of all hotel bookings in Rome and Sicily correspondingly have been canceled and for moderately small tourist places like Ghana, hotel occupancy rates are losing from 70% to less than 30%, with some hotels recording as short as 5%. In the history such incident has never came about, where businesses in almost all the countries have been paralyzed because of a common element. The whole scenario is very wretched and people all over the world have become frightened and frustrated with the existing situation. There is a lot of uncertainty as to when things will get back to normal. Flight connectivity or customer confidence is all essential elements in finding out what the future seems like.

Global Tourism and Hospitality Industry: Pre–coronavirus (COVID-19)

Since one of the leading contributors to the worldwide GDP, this industry straightforwardly employs millions of people worldwide. Global market development identifies that adjacent country tourism, rural and cultural tourism, wellness and health holidays, religious tourism, ecotourism, sports and adventure vacations, and coastal tourism and cruises are some of the promising areas of tourist attention. The main motivational factor for tourism in the past few years was the identification of tourism's participation in employment generation and economic growth, accessibility of better infrastructure, proper marketing and promotion, liberalization of air transport, intra-regional cooperation, and an increasing number of Public–Private-Partnerships (PPPs). In fact, in India, the ministry has taken numerous steps like opening new peaks for mountain climbing that will assist in promoting adventure tourism in the country, dropping e-visa fees and GST rates on hotel room bookings to increase inbound tourism. As per World Travel and Tourism Council (WTTC), the worldwide travel & tourism industry has grown-up from US$ 6.03 Trillion in 2006 and achieve US$ 8.27 trillion by 2017 mounting at a CAGR of 2.9% (PR Newswire, 2019).

According to the United Nations World Tourism Organization (UN-WTO) (January 2020), 2019 witnessed 1.5 billion international tourist arrivals, which signifies a 4% raise from that of 2018. The Middle East was the highest growing region in the world, with an 8% growth in 2019, while Asia and the Pacific region expanded 5%. Europe witnesses a 4% growth in international tourist arrivals and greets 743 million visitors.

Hospitality Industry has evolved enormously over the centuries. Travel bloggers and influencers have broadly used social media or digital platforms such as Facebook, Instagram, or Twitter, travel magazines and further market players like MakeMyTrip, Goibibo, etc., to broadcast tourism and kindle people to discover tourist destinations. A growing association of flights covering every area internationally has sensibly made it much easier to explore as compared to few years ago. Infact, especially a country like India having diversified culture and traditions, the growth in the tourism as well as in hospitality industry is just due to the increase in the influx of more tourists. The expansion and advancement in the hospitality sector and its contributions to the GDP will maintain to be significantly elevated than other sectors of the economy on the back of huge tourism prospective in the country. With a constantly growing middle class and escalating disposable earnings, the tourism and hospitality sector is witnessing a vigorous escalation and accounts for 7.5% of the country's GDP (Malhotra, 2017). With brands like Hilton, Marriott, Starwood, Hyatt etc. the hospitality industry seems to be doing fairly well.

Tourism Industry: The Uncertainty of COVID-19

COVID-19 is a contagious disease caused by a newly discovered corona virus. Till date, there's scarcely a single industry that hasn't experienced from the fallout of COVID-19. According to report on April 2020, UNWTO said 96% of all global destinations have introduced travel limitation in counter to the virus. Around 90 destinations have entirely or moderately closed their borders to tourists, while a further 44 are closed to certain tourists depending on country of origin. According to World Travel & Tourism Council (WTTC), that also found that Asia-Pacific is anticipated to be most heavily impacted with up to 49 million jobs at hazard all through the area, presenting a loss of almost $800 billion to travel and tourism GDP (Keegan, 2020). Also United Nations World Tourism Organization (UNWTO) speaks that the COVID-19 deadly infection *will result in a contraction of the tourism segment* by 20% to 30% in 2020 (Coke, 2020). While many economic sectors are estimated to recuperate once preventive measures are lifted, however this will possibly have a long-term effect on international tourism. This is largely due to squashed consumer confidence and the possibility of longer restrictions on the international movement of people (Dash, 2020). The Indian tourism industry is predicted to have a loss of Rs 1.25 trillion in the year 2020 as a fall out of the closing of hotels and postponement in flight operations after the onset and spread of the *Coronavirus* (Covid-19). With tourism industry there are many other sectors in the economy that are affected during this COVID-19 including hotel, community level operations, monetary, health, travel and transportation, construction, real estate, retail, and vice versa. In the present situation, the tourism industry can only pin its hopes on domestic tourists. According to Deccan Herald – Business News (September 2020), the Coronavirus pandemic has dealt a crippling blow to the Indian travel and tourism industry and the complete value chain connected to the sector is expected to lose roughly Rs 5 lakh crore or USD 65.57 billion; a study by industry chamber CII and hospitality consulting firm Hotelivate.

Hospitality Industry: The Uncertainty of COVID-19

From Summer Olympics to FIFA World Cup speedy approaching, 2020 was believed to be an excellent year for hospitality in Europe and the East. But, things changed with the increase of the Covid-19 virus outbreak, which has previously killed and infected many people around the world. Because of the deferment of all domestic and international flights, combining by a nationwide lockdown together brings an exceptional phase in the history of the hospitality industry. COVID-19, known as Coronavirus, is a new sprain of infection that has developed at the end of 2019 and has spread to all the nations in the world. The hospitality industry, which is directly reliant on tourism, is not only facing huge losses but it also seems very difficult to revitalize in the near future. The COVID-19 pandemic has confounded hotels, bars, restaurants, cafes throughout the world. Hotels are an essential piece of the tourism product. They add to the overall tourism industry through the standards of amenities and services offered by them. In a case if people travel then they will like to reside at their relatives' place as an alternative of hotels. The National Restaurant Association guesstimate the industry will drop $225 billion this year, while 5 to 7 million workers could be jobless (Aka, 2020). The fears are not groundless with the COVID-19 pandemic beginning to leave unforgettable wound on the hospitality industry and its associated services. For example: food delivery player like Zomato, Swiggy let go its staff unemployed, due to this situation. With no money inflow and travel plans being cancelled, resurgence of the industry seems like a far-away dream, at least until mid-2021. Battered and injured by the Covid-19 pandemic, the nation's *travel* and hospitality industry is staring at a Rs 5-trillion income loss more than the subsequently year while 35–40 million jobs, mutually direct and indirect, are at risk (Dash, 2020). However, the moratorium on loans for three months had been provided by the banks for the hospitality sector in India. The significant emergency with the hospitality industry in India is that the most employers functioning in these industries are moreover on contract basis or on informal working and these employer accounts to around 30%–40% of the staff and they all originate from a more fragile foundation so closing the chains and different administrations will influence them monetarily (Chandwani, 2020). According to Hotelivate, the untimely signs of abridged travel became clear in the middle of February but the major terror was felt in March when large-scale cancellations across the corporate, MICE and leisure segments happened. Presently, making no mistake, packed hotels are almost converted into full hospitals. With the imposition of Section 144, there are hardly any bookings being made for the future, and the present ones are all cancelled. Big hotel chains will unquestionably rebound back swiftly; however, for all other establishments, the Covid-19 pandemic is a test of flexibility and creativity (Baynova, 2020).

MICE Industry: The Uncertainty of COVID–19

The Meetings, Incentives, Conventions and Exhibitions (MICE) industry is a significant and embryonic segment of the tourism industry with a great prospect. It shows positive growth in businesses, cities and building destinations image. It wraps various imaginative services that contain show displays, directional signages, banners, kiosks space, event photography, event marketing and sponsorship management, on-site event logistics and staffing, supplier management and virtual meetings. *One of the world's top MICE (Meetings, Incentives, Conventions & Exhibitions)* destinations is Singapore. Regrettably, MICE industry had been strappingly affected by the disruptive effects of COVID-19. It has been a reason for the cancellations of meetings and conferences, public and private, national and international, incentives, conferencing, exhibitions (MICE) events, choking the lifeline of the industry. The Center for Exhibition Industry Research (CEIR) reports that expansion of the exhibition industry throws for the period of the first quarter of 2020 as 72.6% of events initially planned for the second half of March were dropped. The leftover 27.4% of events were delayed and a portion of those occasions may in the long run, be dropped too (Rokou, 2020).

Similar to tourism providers, MICE organizers are similarly susceptible to Covid-19's impact. As the business recoups, coordinators will start with cut back events and expenses with smaller halls and fewer delegates while utilizing digital technologies for broader connect. Since exhibitions require a vast number of participants to be reasonable, digital participation can offer another income creating model (Dutt, 2020).

A Strategy to Attract Tourists

The tourism and hospitality business is on its knees around the world. Considering the way that these two is one of the biggest and quickest developing businesses all-inclusive, a gigantic exertion ought to be attempted to reach back to its center limits in the current circumstance. Domestic tourism and local demand will rise, making India to be more grounded and more impressive than previously. The human nature to travel, to investigate, to find new places and things won't let him limited to one spot however, there won't be any unplanned travelling for sure. It's a matter of time; the industry will practice a positive change once all activities resume on track (EE News Desk 2020). The new metrics dimensions have to be introduced i.e. pre and post COVID-19 is as follows (Table 4.1):

Table 4.1 New dimensions pre and post COVID-19

Pre COVID-19 (Old Dimensions)	Post COVID-19 (New Dimensions)
Global tourist	Local tourist
Socializing	Distancing
Shake hands	Namaskar
Commitment to cleanliness, hygiene	Visible action for hygiene, security, cleanliness and sanitization
Preferences	Priorities
Actual events	Virtual events
International travel	Domestic travel as a new exotic destination
Clustered rooms and common areas	Private and isolated accommodations
Welcome drinks like fruit juices	Immunity boosting 'hot lemon water with raw honey'

Source: Compiled by Author (2021).

COVID-19 and Sustainable Tourism and Hospitality

COVID-19 has a massive impact on travel, tourism and hospitality industry like no other event prior in account of tourism. Governments of every country have put community wellbeing first and introduced complete or fractional limitations on travel. As for some time, tourism is suspended, empty airports, borders closed, hotels shuttered, postponed events, conferences and concerts, the benefits of this sector are under threat. But once this is all over, people will travel again. It is necessary to begin balanced and sustainable tourism, travel, and hospitality industry and recover these both industries post-COVID-19. The following point will be beneficial for sustainable tourism and hospitality after COVID-19 (Figure 4.2).

In today's virus affected environment, where there is a travel restriction, it's essential to hit the above mentioned messages into the right tone and with proper marketing strategy. This is an ideal time to re-organize re-brand and revive and deliver digital solutions like the use of social media, Facebook, TV Commercials while focusing on the above points. There is a chance to expand their offer to more ordinary, rustic locations. As a consequence of COVID-19, outdoor activities and regional tourism is expected to be more important for tourist. Changing the focus from international to domestic tourism is also a requisite now. One must offer the assurance of wellness, protection, security and highlight their benefits. Particularly the countries that have been the hardest hit by the pandemic, such as Italy, US, India and Spain, will have to enlarge the efforts to force tourism and hospitality again to these popular destinations. Creating a 'rebound back' campaign will help in the long run when travellers are keen to travel over again. The COVID-19 outbreak can thus be likely to accelerate the penetration of Artificial Intelligence (AI) and robotics technology

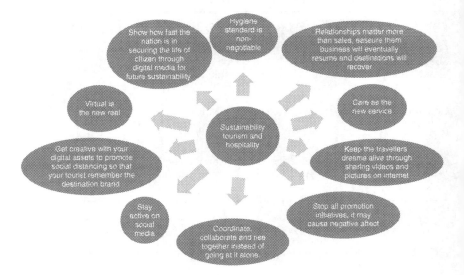

Figure 4.2 Sustainable tourism and hospitality.

into the hospitality industry like robot receptionists, facial scan check-ins, voice guest control, robot delivery soon.

For example, India, as a nation brand, is handling its Covid-19 emergency reveals a few affirmative action's so far. Although India being an emerging economy, distinct it's more affluent counterparts in Europe and North America, India's strong reaction to control the pandemic at an early stage is high that has improved its image and status of being a receptive and proactive nation brand. The Prime Minister's commitment during lockdown "Jaan Bhi, Jahaan Bhi" possibly vibrate as a positive reassurance for moves that would try to balance the most critical problem of sustaining life, first, and then the economy.

Parrish D., the director of the South Carolina Dept. of Parks, Recreation & Tourism (SCPRT), says that South Carolina is to launch tourism recovery campaign in the month of May 'Dream Now, Discover Later' that will encourage consumers to dream about their ideal vacation through iconic beauty shots, sunrise horizons over an oceanfront golf course while their travel is restricted (Anderson, 2020).

The hash tag '#Travel Tomorrow' an online campaign {World Tourism Organization (UNWTO)} had an immense crash on social networks and is being cuddled by a growing number of countries, destinations and companies associated to tourism from all over the world. While staying at home these days, we can travel tomorrow (UNWTO, April 2020). Therefore, it's time to rediscover or re-brand the tourist destination and realign the Messaging. It is time to draw on the passion for the tourism business and the tourism industry.

Areas Need Immediate Attention: Domestic Travel as a Critical Success

Domestic travel is the support the industry is changing its hopes on for the predictable future. The impact of this situation will lower the business savings due to increased insecurity and threat. In the same way, the requirement for the travelling and consumer assurance also may very lower due to uncertainty and fear. But, the magnetism towards events and festivals will be considerably reduced after the COVID pandemic. Therefore, instead of going internationally, the country's heritage, culture, rural places will be more energetic market segments among the travellers. The domestic travel market will considerably rise compared to the international tourism market to liberate the homebound stress of the community as an immediate effect. Travel agencies should modify their packages like Visiting Friends and Relatives (VFR) packages with low-cost alternative. (*The Indian Express*) Prahlad Singh Patel, Minister of Tourism, said in his interview on June 7th, 2020 that the focus should be on rebooting the tourism economy by revitalizing demand. An attempt will be put to encourage domestic tourism through the promotion of 'Dekho Apna Desh' and Incredible India.

With the new normal bringing several new trends like rise in domestic travels with lesser-known destinations so as to avoid human contact and priorities social distancing in the future, health and hygiene being the top priority, solo travelling or road trips and budget-friendly vacations, etc. will be the new trends in tourism and hospitality. The mantra of 'bigger is better' will become an obsolete due to which group tours and activities, or big events, will take a hit. Pal V. (2020) consider that the Government needs to step in and identify the responsibility of hospitality in the expansion of the country while adding that it is the time when Government should understand the role not only to the GDP, but also to employment and to the conservation of prehistoric buildings and cultural traditions. So it is necessary to cut taxes and decrease the costs of bar licenses, visa fees and other related expenses if there is to be any expectation of renaissance in the next five years.

Conclusion

Coronavirus, till today, has become one of the major confrontations that the country is facing, and its impacts will be the last longing. There is a lot of uncertainty, and the future is unpredictable. The key takeaways highlight that the tourism and hospitality industry is that it must stay creative, lively and work together. COVID-19 has changed the situation and will undoubtedly influence the way travellers will think about, plan and consume experiences. Implementing a successful marketing strategy is not just for companies that are under pressure to survive in the market. But it can also be a proactive way out to encourage business development or enlarge to new markets. The suggestion proposed in this paper is not exhaustive but indicates several ways through which tourism and hospitality industry can recover, including AI and robotics, hygiene and sanitation, and health and healthcare. Also destinations has to keep travelling interest alive through so that common people have a desire to travel there once the restrictions are over and this can be done from now onwards i.e. during lockdown period through PR or making proper use of social media or using any digital platform. As people are wedged at home and digital and social media handling has gone up drastically, this is the correct time to acquire people's attention and get them to think about visiting destinations. Try to take the current lockdown as an opportunity.

References

Aka L. (2020). COVID-19: The Hospitality Industry Is Facing an Uncertain Future. *Working Nation.* Retreived from https://workingnation.com/covid-19-the-hospitality-industry-is-facing-an-uncertain-future/. Accessed on 2nd July 2020

Anderson Z. (2020). *South Carolina to Launch Tourism Recovery Campaign Due to COVID-19's Impact.* Retreived from https://wpde.com/news/coronavirus/sc-agency-launches-tourism-recovery-campaign. Assessed on 1st July 2020.

Baynova Y. (2020). *Coronavirus: The Impact on Hospitality Industry and How to Plan Ahead.* Retreived from https://www.clock-software.com/blog/coronavirus-impact-on-hospitality-industry.html. Accessed on 8th July 2020.

Chandwani S. (2020). *Impact of the Novel Coronavirus on the Hospitality Industry. KS Legal & Associates.* Retreived from https://www.lexology.com/library/detail.aspx?g=ac20c4c6-282d-45f6-a84d-201e1ca9899c. Accessed on 3rd July 2020.

Coke P. (2020). *Impact of COVID-19 on Tourism in Small Island Developing States.* Retreived from https://unctad.org/en/pages/newsdetails.aspx?OriginalVersionID=2341. Assessed on 30th June 2020.

Dash J. (April 2020). Covid-19 Impact: Tourism Industry to Incur Rs 1.25 Trn Revenue Loss in 2020. *Business Standard.* Retreived from https://www.business-standard.com/article/economy-policy/covid-19-impact-tourism-industry-to-incur-rs-1-25-trn-revenue-loss-in-2020-120042801287_1.html. Assessed on 30th June 2020.

Deccan Herald – Business News. (September 2020). *Travel and Tourism Sector Likely to Lose Rs 5 Lakh Cr Due to Covid-19 Crisis.* Report Retreived from https://www.deccanherald.com/business/business-news/travel-and-tourism-sector-likely-to-lose-rs-5-lakh-cr-due-to-covid-19-crisis-report-884882.html. Accessed on 5th June 2021.

Dutt V. (2020). *Sustaining India's MICE Segment in the Post-Covid-19 Era. Expressed Food and Hospitality.* Retreived from https://www.foodhospitality.in/guest-column/vijay-dutt-sustaining-indias-mice-segment-in-the-post-covid-19-era/421427/. Accessed on 6th July 2020.

EE News Desk. (2020). *Travel Post COVID-19: Reimagined, Redesigned and Rewired: Vikram Lalvani, Sterling Holiday Resorts Limited.* Retreived from http://everythingexperiential.businessworld.in/article/Travel-post-COVID-19-Reimagined-Redesigned-and-Rewired-Vikram-Lalvani-Sterling-Holiday-Resorts-Limited/04-06-2020-194260/. *Accessed on 3rd July 2020.*

Gursoy D., Chi C. G. and Chi O. H. (2020). COVID-19 Study 2 Report: Restaurant and Hotel Industry: Restaurant and Hotel Customers' Sentiment Analysis. *Would They Come Back? If They Would, WHEN?* (Report No. 2), Carson College of Business, Washington State University.

Keegan M. 2020. Travel Marketing under COVID-19: Is There Any Point? Retreived from https://www.campaignasia.com/article/travel-marketing-under-covid-19-is-there-any-point/459223. Accessed on 29th June 2020.

Malhotra S. (2017). *Hospitality Industry in India: A Big Contributor to Economy's Growth. In Business World.* Retreived from http://www.businessworld.in/article/Hospitality-Industry-In-India-A-Big-Contributor-To-Economy-s-Growth-/16-05-2017-118291/. Accessed on 7th July 2020.

Mensah I. (2020). *Unpacking the Impacts of COVID-19 on Tourism and Repackaging the Hotel Service.* Retreived from https://www.hospitalitynet.org/opinion/4098657.html. Accessed on 11th July 2020.

Page S. (2009). *Tourism management. Managing for Change.* 3rd ed. Oxford: Butterworth-Heinemann/Elsevier.

Pal V. (2020). *Covid-19: What Will It Take for a Revival of the Hospitality Industry.* Retreived from https://www.livemint.com/companies/news/covid-19-what-will-it-take-for-a-revival-of-the-hospitality-industry-11588748217033.html. Accessed on 8th July 2020.

Morgan N. and Pritchard A. (2004). *Meeting the Destination Branding Challenge.* Oxford: Routledge.

PR Newswire. (11th June 2019). *Travel and Tourism Spending Market – Global Industry Analysis, Size, Share, Growth, Trends, and Forecast 2019–2027.* Retreived from https://www.prnewswire.com/news-releases/travel-and-tourism-spending-market---global-industry-analysis-size-share-growth-trends-and-forecast-2019---2027-300865951.html. Accessed on 5th July 2020.

Robinson P., Lück M. and Smith S. (2013). *Tourism.* 1st ed. Wallingford: CABI.

Rokou T. (2020). *Event Cancellations and Postponements Due to COVID-19 Lead to MICE Industry Decline. Travel Daily News.* Retreived from https://www.traveldailynews.com/post/event-cancellations-and-postponements-due-to-covid-19-lead-to-mice-industry-decline. Accessed on 5th July 2020.

Sheller M. (2020). *Some Thoughts on What Comes after a Mobility Shock.* Critical Automobility Studies Lab. https://cas.ihs.ac.at/some-thoughts-on-what-comes-after-a-mobility-shock/. Accessed 4th July 2020.

Sufi T. (2015). Indian Hotel Industry: Past, Present and Future. *PCTE Journal of Hotel Management.* DOI: 10.13140/RG.2.1.3065.1606. Retreived from https://www.researchgate.net/publication/283056992_INDIAN_HOTEL_INDUSTRY_PAST_PRESENT_AND_FUTURE. Accessed on 13th July 2020.

The Indian Express. (7th June 2020). Prahlad Singh Patel, Minister of Tourism. Retreived from https://www.newindianexpress.com/thesundaystandard/2020/jun/07/interview--domestic-tourism-will-revive-sector-post-lockdown-tourism-minister-prahlad-singh-patel-2153219.html. Accessed on 8th July 2020.

Travel Trends Today – T3 News Network (April 2020). Retrieved from https://www.traveltrendstoday.in/news/hotel-and-resorts/item/8333-growth-and-development-likely-to-slow-down-in-the-next-two-years-jll

UNWTO. (April 2020). *Stay Home Today, #travel tomorrow.* Retreived from https://www.unwto.org/news/stay-home-today-traveltomorrow. Assessed on 1st July 2020.

UNWTO. (21st January 2020). *1.5 Bln International Tourist Arrivals Recorded in 2019.* Retreived from https://news.cgtn.com/news/2020-01-21/1-5-bln-international-tourist-arrivals-recorded-in-2019-UNWTO-NqKOuURxZu/index.html. Accessed on 5th July 2020.

Part Two
COVID-19 and Tourism Marketing Sustainability

5 Marketing and Demarketing Strategies for Hotel Operation under Epidemics and Pandemics

Maria José Magalhães and Susana Marques

Introduction

The risk of worldwide dissemination of a pathogenic agent resulting in a pandemic and its economic impact has been studied for many years, mostly as a theoretical exercise that most experts believed that would eventually become a reality, with devastating effects on the economy (Fan et al., 2018). However, the 2020 COVID-19 crisis represented the confirmation of that risk, translated in hundreds of thousands of lives lost and in entire countries locking down their economies to prevent the spread of the virus and the collapse of their health systems.

The COVID-19 pandemic started in late 2019 in Wuhan, province of Hubei, China, and in January 7, 2020, the pathogenic agent was identified as a novel coronavirus, which was named 2019-nCoV. Twelve days later, on January 19, 2020, Guangdong province reports the first case of a COVID-19 outside Hubei (The Novel Coronavirus Pneumonia Emergency Response Epidemiology Team, 2020). By mid-April, many countries had issued stay at home orders, limiting business activities to essential services and services that can be performed remotely. In this process, all across the world, hotels were ordered to close *sine die*, or had to close due to travel restrictions and/or public fear (Chaolan, 2020) (Fox, 2020) (Valadez, 2020).

The reduction in economic activity has a devastating effect on the economy and, therefore, countries have interest in implementing steps to resume normal operation as soon as possible. Nevertheless, that willingness to allow economic operators to resume activity must be balanced with the overall capacity of the health system, resulting in an incremental approach. The Center for Disease Control (CDC) issued guidelines for States and Regions in the United States of America that creates a three phases approach. In Phase One, which should last no less than 14 days, States and Regions that satisfy a set of criteria, should allow certain activities, as long as ("Opening Up America Again," 2020):

- Individuals and business "minimize non-essential travel and adhere to CDC guidelines regarding isolation following travel";

DOI: 10.4324/9781003207467-8

- Large venues, such as sit-down dining, "operate under strict physical distancing protocols".

In Phase Two, which should last no less than 14 days, non-essential travel can resume. However, both in Phase Two and in Phase Three, large venues, such as sit-down dining, can only "operate under strict physical distancing protocols", and bars "Bars may operate with diminished standing-room occupancy, where applicable and appropriate" ("Opening Up America Again," 2020).

It is unclear how long Phase 3 will last and how the general population will behave when the risk of contracting COVID-19 is reduced, but until either a form of treatment or a mass-produced vaccine is available, social distancing will most likely be part of what has been frequently called "the new normal". The hotel industry should prepare for a long Phase 3, not only due to regional regulations, but also as a form of prevention of reputational effects of an outbreak in their facilities. Marketing strategies can be a component of this effort, applying demarketing strategies to audiences that increase operational risks and favoring low-risk audiences in marketing strategies.

Defining Goals

During the mitigation phase of an epidemic/pandemic, authorities tend to implement measures to increase social distancing, which might limit, or even temporarily close, lodging activities. During that period and after the mitigation phase, when regulations implement a slow return to normal operations, hotels have advantages in reducing the risk of their clients, including:

- Reducing liability risks. Depending on the regional legislation, businesses might be liable for any contamination happening in their facilities affecting either employees or clients.
- Reducing reputational risks. Being singled out as a contaminated business has consequences in the capability to attract clients in a situation where the operation margins are already severely constrained.

Reducing the risk of any business amid an epidemic/pandemic outbreak includes increasing social distancing and sanitizing measures. Increasing social distancing is in most situations impossible to do without reducing the number of clients using the business space in any given moment, which results in decreased revenues. Sanitizing measures have operational costs, which result from the need to have more cleaning staff or have the normal team work more hours; increased spending in cleaning products, some of which have specific requirements to be adequate for the concrete situation in hand; and in personal protective equipment, necessary to protect the staff from a contamination. Sanitizing measures can also force some operational units to have reduced operation times, due to the time needed to sanitize the space and the equipment, which might reduce revenue directly and indirectly, by a decrease in sales and by reducing the business capacity to satisfy their clients. Some of the amenities that sanitizing requirements might affect are hotel's bars, gyms, decks, SPAs, pools, and transportation vans (shuttles), given that deep cleaning have to be made periodically and/or equipment must be sanitized every time that a client uses it. Shuttles used, for instance, to drive clients from/to airports and/or city center, not only need frequent sanitizing, but also cannot operate at full capacity. This might force hotels to rent additional vehicles and temporarily hire drivers (which will require some training to meet the expectations of the business), contract with taxi companies a transportation alternative, or reduce the level of service provided to clients. Preparing a hotel room for a new client is also a more time consuming task when extraordinary sanitizing measures are required.

Different clients have different needs and the Marketing/Demarketing strategy has a role to play in defining the characteristics of the clients that will occupy the hotel at each moment in time, with corresponding impacts on the number of users using the available space and on sanitizing needs.

To minimize operational cost and downtime, and to maximize revenue, hotels should pursue a strategy that maximizes the average stay and the revenue associated with client, while controlling the number of clients staying the hotel at a certain period of time and the use of common spaces and free amenities.

The Increased Value of Single Rooms

Under normal operation, hotels have several income streams, associated with different products offered to their clients (restaurant, bar, souvenir shop, etc.), most of which are maximized by maximizing the number of clients in the hotel, if that can be done without lowering mean client's purchasing power. The direct revenue associated with each room (the price payed to occupy that room) is often higher if more clients use the room. That happens because in a hotel the price of a triple room is often greater or equal than the price of a double room, and the price of a double room is often greater or equal than the price of a single room. Some others offer double rooms at the same price of single rooms and/or offer an extra bed for a child without charging any additional fee. This might be part of a strategy to maximize room occupancy rates, or to maximize indirect revenues, or both. In fact, studies have found that double rooms, in some markets, can represent more than 90% of all hotel rooms (Juaneda et al., 2011) (Becerra et al., 2013), despite the fact that several studies have found the price of a double room not to be, on average, twice the price of a single room (Thrane, 2007) (Tavares et al., 2016). There are, however, rare cases where a double room is more than twice the price of a single room (Becerra et al., 2013).

Under social distancing constraints, the available space limits the number of clients in a hotel, beyond what would normally happen. Clients not travelling together must keep a considerable amount of distance between them. For instance, CDC guidelines for the COVID-19 crisis, recommend that everyone should avoid crowded places amid a pandemic (CDC, 2020b) and the recommendations for shared living spaces include "minimize traffic in enclosed spaces, such as elevators and stairwells. Consider limiting the number of individuals in an elevator at one time and designating one directional stairwells, if possible" (CDC, 2020a). These recommendations, and the underlying reasons behind them, reduce the number of guests that a hotel can accommodate, forcing hotels to consider a shift in the business model, given that maximizing revenue is no longer equivalent to maximizing revenue per room.

Traditionally, equation 5.1 models average revenue directly resulting from renting rooms (R_r). This is a function of how much the hotel charges on average, in the period, for each one of the existing rooms (p_i is the average price of room i), of the average rate of occupancy, in the period, of each room (o_i is the average rate of occupancy of room i), and of the number of nights operated in the period (m). In this equation, N is the total number of rooms in the hotel. R_r, in a certain period, is maximized by maximizing the average price of each room, the average occupancy rate of each room, and the number of nights of operation. This normally would mean having as many guests in each room as possible.

$$R_r = m \times \sum_{i=1}^{N}(p_i \times o_i) \tag{5.1}$$

However, under limited conditions of operation, where full capacity is not the goal, the hotel as several options, such as:

- Reduce the total number of rooms available to clients, for instance, by closing one floor. This reduces the total number of people in common areas and frees staff assigned to that floor's maintenance to help on other floors and on common areas sanitization. This option limits the maximum value of R_r, reducing its potential by the value of constant, given that some rooms can longer contribute to its value.
- Reduce the average occupancy rate of all rooms. One strategy might be to close each room for x days in a row when a guest checks-out, to avoid having to deep sanitize it (assuming that the pathogenic agent does not survive for x days in the air or at the surfaces). This strategy reduces the total number of people in common areas and frees maintenance staff, which can help in efforts to sanitize commons spaces. This strategy reduces the rate of occupancy of each room, o_i, and that impact is dependent of the ration between x and the average number of nights that each guest stays at the hotel. For instance, the average number of nights

spent in a hotel/motel by international guests in the United States in 2018 was approximately 10 ("2018 Overseas Market Profile," 2019). Even assuming the best case scenario that all nights were spent in the same hotel room, quarantining each room for the five days needed for the 2019-nCoV to die (van Doremalen et al., 2020) would result in a reduced maximum capacity of 33.3%, corresponding to a reduction of 33.3% of the potential R_r. However, once this reduction is a function of the number of nights spent on average per a guest or group of guests sharing a room, targeting groups of clients with longer stays can result in a higher potential R_r, as discussed later in this work.

- Try to use all rooms while reducing the average number of guests per room, to reduce the number of people in common areas. This has increased sanitizing costs, but it is also the option that has a higher potential R_r, given that all rooms can contribute to revenue at all times.

Furthermore, it is not possible to maximize the average price charged by each room simply by maximizing its occupancy, given that, under reduced capacity constraints, maximizing room capacity would result in a reduction of the number of usable rooms. Reduced capacity might be imposed by local temporary regulations, or be self-imposed, in a strategy to minimize the risk of having to close operations for a certain period, which would lower the value of m.

Under reduced capability, room type and the number of guests in each type of room becomes important in calculating revenue. R_r is now a more complex variable, because the total number of guests at the hotel limits its value (equation 5.2). The number of guests per occupied room (g_i is the number of guests occupying room i) might force to close more rooms than anticipated or close some rooms for longer periods, if the sum of all guests occupying rooms surpasses the defined limit (r_o is the defined maximum rate of occupancy and G is the normal maximum guest capacity of the hotel).

$$\begin{cases} R_r = m \times \sum_{i=1}^{N} (p_i \times o_i) \\ \sum_{i=1}^{N} g_i \leq (r_o \times G) \end{cases} \quad (5.2)$$

Maximizing the number of guests per room, which usually means charging higher rates for the same room, is now not an efficient way of maximizing total revenue, because that would break the defined constraint in the number of guests at the hotel.

Under these constraints, where not all rooms can be occupied at maximum capacity, single rooms, which, as discussed, have a higher price per client, gain an increased value. The ideal number of each type of room depends on the desired rate of reduction, of the number of different types of rooms available, and of the price charged for each type of room.

For instance, the revenue directly resulting from renting rooms (R_r) in a hotel with N standard rooms that can be occupied by either one or two guests, operating under a maximum rate of occupancy of r_o, and charging an average price p_s for a single room and an average price of p_d for a double room, is a function of the number of single rooms, n_s (equation 5.3).

$$R_r = p_s \times n_s + p_d \times \text{minimum}\left(N - n_s, \frac{(2 \times N \times r_o - n_s)}{2}\right) \quad (5.3)$$

The following section presents an illustrative analysis of the value of single rooms, calculated for the average hotel from Thrane's study (Thrane, 2007).

An Example of the Calculation of the Ideal Number of Single Rooms under Reduced Capacity

The average hotel from Thrane's study (Thrane, 2007) has 258 rooms, with the average room rate for a single room being 1,001 NOK (Norwegian krone) and the average rate per night for a double room being 1,247 NOK. In this case, $R_r = 1,001 \times n_s + 1,247 \text{ minimum}\left(258 - n_s, \frac{(516 \times r_o - n_s)}{2}\right)$. Figure 5.1 shows how R_r changes with the number of single rooms (x-axis, ranging from 0 to 258) and with the maximum rate of guest occupancy (y-axis, ranging from 50% to 99%).

Maximum return is found at zero single rooms (all rooms with two occupants) and at total capacity, which corresponds to full operation at full capacity. As the authorized capacity reduces (y decreases), the highest return is achieved with a growing number of single rooms. At a 50% reduction in capacity, the ideal situation is that all rooms are Single. Figure 5.2 shows how R_r changes with the number of single rooms under 10%, 25%, and 40% reductions in guest capacity.

In this illustrative example, at a reduction in guest capacity of 10% the optimal number of single rooms is 52; at a reduction in guest capacity of 25% the optimal number of single rooms is 139; and at a reduction in guest capacity of 40% the optimal number of single rooms is 208. The remaining rooms would be double rooms. At a 50% capacity reduction or at higher rates of reduction, the option that maximizes revenue is to have all rooms (258) with single occupancy. Table 5.1 summarizes the maximum return, for this illustrative example, in the three options discussed above for guest capacity reduction, at several maximum rates of occupancy r_o.

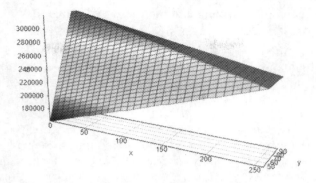

Figure 5.1 Room revenue as a function of both the number of single rooms (*x*-axis) and of the maximum rate of guest occupancy (*y*-axis).

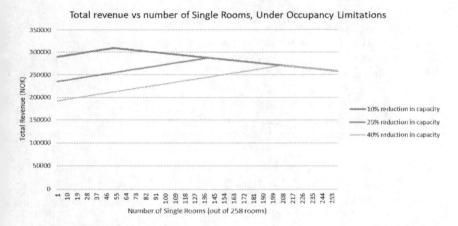

Figure 5.2 Room revenue as a function of the number of single rooms (*x*-axis) at 10%, 25%, and 40% reductions in guest capacity.

Table 5.1 Room revenue as a function of both the number of single rooms (*x*-axis) and of the maximum rate of guest occupancy (*y*-axis)

	R_r (NOK)			
	$r_o = 90\%$	$r_o = 75\%$	$r_o = 60\%$	$r_o = 50\%$
Reduce the total number of rooms available to clients	289,553	193,694	154,955	129,129
Reduce the average occupancy rate of all rooms	289,553	193,694	154,955	129,129
Reduce the average number of guests per room	308,179	287,532	270,558	258,258

Source: own elaboration

Extreme Cleaning/Sanitizing and the Increased Value of Longer Stays

Exceptional sanitizing processes are an opportunity for market differentiation even under normal operation as some clients are willing to pay a premium for highly sanitized rooms. Younger clients, in the 18 to 31 range, are more willing to pay such premium and women are willing to pay a higher premium than men (Zemke et al., 2015). Epidemics/pandemics are situations where clients are more aware of the risk of contamination and deep sanitizing becomes more than a possible marketing strategy, becoming a risk management strategy and sometimes a legal operational requirement.

Cleaning and sanitizing a hotel room under pandemic guidelines has several types of additional costs. There are, at least, the following additional costs to consider:

- Personal Protective Equipment (PPE);
- Sanitizing products;
- Loss in efficiency due social distancing and increased cleaning/sanitizing requirements;
- Sanitizing equipment;
- Staff training;
- Additional cleaning staff and/or additional working hours;
- Additional hours associated with creating and managing new processes and compliance checks;

During a health emergency, PPE is a critical tool to protect workers from contamination, to prevent guests from being contaminated by the previous guests occupying their room, and to prevent workers, such as cleaning crews, from spreading a virus from a contaminated room to other spaces in the hotel. When considering this, it is important to remember that the contamination phase of a pathogenic agent might coincide with an asymptomatic phase.

Sanitizing should only happen after cleaning "the surface or object with soap and water" (CDC, 2020a) and should be done, if possible, with approved, safe, and effective products, such as those approved by the United States Environmental Protection Agency (EPA). In a situation where the threat is a novel pathogenic agent, as it is the case of the COVID-19 pandemic, EPA uses general efficiency criteria (US EPA, 2020). The use of these products might require the use of additional PPE. The fewer the times each room needs to be sanitized, the lower the cost with these products and related PPE, which is another reason to implement Marketing/demarketing strategies that increase the average duration of stay.

Cleaning a hotel while increasing social distancing reduces operation efficiency. The best way to limit contamination risks is to have small teams performing each work and to change the cleaning routine. To guarantee proper room sanitization, cleaning and room preparation cannot happen at the same time when a room is being prepared for a new client. The process should now start with room cleaning (including removing all linen), then sanitizing, and, only then, room preparation (making bed and replenishing complementary items). This change requires more staff and/or more time to do the same operations. Hallways and other common areas also needed more frequent and deep cleaning and periodic sanitizing. Every time that there's a guest change in a room, staff must remove all complementary products, such as tea bags, coffee K-cups pods, or pencils, and then sanitize them, which is more efficient than sanitizing them as part of room sanitizing processes. All these changes require staff training, induce more cleaning working hours, and might require more cleaning staff, which requires even more training.

Sanitizing might also require the use of new equipment. New equipment has several types of associated costs, besides the investment needed to acquire it. New equipment induces increased utilities costs (energy and/or water and/or consumables), staff training costs, compliancy checks, and inventory management costs (Zemke et al., 2015). While new equipment also require time to operate it, it might also increase staff productivity when sanitizing, compared with the alternative option of sanitizing with that equipment. Examples of sanitizing equipment are Ultraviolet devices and Ozone disinfection systems (Zemke et al., 2015). Staff might also need training on the use of sanitizing products, given that employers are mandated to train their staff on the use of sanitizing agents ("Hazard Communication | Occupational Safety and Health Administration," 2012).

Process changes include changes in room cleaning, sanitizing, and preparation; hallways and common areas cleaning and sanitizing; bar, restaurant, and breakfast area operational procedures. Developing, maintaining/update these processes, and managing reports of breaches in PPE, such as tear in gloves, are part of the business responsibility (CDC, 2020a) and require staff with expertise that are not always available in hotels that are not part of a hotel chain. These plans, must also take in consideration the need to protect cleaning staff from increased occupational hazards, which even under normal operation include physical, chemical, biological, and psychosocial hazards (Hsieh et al., 2013). This might require the business to hire a new collaborator, train existing staff and/or hire a consultant firm.

It is clear that, given the sanitizing requirements when there will be new guests occupying a room, that longer stays have an increased value when operating under constraints induced by an epidemic/pandemic.

Demarketing under an Epidemic/Pandemic Health Crisis

Kotler & Levy introduced the concept of demarketing, defining it as "as that aspect of warketing that deals with discouraging customers in general or a certain class of customers in particular on either a temporary or permanent basis" (Kotler and Levy, 1971). According to these authors, there are three types of demarketing:

- General demarketing: where companies seek to reduce demand;
- Selective demarketing: where demand for certain market segments is discouraged;
- Ostensive demarketing: in which the perception of consumers is that the business intents to discourage the demand when in fact it want to increase it. In practice, there will be an increase of the demand of the more and more desired product, in consequence of the difficulty to obtain it.

The first published paper on the application of demarketing directly to tourism is by Clements in 1989, who refers the use of demarketing as a tool to discourage a certain segment of tourists from visiting Cyprus, thus using selective demarketing (Clements, 1989).

As previously discussed, under operation constrains created by an epidemic/pandemic health crisis, hotels should try to model their clients' profiles with the purpose of:

- Increase the guests' average length of stay;
- Decrease the average number of guests staying in each room;
- Decrease the use of common use amenities, such as pools, gyms, and shuttles.

The marketing strategy must serve the hotel's needs and, therefore, marketing tactics should aim to increase the demand in groups that fit the hotel's goals, and all client profiles that do not help reach those goals should be covered by a selective demarketing strategy.

Hotels operate in a certain geographical region, which itself has a specific tourism demand. Therefore, each hotel needs to follow specific marketing/demarketing strategies. Also, some hotels serve a very specific audience, and have no possibility of changing their client profile to the same extent as a hotel that serves a region that has business tourism and cultural tourism. That is the case, for instance, of hotels located inside family oriented amusement parks, which cannot target, for instance, business clients as their main source of revenue. Hotels that are located in convention centers or in casinos face different challenges.

Business Clients

When it is possible to target business clients, hotels should recognize the important of this market. Business clients have several advantages in the context of the hotel strategy presented in this work. These include the facts that:

- Business clients travel alone more often than leisure travelers do. Looking at overseas visitors to the United States in 2018, while 58.1% of "all overseas visitors" were travelling alone, 82.3% of "all business visitors" were travelling alone which compares with only 42.9% of "all leisure visitors" ("2018 Overseas Market Profile," 2019).
- Business tourists choose hotels and motels more often than leisure tourists do. Looking at overseas visitors to the United States in 2018, 87.7% of "all business visitors" stayed in a hotel or motel, while that was the choice of only 79.9% of "all leisure visitors" ("2018 Overseas Market Profile," 2019).
- Business tourists stay longer when staying in a hotel or motel than leisure visitors do. Looking at overseas visitors staying in hotels or motels in the United States in 2018, the average stay for "all business visitors" was 11 nights, while "all leisure visitors" stayed on average 9 nights ("2018 Overseas Market Profile," 2019).
- Business clients spend more on lodging per visitor. Looking at overseas visitors to the United States in 2018, the average expense in lodging per visitor was $758 in the "all business visitors" and $399 in the "all leisure visitors" nights ("2018 Overseas Market Profile," 2019).
- Business tourists make their traveling decisions closer to the date of travelling, making this market more responsive to the changes in hotel marketing strategies that result from a health emergency. Looking at overseas visitors to the United States in 2018, the group "all business visitors" made, on average, the trip decision 45.2 days in advance, while the group "all leisure visitors" made the trip decision, on average, 120.1 days in advance ("2018 Overseas Market Profile," 2019).
- While still valuing safety and security, business clients have less concerns for safety and security than leisure travelers (Knutson, 1988), and they travel due a business need, which makes them more likely to travel in situations where health safety is a general concern in the population.

Business clients are less sensitive to room rates than leisure travels (Knutson, 1988), which allows for the use of price as a demarketing tool to reduce attractivity to leisure clients while retaining business clients.

Business clients value green hotel policies more than leisure guests (Millar et al., 2012), which makes them more prone to engage in practices that reduce the use of chemical products in cleaning and sanitization of rooms, as long as safety is not endangered.

Strategies to attract business guests include:

- Offering earlier breakfast. Increasing the operation period of breakfast rooms spreads demand, making it easier to meet social distance

requirements. When doing so, hotels should favor opening breakfast rooms sooner, rather than closing later, favoring business clients (Sogar and Jones, 1993).
- Create of enhance loyalty programs, designed to target business tourists. Hotels should consider immediate rewards that are valued by this market, given that studies have shown that reward timing has a direct effect on the efficiency of these programs ("Sunny" Hu et al., 2010). Some programs have found that clients that are members of a loyalty program are more likely to bring their families with them (McCleary et al., 1994). Therefore, the structure of the immediate reward program should adapt when operations are constrained by a health emergency, giving better rewards for occupying single rooms in periods when that best serves the hotel overall strategy.
- Direct advertising strategies to reservation channels that are preferred by business travels and not by leisure travelers. In the US overseas market, the channel that should be prioritized is reservations through corporate travel departments, which account for more than a third of all international business tourists ("2018 Overseas Market Profile", 2019).

On a symmetric perspective, complementary strategies can be used to reduce the attractivity of the hotel to leisure travels to the extent needed. Demarketing strategies might include:

- Close breakfast areas earlier;
- Reduce loyalty program rewards for the occupation of double rooms.
- Increase the price for an extra bed in a room.
- Reduce the limit age of children allowed to stay in their parents' bed.
- Remove from the website any pictures of amenities available to children, as well as pictures that create the feeling that the hotel is family friendly, replacing the latter by pictures that business travels can relate to.
- Do not promote childcare programs, which are more likely to attract leisure travelers (Victorino et al., 2005).
- Direct advertising away from reservation channels preferred by leisure tourists. In the US overseas market, the channels that attract more leisure tourists in detriment of business tourists are Internet Booking services and tour operators or travel clubs ("2018 Overseas Market Profile," 2019).

Choosing to target the business tourist market must be a deliberate choice, embraced by all staff in an effort even bigger than usual to achieve client satisfaction, because business tourists tend to be more critical when rating hotels (Radojevic et al., 2018), which has impact in Word of Mouth marketing and in digital marketing.

Female Business Travelers

Female business travelers represent less than half of the business tourism market (Brownell, 2011) ("2018 Overseas Market Profile," 2019), but the specific characteristics of part of this group make it particularly attractive for the hotel industry when operating under sanitizing and social distancing constraints.

The first relevant fact about female business travelers is that, while they tend to travel less often, they also tend to stay longer, up to almost twice as long as male business travelers do (McCleary et al., 1994) (Smith and Carmichael, 2007). The value of longer average stays has already been established in this work, therefore this is a very important element to consider when deciding the market mix of a hotel.

Women rate business services and facilities as less important than men do (McCleary et al., 1994), which makes this an easier market to target to hotels that haven't been focusing on business markets and/or do not have facilities, and reduces the intensity of use, easing social distancing, of existing facilities.

While all female business travelers share an interest in meeting their clients/customers and meeting new people, as almost any business tourist, they also have different socioeconomic characteristics, different focus if interest and different behaviors when travelling, which results in three relevant classification clusters (Newth, 2009).

- More experienced travelers (10+ years), in their 50s, occupying middle management positions, and holding graduate education, constitute Cluster 1. Women in this group particularly value travelling to new places, and connecting with other female business travelers (Newth, 2009).
- Women with seven to ten years of travelling experience, mostly in their 40s, holding senior positions, graduate education, and with higher incomes ($250,000+), constitute Cluster 2. Women in this group value, connecting with other female business travelers, and staying at a great hotel/room. These women strong correlate empowerment with freedom (Newth, 2009).
- Women with four to six years of travelling experience, mostly in their 40s, with undergraduate education, occupying middle management positions, and earning $150,000 to $200,000 constitute Cluster 3. These women focus on productivity and their focus is essentially meeting their clients/customers (Newth, 2009).

Hotel marketers should be aware of these clusters when deciding on a marketing mix. If the hotel does not have the characteristics for female business tourists to classify it as a "great hotel" or the rooms as "great rooms" and if it is not possible or desired to do those improvements, then it will be harder to capture women in Cluster 2.

Women in Cluster 1 and in Cluster 2 value a set of activities, related to interacting with other female business travelers, that hotels can offer as part of the loyalty program or of the "do not clean my room every day" rewards strategy discussed later in this paper. These activities include going to a place to meet, sightseeing, visiting museums and art galleries, walking, hiking, and shopping, which all happen outside the hotel, reducing people concentration inside the hotel (Newth, 2009).

Women in Cluster 3 are an important market for all hotels, given that they focus on meeting with their clients/customers (Newth, 2009) and, therefore, it is not expected that they will be using the hotel facilities intensively.

Female travelers are also among the most likely clients to order room service (Hao and Har, 2014), which is a source of revenue for hotels and is also an important tool to reduce the number of people using shared spaces, like restaurants, bars, and breakfast areas.

When trying to attract female business tourists, hotel should consider:

- Adding activities to the loyalty program that promote interaction between female business travelers outside of the hotel, and highlight those benefits in their marketing efforts.
- Choose advertising images that women can relate to might help to overcome the fact that female business value emotional relations and often feel that they are not valued by the travel industry (Brownell, 2011).
- Because women are more likely to use hair dryers, irons and ironing boards, and bathrobes (McCleary et al., 1994), add those items to the hotel rooms and highlight that when promoting them.
- Include room service discounts in loyalty programs. This option meets the needs of female travelers, and increases the immediacy of the rewards, which travelers' perception of the value of the program.

Do Not Clean My Room Every Day

Travelers are usually not willing to pay a premium for green hotel policies, but they do take green policies in consideration when choosing a hotel and they value options like "do not change my sheets every day unless specifically requested" and "do not change my towels every day unless specifically requested" (Watkins, 1994). Cleaning a room induces energy consumption, water consumption, and the use of chemical products. Therefore, not cleaning the room every day is also a green policy. Even though some travelers might see this as extreme under normal conditions, some are willing to make that choice if they can benefit from it. Many Starwood Hotels & Resorts have been offering the "make a green choice" option for more than ten years, allowing clients to forgo housekeeping services for up to two consecutive days, in exchange for loyalty points ("What Is 'Make a Green Choice'?," n.d.). Some of the concerns associated with this type of program have to do with concerns that companies might reduce housekeeper hours, and that rooms will need a deeper cleaning after the stay, inducing the use of chemicals that harm the environment and represent a risk to housecleaners (Hasek, 2018). Knowing that a "do not clean my room every day" policy will serve to use less cleaning products and to prevent the housekeeping staff from being overwhelmed, and that a deep cleaning and sanitizing would happen anyway when guests checkout, properly addresses these questions.

By having clients opting-out of housekeeping services, hotels save cleaning time and products; release housekeeping staff for other tasks, such as sanitizing rooms and commons spaces; save PPE; and reduce the risk of staff exposure to the pathogenic agent. Hotels should consider not only offering loyalty points to guests that opt-out of housekeeping services, which mainly targets frequent travelers, but also to:

1 Offer discounts that are still cost-effective considering the savings that result from this choice.
2 Offer discounts to local attractivities. This enriches the guests' local experience, increasing destiny satisfaction, and invites them to get out of the hotel, which in turn favors social distancing in hotel amenities.

Conclusions

Running a hotel amid an epidemic/pandemic scenario forces management to adopt protective measures that induce increased operation costs while, simultaneously, enforcing social distancing and/or operating with reduced limited capacity. To minimize costs and maximize revenue, the lodging industry should adopt a different marketing mix, designed to fit the hotel desired single room capacity. For most hotels, operating under limited occupancy increases the value of single room guests, decreases the value of high occupancy rooms, and increases the value of extended stays. The marketing mix is a tool to achieve those goals, and it is important to include both marketing and demarketing strategies, to fully achieve them. Figure 5.3 presents a summary of the different types of hotel guest profiles, and several options, as discussed, for demarketing strategies. Lodging business that can target both business and leisure markets should adopt strategies to prioritize the business tourists market and then implement the same measures that leisure specific or business specific hotels should implement.

Limitations

The strategies presented in this work do not take in consideration the category of the hotel, or non-generalizable context constraints that might affect a specific hotel. This study also does not cover situations where the hotel is an operational tool, or is strongly associated and fully dependent of, a larger main business, such as hotels serving casinos or family recreation parks.

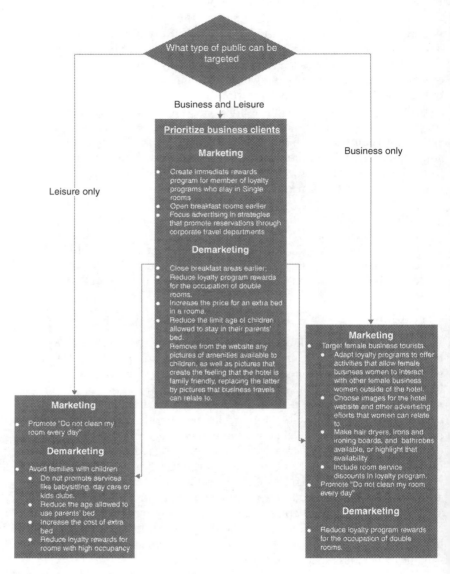

Figure 5.3 Summary of Marketing and Demarketing strategies.
Source: own elaboration.

References

Becerra, Manuel, Juan Santaló, and Rosario Silva. 2013. "Being Better vs. Being Different: Differentiation, Competition, and Pricing Strategies in the Spanish Hotel Industry." *Tourism Management* 34 (February): 71–79. https://doi.org/10.1016/j.tourman.2012.03.014.

Brownell, Judi. 2011. "Creating Value for Women Business Travelers: Focusing on Emotional Outcomes." *Cornell Hospitality Report* 11 (12). https://scholarship.sha.cornell.edu/chrpubs/10/.

CDC. 2020a. "Communities, Schools, Workplaces, & Events." Centers for Disease Control and Prevention. April 30, 2020. https://www.cdc.gov/coronavirus/2019-ncov/community/shared-congregate-house/guidance-shared-congregate-housing.html.

CDC. 2020b. Coronavirus Disease 2019 (COVID-19) [WWW Document]. Centers for Disease Control and Prevention. URL https://www.cdc.gov/coronavirus/2019-ncov/prevent-getting-sick/social-distancing.html.

Chaolan, Supagong. 2020. "Hotels Ordered to Close in Surat Thani." Https://Www.Bangkokpost.Com. April 7, 2020. https://www.bangkokpost.com/thailand/general/1895000/hotels-ordered-to-close-in-surat-thani.

Clements, M. A. 1989. "Selecting Tourist Traffic by Demarketing." *Tourism Management* 10 (2): 89–94.

Doremalen, Neeltje van, Trenton Bushmaker, Dylan H. Morris, Myndi G. Holbrook, Amandine Gamble, Brandi N. Williamson, Azaibi Tamin, et al. 2020. "Aerosol and Surface Stability of SARS-CoV-2 as Compared with SARS-CoV-1." *New England Journal of Medicine* 382 (16): 1564–67. https://doi.org/10.1056/NEJMc2004973.

Fan, Victoria Y., Dean T. Jamison, and Lawrence H. Summers. 2018. "Pandemic Risk: How Large Are the Expected Losses?" *Bulletin of the World Health Organization* 96 (2): 129–34. https://doi.org/10.2471/BLT.17.199588.

Fox, Cooper. 2020. "Governor Mills Orders Hotels and Motels Closed." April 3, 2020. https://92moose.fm/governor-mills-orders-hotels-and-motels-closed/.

Grimm, Christi A. 2020. "Hospital Experiences Responding to the COVID-19 Pandemic: Results of a National Pulse Survey March 23–27, 2020." April, 41.

Hao, Jocelyn Siah Chee, and Chris Ong Siew Har. 2014. "A Study of Preferences of Business Female Travelers on the Selection of Accommodation." *Procedia - Social and Behavioral Sciences* 144 (August): 176–86. https://doi.org/10.1016/j.sbspro.2014.07.286.

Hasek, Glenn. 2018. "'Make a Green Choice' Not Always the Best Choice? | Green Lodging News." November 16, 2018. https://www.greenlodgingnews.com/make-a-green-choice-not-always-the-best-choice/.

"Hazard Communication | Occupational Safety and Health Administration." 2012. https://www.osha.gov/dsg/hazcom/index.html.

Hsieh, Yu-Chin (Jerrie), Yorghos Apostolopoulos, and Sevil Sönmez. 2013. "The World at Work: Hotel Cleaners." *Occupational and Environmental Medicine; London* 70 (5): 360. http://dx.doi.org.cobalt.champlain.edu/10.1136/oemed-2012-100986.

Juaneda, Catalina, Josep Maria Raya, and Francesc Sastre. 2011. "Pricing the Time and Location of a Stay at a Hotel or Apartment." *Tourism Economics* 17 (2): 321–38. https://doi.org/10.5367/te.2011.0044.

Knutson, Bonnie J. 1988. "Frequent Travelers: Making Them Happy and Bringing Them Bac." *Cornell Hotel and Restaurant Administration Quarterly; Ithaca* 29 (1): 83.
Kotler, Philip, and Sidney Levy. 1971. "Demarketing, Yes, Demarketing." *Harvard Business Review* 49: 74–80.
McCleary, Ken W., Pamela A. Weaver, and Li Lan. 1994. "Gender-Based Differences in Business Travelers' Lodging Preferences." *Cornell Hotel and Restaurant Administration Quarterly* 35 (2): 51–58.
Millar, Michelle, Karl J. Mayer, and Seyhmus Baloglu. 2012. "Importance of Green Hotel Attributes to Business and Leisure Travelers." *Journal of Hospitality Marketing & Management* 21 (4): 395–413. https://doi.org/10.1080/19368623.2012.624294.
Newth, Francine. 2009. "The New Strategic Imperative: Understanding the Female Business Traveler." *International Business & Economics Research Journal (IBER)* 8 (11). https://doi.org/10.19030/iber.v8i11.3185.
"Opening Up America Again." 2020. The White House. Accessed April 26, 2020. https://www.whitehouse.gov/openingamerica/.
Radojevic, Tijana, Nemanja Stanisic, Nenad Stanic, and Rob Davidson. 2018. "The Effects of Traveling for Business on Customer Satisfaction with Hotel Services." *Tourism Management* 67 (August): 326–41. https://doi.org/10.1016/j.tourman.2018.02.007.
Smith, Wayne W., and Barbara A. Carmichael. 2007. "Domestic Business Travel in Canada with a Focus on the Female Market." *Journal of Travel & Tourism Marketing* 21 (1): 65–76. https://doi.org/10.1300/J073v21n01_05.
Sogar, David H., and H. Michael Jones. 1993. "Attracting Business Travelers to a Resort." *Cornell Hotel and Restaurant Administration Quarterly* 34 (5): 43–47.
"Sunny" Hu, Hsin-Hui, Chun-Te Huang, and Po-Tsang Chen. 2010. "Do Reward Programs Truly Build Loyalty for Lodging Industry?" *International Journal of Hospitality Management* 29 (1): 128–35. https://doi.org/10.1016/j.ijhm.2009.07.002.
Tavares, Fernando Oliveira, Luis Pacheco, and Jorge Borges. 2016. "Fatores Indicadores Do Preço de Um Quarto de Hotel: Uma Aplicação a Uma Amostra de Hotéis Portugueses." *Revista ESPACIOS* 37 (26): 10–20.
The Novel Coronavirus Pneumonia Emergency Response Epidemiology Team. 2020. "The Epidemiological Characteristics of an Outbreak of 2019 Novel Coronavirus Diseases (COVID-19) — China, 2020." China CDC Weekly. China CDC. https://cdn.onb.it/2020/03/COVID-19.pdf.pdf.
Thrane, Christer. 2007. "Examining the Determinants of Room Rates for Hotels in Capital Cities: The Oslo Experience." *Journal of Revenue and Pricing Management* 5 (4): 315–23. https://doi.org/10.1057/palgrave.rpm.5160055.
"2018 Overseas Market Profile." 2019. National Travel and Tourism Office. https://travel.trade.gov/outreachpages/download_data_table/2018-Overseas-Market-Profile.xlsx.
US EPA, OA. 2020. "How Does EPA Know That the Products on List N Work on SARS-CoV-2?" Overviews and Factsheets. US EPA. March 19, 2020. https://www.epa.gov/coronavirus/how-does-epa-know-products-list-n-work-sars-cov-2.
Valadez, Roberto. 2020. "Por Coronavirus, Todos Los Hoteles Deberán Cerrar En CdMx." February 4, 2020. https://www.milenio.com/negocios/por-coronavirus-todos-los-hoteles-deberan-cerrar-en-cdmx.

Victorino, Liana, Rohit Verma, Gerhard Plaschka, and Chekitan Dev. 2005. "Service Innovation and Customer Choices in the Hospitality Industry." Edited by Allard C. R. van Riel. *Managing Service Quality: An International Journal* 15 (6): 555–76. https://doi.org/10.1108/09604520510634023.

Watkins, Edward. 1994. "Do Guests Want Green Hotels?" *Lodging Hospitality* 50 (4): 70.

"What Is 'Make a Green Choice'?" n.d. Accessed May 12, 2020. https://help.marriott.com/s/article/Article-22164.

Zemke, Dina Marie V., Jay Neal, Stowe Shoemaker, and Katie Kirsch. 2015. "Hotel Cleanliness: Will Guests Pay for Enhanced Disinfection?" *International Journal of Contemporary Hospitality Management* 27 (4): 690–710. https://doi.org/10.1108/IJCHM-01-2014-0020.

6 Futurology of Ethical Tourism Digital & Social Media Marketing Post COVID-19

Brighton Nyagadza and Farai Chigora

Ethics are utilitarian and deontological based on reason, intention and duty.
(Kant 1788)

Introduction

The aim of the chapter is to examine ethical tourism digital and social media marketing predictive trends that will take place globally post COVID-19 period. As of 1 March, 2020, there was a recording of 79,968 cases of the virus and 2,873 deaths confirmed in China. The deadly virus has been observed as spreading at 2.2, or even greater (averaging from 1.4 to 6.5), and familial clusters of pneumonia as it goes human to human transmissions (Chan et al. 2019; Liu et al. 2019; Guo et al. 2020; Riou and Althaus 2020). The World Health Organisation (WHO), has formally named the diseases coronavirus disease 2019 (COVID-19) and the Coronavirus Study Group (CSG) of the International Committee suggested to call it SARS-CoV-2, both heralded on February 11, 2020 (Guo et al. 2020). Research suggests that the virus causes acute respiratory problems, with its reservoirs probably from bats and sea foods, although no scientific evidence has been provided to explain this (Giovanetti et al. 2020; Guo et al. 2020; Paraskevis et al. 2020). Due to this dangerous SARS-CoV-2 disease viral pandemic, digital disruption that it has prompted has the power to reshape conventional tourism markets faster than any other force in history. The author saw that the reason behind this could be that the whole world was brought to stand still, forcing heavy lockdowns cutting across continents in a bid to reduce the fast spread of the virus.

The chapter motivation logic was in a bid to offer pragmatic advice to tourism business practitioners in crafting ethical digital marketing strategies amid COVID-19 ravages. Ethical tourism digital and social media marketing concepts were critically analysed and evaluated to determine their link to the current research focus area. In addition theoretical concepts related to ethics were consulted as anchors of the chapter, such as nudges or ethics of influence, privacy ethics, ethical representation and graphic ethics, utilitarianism & the common good, deontological philosophies, as well as the framework for ethical tourism digital and social media marketing decision making. Main literature findings have pointed to the fact that the main predictive trends in Ethical Tourism Digital and Social Media Marketing include use of Accelerated Mobile Pages (AMP), Micro Vlogging, Voice Search, Blogging, Social messaging. With the continuous dynamic digital landscape, tourism marketers need to embrace the art of doing business by adopting new ethical tourism digital and social media marketing techniques, to curb challenges brought by the COVID-19. Given this reality, it is useful for tourism organisations need to integrate ethical digital and social media marketing into their corporate marketing strategies. Viral quality of digital and social media marketing makes it an appealing tool for businesses to market tourism products and services. The chapter also give an intuitive apprehension of the predictive trends in Ethical Tourism Digital and Social Media Marketing strategies vital for developing an agile stance to outwit rivals in the post COVID-19 era.

Tourism Digital and Social Media Marketing Ethical Issues

Tourism digital and social media marketing ethics can be defined as the subsets of tourism business ethics (Murphy 2002) that are focused on how moral standards are applied to tourism digital and social media marketing decisions, behaviours and institutions (Murphy et al. 2005; Pallab 2019). The concept of ethics in tourism digital and social media marketing is deemed to be very subjective and complicated in nature, while on the other hand it all amounts to advice on abiding existing principles of law and self-interest (Gaski 1999; Pallab 2019). Although the tourism organisations have made significant progress in establishing ethical knowledge, both professional and academic, has made significant steps in increasing tourism digital and social media marketing values, there is still some literature and theoretical gaps between the depth and specifity related to this issue, as aimed to be addressed in this chapter. Tourism digital and social media marketing ethics are philosophy focused, managerial, cross-cultural, stakeholder focused and society focused (Pallab 2019). The coming in of the Fourth Industrial Revolution (4IR) world-wide has brought in some new developments commonly known as the 'new normal' in the tourism industry. In support of this, several scholars have researched on the adoption of Internet of Things (I.o.Ts) and/or social media platforms for tourism activities (Nyagadza and Nyauswa 2019) and others have described this new development with terms such as digital, online or electronic tourism marketing. Internet as a common connecting pool of information for many, it has revolutionised the tourism businesses and destinations services. Digital and social media platforms shall make the visitors to evaluate photos, videos, and even corporate stories, regardless of where they are located in the world. Digitally connected tourism technologies with intelligent systems, will revolutionize and optimise digital social media platforms with interconnection of network systems, thus Internet-of-Things (Nyagadza 2020). Visitors with this will be able to develop an image about the target areas of visit based mainly on the digital and social media platforms, upon their reasoned opinions, emotional interpretation and feelings. This has forced the tourism practitioners to have a strong drive towards digital and social media platforms leverage in a way to make sure that they can market and sell their products and services. Tourism corporate websites and social media platforms such as Facebook and Google have deep learning algorithms that have been developed with the digital expertise which can have interactivity that allow how tourists, travel, see and consume services among other issues. As of now Google (and other organisations) has developed robots that are meant to behave like humans and can be able to watch videos on YouTube (Bagot 2017; Jurkiewicz 2018). More of the decisions currently being made by human beings (the tourism practitioners) shall be made by the digital algorithms which are much sharper in accuracy, provided there is no unbiased data, which maybe erroneous (Manyika 2013; McAfee and Brynjolfsson 2017; Kim 2020). Concerns are more on the ethical side of using the Artificial Intelligence (AI) in tourism digital and social media marketing, which has been viewed by scholars such as Cellan-Jones (2014), Garling (2014), Simonite (2017) and Jurkiewicz (2018), to be dehumanizing the choices of individuals by evidently replacing individual identity with collective, computerised model citizens and employees.

In addition to this, tourism digital social media marketing sites have been subjectively viewed to be specifically focusing on certain demographics. This has triggered hate groups which might have led to accumulation of information on users and some segments for discrimination, not for tourism business. Further to this, digital platforms such as spam emails and unsolicited ads, encourages prejudice, where the viewers are lured to unethically show hate to some groups through their derogatory speech (Byrne 2017; Collins et al. 2017; Chiel 2018; Jurkiewicz 2018). Thus, in the end, the tourists tend to be limited in turn on how they are likely to use the social media platforms to access information to access. Ethical challenges of the Fourth Industrial Revolution (4IR) emerging technologies in the delivery of the tourism marketing include, but not limited to, sufficiency issues related to maturity befitting technological disruption and whether there can be affordability to the costs faced (Ordoobadi 2011; Micheler et al. 2019) for interoperability reasons (Micheler et al. 2019). The major concern on ethical tourism digital and social media marketing is due to the problems related to what is good and ethical in philosophical meanings. Decision making as a key component in any organisation, there is need to follow a structured way on what is required. The purpose is not express the ways in which decisions are made but how to understand the process of ethics decision making in an organisational environment. Management responsible for the tourism digital and social media marketing are to make specific decision demands knowledge of the tourism, an assessment of risk, and the experience to know the effects to the concerned stakeholders (Ferrell 2005). The succeeding section accounts for the decision making framework related to ethical tourism digital and social media marketing.

Ethical Tourism Digital and Social Media Marketing Decision Making Framework

In every organisation decision making is one of the key matters of concern. It affects the way things are handled and operate at any given circumstance. Values-motivated ethical tourism leadership, corporate management training, monitoring and reporting systems, are necessary for an ethical tourism corporate culture. Figure 6.1 depicts Ethical tourism digital and social media marketing decision making framework.

Corporate values are important elements of corporate stories for branding and they denote the core purpose of an organisation which is guided by its mission and vision (Nyagadza et al. 2020a). A tourism organisation need to understand what drives behaviour of individuals and how to align them with integrity goals (Ferrell 2005). What is key is to know the nexus between general personal characters and corporate values, so as to make an effective making process, in line with the stakeholders' (internal and external) expectations (Ferrell and Gresham 1985; Kaplan and Haenlein 2010). This is so because there is a distinction between organisational and personal ethics. The legal system usually assists in dealing with the ethical issues. The next section accounts for the theoretical underpinnings related to ethical philosophies.

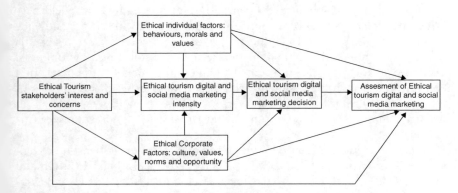

Figure 6.1 Ethical tourism digital and social media marketing decision making framework.
Source: Author's conception.

Theoretical and Ethical Philosophies for Tourism Digital and Social Media Marketing

Normative ethical theories in moral philosophy are either subdivided into teleological or deontological in nature (Murphy and Laczniak 1981; Gould 1994; LaTour and Henthorne 1994), depending on the focus. Any action that is deemed to be morally right in tourism digital and social media marketing if and only the act is something that a virtuous agent might characteristically do in the agent's circumstances except for tragic dilemmas in which a decision is morally right and only if is what such an agent might decide, but the action decided upon maybe too terrible to called right or good (Hursthouse 1999; McElreath 2018).

Teleological philosophies can be viewed as concerned with the moral worth of an individual tourism organisational behaviour, in the determination of worth and the consequences related. The organisation should examine and decipher the consequences, whether good or bad, of alternative actions and behaviours in a certain situation (McElreath 2018). When conducting tourism digital and social media marketing activities there is need to strike a balance of good over bad when compared with alternative actions (Hunt and Vitell 1986).

On the other hand, the actions which tourism organisations make without considering the results of the actions relates to deontological philosophies. The latter is opposite to the strategic views of teleology (Fraedrich and Ferrell 1992). Therefore, the deontological perspective on rightfulness or wrongness of tourism digital and social media marketing should be judged based on actions without much focus on the outcomes (LaTour and Henthorne 1994). Due to this, the teleological perspective, tourism digital and social media marketing activities should be punctuated with ethical actions. The use of unorthodox and/or uncouth content to market a product via paid for tourism digital and social media marketing media channel can yield negative side effects (sexual obsessions, gratuitous sex) to the target audience (Gould 1994; LaTour and Henthorne 1994). The results of sexual appeals in tourism digital and social media marketing have some moral wrongness. Using sex as form of appeal in tourism digital and social media marketing continues to be a highly controversial issue, considering the variations of religion and strength as well as diverse reactions to it. Both positive and negative emotions are evoked from the target audiences, in response to this matter.

Some authorities due to this value the idea of considering the state of balance in considering use of deontological and teleological ethical decisions and judgements. Thus, this leads to the norm development (Reidenbach and Robbin 1988) in the adoption of those balanced ethical stances (Frankena 1963). However, on the other hand, some view this as opposing, since the two philosophical ethical stances are deemed to be different in terms of application and relativity. In line with this, the next sections address the predictive trends related to tourism digital and social media marketing (Nyagadza et al., 2022).

Predictive Tourism Digital and Social Media Marketing Trends Post Covid-19

The swiftness of social media messages and images circulation has made it more appealing for organisations (Xiang and Gretzel 2010; Nadaraja and Yazdanifard 2013; Nyagadza 2020a). Social Media Marketing is the use of digital marketing activities on social media platforms. In other meaning, it can be viewed as the use of social media platforms to develop an organisation's online brand, its products and services (Nadaraja and Yazdanifard 2013; Nyagadza et al. 2020a). Researchers argue that various social network platforms enable the sharing of podcasts, videos, which fuel viral marketing. A variety of academic researchers proposed that social media marketing develops much bigger portion in networking people for interaction and improving the room for their voices to be understood and being heard (Mangold and Faulds 2009; Lipsman et al. 2012; Malthouse et al. 2013; Peters et al. 2013; Pereira et al. 2014; Tafesse and Wien 2017). The leading social networks compilation show that social networks are raking up more and more active users (Statista 2018). Fostering of the idea of sharing social messages, via social media platforms to personalised contacts, has bred a new paradigm shift towards exponential social media marketing growth and massive communication trust amongst the users (Hafele 2011). Further to this, it makes consumers share and link information and stories related to great brands and being able to diagnose their views, espoused experiences and creation of customised personal branded content (Gensler et al. 2013; Davis et al. 2014; Tafesse and Wien 2017). The virality effect of social media has brought a great multiplier effect. Through the networking of friends and contacts, this leads to higher direct leverage to the digital marketers who heavily rely on the social media as a key platform and level field to deliver valued promises and better customer experiences (Berthon et al. 2012; Peters et al. 2013; Ashley and Tuten 2015; Kim et al. 2015; Tafesse and Wien 2017). The next section gives an address of predictive trends in social media marketing.

Micro-Vlogging

Micro-Vlogging is the term that is used to describe the sharing of short videos on tourism digital and social media marketing platforms (Nyagadza et al. 2020b). Social media networks were created for the users to share pictures and textual posts. However, tourism digital and social media marketing networks have updated their applications to accommodate video sharing which is a growing trend among users. Statistics show that 85% of the internet is now video and most social media users prefer sharing videos as compared to other forms of sharing information with their followers. This trend has affected how companies produce, amplify and distribute content. Social media platforms have tapped into Micro-Vlogging, which organisations can use to target their customers who do not have time to watch full videos and/or tutorials. These include Instagram Live, Facebook Live, Twitter videos and

Snapchat. These are key in brand resonance with the customers where there is reaffirmation of the brand promise and identity (Puto and Wells 1984; Laskey et al. 1989). Instagram Live, Facebook Live, Twitter videos, Snapchat build digital self-identity and self-image (Wallace et al. 2014; Vernuccio et al. 2015), as people tend to be emotionally attached to them. In sync to this, the researchers understand that Micro-Vlogging helps people make an informed decision. A lot of people who turn to video reviews learn better through a more visual medium. People crave authenticity and credibility when it comes to vlogs. While there will always be room for growth when it comes to blogging, vlogging can help one learn new skills (Roces 2018; Nyagadza 2020). One's audience would have to watch the video. Even though blogging does take more work than what most people think, vlogging takes up twice the time and effort (Roces 2018; Nyagadza 2019b). There's setting up the camera, checking the sound quality, and finding and creating a well-lit environment. And that's just the production work. Vloggings yields multiple interactivity (Zaglia 2013; Tafesse 2016; Nyagadza et al. 2020c). Post-production refers to time-consuming and editing and rendering of the final video.

Social Messaging

Furthermore, future trend in tourism digital and social media marketing is companies moving from social network platforms to social messaging. In the beginning companies focused efforts on social networks. However, future trends are showing that more and more companies are investing massively in social messaging applications, which educate and stimulate purchases amongst customers (Kim et al. 2015; Taecharungroj 2016). The applications give a company's audience a platform for client support, as well as the brand features for e-commerce. These also are platforms to effectively implement electronic customer relations management strategies such as database marketing after profiling its customers digitally (Kim et al. 2015; Taecharungroj 2016).

Based on the above, Facebook is deemed to be the better chosen social media platform, so frequently used, popular and has greater chances of executing social media marketing on it. The costs and efforts invested in building the nomenclature and structure of the social media platforms such as the mentioned, Facebook, Twitter, Instagram and others has made it possible to increase the speed of message sharing (DiMicco et al. 2008; Lorenzo et al. 2011; Hohenthal et al. 2014; Jurado et al. 2019). Through direct consequence of experience in the social media platforms, the researcher observed that the use of hashtags with a sign # and "at" with a sign again of @, has made it possible to push the messages so fast to reach audience and engage them like never before. The majority of social media users get to interact with their corporate and product brands either through Facebook or LinkedIn for instance, may be astounded to see if one of their corporates reaches out (Sweeney 2013; Nyagadza 2019a).

Blogging

Blogging is an important element of tourism digital and social media marketing technique for several reasons. Blogging and Wikipedia are typical examples of online content that is generated or created by users (Bruns 2008; Madsen and Slatten 2015). Authorities contend that blogging influences a large number of people with minimal efforts (Bilos and Kelic 2012), although it has its own inefficiencies due to informational factors (Calvo and Zenou 2005; Kaplan and Haenlein 2010; Torrent 2015). An argument is that Blogs provide room for everyone in expressing views and comments independently and freely (Van der Heide and Lim 2016), in response to brand communication as a result of social ties (van Noort et al. 2012; Shan and King 2015; Hayes et al. 2018). Blogs allow experts to share their expertise openly and assist the latter to present themselves within specific social settings (Goffman 1959; Boyd 2008; Swart et al. 2019). Blogging can help a company to obtain more customers for an existing running business and enhance interactivity (Lai et al. 2011; Radu 2016). Under usual circumstances, if online customers are not able to see the product brands or services they might be looking for on the blogs, chances are so high that they will not repeat revisit of the same site.

On the other hand, the researcher found that blogs cannot have most relevant and recent information if the bloggers are not always updating their blog spots (Lai et al. 2011; Radu 2016). Other proponents argue that blogs are naturally followed by rather lesser stakeholders, but in politics and business, elites tend to read them (Farrell and Drezner 2008; Madsen and Slatten 2015). Blogs are deemed to be a bit cheap to start up in terms of content creation (Farrell and Drezner 2008; Madsen and Slatten 2015). However, for bloggers to realise returns from them, a considerable investment is supposed to be necessitated (Farrell and Drezner 2008; Madsen and Slatten 2015; Nyagadza 2019a). Research has suggested that blogs are one of the most important social media platforms which have transformed even broadcast newsroom practices such as sourcing, gatekeeping, and verifying (Lasorsa et al. 2012; Broersma and Graham 2013, 2016; Canter 2015; Brems et al. 2017).

Discussion

Tourism digital and social media marketing challenges and limitations may come and go, but the power of reaching customers through search engines and social media never changes. Currently, the world has more than a thousand active social media marketing platforms. This is a result of the drive towards focusing on tourism digital and social media marketing channels, in response to customer demand and dynamics taking place globally. Within these social media marketing platforms, they are seen as strategic places where customers desire to be updated regularly on the information relating to their product brand choices. The level of loyalty tourism digital and social media marketing platforms leads to the development of brand advocates who have bold emotional attachment to product and service brands. Further to this, tourism digital and social media marketing platforms can always be a room to express corporate storytelling for branding in terms of how matters on corporate associations, corporate values, corporate personalities and corporate benefits can be conveyed to intended internal and external stakeholders (Nyagadza et al. 2019).

Similarly, tourism digital and social media marketing platforms are now being used amongst migrants and tourists to consistently get enough connection with kinsmen from their nations of origin as well as social-cultural adaptation (Brekke 2008; Komito 2011; Croucher 2011; Sawyer and Chen 2012). When used effectively, both tourism digital and social media marketing, could have several valuable outputs (Archambault and Grudin, 2012; COMCEC 2015).

The volatility of tourism digital and social media marketing has caused divisions and business wars. The two, tourism digital and social media marketing, present massive advantages to customers and owners of businesses. Nevertheless, problems are also generated in the process as a result of negative impact of social media. This is so because social media marketing and search engine marketing platforms can magnify matters of concern. It can be associated with deception. Sometimes brand promises can never be fulfilled. There are a lot of legal cases related to character defamation and/or assassination, frauds, embezzlement of funds, corporate reputation problems, dystopic digital marketing cultural development, negative hypnotisation of customers, cyber bullying, pornography, personalised imposters and impersonation!

Conclusion

Learning the new trends brought by social media marketing and search engine marketing is a necessity for business survival and growth. The trends constitute the digital marketing futures for the art of doing business. Findings in this chapter depicts that, predictively, digital marketers need to consider involving more closely, social media marketing and search engine marketing, as efforts to improve corporate strategies viability. Furthermore, the study indicates that there is ease of use in embracing social media marketing platforms as well as speed and better reach of target audience. These platforms, besides being meant for social and business purposes, are increasing in terms of usage by politicians, musicians and arts sectors to promote their product brands and services.

Tourism digital and social media marketing outlets are highly self-propagating in that the people who use them spread in terms of numbers. Due to the speed of spread in expressing messages and information, social media marketing is predictively deemed to be the most appealing digital platform, where business organisations and entrepreneurs can sell products and services (Xiang and Gretzel 2010). Tourism digital and social media marketing is now a developing phenomenon in marketing. Thus, tourism digital and social media marketers need to embrace and understand the use of social media marketing and search engine marketing predictive trends as components in their marketing strategies and campaigns to reach out to more customers. Critics cite that the behaviour of customers, whilst they purchase and socialise online, have an impact on the way profits are realised within the concerned businesses (Zhao and Elesh 2008; Huberman et al. 2009; Miles 2018).

The coming in of artificial intelligence, machine learning, availability of big data and algorithms has made it easier to better target tourism consumers. The post 2000 period has witnessed great growth in the numbers of social media followers who are very active almost on a daily basis (Kaplan and Haenlein 2010; Wilson et al. 2011; Wilson et al. 2012). This has lured business operators to shift their marketing efforts to social media marketing, as better leverage to engage customers (Kaplan and Haenlein 2010; Wilson et al. 2011; Wilson et al. 2012) together unifying social communities with the commerce and industry fraternity (Skeels and Grudin 2009; Madsen and Slatten 2015). At times the transactions done on tourism digital and social media marketing can be a bit costly in nature Padel and Foster 2005; Roitner et al. 2008; Tsakiridou et al. 2008; Rousseau and Vranken 2013). In terms of messaging, Sweeney (2013) argues that, majority of businesses are rightfully taking advantage of social media marketing to push their messages directly to customers.

References

Archambault, A. and Grudin, J. 2012. "A longitudinal study of Facebook, LinkedIn, & Twitter use", In *Proceedings of the SIGCHI Conference on Human Factors in Computing Systems*, 2741–2750. Austin, TX: ACM.
Ashley, C. and Tuten, T. 2015. "Creative strategies in social media marketing: an exploratory study of branded social content and consumer engagement", *Psychology and Marketing*, 32: 15–27. https://doi.org/10.1002/mar.2015.32.issue-1.
Bagot, M. 2017. "Google is training robots to understand humans by making them binge-watch YouTube videos", *The Mirror*. Retrieved from http://www.mirror.co.uk/tech/google-training-robots-understand-humans-11413196.
Berthon, P. R., Pitt, L. F., Plangger, K. and Shapiro, D. 2012. "Marketing meets Web 2.0, social media, and creative consumers: implications for international marketing strategy", *Business Horizons*, 55(3): 261–271. https://doi.org/10.1016/j.bushor.2012.01.007.
Bilos, A. and Kelic, I. 2012. "Marketing aspects of social networks", *Economic research Ekonomska Istrazivanja*, 25(2): 155–174.
Boyd, D. 2008. "Why youth (heart) social network sites: the role of networked publics in teenage social life", In *Youth, Identity, and Digital Media*, edited by David Buckingham, 119–142. Cambridge: MIT.

Brekke, M. 2008. "Young refugees in a network society", In *Mobility and Place: Enacting Northern European Peripheries*, edited by J. O. Bærenholdt and B. Granas, 103–114. Aldershot: Ashgate.

Brems, C., Temmerman, M., Graham, T. and Broersma, M. 2017. "Personal branding on Twitter", *Digital Journalism*, 5(4): 443–459. https://doi.org/10.1080/21670811.2016.1176534.

Broersma, M. and Graham, T. 2013. "Twitter as a news source", *Journalism Practice*, 7(4), 446–464. https://doi.org/10.1080/17512786.2013.802481.

Broersma, M. and Graham, T. 2016. "Tipping the balance of power social media and the transformation of political journalism", In *The Routledge Companion to Social Media and Politics*, edited by Axel Bruns, Eli Skogerbø, Christian Christensen, Anders Olaf Larsson and Gunn Enli, 89–103. New York: Routledge.

Bruns, A. 2008. *Blogs, Wikipedia, Second Life, and Beyond: From Production to Produsage*. New York: Peter Lang.

Byrne, B. P. 2017. "Twitter says it fixed 'bug' that let marketers target people who use the N-word", *The Daily Beast*. Retrieved from http://www.thedailybeast.com/twitter-lets-you-target-millions-of-users-who-may-likethe-n-word.

Calvo, A. and Zenou, Y. 2005. "Job matching, social network and word-of-mouth communication", *Journal of Urban Economics*, 57(3): 500–522. https://doi.org/10.1016/j.jue.2005.01.001.

Canter, L. 2015. "Personalised tweeting", *Digital Journalism*, 3(6): 888–907. https://doi.org/10.1080/21670811.2014.973148.

Cellan-Jones, R. 2014. "Stephen Hawking warns artificial intelligence could end mankind", *BBC News*. Retrieved from http://www.bbc.com/news/technology-30290540.

Chan, J. F., Yuan, S., Kok K. H., To, K. K., Chu, H. and Yang, J. 2019. "A familial cluster of pneumonia associated with the 2019 novel coronavirus indicating person-to-person transmission: a study of a family cluster", *Lancet*, 395v(10223): 514–523.

Chiel, E. 2018. "The injustice of algorithms", *New Republic*. Retrieved from https://newrepublic.com/article/146710/injustice-algorithms.

Collins, B., Poulsen, K. and Ackerman, S. 2017. "Russia used Facebook events to organize anti-immigrant rallies on U.S. soil", *The Daily Beast*. Retrieved from http://www.thedailybeast.com/exclusive-russia-used-facebookevents-to-organize-anti-immigrant-rallies-on-us-soil.

COMCEC. 2015. "Effective tourism marketing strategies: ICT-based solutions for the OIC member countries", http://www.comcec.org/en/wp-content/uploads/2016/05/6-Tourism-Proceed.pdf, Accessed June 13, 2020.

Croucher, S. M. 2011. "Social networking and cultural adaptation: a theoretical model", *Journal of International and Intercultural Communication*, 4(4): 259–264. https://doi.org/10.1080/17513057.2011.598046.

Davis, R., Piven, I. and Breazeale, M. 2014. "Conceptualizing the brand in social media community: the five sources model", *Journal of Retailing and Consumer Services*, 21(4): 468–481. https://doi.org/10.1016/j.jretconser.2014.03.006.

Dimicco, J., Millen, D. R., Geyer, W., Dugan, C., Brownholtz, B. and Muller, M. 2008. "Motivations for social networking at work", In *Proceedings of the 2008 ACM Conference on Computer Supported Cooperative Work*, 711–720, California: ACM.

Farrell, H. and Drezner, D. W. 2008. "The power and politics of blogs", *Public Choice*, 134: 15–30. https://doi.org/10.1007/s11127-007-9198-1.

Ferrell, O. C. 2005. "A framework for understanding organisational ethics", In *Business Ethics: New Challenges for Business Schools and Corporate Leaders*, edited by R. A. Peterson and O. C. Ferrell, 3–17. Armonk, NY: Sharpe, M. E.

Ferrell, O. C. and Gresham, L. 1985. "A contingency framework for understanding ethical decision making in marketing", *Journal of Marketing*, 49 (Summer): 87–96.

Fraedrich, J. and Ferrell, O. C. 1992. "Cognitive consistency of marketing managers in ethical situations", *Journal of the Academy of Marketing Science*, 20 (Summer): 245–252.

Frankena, W. 1963. *Ethics*, Englewood Cliffs, NJ: PrenticeHall, Inc.

Garling, C. 2014. "As artificial intelligence grows, so do ethical concern", *SFGate*. Retrieved from http://www.sfgate.com/technology/article/As-artificial-intelligence-grows-so-do-ethical-5194466.php.

Gaski, J. 1999. "Does marketing ethics really have anything to say? – A critical inventory of the literature", *Journal of Business Ethics*, 18(3), 315–334.

Gensler, S., Völckner, F., Liu-Thompkins, Y. and Wiertz, C. 2013. "Managing brands in the social media environment", *Journal of Interactive Marketing*, 27(4): 242–256. https://doi.org/10.1016/j.intmar.2013.09.004.

Giovanetti, M., Benvenuto, D., Angeletti, S. and Ciccozzi, M. 2020. The first two cases of 2019-nCoV in Italy: where they come from? *Journal of Medical Virology*, 2020: 1–4. https://doi.org/10.1002/jmv.25699 [Epub ahead of print].

Goffman, E. 1959. *The Presentation of Self in Everyday Life*. Garden City, NY: Doubleday Anchor Books.

Gould, S. J. 1994. "Sexuality and ethics in advertising: a framework and research agenda", *Journal of Advertising*, 23:3 13–80.

Guo, Y.-R., Cao, Q.-D., Hong, Z.-S., Tan, Y.-Y., Chen, S.-D., Jin, H.-J., Tan, K.-S., Wang, D.-Y. and Yan, Y. 2020. "The origin, transmission and clinical therapies on coronavirus disease 2019 (COVID-19) outbreak – an update on the status", *Military Medical Research*, 7(11). https://doi.org/10.1186/s40779-020-00240-0.

Hafele, N. 2011. "Social media marketing: interaction, trends & analytics", *ICT 511 Fall*, 51(3): 1–6.

Hayes, J. L., Yan, S. and King, K. W. 2018. "The interconnected role of strength of brand and interpersonal relationships and user comment valence on brand video sharing behaviour", *International Journal of Advertising*, 37(1): 142–164. https://doi.org/10.1080/02650487.2017.1360576.

Hohenthal, J., Johanson, J. and Johanson, M. 2014. "Network knowledge and business-relationship value in the foreign market", *International Business Review*, 23(1): 4–19. https://doi.org/10.1016/j.ibusrev.2013.08.002.

Huberman, B., Romero, D. and Wu, F. 2009. "Social networks that matter: Twitter under the microscope", *First Monday: Journal*, 14(5): 1–9. https://arxiv.org/pdf/0812.1045.pdf.

Hunt, S. D., and Vitell, S. (1986). "A general theory of marketing ethics", *Journal of Macromarketing*, 6(1): 5–16.

Hursthouse, R. 1999. *On Virtue Ethics*. New York: Oxford University Press.

Jurado, E. B., Uclés, F. B., Moral, A. M. and Viruel, M. J. M. 2019. "Agri-food companies in the social media: a comparison of organic and non-organic firms", *Economic Research-Ekonomska Istraživanja*, 32(1): 321–334. https://doi.org/10.1080/1331677X.2018.1547203.

Jurkiewicz, C. L. 2018. "Big data, big concerns: ethics in the digital age", *Public Integrity*, 20:1, 46–59.

Kant, I. 1788. "Cambridge Texts in the History of philosophy", In *Critique of Practical Reason*, edited by J. G. Mary, 1–35. Cambridge, MA: Cambridge University Press, 1997.
Kaplan, A. M. and Haenlein, M. 2010. "Users of the world, unite! The challenges and opportunities of social media", *Business Horizons*, 53(1): 59–68.
Kim, B. 2020. *"Moving Forward with Digital Disruption: What Big Data, IoT, Synthetic Biology, AI, Blockchain, and Platform Businesses Mean to Libraries"*, Chicago: American Library Association.
Kim, D., Spiller, L. and Hettche, M. 2015. "Analyzing media types and content orientations in Facebook for global brands", *Journal of Research in Interactive Marketing*, 9: 4–30. https://doi.org/10.1108/JRIM-05-2014-0023.
Komito, L. 2011. "Social media and migration: virtual community 2.0", *Journal of the American Society for Information Science and Technology*, 62: 1075–1086. https://doi.org/10.1002/asi.21517.
Lai, I. K. W., Tong, V. and Lai, D. 2011. "Trust factors influencing the adoption of internet based inter-organizational systems', *Electronic Commerce Research and Applications*, 10(1): 85–93. https://doi.org/10.1016/j.elerap.2010.07.001.
LaTour, M. S. and Henthorne, T. L. 1994. "Ethical judgments of sexual appeals in print advertising", *Journal of Advertising*, 23(3): 81–90. https://doi.org/10.1080/00913367.1994.10673453.
Laskey, H. A., Day, E. and Crask, M. R. 1989. "Typology of main message strategies for television commercials", *Journal of Advertising*, 18: 36–41. https://doi.org/10.1080/00913367.1989.10673141.
Lasorsa, D. L., Lewis, S. C. and Holton, A. E. 2012. "Normalizing Twitter. Journalism practice in an emerging communication space", *Journalism Studies*, 13(1): 19–36. https://doi.org/10.1080/1461670X.2011.571825.
Lipsman, A., Mudd, G., Rich, M. and Bruich, S. 2012. "The power of "like"", *Journal of Advertising Research*, 52: 40–52. https://doi.org/10.2501/JAR-52-1-040-052.
Liu, Y., Gayle, A. A., Wilder-Smith, A. and Rocklov, J. 2020. "The reproductive number of COVID-19 is higher compared to SARS coronavirus", *Journal of Travel Medicine*. https://doi.org/10.1093/jtm/taaa021.
Lorenzo, C., Constantinides, E. and Alarcon, M. D. C. 2011. "Consumer adoption of social networking sites: implications for theory and practice", *Journal of Research in Interactive Marketing*, 5(2–3): 170–188. https://doi.org/10.1108/17505931111187794.
McAfee, A. and Brynjolfsson, E. 2017, *"Machine, Platform, Crowd: Harnessing Our Digital Future"*, New York: W.W. Norton.
Madsen, D. O. and Slåtten, K. 2015. "Social media and management fashions", *Cogent Business & Management*, 2: 1–17. http://dx.doi.org/10.1080/23311975.2015.1122256.
Malthouse, E. C., Haenlein, M., Skiera, B., Wege, E. and Zhang, M. 2013. "Managing customer relationships in the social media era: introducing the social CRM house", *Journal of Interactive Marketing*, 27: 270–280. https://doi.org/10.1016/j.intmar.2013.09.008.
Manyika, J. 2013. *"Disruptive technologies: advances that will transform life, business, and the global economy"*, McKinsey Global Institute, May. http://www.mckinsey.com/insights/business_technology/disruptive_technologies.
Mangold, W. G. and Faulds, D. J. 2009. "Social media: the new hybrid element of the promotion mix", *Business Horizons*, 52: 357–365. https://doi.org/10.1016/j.bushor.2009.03.002.

McElreath, F. S. 2018. "Contemporary virtue ethics and action-guiding objections", *South African Journal of Philosophy*, 37(1): 69–79. https://doi.org/10.1080/02580136.2017.1419330.

Micheler, S., Goh, Y. M., & Lohse, N. (2019). "Innovation landscape and challenges of smart technologies and systems – a European perspective", *Production & Manufacturing Research*, 7(1): 503–528.

Miles, S. 2018. "Do we have lift-off?' Social media marketing and digital performance at a British Arts Festival", *The Journal of Arts Management, Law, and Society*, 48(5): 305–320. https://doi.org/10.1080/10632921.2017.1366379.

Murphy, P. and Laczniak, G. R. 1981. "Marketing ethics: a review with implications for managers, educators and researchers", *Review of Marketing*, 2: 251–266. Chicago, IL: American Marketing Association.

Murphy, P. E. 2002. "Marketing ethics at the millennium: review, reflections and recommendations", In *The Blackwell Guide to Business Ethics*, edited by N. E. Bowie, 165–185. Malden, MA: Blackwell.

Murphy, P. E., Laczniak, G. R., Bowie, N. E. and Klein, T. A. 2005. *Ethical Marketing*. Upper Saddle River, NJ: Pearson Prentice-Hall.

Nadaraja, R. and Yazdanifard, R. 2013. "Social media marketing: advantages and disadvantages", https://www.researchgate.net/publication/256296291_Social_Media_Marketing_social_media_marketing_advantages_and_disadvantages, Accessed June 13, 2020.

Nyagadza, B., Pashapa, R., Chare. A., Mazuruse, G. and Hove, P. K. 2022. "Digital technologies, Fourth Industrial Revolution (4IR) & Global Value Chains (GVCs) nexus with emerging economies' future industrial innovation dynamics", *Cogent Economics & Finance*, 9(1), pp. 1–23.

Nyagadza, B. 2020. "Search engine marketing and social media marketing predictive trends", *Journal of Digital Media & Policy*, Intellect publishers, Bristol, United Kingdom. https://doi.org/10.1386/jdmp_00027_1.

Nyagadza, B., Kadembo E. M. and Makasi, A. 2020a. "Exploring internal stakeholders' emotional attachment & corporate brand perceptions through corporate storytelling for branding", *Cogent Business & Management Journal*, 7(1): 1–22, Taylor & Francis Publishers, England & Wales, United Kingdom (UK). https://www.tandfonline.com/doi/full/10.1080/23311975.2020.1816254.

Nyagadza, B., Kadembo E. M. and Makasi, A. 2020b. "Corporate storytelling for branding: underpropping or thwarting internal stakeholders' optimistic corporate brand perceptions?", *Cogent Social Sciences Journal*, 6(1): 1–27, Taylor & Francis Publishers, England & Wales, United Kingdom (UK). https://www.tandfonline.com/doi/full/10.1080/23311886.2020.1845926.

Nyagadza, B., Kadembo, E. M. and Makasi, A. 2020c. "Structurally validated scale of appraising the nexus between corporate storytelling for branding & internal stakeholders' corporate brand perceptions", *Cogent Business & Management Journal*, Taylor & Francis Publishers, England & Wales, United Kingdom (UK). https://www.tandfonline.com/doi/full/10.1080/23311975.2020.1858524.

Nyagadza, B. and Nyauswa, T. 2019. "Parametric insurance applicability in Zimbabwe: a disaster risk management perspective from selected practicing companies", *Insurance Markets and Companies (IMC), Business Perspectives*, 10(1): 36–48, Ukraine. https://doi.org/10.21511/ins.10 (1).2019.04.

Nyagadza, B. 2019a. "Responding to change and customer value improvement: pragmatic advice to banks", *The Marketing Review (TMR)*, 19(3–4): 235–252,

West Burn Publishers, Scotland, United Kingdom (UK). https://doi.org/10.1362/146934719X15774562877719.

Nyagadza, B. 2019b. "Conceptual model for financial inclusion development through agency banking in competitive markets", *Africanus: Journal of Development Studies*, 49(2): 2663–6522. https://doi.org/10.25159/2663-6522/6758.

Padel, S. and Foster, C. 2005. "Exploring the gap between attitudes and behaviour: understanding why consumers buy or do not buy organic", *British Food Journal*, 107(8): 606–625. https://doi.org/10.1108/00070700510611002.

Ordoobadi, S. M. 2011. "Application of ANP methodology in evaluation of advanced technologies", *Journal of Manufacturing Technology Management*, 23(2), 229–252.

Pallab, P. 2019. "A gap analysis of teaching marketing ethics: desired versus current state", *Journal of Education for Business*, 94(7): 460–470. https://doi.org/10.1080/08832323.2019.1568221.

Paraskevis, D., Kostaki, E. G., Magiorkinis, G., Panayiotakopoulos, G., Sourvinos, G. and Tsiodras, S. 2020. "Full-genome evolutionary analysis of the novel corona virus (2019-nCoV) rejects the hypothesis of emergence as a result of a recent recombination event", *Infection, Genetics and Evolution*, 79: 104212.

Pereira, H. G., de Fátima Salgueiro, M. and Mateus, I. 2014. "Say yes to Facebook and get your customers involved! Relationships in a world of social networks", *Business Horizons*, 57: 695–702. https://doi.org/10.1016/j.bushor.2014.07.001.

Peters, K., Chen, Y., Kaplan, A. M., Ognibeni, B. and Pauwels, K. 2013. "Social media metrics—A framework and guidelines for managing media", *Journal of Interactive Marketing*, 27: 281–298. https://doi.org/10.1016/j.intmar.2013.09.007.

Puto, C. P. and Wells, W. D. 1984. "Informational and transformational advertising: the differential effects of time", *Advances in Consumer Research*, 11: 638–643, edited by Thomas C. Kinnear, Provo, UT: Association for Consumer Research.

Radu, A. 2016. "The pros and cons of blogging professionally", https://workology.com/the-pros-and-cons-of-blogging-professionally/, Accessed June 13, 2020.

Riou J, and Althaus, C. L. 2020. "Pattern of early human-to-human transmission of Wuhan 2019 novel coronavirus (2019-nCoV), December 2019 to January 2020", Euro Surveill. 2020; 25(4): 2000058. https://doi.org/10.2807/1560-7917.ES.2020.25.4.2000058.

Reidenbach, R. E. and Robin, D. P. 1988. "Some initial steps toward improving the measurement of ethical evaluations of marketing activities", *Journal of Business Ethics*, 7: 871–879.

Roces, M. 2018. "Pros and cons of turning all your blogs into vlogs", https://theinscribermag.com/pros-and-cons-of-turning-all-your-blogs-into-vlogs/, Accessed June 13, 2020.

Roitner, B., Darnhofer, I., Somsook, S. and Vogl, C. R. 2008. "Perceptions of organic foods in Bangkok, Thailand", *Food Policy*, 33(2): 112–121. https://doi.org/10.1016/j.foodpol.2007.09.004.

Rousseau, S. and Vranken, L. 2013. "Green market expansion by reducing information asymmetries: evidence for labelled organic food products", *Food Policy*, 40: 31–43. https://doi.org/10.1016/j.foodpol.2013.01.006.

Sawyer, R. and Chen, G. 2012. "The impact of social media on intercultural adaptation", *Intercultural Communication Studies*, 21: 151–169. https://web.uri.edu/iaics/files/09RebeccaSawyerGuoMingChen.pdf.

Shan, Y. and King, K. W. 2015. "The effects of interpersonal tie strength and subjective norms on consumers' brand-related eWOM referral intentions", *Journal of Interactive Advertising*, 15(1): 16–27. https://doi.org/10.1080/15252019.2015.1016636.

Simonite, T. 2017. "Two giants of AI team up to head off the robot apocalypse", *Wired*. Retrieved from https://www.wired.com/story/two-giants-of-ai-team-up-to-head-off-the-robot-apocalypse.

Skeels, M. M. and Grudin, J. 2009. "When social networks cross boundaries: a case study of workplace use of Facebook and LinkedIn", Paper presented at the *Proceedings of the ACM 2009 International Conference on Supporting Group Work*, New York. https://doi.org/10.1145/1531674.1531689.

Statista. 2018. "Social media statistics and facts", https://www.statista.com/topics/1164/social-networks/, Accessed June 13, 2020.

Swart, J., Peters, C. and Broersma, M. 2019. "Sharing and discussing news in private social media groups", *Digital Journalism*, 7(2): 187–205. https://doi.org/10.1080/21670811.2018.1465351.

Sweeney, D. 2013. "The pros and cons of direct messaging on Facebook, Twitter, and LinkedIn", https://www.socialmediatoday.com/content/pros-and-cons-direct-messaging-facebook-twitter-and-linkedin, Accessed June 13, 2020.

Taecharungroj, V. 2016. "'Starbucks' marketing communications strategy on Twitter'", *Journal of Marketing Communications*, 23(6): 552–571. https://doi.org/10.1080/13527266.2016.1138139.

Tafesse, W. 2016. "An experiential model of consumer engagement in social media", *Journal of Product & Brand Management*, 25: 424–434. https://doi.org/10.1108/JPBM-05-2015-0879.

Tafesse, W. and Wien, A. 2017. "A framework for categorizing social media posts", *Cogent Business & Management*, 4: 1–22. https://doi.org/10.1080/23311975.2017.1284390.

Torrent, J. 2015. "Knowledge products and network externalities: implications for the business strategy", *Journal of the Knowledge Economy*, 6(1): 138–156. https://doi.org/10.1007/s13132-012-0122-7.

Tsakiridou, E., Boutsouki, C., Zotos, Y. and Mattas, K. 2008. "Attitudes and behaviour toward organic products: an explanatory study", *International Journal of Retail & Distribution Management*, 36(2): 158–175. https://doi.org/10.1108/09590550810853093.

Van Der Heide, B. and Lim, Y.-S. 2016. "On the conditional cueing of credibility heuristics: the case of online influence", *Communication Research*, 43(5): 672–693. https://doi.org/10.1177%2F0093650214565915.

van Noort, G., Antheunis, M. L. and van Reijmersdal, E. A. 2012. "Social connections and the persuasiveness of viral campaigns in social network sites: persuasive intent as the underlying mechanism", *Journal of Marketing Communications*, 18(1): 39–53. https://doi.org/10.1080/13527266.2011.620764.

Vernuccio, M., Pagani, M., Barbarossa, C. and Pastore, A. 2015. "Antecedents of brand love in online network-based communities. A social identity perspective", *Journal of Product and Brand Management*, 24: 706–719. https://doi.org/10.1108/JPBM-12-2014-0772.

Wallace, E., Buil, I. and de Chernatony, L. 2014. "Consumer engagement with self-expressive brands: brand love and WOM outcomes", *Journal of Product & Brand Management*, 23: 32–42. https://doi.org/10.1108/JPBM-06-2013-0326.

Wilson, H. J., Guinan, P., Parise, S. and Weinberg, B. D. 2011. "What's your social media strategy?", *Harvard Business Review*, 89: 23–25. https://hbr.org/2011/07/whats-your-social-media-strategy.

Wilson, R. E., Gosling, S. D. and Graham, L. T. 2012. "A review of Facebook research in the social sciences", *Perspectives on Psychological Science*, 7: 203–220. http://dx.doi.org/10.1177/1745691612442904.

Xiang, Z. and Gretzel, U. 2010. "Role of social media in online travel information search", *Tourism Management*, 31: 179–188. https://doi.org/10.1016/j.tourman.2009.02.016.

Zaglia, M. E. (2013), "Brand communities embedded in social networks", *Journal of Business Research*, 66: 216–223. https://doi.org/10.1016/j.jbusres.2012.07.015.

Zhao, S. and Elesh, D. 2008. "Co presence as 'being with': social contact in online public domains', *Information Communication & Society*, 11(4): 565–583. https://doi.org/10.1080/13691180801998995.

7 Rebranding Destinations for Sustainable Tourism Recovery Post COVID-19 Crisis

Zanete Garanti, John Violaris, Galina Berjozkina and Iordanis Katemliadis

Introduction

The tourism industry was one of the largest and fastest-growing industries until the end of 2019, when all the world was challenged because of COVID-19. The national and international economy, including tourism networks, i.e. international travel, domestic tourism, day trips and various divisions, such as air transport, cruises, public transport, hotels, cafes and restaurants, conferences, concerts, meetings or sporting events, was suddenly affected by international, regional and local travel restrictions (Gössling et al., 2020). The pandemic has affected all parts of the tourism and hospitality sectors. Within a few months, the situation has changed rapidly, affecting tourism itself and tourist sites. Most of the words over tourism sites have become under or non-tourism objects. The extraordinary conditions have led to closed borders in nearly all countries or at least entrance controls, selective country travel bans, entry quarantines, and health certificates (Gössling et al., 2020). With more than 100 million direct tourism jobs at risk, it is tempting to aim for quick tourism recovery as soon as the health situation stabilizes. And while recovery is important, the new norm for the tourism industry is transformation (Ateljevic, 2020) to avoid further unsustainable practices in the industry. UN Secretary-General Antonio Guterres emphasized this as an opportunity to rethink tourism and rebuild it in a "safe, equitable and climate friendly manner" (UNWTO, 2018). UNWTO Global Guidelines to Restart Tourism as well as One Planet Vision for a Responsible Recovery of the Tourism Sector, an all-defined innovation and sustainability, as the new norm in the industry, and call for responsible recovery for people, the planet and its prosperity.

It is obvious that each country, on a macro level, depending on its resources, vision and capabilities, has responded in its own way to the COVID-19 challenges. Also, on a micro level, each tourism related enterprise has also responded in its own way. Some enterprises have chosen to cease their operations completely. Others, to redirect their efforts and product to the local customers. Others still, have seen COVID-19 as an opportunity to redirect their business to other directions that perhaps were in their plans, yet not their immediate ones. In other words, the COVID-19 triggered

DOI: 10.4324/9781003207467-10

the necessity to expedite decisions and changes. In the context of the "new norm" in tourism (Analytica, n.d.), the whole tourism sector is gradually being rebranded. Traditionally mass tourism and large arrivals were satisfying the hoteliers and other related businesses. Now, the reality of the health crisis forces the governments, industries and stakeholders to rethink the product (Jugănaru, n.d.; Hung et al., 2020; Renaud, 2020) and to think out of the safe box that was sustaining the tourism sector for so many years. Immediately, local customers became much more important and valuable than before. They also, not being able to travel abroad, started seeking local destinations on an unprecedented scale. And they started 'discovering' little villages that had to offer local products and services. Although this process has taken place in such a short time and under difficult conditions, it seems it has managed to a satisfactory degree make-up for a substantial percentage of the income loss from foreign arrivals, yet only for a few months. The COVID-19 has taught an important lesson to all economies. A lesson that was always known, yet not applied: Economies need to be as diverse as possible. They also need to be flexible and able to adjust as quickly as possible.

The new norm for tourism means that destinations will have to rethink how they are branded and positioned for the potential future, as the demand for tourism will change significantly. A shift in demand for more safe and sustainable tourism practices will mean that supply will have to adjust and come forward with the strategies to transform the existing tourism experiences. In this chapter, we discuss the tourism industry rebranding for sustainable tourism recovery after COVID-19, by

1   exploring the tourism destination branding,
2   describing the aspects of sustainable tourism development and recovery, and finally
3   discussing destination rebranding strategies for sustainable tourism recovery.

Tourism Destination Branding

In today's highly competitive and dynamic environment branding products and services mean that also destinations, whether individual resorts, cities, villages, regions or countries, are adopting branding techniques (Jago et al., 2003; Qu et al., 2011; Malerba et al., 2020). Destination branding can be defined as

> a name, symbol, logo, word mark or other graphic that both identifies and differentiates the destination; furthermore, it conveys the promise of a memorable travel experience that is uniquely associated with the destination; it also serves to consolidate and reinforce the recollection of pleasurable memories of the destination experience.
> (Ritchie and Ritchie, 1998)

With destinations being multidimensional (Pike, 2005), the challenge is to ensure sufficient differentiation of the destination (Aaker, 2009) and ensure its uniqueness (Morgan et al., 2007). Destination branding involves different levels of stakeholders (Blain et al., 2005) and the combination of various industries (Upadhya and Vij, 2020) (e.g., city brand would be a result of local government, public, businesses, local restaurants, hotels and other relevant stakeholder collaborative efforts, which appears to be the key success factor of destination branding) (Antónia et al., 2020; Perkins et al., 2020). As destination branding is a broad process (Ruiz-Real et al., 2020), it is not uncommon for destination management organizations (DMOs) to attempt both external destination marketing as well as internal destination development (Presenza et al., 2005) to achieve the main objectives of destination management.

The main objective of a DMOs is in marketing, promotion and sales tasks, as well as coordinating long-term destination planning and management since the consumer perceives and buys a destination as one integrated product (Mead, 1983; Pearce, 1992; Keller and Bieger, 2008; Bieger et al., 2011). Tourists look at the destination as a whole touristic product and therefore tourism authorities need to approach their destination as a whole and not as individual unit that compete, otherwise they can lose the competition. Varraa, Buzzigoli and Loro (2011) suggest that "destination management is an approach which can raise the value of territory users, organizations, citizens, and the whole community, not only for the tourist, using local products and services". Therefore, the importance of DMOs to coordinate tourism destination marketing is undeniable, and many countries have created and funded DMOs in order to support the development of their tourism industry.

DMOs as organizations want to achieve specific targets and are trying to create factors and synergy that will lead to the creation of unique tourist products. They are trying to accomplish this by combining different resources in order to achieve financial and socio-economic goals. One of the major roles that led to the creation of the DMOs are that they are primarily responsible to promote and sell the destination. The DMOs are getting in touch not only with the end customers but very importantly with professional groups such as journalists of tourism magazines, organizers of incentive travels, tour operators and travel agents. They organize familiarization trips, where journalists are invited to experience the destination and go back to their countries and publications and write about the host destination. Presenza et al. (2005) categorize their marketing activities to (a) External Destination Marketing (EDM), whereas DMOs are carrying out activities like web marketing, advertising through classic and new media (e.g. Facebook, Instagram), sales blitzes, direct sales, direct mail, events, festivals, conferences, fairs; (b) Internal Development Role (IDD), which are all the activities that the DMOs are undertaking within the destination such as visitor management, measuring visitor satisfaction, market research, development of the human resources of the destination, helping to attract and raise financial resources; and finally (c) Overall Destination Management (ODM), which refers to the coordination of stakeholders and management of crises. Destination Management should be considered as an activity aimed at achieving a balance between each operator's interests and the community's interests, between formal and informal relations, between public and private targets (Varra et al., 2011).

DMOs ownership varies amongst countries, in some they are entirely public owned, while in other countries they are a consortium of public-private sectors. DMOs offer an integrated and holistic outlook of the destination and because of the fact that they are not solely there to make a profit they have set other goals apart from profit in their agenda. As Bosnic et al. (2014) put it DMOs long term goals can be broken down to optimal economic development of destination, a higher quality of life standard for the local population, preservation of necessary levels of ecology, cultural and historic heritage preservation and use of heritage in economic and general growth, ensure normative framework, ensuring cooperative and complex activities of various groups within the system of an organization.

Destination branding is a joint effort amongst stakeholders and DMOs to create a unique and distinct destination image (San Martín et al., 2019) and personality (Vinyals-Mirabent et al., 2019; Yang et al., 2020) that would contribute towards destination brand equity (Gartner and Ruzzier, 2011; Sartori et al., 2012; Dedeoğlu et al., 2019) and loyalty (Chen et al., 2020) and ensure that tourists visit the destination (Rodríguez-Molina et al., 2019). The evidence from the empirical literature shows that destination branding efforts do affect tourist spending (Khan et al., 2019) and alternate their behavior towards visiting and re-visiting the destination (Blasco-Lopez et al., 2019; Yin et al., 2020). Moreover, the destination branding efforts also ensure local residents' participation (Mai et al., 2019) and allow them to become ambassadors of the destination brand (Wassler et al., 2019). Several studies that show how successful destination brands have been created for various destinations (Dieguez and Conceição, 2020), also it indicates that each destination attempt the branding process through their own unique approaches, e.g. storytelling (Lund et al., 2019), creativity, innovation and smartness (Trinchini et al., 2019) or through promoting local foods (Macelloni and Felder, 2020). With the complexity of destination branding, it is important to identify the unique attributes of the destination that further serve as a basis for the destination image, personality and brand building.

Sustainable Tourism Recovery

Sustainability is a desired goal of development (Brown et al., 1987), and is often seen as integration of economic, social and environmental considerations (Munasinghe et al., 2019) also known informally as earnings, earth, and people (Grant, 2020) into activities so that interests of future generations are emphasized (Bogacki and Letmathe, 2020). It has become clear at the global level that awareness of the ability of tourism to drive sustainable development is increasing. The United Nations have proposed 17 sustainable development goals (UNSDG) that is the comprehensive guide of sustainability for planet, people and future in the 21st century, and year of 2017, as the International Year of Sustainable Tourism for Development, was an occasion to increase public and private sector awareness of the importance of sustainable tourism to development (Tourism and the Sustainable Development Goals – Journey to 2030, Highlights, 2018).

Tourism has been applied to the underlying theories and values of sustainable growth, as a result of philosophical difficulties, disputes, and the multiplicity of both ideologies (Saarinen, 2006). By comparison, the definition sustainable development in tourism is favored by some scholars (Butler, 1999). Sustainable tourism is described by the United Nations World Tourism Organization as "tourism that takes full account of its current and potential economic, social and environmental effects, meeting the needs of tourists, business, the environment and host communities" ("EU Guidebook on Sustainable Tourism for Development," n.d.). Despite many decades of theoretical and practical discussion on the sustainability of tourism, it is usually described as a good awareness of the processes of how a responsible destination actively executes a sustainability policy and how it is called for in the dominant tourism debate on sustainability (theory, seen as a concept) and accountability (practice, seen as appropriate action) (Mihalic, 2016). Definitions like these highlight the needs of the industry and the products being used sustainably.

It is not possible to regard tourism that ruins the environment as sustainable; tourism that causes disparity between residents and visitors is not appropriate and tourism in the hands of a few multinational intermediaries does not enhance the hosting area (Saravitali, 2020). Similarly, the Road to 2023 study on Tourism and the Sustainable Development Goals indicates that 'Tourism's role in achieving the 17 SDGs can be greatly improved as sustainable development becomes a joint responsibility and shifts to the heart of tourism sector decision-making' (Sharpley, 2020). The Tourism and Hospitality sector can be sustainable if policymakers, corporate officials, educators, civil society and travelers will reform tourism and themselves into more sustainable practices, and they should be willing to contribute and function together in order to meet the essential values of sustainable growth. Policymakers have to put the ability to leverage the potential of tourism to provide countries and their people with long-lasting advantages, while traditional and non-traditional investors have the opportunity to engage in tourism to improve meaningful growth outcomes.

The approach to sustainable growth can be extended to any scale of tourism production, from larger resorts to special interest tourism of small size (Inskeep and Others, 1991). Scholarly literature shows that a variety of positive impacts and rewards are created by the travel trade industry, but it also stresses that if travel and tourism are not handled and controlled appropriately, it may lead to negative effects for the climate, culture and local economies (Ventriglia and Rios-Morales, 2013). It also shows that the role of the media is essential to environmental growth and sustainable tourism (Lane, 2009). Since social media seeks to reach and influence large audiences it has a huge impact on the tourism and hospitality industry. In order to reach sustainability in tourism and hospitality sector associations and government bodies have sought to identify and honor good practices and achievements by certificates, eco-labels and environmental certification programs (Ventriglia and Rios-Morales, 2013). The study of Richards and Font (2019) indicates that a positive corporate culture for businesses that want to ramp up the amount of sustainable products they purchase and distribute is a requirement for success. Sustainability is marketed only where it relates to the ability of a company to fulfill the quality-of-service needs, especially in relation to the suitability of the goods to its target audiences and the development of technical and trustworthy relationships. Buyers and sellers also lack the incentive to accept environmental criteria for commodities that are heavily priced and/or that have strict health and safety controls, because they are strongly valued and promoted.

It could take years or even decades to recover from the pandemic, however, to help tourism recovery, approaches to recovery should be taken currently. COVID-19 pandemic was not the first pandemic that has affected the tourism sector and led to a crisis at this point. Twenty years earlier, it was concluded that sustainable tourism growth was an unviable target (Sharpley, 2020). Although the idea of sustainable tourism continues to be the topic of intense and often divisive discussion, since the 1990s, the sector has evolved and expanded immensely. In recent years, there has been growing debate on how sustainable tourism studies and policies should often rely more on recognizing and modifying the perceptions, habits, and preferences of human actors (Bramwell et al., 2017). For many, sustainable tourism is not even an option; every tourism needs to be sustainable to function in the 21st century; otherwise it cannot exist (Moscardo and Murphy, 2014). Despite these outcomes, the industry's long-term survival faces considerable challenges in terms of keeping the growth model consistent with the local community's quality of life, especially in cities or mature destinations ("How Global Tourism Can Be More Sustainable," n.d.).

Sustainable tourism is responsible tourism. According to current academic literature, it is clear that future tourism will be forced to operate differently and to some extent transformed. The tourism industry has also been stated to have strong durability and the potential to respond to and rebound from devastating or unforeseen phenomena. However, this time, the industry would have a very serious stress test to overcome (Romagosa, 2020). From this point of view, the present downturn does not, at least in terms of its potential management and planning, suggest a significant improvement in the tourism industry. Rather, a philosophy of 'business as normal' will prevail. The survival of destinations and tourism firms is of great concern. Faced with an unpredictable future, those destinations who seem to be less disadvantaged and more stable places are those who provide more diversity and are less reliant on a single demand and have preferred qualitative rather than quantitative parameters of growth. Companies who, regardless of their scale, have invested in and been committed to the ideals of sustainable tourism are those that would be best placed in the current setting (Higgins-Desbiolles, 2020a). The goal for global sustainable tourism would also be to strike a balance between sustaining activity in rich countries while minimizing overcrowding and taking development to developing countries, some of which are too reliant on the sector and economies that will need a lot of incentives to recover. Sustainability teaches us to look for alternatives.

Destination Rebranding Strategies for Sustainable Tourism Recovery

In the branding literature, branding is seen as a dynamic and interactional process (Helle et al., 2011), which requires that developed brand and branding strategies are updated and continuously adjusted (Mary and Schultz, 2003) to keep up with the changes in organizational strategy and vision, as well as external factors that affect the organization or de-stigmatization. Rebranding is an especially effective tool for rebuilding an image and trust for product, service or destination after a crisis (Brophy, 2014), for example rebranding was used to build a new image of Lesvos Island after immigration crisis that started in 2015 (Donovic, 2020) and rebuild an image of Nigeria with the help of filmmakers to fight negative stereotypes on Nigeria and Nigerians (Endong, 2020). Therefore, the crisis that the world faces in 2019/2020 is also an opportunity to adjust and rebuild the image of the places and ensure the future recovery of the tourism and travel industry.

COVID-19 has brought many challenges for the tourism industry, but amongst the general public, academics and practitioners there is a hope that changes made during the crisis would contribute towards more sustainable tourism development in the future (Gössling et al., 2020). The world needs reshaping tourism and resetting tourism research agendas (Rogerson and Baum 2020) to ensure that growing numbers of people, professionals and governments become conscious and rebuild their operations towards sustainable tourism development goals (Galvani et al., 2020). There is currently a "war" ongoing amongst those that advocate quick tourism recovery that would help nations economically, especially countries that heavily depend on tourism income, and tourism reform, which would take a slow turn on tourism recovery, but ensure more sustainable, ethical and responsible tourism in the future (Higgins-Desbiolles, 2020b). Academics do advocate for tourism reforms and transformation but recognize that the change has to happen from both the demand and supply side of the tourism industry, and only if substantial institutional innovation happens in both (Brouder, 2020) and new approaches to travel and tourism are introduced (Nepal, 2020; Romagosa, 2020) we can ensure the sustainable future of the industry.

The recent literature from industry professionals and academics draws several future tourism directions that would contribute to sustainable tourism recovery. In September 2020, Andrew Nelson interviewed industry professionals for a Wall Street Journal article on "How Travel Will Change Post Pandemic: 10 Expert Predictions", and it outlines the importance of less crowded, clean air, secret destinations that offer esoteric food, vanishing species and nature conservation would be the top priorities in post COVID-19 era. Academics agree that the speed we consume the world will slow down (Benjamin et al., 2020), and tourism recovery will be public-private consolidation and collaboration effort (McCartney, 2020). Destination rebranding efforts will have to focus on emphasizing unique attributes of the destinations that will allow tourists to experience safe and sustainable tourism.

Taking into account the above mentioned, it is clear that collaboration amongst DMOs and all stakeholders will be the key success factor when it comes to rebranding destinations. DMOs have an important role to play as they can work as the entity that can bring the different stakeholders together. DMOs are in many cases in position to have a clearer picture coming from collected data, of the impact of COVID-19 and are able to understand the consequences and solutions that are needed more holistically. By many academics and people in the industry this health crisis is considered a golden opportunity for destinations to rebrand their image. They urge destinations to project a cleaner, less crowded, more resilient and sustainable image that will attract less tourists but with higher spending power. By doing so they will meet the Sustainable Development Goals (SDGs) that were laid out by the UNWTO in 2015 with the 2030 Agenda for Sustainable development and will also fulfill the long term goals that were broken down by Blažević and Peršić (2007) and Bosnić et al. (2014), namely optimal economic development of destination, a higher quality of life standard for the local population and preservation of necessary levels of ecology.

To do so DMOs should work on three different levels: short term, medium and long term. The short-term level is still very unpredictable since the pandemic is still in full swing. But DMOs can try to mitigate the consequences working with the authorities, put safety first and create strong protocols that will be decided with the key industry players and followed by everyone. Destinations that deal with the pandemic successfully will come out of this crisis stronger and with a positive image to rebrand the destination. DMOs should also gather data and develop plans and scenarios on how to deal with the crisis. At this level they should take on new roles and work also as crisis management organizations that provide leadership to the destination.

On a medium term DMOs can play an important role in co-creating initiatives that will boost domestic tourism and will benefit local businesses.

DMOs should stay active and relevant on the social media platforms and keep reminding customers that they are ready to welcome them when the pandemic is over. On a longer term DMOs should rethink their approach on how the visitor economy can add maximum value to the local communities and readjust the product offerings together with the destination's stakeholders to create a product that is greener, more sustainable and more authentic. The digital transformation of DMOs will help to realize the above goals. As Gössling et al. (2020) put it "the challenge is now to collectively learn from this global tragedy to accelerate the transformation of sustainable tourism".

Conclusion and Discussion

The current study aimed to (1) explore the tourism destination branding (2) describe the aspects of sustainable tourism development and recovery and finally (3) discuss destination rebranding strategies for sustainable tourism recovery. The study has shown that tourism got affected on macro and micro level, forcing countries and enterprises to rapidly change the strategy in order to adjust to new circumstances. The situation with pandemic has reshaped the way destination management is managed. Now all the attention has been placed on rural, less visited areas, where tourism stakeholders started to explore local tourism and production opportunities.

Destination branding, shown by current research, is a complex and challenging task, especially taking into consideration effects of crisis, and involves differentiation and multidimensionality of the destination, combining various industries and levels of stakeholders. Moreover, the destination branding efforts also ensure local residents' participation and allows them to become ambassadors of the destination brand. DMOs are playing a major role in destination branding and attracting more locals and, as an organization, aims to achieve certain goals by creating factors of synergy that will develop a unique tourism product. The important contribution of the DMOs in rebranding strategies cannot be unseen- reaching out to tourism magazines, local tourism organizations, industry professionals, organizing familiarization trips and writing about the destination in order to make it popular and attract potential tourists. In spite of the above mentioned, long-term priorities of the DMOs can be broken down in order to maximize the economic development of the destination, boost the quality of life of the local population, maintain the required levels of biodiversity, protection of cultural and historical heritage and use of heritage for economic and general growth.

Sustainability is another goal towards responsible and swift tourism recovery. Nowadays, the awareness for sustainable tourism recovery is increasing and as a result 17 sustainable development goals were proposed by the United Nations. The goals are focused on increasing public and private sector awareness of the importance of sustainable tourism development. The society needs to get involved in promoting the area they live in, make sure that sustainable tourism practices are there and that tourism does not ruin or harm the environment. The collaboration between the community, governmental bodies and stakeholders needs to be invented and all three need to agree on promoting sustainable tourism practices in local areas. Whenever the post crisis period approaches, sustainability becomes an especially effective tool for rebuilding an image and trust for product, service or destination. The new normal for tourism in the future will mean rebranding and repositioning towards sustainable practices.

The growing number of academic literature looks and projects tourism destinations post crisis. Rebranding destinations for sustainable tourism are a topic of particular interest in the discussion that is taking place now. A lot of researchers underline the fact that the sustainable transformation of destinations was already underway, and the health crisis has accelerated this trend. Researchers and the industry are thinking ways on how to mitigate the consequences of the pandemic but also plan for the future. The United Nations back in August 2020 has issued a roadmap towards a more sustainable and inclusive tourism sector that will build international cooperation among the stakeholders to transform the destinations in a way that they will embrace local values and community (Back, 2020). Sigala (2020) pointed out that the COVID-19 crisis has seen an unprecedented intervention of governments to boost the economic recovery and save jobs. Together with the destinations' authorities, governments have acted very nationalistic by signing, for example bilateral agreements, even though the response should be more collective. Another angle on the impact of the COVID-19 was highlighted by Zenker and Kock (2020) in their article for the tourism agenda that should be put forward post COVID-19. Authors claim that two consequences emerge regards destinations and their effort to rebrand and reposition. First, destination may be approached by tourists as a place that should not be considered to visit due to the high levels of infections. On the other hand, destinations might be branded in charitable manner so that tourists want to visit them in order to support the local economy. These two approaches should be accompanied with a tourist segmentation/targeting strategy the authors suggest. For other academics it is suggested that the COVID-19 crisis will force destinations to rebrand and focus their efforts towards source markets that are regional, national or continental (Jiricka-Pürrer et al., 2020). Authors suggest that when the pandemic is over destinations should not return back to the same practices and limit the trips that are too cheap and promote those that are thoughtfully planned, as this was anyway not a sustainable approach. To conclude, it is important to add that researchers, tourism (UNWTO) and not tourism authorities (OECD) agree that the recovery will take two to three years depending on the destination and it will be asymmetrical. In the meantime, destinations need to stay relevant to the minds of the tourists, try to mitigate as possible the consequences of the pandemic and draw a plan in which the destinations will come out more resilient, greener and more sustainable.

The main limitations of this study lie with the uncertainty related to the COVID-19 final outcome. At the time of writing, it has been ten months into pandemic and scientists around the world are uncertain as to the outcome, as well as the possibility of providing an effective vaccine and/or medicine to combat the disease. Given this, it is quite impossible for governments as well as business organizations to wisely plan for the future of the economy and their enterprises, respectively. Any measures already taken, any plans already drafted depend on the pandemic's final outcome. Additionally, investors are reluctant to place their funds into businesses that might as well be negatively affected, should the situation get worse. In fact, the trend currently is for investors to prefer investing in real estate assets, that they consider more secure, rather than investments in businesses. It is obvious that the pandemic has greatly affected the 'modus operandi' of the totality of the economy and society. Additionally, it is also certain that certain things, that in the early stages of the pandemic seemed to be temporary, for example tele-work, digital, virtual travel will probably become the norm in the post COVID-19 era.

In the context of this study, authors have identified certain key areas that led to the rebranding of the tourist product and the sustainability of the tourism sector. These will continue expanding in the future and will be blended with the changes that the pandemic has necessitated. Future studies might as well focus on attempting to forecast the next pandemic or other major event and get the economies and societies more prepared to face them, as it is more than obvious that no country was prepared to face the COVID-19 pandemic.

References

"EU Guidebook on Sustainable Tourism for Development." n.d. Accessed October 1, 2020. https://www.unwto.org/EU-guidebook-on-sustainable-tourism-for-development.

"How Global Tourism Can Be More Sustainable." n.d. Accessed September 30, 2020. https://www.weforum.org/agenda/2019/09/global-tourism-sustainable/.

Aaker, David A. 2009. *Managing Brand Equity.* Simon and Schuster.

Analytica, Oxford. n.d. "Tourism Will Settle to a New Normal after the Pandemic." *Emerald Expert Briefings.* https://www.emerald.com/insight/content/doi/10.1108/OXAN-DB253012/full/html.

Antónia, Martins Catarina, Carneiro Maria João Aibéo, and Pacheco Osvaldo Rocha. 2020. "Key Factors for Implementation and Success of Destination Management Systems. Empirical Evidence from European Countries." *Industrial Management & Data Systems* (ahead-of-print). https://doi.org/10.1108/IMDS-11-2019-0598.

Ateljevic, Irena. 2020. "Transforming the (Tourism) World for Good and (Re)generating the Potential 'New Normal.'" *Tourism Geographies: An International Journal of Tourism Place, Space and the Environment,* 22(3): 1–9.

Back, K. (2020, September 27). Commentary: Policy Brief on COVID-19 and Transforming Tourism. Retrieved November 04, 2020, from https://www.un.org/en/commentary-policy-brief-covid-19-and-transforming-tourism.

Benjamin, Stefanie, Alana Dillette, and Derek H. Alderman. 2020. "'We Can't Return to Normal': Committing to Tourism Equity in the Post-Pandemic Age." *Tourism Geographies: An International Journal of Tourism Place, Space and the Environment*, 22(3): 1–8.

Bieger, Thomas, Christian Laesser, and Pietro Beritelli. 2011. *Wettbewerb im alpinen Tourismus - Herausforderungen und Innovationen*. Erich Schmidt Verlag GmbH & Co. KG.

Blain, Carmen, Stuart E. Levy, and J. R. Brent Ritchie. 2005. "Destination Branding: Insights and Practices from Destination Management Organizations." *Journal of Travel Research*, 43(4): 328–38.

Blasco-Lopez, Francisca, Nuria Recuero Virto, Joaquin Aldas Manzano, and Daniela Cruz Delgado. 2019. "Facebook's Power: Factors Influencing Followers' Visit Intentions." *Spanish Journal of Marketing-Esic*. https://www.emerald.com/insight/content/doi/10.1108/SJME-06-2018-0032/full/html.

Blažević, B., and Peršić, M. (2007). "Assessing the Kvarner Tourism Offering." *Tourism and Hospitality Management*, 13(1): 435–41.

Bogacki, J., and P. Letmathe. 2020. "Representatives of Future Generations as Promoters of Sustainability in Corporate Decision Processes." *Business Strategy and the Environment*. https://onlinelibrary.wiley.com/doi/abs/10.1002/bse.2618.

Bosnić, I., Tubić, D., and Stanišić, J. (2014). Role of Destination Management in Strengthening the Competitiveness of Croatian Tourism. *Ekonomski vjesnik: Review of Contemporary Entrepreneurship, Business, and Economic Issues*, 27(1), 153–70.

Bramwell, Bill, James Higham, Bernard Lane, and Graham Miller. 2017. "Twenty-Five Years of Sustainable Tourism and the Journal of Sustainable Tourism: Looking Back and Moving Forward." *Journal of Sustainable Tourism*, 25(1): 1–9.

Brophy, Richard. 2014. "Rebrand in Crisis: How Liberty Came to Ireland." *Journal of Strategic Marketing*, 22(2): 93–103.

Brouder, Patrick. 2020. "Reset Redux: Possible Evolutionary Pathways towards the Transformation of Tourism in a COVID-19 World." *Tourism Geographies*, 22(3): 484–90.

Brown, Becky J., Mark E. Hanson, Diana M. Liverman, and Robert W. Merideth. 1987. "Global Sustainability: Toward Definition." *Environmental Management*, 11(6): 713–19.

Butler, Richard W. 1999. "Sustainable Tourism: A State-of-the-Art Review." *Tourism Geographies*, 1(1): 7–25.

Chen, Ruixia, Zhimin Zhou, Ge Zhan, and Nan Zhou. 2020. "The Impact of Destination Brand Authenticity and Destination Brand Self-Congruence on Tourist Loyalty: The Mediating Role of Destination Brand Engagement." *Journal of Destination Marketing & Management*, 15(March): 100402.

Dedeoğlu, Bekir Bora, Mathilda Van Niekerk, Jeffrey Weinland, and Krzysztof Celuch. 2019. "Re-conceptualizing Customer-Based Destination Brand Equity." *Journal of Destination Marketing & Management*, 11(March): 211–30.

Dieguez T., Conceição O. 2020 Innovative Destination Branding: "Porto.". In: Rocha Á., Abreu A., de Carvalho J., Liberato D., González E., Liberato P. (eds).

Advances in Tourism, Technology and Smart Systems. Smart Innovation, Systems and Technologies, 131–140. Springer, Singapore.

Donovic, Danica. 2020. "Rebranding Places Affected by Immigration Crisis: The Case of Lesvos Island in Greece." Aristotle University of Thessaloniki. http://ikee.lib.auth.gr/record/316285/files/GRI-2020-26822.pdf.

Endong, Floribert Patrick, C. 2020. "Tackling Nigeria's Image Crisis with the Aid of Popular Cinema: A Study of Nollywood Filmmakers and the Nigeria's Nation-Branding Efforts." In Endong, Floribert Patrick, C. (eds). *Deconstructing Images of the Global South Through Media Representations and Communication*, 187–206. IGI Global.

Galvani, Adriana, Alan A. Lew, and Maria Sotelo Perez. 2020. "COVID-19 Is Expanding Global Consciousness and the Sustainability of Travel and Tourism." *Tourism Geographies*, 22(3): 567–76.

Gartner, William C., and Maja Konecnik Ruzzier. 2011. "Tourism Destination Brand Equity Dimensions: Renewal versus Repeat Market." *Journal of Travel Research*, 50(5): 471–81.

Gössling, Stefan, Daniel Scott, and C. Michael Hall. 2020. "Pandemics, Tourism and Global Change: A Rapid Assessment of COVID-19." *Journal of Sustainable Tourism*, 29(1), 1–20.

Grant, Mitchell. 2020. "Sustainability." August 27, 2020. https://www.investopedia.com/terms/s/sustainability.asp.

Helle, Kryger Aggerholm, Esmann Andersen Sophie, and Christa Thomsen. 2011. "Conceptualising Employer Branding in Sustainable Organisations." *Corporate Communications: An International Journal*, 16(2): 105–23.

Higgins-Desbiolles, F. 2020a. "The End of Global Travel as We Know It: An Opportunity for Sustainable Tourism." *The Conversation*: 17. Retrieved From https://theconversation.com/the-end-of-global-travel-as-we-know-it-an-opportunity-for-sustainable-tourism-133783 [Accessed on 25 July, 2021]

Higgins-Desbiolles, Freya. 2020b. "The 'War over Tourism': Challenges to Sustainable Tourism in the Tourism Academy after COVID-19." *Journal of Sustainable Tourism*, August, 29(4): 1–19.

Hung, K., H. Huang, and J. Lyu. 2020. "The Means and Ends of Luxury Value Creation in Cruise Tourism: The Case of Chinese Tourists." *Journal of International Hospitality, Leisure & Tourism Management*. https://www.sciencedirect.com/science/article/pii/S1447677020301467.

Inskeep, Edward, and Others. 1991. *Tourism Planning: An Integrated and Sustainable Development Approach*. Van Nostrand Reinhold.

Jago, Leo, Laurence Chalip, Graham Brown, Trevor Mules, and Shameem Ali. 2003. "Building Events into Destination Branding: Insights from Experts." *Event Management*, 8(1): 3–14.

Jiricka-Pürrer, A., Brandenburg, C., and Pröbstl-Haider, U. (2020). City Tourism Pre- and Post-Covid-19 Pandemic–Messages to Take Home for Climate Change Adaptation and Mitigation? *Journal of Outdoor Recreation and Tourism*, 31: 100329.

Jugănaru, I. D. n.d. "Mass Tourism during the Coexistence with the New Coronavirus. The Predictable Evolution of the Seaside Tourism in Romania." *Stec.univ-Ovidius.ro*. http://stec.univ-ovidius.ro/html/anale/RO/2020/Section%202/11.pdf.

Keller, Peter, and Thomas Bieger. 2008. *Real Estate and Destination Development in Tourism: Successful Strategies and Instruments.* Erich Schmidt Verlag GmbH & Co KG.

Khan, Jashim, Vivi Maltezou, and Chang He. 2019. "The Role of Destination Brand Image and Revisit Intention on Tourist Spending." In Androniki Kavoura, Efstathios Kefallonitis, Apostolos Giovanis (eds) *Strategic Innovative Marketing and Tourism*, 371–76. Springer International Publishing.

Lane, Bernard. 2009. "Thirty Years of Sustainable Tourism." In Stefan Gössling, C. Michael Hall, David Weaver (eds). *Sustainable Tourism Futures Perspectives on Systems, Restructuring and Innovations*, 19–32. Routledge.

Lund, Niels Frederik, Caroline Scarles, and Scott A. Cohen. 2019. "The Brand Value Continuum: Countering Co-Destruction of Destination Branding in Social Media through Storytelling." *Journal of Travel Research*, November, 59(8), 0047287519887234.

Macelloni, Edoardo, and Florian Felder. 2020. "Destination Branding through Local Food Products: The Case of Südtirol / Alto Adige." https://lup.lub.lu.se/student-papers/record/9019814.

Mai, Xianmin, Chuntao Wu, Tingting Zhang, Zhixiang Zhou, Haiyan Zhong, and Others. 2019. "The Impact of Local Community Participation on Branding Ethnic Tourism Destination: A Case Study of House Renovation in Jiaju Tibetan Village." *Open Journal of Social Sciences*, 7(01): 178.

Malerba, Rafaela Camara, Cristina I. Fernandes, and Pedro Veiga. 2020. "What Do We Know about Destination Branding?" In Sérgio Jesus Teixeira and João Matos Ferreira (eds). *Multilevel Approach to Competitiveness in the Global Tourism Industry*, 211–28. IGI Global.

Mary, Jo Hatch, and Majken Schultz. 2003. "Bringing the Corporation into Corporate Branding." *European Journal of Marketing*, 37(7/8): 1041–64.

McCartney, Glenn. 2020. "The Impact of the Coronavirus Outbreak on Macao. From Tourism Lockdown to Tourism Recovery." *Current Issues in Tourism*, 24(19), 1–10.

Mead, Barney. 1983. "Book Reviews: TOURISM, AN EXPLORATION By Jan van Harssel (National Publishers of the Black Hills, Inc., 521 Kansas City Street, Rapid City, South Dakota 57701, 1982, 373 Pp., $18.00." *Journal of Travel Research.* https://doi.org/10.1177/004728758302200269.

Mihalic, Tanja. 2016. "Sustainable-Responsible Tourism Discourse – Towards 'Responsustable' Tourism." *Journal of Cleaner Production*, 111(January): 461–70.

Morgan, Nigel, Annette Pritchard, and Roger Pride. 2007. *Destination Branding.* Routledge.

Moscardo, Gianna, and Laurie Murphy. 2014. "There Is No Such Thing as Sustainable Tourism: Re-conceptualizing Tourism as a Tool for Sustainability." *Sustainability: Science Practice and Policy*, 6(5): 2538–61.

Munasinghe, Mohan, Priyangi Jayasinghe, Yvani Deraniyagala, Valente José Matlaba, Jorge Filipe dos Santos, Maria Cristina Maneschy, and José Aroudo Mota. 2019. "Value–Supply Chain Analysis (VSCA) of Crude Palm Oil Production in Brazil, Focusing on Economic, Environmental and Social Sustainability." *Sustainable Production and Consumption*, 17(January): 161–75.

Nepal, S. K. 2020. "Travel and Tourism after COVID-19–Business as Usual or Opportunity to Reset?" *Tourism Geographies: An International Journal of Tourism Place, Space and the Environment.* https://www.tandfonline.com/doi/full/10.1080/14616688.2020.1760926.

Pearce, Paul. 1992. "Construction Marketing a Professional Approach." https://doi.org/10.1680/cmapa.16521.
Perkins, Rachel, Catheryn Khoo-Lattimore, and Charles Arcodia. 2020. "Understanding the Contribution of Stakeholder Collaboration towards Regional Destination Branding: A Systematic Narrative Literature Review." *Journal of International Hospitality, Leisure & Tourism Management*, 43(June): 250–58.
Pike, Steven. 2005. "Tourism Destination Branding Complexity." *Journal of Product & Brand Management*, 14(4): 258–59.
Presenza, Angelo, Lorn Sheehan, and J. R. Brent Ritchie. 2005. "Towards a Model of the Roles and Activities of Destination Management Organizations." *Journal of Hospitality, Tourism and Leisure Science*, 3(1): 1–16.
Qu, Hailin, Lisa Hyunjung Kim, and Holly Hyunjung Im. 2011. "A Model of Destination Branding: Integrating the Concepts of the Branding and Destination Image." *Tourism Management*, 32(3): 465–76.
Renaud, Luc. 2020. "Reconsidering Global Mobility--Distancing from Mass Cruise Tourism in the Aftermath of COVID-19." *Tourism Geographies: An International Journal of Tourism Place, Space and the Environment*, 22(3): 1–11.
Richards, P., and X. Font. 2019. "Sustainability in the Tour Operator – Ground Agent Supply Chain." *Journal of Sustainable Tourism*, 27(3): 277–91.
Ritchie, J. R. B., and J. R. R. Ritchie. 1998. "The Branding of Tourism Destinations." *Association of Scientific Experts in Tourism*. http://citeseerx.ist.psu.edu/viewdoc/download?doi=10.1.1.201.9520&rep=rep1&type=pdf.
Rodríguez-Molina, M. A., D. M. Frías-Jamilena, S. Del Barrio-García, and J. A. Castañeda-García. 2019. "Destination Brand Equity-Formation: Positioning by Tourism Type and Message Consistency." *Journal of Destination Marketing & Management*, 12(June): 114–24.
Rogerson, Christian, and Tom Baum. 2020. "COVID-19 and African Tourism Research Agendas." *Development Southern Africa*, 37(5): 17–29.
Romagosa, Francesc. 2020. "The COVID-19 Crisis: Opportunities for Sustainable and Proximity Tourism." *Tourism Geographies*, 22(3): 690–94.
Ruiz-Real, José Luis, Juan Uribe-Toril, and Juan Carlos Gázquez-Abad. 2020. "Destination Branding: Opportunities and New Challenges." *Journal of Destination Marketing & Management*, 17(September): 100453.
Saarinen, Jarkko. 2006. "Traditions of Sustainability in Tourism Studies." *Annals Of Tourism Research*, 33(4): 1121–40.
San Martín, Héctor, Angel Herrero, and María del Mar García de los Salmones. 2019. "An Integrative Model of Destination Brand Equity and Tourist Satisfaction." *Current Issues in Tourism*, 22(16): 1992–2013.
Saravitali. 2020. "Sustainable Tourism: The Theory." July 26, 2020. https://www.sustainabletourismworld.com/sustainable-tourism-the-theory/.
Sartori, Andrea, Cristina Mottironi, and Magda Antonioli Corigliano. 2012. "Tourist Destination Brand Equity and Internal Stakeholders: An Empirical Research." *Journal of Vacation Marketing*, 18(4): 327–40.
Sharpley, Richard. 2020. "Tourism, Sustainable Development and the Theoretical Divide: 20 Years on." *Journal of Sustainable Tourism*, 28(11): 1932–46.
Sigala, Marianna. 2020. "Tourism and Covid-19: Impacts and Implications for Advancing and Resetting Industry and Research." *Journal of Business Research*, 117: 312–21.

Trinchini, Lino, Kolodii Natalia Andreevna, Goncharova Natalia Aleksandrovna, and Rodolfo Baggio. 2019. "Creativity, Innovation and Smartness in Destination Branding." *International Journal of Tourism Cities*, 5(4): 529–43.

Upadhya, Amitabh, and Mohit Vij. 2020. "Creative Tourist Experience: Role of Destination Management Organizations." In Information Resources Management Association (eds). *Destination Management and Marketing: Breakthroughs in Research and Practice*, 763–83. IGI Global.

Varra, Lucia, Chiara Buzzigoli, and Roberta Loro. 2012. "Innovation in Destination Management: Social Dialogue, Knowledge Management Processes and Servant Leadership in the Tourism Destination Observatories." *Procedia-Social and Behavioral Sciences* 41: 375–85.

Ventriglia, Britt, and Ruth Rios-Morales. 2013. "The Shift toward Sustainability in the Travel Trade Industry." In *Sustainability in Tourism: A Multidisciplinary Approach*, edited by Ian Jenkins and Roland Schröder, 103–22. Springer Fachmedien Wiesbaden.

Vinyals-Mirabent, Sara, Mihalis Kavaratzis, and José Fernández-Cavia. 2019. "The Role of Functional Associations in Building Destination Brand Personality: When Official Websites Do the Talking." *Tourism Management*, 75(December): 148–55.

Wassler, Philipp, Liang Wang, and Kam Hung. 2019. "Identity and Destination Branding among Residents: How Does Brand Self-Congruity Influence Brand Attitude and Ambassadorial Behavior?" *International Journal of Tourism Research*, 21(4): 437–46.

World Tourism Organization (UNWTO). (2018). Tourism and the Sustainable Development Goals – Journey to 2030, Highlights [Ebook] (p. 15). Madrid. Retrieved from https://www.undp.org/content/dam/undp/library/Sustainable%20Development/UNWTO_UNDP_Tourism%20and%20the%20SDGs.pdf.

Yang, Shaohua, Salmi Mohd Isa, T. Ramayah, Ramona Blanes, and Shaian Kiumarsi. 2020. "The Effects of Destination Brand Personality on Chinese Tourists' Revisit Intention to Glasgow: An Examination across Gender." *Journal of International Consumer Marketing*, 32(5): 1–18.

Yin, Cheng-Yue, Nan Bi, and Yong Chen. 2020. "You Exist in My Song! How a Destination-Related Popular Song Enhances Destination Image and Visit Intentions." *Journal of Vacation Marketing*, 26(3): 305–19.

Zenker, S., and Kock, F. (2020). "The Coronavirus Pandemic–A Critical Discussion of a Tourism Research Agenda." *Tourism Management*, 81: 104164.

Part Three
Tourism Education and Research for Tourism Sustainability

8 Why Do We Teach Tourism?

Johan R. Edelheim

Introduction

Imagine the history of humanity through a metaphor of a train ride that can only go forward, just like time. Humanity has travelled far along tracks that have turned, crossed swamps, slowly ascended and rapidly descended mountains, and navigated several historical forks that could have led to a totally different ride. The emergence of COVID-19 was one of these forks, and we will never travel on the same tracks that we did before, we are on a different trajectory now.

I was recently told by a colleague that "post" COVID-19 is in some circles understood as any time after the emergence of the SARS Cov-2 virus, not, as I had so far interpreted the term, after we eventually have learned to live with this pandemic. The significance of learning this was surprisingly big – it reminded me of how the interpretation of one word can take on totally different connotations and realities for different people, and how easy it is for us humans to discuss an issue, and to totally misunderstand one another whilst imagining that we discuss the same matter.

Let me therefore start by outlining how I visualise a "Post COVID-19 Period". The vision I have, and that this chapter aims to share, refers to a world where COVID-19 no longer is an uncontrollable threat to all lives, livelihoods, and lifestyles on Earth. Let me reiterate that this is to ALL life, not just to a select privileged group of humans. The vision includes the kind of tourism education that could, and in my mind should take place at such a stage. Post COVID-19 is thus not a magical leap back to the "train tracks we were riding" in the past, but an acceptance that this virus, and its mutations will be a part of our future realities and decisions.

The perspective that I write from is additionally that tourism acts as a force in society that requires true multi-, cross, and indisciplinary investigations (Echtner and Jamal 1997) in order to come to its right. Tourism does more than the mobility it requires, more than the impacts it produces and causes, and more than the realities it creates, re-creates, and de-creates. Thus, tourism can be a force for good in many respects, and it should therefore not be imagined to be purely the responsibility of a few fields of interest, but rather a holistic concern for society as a whole.

DOI: 10.4324/9781003207467-12

It is fair to say that I am critical to how tourism has been taught, researched, and practiced in many places of the world in the decades leading up to the COVID-19 pandemic, but that does not mean that I would be "anti-tourism" (Higgins-Desbiolles 2021). Quite the opposite, I am very positive to the powers inherent in tourism; for example: Tourism might bring great social benefits to communities through improved infrastructure that serves locals as well as visitors. There can be cultural benefits through revitalisation and pride in traditions for Indigenous people and minorities. Tourism can entail ecological benefits through a focus and interest in preserving and learning more about distinct biospheres. Additionally, local communities can receive economic benefits through monetary activities related to tourism. Though, the enormous emphasis this last dimension has received is in my mind disproportional to its importance for the local communities that also bear the greatest overall cost of tourism.

To be critical is not the same as rejecting, but rather to care for something, and wanting it to develop into something even better. We need to stay away from strong dualisms, the world is not just hot or cold, light or dark, but it is temperate and multichromatic, and it is by acknowledging this multitude, and respecting different views that we progress. Simultaneously, we do not want to sink into relativism where nothing matters or have any preference, but rather need to have some guidelines for how to progress, and I will in this chapter claim that it is by examining and being conscious of lived and aspirational values in ourselves that this can be done.

Research Problem

We learn through hermeneutics that the only way to formulate a question is by having some sort of idea about what the answers might be. People are therefore always grappling for solutions to upheavals by examining what they already know. The urge to discuss "post" COVID-19 when the world is still very much in the midst of the pandemic, is because we do not know how to act in a world where none of the certainties of the past hold true.

By imagining a time post this pandemic we pin our hopes on a technofix (Huesemann and Huesemann 2011) that again make unhindered mobility possible, at least until the next pandemic, or other global change to the equilibrium of modern society, arrives. The talk about rapid tests, vaccines, travel bubbles, vaccination passports, and similar, are all examples of technofixes. Therein lies the problem plaguing contemporary civilisations; we put our trust in technology and sciences to fix what we are simultaneously destroying, whereas we seldom stop long enough to actually consider the cause of the current state. Instead, we immediately start searching for solutions to the symptoms, or even worse – we just wish the symptoms were not there, and we refuse to engage with the actual problem, and will therefore never be prepared for the next turmoil.

This problem is based, I will argue, on a lack of reflection, a deterministic tunnel vision that sees a current state of affairs as the only possible state of affairs, and a total belief in meliorism (Pernecky 2020) that disregard traditional knowledges and puts its hopes on developments of the future. In order to provide some solutions to this problem the following research questions were formed:

Research Questions

Why do we teach tourism in modern societies? Why is tourism education linked to the same economic path of dependency that modern states and governments follow? Why should future tourism education prepare students to formulate new questions that would open up new realities?

Research Significance

To question a matter with the word "why" brings the field of enquiry to *values*, rather than a "what" which aims for matters of *knowledge*, or a "how" which aims for matters of *being*. If the subtitle of this chapter would have been "What, do we teach in tourism?" or "How, do we teach tourism?" the answers would have led us back to issues in existence. The significance of asking a "why" question, is its forward aim. It is linked to ethics, and the response-ability we all have.

The core question that every academic involved in the field of tourism higher education should be able to answer is "Why do I teach/research tourism?" And we should never settle for the first response, we should continue asking "why" until we come to a core that shows us the values the action is built upon, and the purpose the action is directed towards.

Research Context

Tourism is taught all over the worldF, in secondary and in tertiary institutions, in public and in private institutions, as a major on its own, as a minor connected to a complementary major, or simply as an extension to a different field of studies. To investigate tourism education is therefore always fraught with challenges, including how to scope, how to delineate, and how to generalise – if that is the wish. This chapter will focus on tourism higher education in a distinct geographical region, but as the region contains five separate nation-states, all with their own higher education traditions, systems, and legislations, it is intended to exemplify tourism higher education more broadly.

The Nordic countries – hereafter the Nordics, are five nations (Denmark, Finland, Iceland, Norway, and Sweden) making up the North-west of Europe. The countries (including the self-governing regions of Greenland, Faeroe Islands, and Åland Islands) have a combined area of 3,426 mil square kilometres, with merely 27.36 million inhabitants in total (The Nordic Council 2021). This means that less than 4% of Europe's population lives in the Nordics, whilst their combined land mass is more than a third of Europe's size. The land mass would, if it were one single nation, be the world's seventh biggest nation, larger than India, alternatively a third of the size of either Canada, China, or the USA. As a result, education is spread out over a large geographic area, and comprises dominantly many smaller institutions. This is also true for the Higher Education (HE) sector with 179 institutions in total, see Table 8.1 below.

HE in the Nordics has in the past two decades gone through several reforms in the wake of the Bologna process, instilled by the European Union (EU). Iceland and Norway are not EU members, but all Nordic countries follow roughly the European Qualifications Framework (EQF) in their current educational set-ups (Gornitzka 2007). The four HE levels of the EQF are 5–8, where Level 5 is called a short cycle, generally referring to a post-secondary certificate or diploma. Level 6 is a bachelor education, Level 7 a masters', or postgraduate education, and Level 8 a doctoral education.

Higher Education is offered in a range of different institutions. Iceland is the only country that does not separate these into different entities. Finland has two types of HE providers, Norway and Sweden have four types, and Denmark has five types of HE providers (see Table 8.1).

To the rest of the world, many of these different types of providers are presenting themselves as "universities", and students, for example enrolled in a bachelor's degree at any of these providers graduate to the same EQF level six, but internally in the countries there are marked status and task differences. Traditional, or "research-intensive" universities, are listed in the first column in Table 8.1, whereas applied, technical, and private universities and university colleges to the right-hand of this.

Literature Review – Frameworks

A Purpose of Tourism Higher Education (THE)

Tourism (in this chapter used as a collective word also including hospitality, events, and gastronomy) has been taught as its own Major in HE institutions around the world for roughly 50 years (Airey, Dredge, and Gross 2015). The field was initially taught as a Minor in different faculties, but a substantial growth in programs happened from the 1980s to the 2000s, and many separate schools were created in that time (Catrett 2018). Page and Connell

Table 8.1 Types of Nordic HEs

Nordic Countries	Types of Higher Education institutions							
Iceland	Universities and university colleges	7						7
Finland	Universities	14	Universities of applied sciences	21				35
Norway	Universities	10	Scientific colleges	9	Colleges	13	Colleges with accredited study programs	17	49
Sweden	Universities	18	University colleges	12	Art, design, and music academies	5	Independent education providers	13	48
Denmark	Universities	8	University colleges	7	Artistic higher education institutions	12	Schools of maritime education and training	5	Business academies	8	40
Total		57		49		30		35		8	179

(2020) remind that tourism was not considered an intellectual pursuit before the 1980s, but rather "superficial and not really worthy of academic respect", however, this changed during the 1990s (2020, 4).

Though, the creation of schools focused on the study of tourism has not settled all discrepancies. An ongoing debate within tourism schools, but equally much amongst tourism stakeholders, is an ultimate purpose of THE. Many studies investigating THE curricula compare perceptions amongst academics, students, and operational tourism stakeholders. Gaps between the different views are commonly highlighted and presented as challenges for the field (Mei 2019). Dredge et al. (2012) named the curriculum space a "force field", drawn between two separate forces: skills (techne) and knowledge (episteme). Their study emphasised the need for both perspectives in order for students to graduate with practical wisdom (phronesis).

Page and Connell (2020, 5–7) list eight reasons for why the study of tourism is not as straight forward as many other academic fields, they are: (1) *Recognition*, whether tourism should be approach as a phenomenon, or as an assembly of industries, or even as one single industry – each perspective recognises different sets of approaches and entails different beliefs. (2) *Conceptualisation*, due to the multiscientific nature of tourism, and without a joint "tourismology" that would combine all tourism research to one set epistemological basis, researchers are spread over many fields, inhabiting different ontological realities, and not cross-fertilising fully within the field. (3) *Terminology*, a drive for creating the "next new", and for accumulating more publications, leads to a continuous reinvention of labels often for the same matter, such as ecotourism, green tourism, etc. This makes both research and practice unnecessary complex and steals time and effort from actual advances in the field. (4) *Data sources* used in tourism are fluid, and not generalisable – in comparison to many other fields. Different countries and stakeholders report on, define and emphasise different maters, for whichever purpose they want to progress. (5) *Reductionism* refers to the lack of overarching analytical frameworks that would allow for holistic interpretations, due to the multiscientific background of involved stakeholders. The study of tourism is instead reduced to separate interactions and activities. (6) *Rigour* highlights the earlier mentioned perception of tourism as something superficial which leads laypersons to imagine that they "understand" tourism and publish "expert" opinions. (7) *Theory*, or the lack thereof, hinders tourism from developing. Most tourism research is descriptive rather than advancing the field theoretically. Finally, (8) the *Academic/Practitioner divide* which highlight the different agendas, timescales, and values among academics and operational tourism stakeholders.

As a whole, global THE curricula are definitely caught in the "force field" that Dredge et al. (2012) described, pulled and pushed in different directions depending on the bargaining power held by different stakeholders. A very rough division into two schools of thought perceive tourism either as an *industry* whereby they find that education should be operationally vocational leading to a competent workforce, or those that see tourism as a *phenomenon* and through that perspective consider liberally theoretical education to be most suitable in order to prepare students to become knowledgeable members of society (Tribe 2005). However, I state in the introduction that we should avoid dualisms, and instead progress the field consciously together, like Dredge et al. proposed (2012). We need to acknowledge what we see as the purpose of THE and how we value THE personally. This leads us to an investigation of foundational philosophies, and especially axiology, because the values we hold determine how we can shape our future actions.

Foundational Philosophies

Different THE curricula can be investigated based on their foundational philosophies. Firstly, we can study *what* is being taught, what knowledge is included, and what sort of truth claims are created. All of these concerns focus on epistemology, and this is where a majority of research of THE is centred (Edelheim 2020). Epistemological arguments are necessary for many fields. However, purely epistemological arguments are not as helpful when investigating humanities and social sciences due to their inherent linguistic power structure (Belhassen and Caton 2009). To determine what a THE curricula should be like from an epistemological perspective will always be based on the reality of that author, how they value THE.

Thus, an alternative foundational philosophy is to examine *how* THE is taught, how courses are created, and how assessments are set. These questions of "how" are interested in the meanings and the realities of the matters, thus their ontology. Ontological questions are also necessary, for example by establishing that people adhering to different scientific fields will interpret reality in different ways, and thus reach mutually exclusive results, whereas both are epistemologically created correctly, in their own field (Hollinshead 2004).

Axiology as a final foundational philosophy can help us investigate *why* THE is taught. The core of using axiology as a foundational philosophy is the quest to examine values, and value-decisions involved in locating tourism schools in specific faculties, creating tourism programs, determining their content, now and in the future. Values are complex to investigate, and axiology is by no means a simple foundational philosophy to follow, but my aim in the next section is to show how it can usefully be applied in this chapter, beyond accusations of relativism or extreme essentialism (Gallarza and Gil 2008).

Axiology and Values

Acknowledging one's own values and unravelling in-built values of the world around us is important. The importance stems from the fact that values are always active. They are the result of constant evaluation, which is something all of us do every day, every moment of our lives, consciously and unconsciously. From the moment we wake up until we have fallen asleep again, we evaluate how to act, what to do, what to believe in and what not. We live through values, we live axiologically. Axiology is often confused with studies of ethics or aesthetics, but that is a fallacy. Axiology, as a field of investigation, is according to Hartman (2019) not about determinations of what is good or bad in a moral sense, or in the sense of taste. Instead, it is about "the principle of value" (2019, 23) or, more precisely, "a method of thinking which one is free to use and, consequently, develop one's own sense of value" (2019, 53).

Stating that values are subjective, or objective are epistemological claims, undermined by the fact that all truth claims come from evaluations of set perimeters, created by humans, not existing in an own "untainted" realm. Similarly, investigating what we "mean" by values, or what their "existence" could be, are ontological problems, and thus outside the scope of an axiological study (McDonald 2004). But to claim, as I will below, that there are values that could be considered better or worse than others might sound permissive to an own agenda. However, in this I am following the lead of McMurtry's axiom of life-value (2009–2010, 2013), and of Hartman's (2019) hierarchy of values.

McMurtry's primary axiom of value states that:

> X is value if and only if, and to the extent that, X consists in or enables a more coherently inclusive range of *thought* (T = internal image and concept) / *feeling* (F = the felt side of being; senses, desires, emotions, moods) / *action* (A = animate movement across species and organizations) than without it
> Conversely:
> X is disvalue if and only if, and to the extent that, X reduces/disables any range of thought/experience/action.
> (McMurtry 2009–2010, 213)

This axiom gives us an opening to what values, and disvalues are. Rather than being seen as relative opinions that different people hold, they refer to entities with either positive or negative effects on thoughts, feelings, and actions. Though, as that is still rather theoretical, McMurtry goes on by explaining what a life-value is:

> the most basic and universal life-matters are already decided beneath the social rules and people's opinions – such as that all people need sufficient nutriment, clean water, sewage facilities, learning of society's symbol systems, home and love, and expert care when ill if their life-capacities are not to be reduced or destroyed. […]

Why Do We Teach Tourism? 135

For whatever the self's desires, deprivation of any of these life goods leads to loss of life-capacity towards dehumanization and physical death. Yet which life-good and its provider is not in increasing peril for a growing majority of the world in our global value and rule system?
(2013, 1)

The most important aspect is thus life, not just human life, but all life. As a premise for all value and for all values is life in different ways. Without ensuring life, nothing else maintains value. This leads us to Hartman and the hierarchy of values he created with three dimensions: *intrinsic* (internal, affective or singular), *extrinsic* (behavioural or external), and *systemic* (conceptual, or synthetic) values.

In this hierarchy, intrinsic values are those that are good for their own sake, namely living things. Edwards (2010) states that intrinsic values are based on the entity's consciousness and self-awareness, its creativity and capacity to value, an end *to*, *in*, and *for* itself. Extrinsic values are, in Edwards' (2010) terms, useful or potentially useful objects, processes, or activities. He states, "Extrinsic properties are spatiotemporal properties existing in our common perceptual environment, our shared everyday world of space-time as given to us in ordinary sense experience" (2010, 60). The third layer, systemic values, is important because it signals a rejection of abstractions as a central component. An idea can be limitlessly worthy and good, but it can never think itself. It has to be thought by a living entity.

Methods

My chapter is set within a critical constructivist paradigm that highlights the multitude of ontologies in existence in the field of tourism higher education. It examines a set of tourism programs in order to illustrate that the academic system is reproducing values of societies, and that this circularity makes graduands from tourism programs vulnerable to possessing irrelevant skills and knowledges in an uncertain future. In order to visualise tourism education, post any future upheavals, it is of essence to start from where we are standing, and question why it is created as it is.

Data Selection and Collection

Having worked in the Nordics for almost ten years before moving to Asia, I argue that the region function as an interesting case on a global scale as it exemplifies neoliberal commodification of the HE sector in action. Their education systems were long known as publicly funded, free for anyone to attend, and inclusive in that they were geographically present all over the region (Vabø and Aamodt 2008). Whereas the public investment is still large in an international comparison, other things have changed quite a lot now that most have some form of fee structures (Vabø and Wiers-Jenssen 2017), and many smaller institutions have been merged together, or amalgamated into larger HE providers.

This study is focusing only on institutions offering tourism as an own major degree, thus limiting out providers offering tourism as a minor inside other disciplines. The data was collected between December 2020 and March 2021 from publicly available online sources, with a previous round of data collection done in January 2019. The first step was to find all programs available for students to apply to, either in English, or in one of the five native languages spoken in the Nordics. The official pages for student applications were used in each country, and the search terms were (both in English and in the separate languages): "Tourism", "Hospitality", "Events", "Hotels", "Restaurant", "Gastronomy" and "Meals". The following related, but in this study deemed tangential, terms were limited out of this study: "Leisure", "Outdoor programs", "Food technology", "Nutrition", "Guiding", "Sport", "Service", "Experience design", "Transport", "Logistics". Some degrees carrying aspects of these latter terms were included if a major part of their programs focused on tourism.

Separate spreadsheets were created for each country collecting information about the schools and departments, the faculties they belonged to, each program's mission statements (general overviews, program descriptions, structures, learning outcomes and, prospective career outcomes), the languages they were taught in, and each individual unit included in the programs. The units' names, objectives, outcomes, teaching methods, and assessable items were individualised to further analyse what kind of purposes and values the separate syllabi and curricula were based on.

Methodology

All data was transcribed, and collected in comparable formats, making it possible to see broader pictures. A critical content analysis followed (Manning and Cullum-Swan 1994) analysing what the separate programs included, how the programs were taught, and most importantly why different components, methods, objectives, and assessments were included. Naturally, this final dimension is a case of inference of purposes, rather than a direct reading. This is the reason why a critical content analysis, rather than a quantitative content analysis was used (Saukko 2003), as it allows for results to be reported also through discourses uncovered.

The most significant values laden sections are the introductory paragraphs outlining programs on the institutions' websites. This is where the institution and their representatives, often the faculty in cooperation with communication and marketing specialists, describe their programs based on everything they personally value, and what they imagine that others will value too. The other values-rich components of programs' mission statements are the outcomes of the degrees, both the academic ones, and those relating to career options after graduation. Many countries have set standards for what universities need to report on, such as explicating what graduating students should possess for knowledge, skills, and competences. However, many are also reporting on what kind of tasks alumni from the programs are involved in, in order to give interested stakeholders (in many cases prospective applicants and current students), and idea of the diverse options that await after graduation.

The underlying analytical framework is the earlier presented axiological hierarchy, it allows me to highlight the intrinsic, extrinsic, and systemic values in play in the data.

Findings

What and How THE Is Offered

Approximately a quarter of the total 179 HE providers in the Nordics have Tourism majors at some level, see Table 8.2 below. There are a total of 100 separate degrees on offer, thus approximately 2.5 degrees per institution that are offering some kind of tourism program. More than half of these degrees are bachelor level, another third are masters' degrees, the rest are certificates, diplomas, and one combined degree.

More than half of tourism majors are housed in faculties of social sciences, approximately 15% in natural sciences, 11% in humanities, almost 16% of the institutions do not belong to separate faculties, this is especially the case for university colleges in Denmark and Finland. It is noteworthy, especially with the strong emphasis on tourism's connection with design, culture, and creative industries that only one program is housed in a combined arts and humanities faculty (Table 8.3).

Table 8.2 Number and type of Nordic THEs

Institutions	44	24.44%
Degrees	100	227.27%
Certificate – Diploma	12	12.00%
Bachelor	55	55.00%
Master	32	32.00%
Bachelor & Master	1	1.00%

Table 8.3 Faculty belonging of Nordic THEs

Natural sciences	6.5	14.77%
Social sciences	25	56.82%
Humanities	5	11.36%
Arts	0.5	1.14%
None	7	15.91%
Total	**44**	**100.00%**

138 *Johan R. Edelheim*

Examining the type of institution that offers tourism degrees gives an indication of how tourism is perceived in that country. As mentioned earlier (Page and Connell, 2020), tourism used not to be considered worthy of scientific focus. An indication if this is still the case can be found from what institutions offer tourism programs. Table 8.4 shows that 87% of tourism programs in Finland are offered at applied science universities, whereas only 30% of the Swedish programs are based at university colleges. Iceland being an outlier here as their higher education institutions are not officially separated. In total, less than half of all institutions offering tourism programs are "traditional" universities, thus exemplifying the applied and non-theoretical perception decision makers have of tourism as a whole.

A trend in recent years has been to offer an increasing number of degrees in English. The argument is often that tourism is an international field, and students graduating are therefore in an advantage if they do already speak a global Lingua Franca. Another reason is, naturally too, that programs offered in English are more attractive to international applicants. The Nordics have very different approaches to this issue, Norway offers, for example, no bachelor's degrees in English, only masters' level programs, Denmark and Sweden are the opposite, a majority of their program are offered either just in English, or alternatively in a dual mode – English and the native language. Finland has two native languages and are thus offering degrees in both of them. Iceland is the only country offering another "international" language with a degree offered in Icelandic and German (see Table 8.5).

Why THE Is Taught

An analysis of the names of the 100 THE programs on offer give, not surprisingly the most common word as "tourism", appearing in 70 of the names. The Swedish degrees were the only exception, here where the word "destination" is commonly used as a synonym to tourism. The second most common word is "management" which is found in 46 instances, thus almost half of the degree names, another 27 programs have related words, such

Table 8.4 Research intensive institutions offering THE programs, number and percentage of total

Denmark	3	30%
Finland	2	13%
Iceland	4	100%
Norway	4	57%
Sweden	7	70%
Total	**20**	**45%**

Why Do We Teach Tourism? 139

Table 8.5 Languages Nordic THEs are offered in

Denmark			Finland			Iceland			Norway			Sweden		
Danish	2	13%	Finnish	23	66%	Icelandic	5	50%	Norwegian	14	88%	Swedish	8	33%
			Swedish	1	3%	Icelandic/English	3	30%						
Danish/English	1	7%				Icelandic/German	1	10%				Swedish/English	1	4%
English	12	80%	English	11	31%	English	1	10%	English	2	13%	English	15	63%
	15			35			10			16			24	

as "business, economy, marketing, industry, administration, and entrepreneurship" as part of their names.

This is followed by "service" (20) and, "hospitality" (18) thus, each found in approximately a fifth of all the programs respectively. Words related to hospitality, such as "hotel, restaurant, food, meal, gastronomy, sommelier, and culinary chef" appear a further 19 times.

The sixth most used word is "development", which appear in ten programs' names, another six have the word "sustainable" and three use "nature". Here we find a substantial portion of the programs in Sweden, none in Iceland, and only one in Denmark. A further reading of mission statements will indicate if this value choice is consistent. However, names tend to be rather static, and in many cases also generic due to government regulations, so a more detailed examination of mission statements will be done below. An analysis of all courses included, their learning outcomes, assessment methods, and teaching methods reveal more about *what* and *how* tourism is taught, these findings will be the topic of other articles based on the data.

The applied character of the field, and the strong connection to an "industry" that studies are connected to is highlighted in many of the mission statements. Opening sentences stating: "Tourism is a major growth industry", or "The tourism industry is one of the fastest growing industries" are common, some even more blatantly state "Prepare for a career in the World's fastest growing industry" and lay thus the foundation for what that institution, and their faculty members represent for values. These sentences explain the ontological reality the program is located in, and the axiological purpose that institution sees for education. A minority of programs have broader mission statements, including phrases like "prepare for the anthropocene", "to become philosophic practitioners", or "embrace ecological, ethical and social considerations". Out of the 100 program mission statements only one (!) refer directly to COVID-19 and the challenges this creates for everything related to tourism. More about these findings in the discussion below which I tie back to the research questions for this chapter.

Discussion and Conclusion

Why Do We Teach Tourism in Modern Societies?

A minority of tourism programs focus on intrinsic values, entities that are good to, in, and for themselves in any form, either in their names, the units that are compulsory to study, or the mission statements outlining their purpose. Knowledge, skills, and competencies listed are in a majority of the programs examined bypassing intrinsic values totally. Swedish programs had a slightly higher tendency than the other countries examined to highlight intrinsic values relating to ethics of practice, ecological environments, and people's well-being as some examples. Extrinsic values are more common, such as communal health practices. The overwhelming majority of values on display are, however, systemic, such as employment, growth, finance, management – all logical and self-evident, but not visionary for an uncertain future.

The schools housing tourism programs include words such as "experience, wellness, hospitality, service, food, rural, management, culinary arts, meal science, management, innovation, business, economy, and marketing". The names of the schools describe how decision makers understand tourism as a discipline. It is natural that no large changes have taken place yet in how tourism is perceived inside the higher education sector. The sector is by nature rather conservative, moves generally quite slowly, and decision making involve multiple layers of workgroups, consultation rounds and board meetings before any substantial changes are made.

Part of this is to protect students studying programs, they should have the right to finish their studies doing the same program that they applied to. Another reason is the expertise held by staff members. Having researched a field, and specialised in some sector of it, we tend to become protective, and insular in our views of how our places of employment should develop in the future. Finally, it is also due to other stakeholders, such as funding agencies (be they private or public), potential industry representatives, or community members who all perceive tourism education that is provided from their own perspectives, and with their own agendas. Within this force field of different interests, with competing ontological views of reality, and conflicting epistemological views of needed data, value decisions tend to aim for maintaining commonly held norms (Türkkahraman 2014). The old emphasis is maintained, even in the light of a new reality appearing. Thus, we are teaching tourism for reasons of the past, not for the future.

Why Is Tourism Education Linked to the Same Economic Path of Dependency That Modern States and Governments Follow?

The COVID-19 outbreak is a sobering reminder of why overdependence on any one thing is not feasible. Now, more than a year since WHO declared COVID-19 a global pandemic, a vast majority of tourism programs that are actively recruiting new students have done no substantial changes to how they describe the sector they are involved in, and what students need to prepare themselves for. It is alarming that such a large proportion of the people involved in managing these programs behave like ostriches, instead of proactively managing their challenge. The COVID-19 pandemic that is raging when this book is being written will not be the last upheaval to the world order and serves therefore as an example of warning for the future.

Though, despite a majority of the Nordics having had different levels of lockdowns, states of emergency, and restrictions to "non-essential" movement and services, which entails all of the tourism sector, almost none of the programs acknowledge this openly. COVID-19 is referred to in passing as an operational inconvenience with statements such as: "depending on the situation, classes will either be delivered virtually or in person", but no direct reference is made to how the pandemic changes and challenges the whole sector. It is as if decision makers would be afraid to openly admit that the sector is in dire crisis, and by not saying so imagine that students will forget it and go on like before.

A general indication is that tourism also in higher education institutions is perceived rather vocationally, and that a strong focus is on operations. This might serve existing tourism stakeholders' interests rather well, as long as no external shocks upset the field. However, we inhabit a world where international, and domestic long-haul travel is restricted due to a pandemic. And we know also that the future contains catastrophic climate change. The current educational focus is thus becoming ever less relevant. But therein lies the challenge of path dependency, we have paved a certain course so well, that we consider it impossible to change.

Secondary vocational colleges should provide employees for the present, but higher education should also be aimed at preparing society for the future. It is therefore in the interest of all tourism academics to critically ask oneself why one teaches tourism, and what one wants to pass on to future professionals.

Why Should Future Tourism Education Prepare Students to Formulate New Questions That Would Open Up New Realities?

Firstly, in order to vision tourism education in the future, let me start from the faculties and schools housing the programs. The current large emphasis on management, economics and business all go hand in hand with economic values such as growth, labour, and development. If we are serious about using tourism to make the world a better place for all living beings to exist, then we also need to re-think its educational focus. We need professionals who can see beyond current paths of dependency, and who can re-imagine how we define success.

Tourism should always firstly be good for the communities and ecosystems that are being visited. Tourism should naturally provide well-being for those involved, and it should not be to the detriment of others. But we should not confuse well-being with monetary wealth – they have statistic correlations to some extent, but they are definitely not synonyms. Growth, as an example, was a potent concept in the 1960s before jet engines, mass consumption, and globalisation, but it is no longer what we should strive for on a finite planet with imminent ecological and health crises.

Secondly, the mission statements of our programs need to go beyond their current simplistic marketing discourse, and actually treat prospective and current students as the intelligent and concerned individuals they are. Tourism is not just an industry, or a conglomeration of industries, it is also a phenomenon, and an activity which causes reactions, and reacts to all sorts of input in the open system making up the Earth and social realities. We should emphasise words such as responsible, equitable, and holistic in our program descriptions and graduate outcomes.

Finally, I challenge you all to go to your institution's webpages, social media sites, and brochures and read the opening paragraphs for the tourism programs, to determine values emphasised. My guess is that a majority will, just like in the Nordics, be systemic values, related to ideas about an industry, management, growth, and similar features. Other values will be extrinsic, and relate to actions that might enhance life, and only a minority will relate to intrinsic values. Now, if those are the foundations that we lay for future tourism professionals, why were we wondering about overtourism and disenfranchised local communities before COVID-19? We should naturally still prepare students to become tourism professionals, but we need to pay attention to the values we instil in them.

Let us put the dualisms of professional versus liberal tourism education behind us and jointly work towards creating programs that aim for practical intelligence. We need students graduating with an awareness of the world-making capabilities they all possess. The key will be to acknowledge that all decisions are values-bound at their core. The purpose we see for THE highlights our values. If we want tourism education post COVID-19 to lead to a better world, then we need to take the first steps on that way ourselves.

References

Airey, David, Diane Dredge, and Michael Gross. 2015. "Tourism, Hospitality and Events Education in an Age of Change." In *The Routledge Handbook of Tourism and Hospitality Education*, edited by Dianne Dredge, David Airey and Michael Gross, 3–14. London: Routledge.

Belhassen, Yaniv, and Kellee Caton. 2009. "Advancing Understandings – A Linguistic Approach to Tourism Epistemology." *Annals of Tourism Research* 36 (2):335–352. doi: 10.1016/j.annals.2009.01.006.

Catrett, Jeffrey B. 2018. "Hospitality Education: A Third Paradigm." In *Innovation in Hospitality Education: Anticipating the Educational Needs of a Changing Profession*, edited by Jeroen Oskam, Daphne M. Dekker and Karoline Wiegerink, 15–32. Cham: Springer.

Dredge, Dianne, Pierre J. Benckendorff, Michelle Day, Michael Gross, Maree Walo, Paul Weeks, and Paul A. Whitelaw. 2012. "The Philosophic Practitioner and the Curriculum Space." *Annals of Tourism Research* 39 (4):2154–2176.

Echtner, Charlotte M., and Tazim B. Jamal. 1997. "The Disciplinary Dilemma of Tourism Studies." *Annals of Tourism Research* 24 (4):868–883.

Edelheim, Johan. 2020. "How Should Tourism Education Values Be Transformed after 2020?" *Tourism Geographies* 22 (3):547–554. doi: 10.1080/14616688.2020.1760927.

Edwards, Rem B. 2010. *The Essentials of Formal Axiology*. Lanham, MD and Plymouth: University Press of America.

Gallarza, Martina G., and Irene Gil. 2008. "The Concept of Value and Its Dimensions: A Tool for Analysing Tourism Experiences." *Tourism Review International* 63 (3):4–20. doi: 10.1108/16605370810901553.

Gornitzka, Åse. 2007. "What Is the Use of Bologna in National Reform?" In *Creating the European Area of Higher Education – Voices from the Perifery*, edited by Voldemar Tomusk, 19–41. Dordrecht: Springer.

Hartman, Robert S. 2019. "Five Lectures on Formal Axiology." In *Rober S. Hartman Institute – Axiology Studies Series*, edited by Clifford G. Hurst, 1–133. Salt Lake City, UT: Izzard Ink Publishing Company. Book version of a series of lectures given in the late 1960s and early 1970s.

Higgins-Desbiolles, Freya. 2021. "The "War over Tourism": Challenges to Sustainable Tourism in the Tourism Academy after COVID-19." *Journal of Sustainable Tourism* 29 (4):551–569. doi: 10.1080/09669582.2020.1803334.

Hollinshead, Keith. 2004. "A Primer in Ontological Craft: The Creative Capture of People and Places through Qualitative Research." In *Qualitative Research in Tourism: Ontologies, Epistemologies and Methodologies*, edited by Jenny Phillimore and Lisa Goodson, 63–82. Oxon and New York: Routledge.

Huesemann, Michael, and Joyce Huesemann. 2011. *Techno-Fix: Why Technology Wont Save Us Or the Environment*. Gabriola Island: New Society Publishers.

Manning, Peter K., and Betsy Cullum-Swan. 1994. "Narrative, Content, and Semiotic Analysis." In *Handbook of Qualitative Research*, edited by Norman K. Denzin and Yvonna S. Lincoln, 463–477. Thousand Oaks, CA: Sage Publications.

McDonald, Hugh P. 2004. *Radical Axiology: A First Philosophy of Values*. Amsterdam and New York: Rodopi.

McMurtry, John. 2009–2010. "The Primary Axiom and The Life-Value Compass." In *Encyclopedia Life Support Systems (EOLSS)*, edited by John McMurty, 212–256. Paris: Developed under the Auspices of the UNESCO, Eolss Publishers.

McMurtry, John. 2013. *The Cancer Stage of Capitalism – From Crisis to Cure*. 2 ed. London: Pluto Press.

Mei, Xiang Ying. 2019. "Gaps in Tourism Education and Workforce Needs: Attracting and Educating the Right People." *Current Issues in Tourism* 22 (12):1400–1404. doi: 10.1080/13683500.2017.1402870.

Page, Stephen J., and Joanne Connell. 2020. *Tourism – A Modern Synthesis*. 5 ed. Oxon: Routledge. Textbook.

Pernecky, Tomas. 2020. "Critical Tourism Scholars: Brokers of Hope." *Tourism Geographies* 22 (3):657–666. doi: 10.1080/14616688.2020.1760925.

Saukko, Paula. 2003. *Doing Research in Cultural Studies – An Introduction to Classical and New Methodological Approaches*. London: SAGE Publications.

The Nordic Council. 2021. "Facts about the Nordic Countries." The Nordic Council and the Nordic Council of Ministers, accessed 22 February, 2021. https://www.norden.org/en/information/facts-about-nordic-countries.

Tribe, John. 2005. "Tourism, Knowledge and the Curriculum." In *An International Handbook of Tourism Education*, edited by David Airey and John Tribe, 47–60. Oxford: Elsevier.

Türkkahraman, Mimar. 2014. "Social Values and Value Education." *Procedia – Social and Behavioral Sciences* 116:633–638. doi: 10.1016/j.sbspro.2014.01.270.

Vabø, Agnete, and Per Olaf Aamodt. 2008. "Nordic Higher Education in Transition." In *Structuring Mass Higher Education. The Role of Elite Institutions*, edited by David Palfreyman and Ted Tapper, 57–71. New York: Routledge.

Vabø, Agnete, and Jannecke Wiers-Jenssen. 2017. "Europe: Different Approaches to Fees for International Students." In *Understanding Global Higher Education. Insights from Key Global Publications*, edited by Georgiana Mihut, Philip G. Altbach and Hans deWit, 66–69. Rotterdam: Sense Publishers.

9 Students Shaping Their Future

Virtual Reality Interactive Exercises to Engage in for Learning

Nuria Recuero Virto

Introduction

Lockdowns to contain the spread of the COVID-19 pandemic is posing many challenges in the tourism industry, and precisely toward qualifying these professionals and, thus, for prolonged out-of-university tech learning (Chiao et al., 2018). Universities are struggling with how to face the probable demotivation and lack of implication from tourism students by speedily and competitively adapting to this technological transition with high-quality e-lectures that improve teaching and educational content (Pham and Ho, 2020). While this current crisis is triggering a lasting technological disruption, cultivating future tourism workers' communication creativity and attracting students' attention also prove to be pain points.

Notwithstanding the relevance of virtual reality (VR) in higher education institutions and the tourism industry (Kim et al., 2019), up to date no study has been found that deals with students' perceptions regarding VR Tour Creator applications. The use of VR in tourism is a key innovative technology that allows people to travel anywhere across tour guiding that permits them obtain educational, meaningful and enjoyable experiences (Chiao et al., 2018).

A case study has been developed based on tourism postgraduate students that were asked to design and create a VR tour; offering them an immersive, memorable educational opportunity related to the communication aspects. Once the assignment has been accomplished, students will be requested to answer an online questionnaire which comprises different concepts that pretend to embrace a complete overview of the VR tour creator experience. To address the gap concerning students' adoption of VR Tour Creator tool, an extended version of the Technological Acceptance Model (TAM) has been proposed considering the factors satisfaction and student engagement.

The study will be analysed using structural equation modelling to predict students' attitude and behavioural intention to designing and creating VR. The findings will be discussed offering contributions to the field of management in tourism higher education and VR resources driving future tourism education post COVID-19. The interest of this research is also motivated by the undeniable popularity of the VR device in the tourism sector.

DOI: 10.4324/9781003207467-13

Literature Review and Hypotheses Development

A literature review is proposed in order to contextualise the research problem with a comprehensive theoretical framework. It summarizes literature regarding the TAM model to explain the factors that have an effect on the acceptance of e-learning tools. Researchers have used different theories to describe subjects' predisposition to accept and use technological advances. The most widespread theories are t TAM (Davis, 1989; Davis and Venkatesh, 1996), Theory of Planned Behaviour (Mathieson, 1991) and Unified Theory of Acceptance and Use of Technology (UTAUT) (Guo and Liu, 2013; Parameswaran et al., 2015). Among these theories, this study has used TAM as the foundation of the proposed model as it is considered to offer the best explanations regarding subjects' attitudes and behaviour (Abdullah et al., 2016; Moon and Kim, 2001).

Technology Acceptance Model

Although many researchers have examined the TAM model in different educational contexts, such as Wu and Chen (2016) in the use of MOOCs or Al-Emran, Arpaci, and Salloum (2020) in the adoption of mobile learning, VR remains understudied. In the same vein, a broad number of studies have analysed consumers' and employees' predisposition to adopt VR (such as Manis and Choi 2019; Sagnier et al., 2020) and precisely regarding the acceptance of this technology in the tourism industry (e.g., Disztinger et al., 2017; Gibson and O'Rawe, 2018; Huang et al., 2015; Lee et al., 2019), but little research has been conducted regarding the adoption of VR in tourism education (Chiao et al., 2018). Moreover, no study has been found that deals with the adoption of a tool that trains students in creating VR tours.

The TAM model was been widely empirically accepted, proving that users' adoption and effective use of technology are defined by their intention to use it, which is affected by the perceptions' users have of their ease of use, usefulness and attitude (Abdullah et al., 2016; Lin, 2009; Padilla-Meléndez et al., 2013).

For the main objective of this research, the TAM model constructs of perceived ease of use and perceived usefulness are the most linked to the characteristics of the technology and, hence, the key purpose of this research (Visinescu et al., 2015). Perceived ease of use has been conceptualized as the level in which users consider that the use of the technology does not require efforts (physical or mental), whereas perceived usefulness is described as the extent in which a user feels that the technology will assist their job performance (Davis, 1989; Lee et al., 2019; Roca et al., 2006).

It has been widely proved that perceived ease of use has a positive and significant effect on perceived usefulness and precisely in the education system, concerning MOOcs (Wu and Chen, 2016), blended learning scenarios (Padilla-Meléndez et al., 2013) and e-learning environments (Chang et al.,

2017). Likewise, this study examines students' perceptions regarding their ease of use (i.e., level of effortless) and their perceived usefulness (i.e., assistance in the performance) in the adoption of the VR Tour Creator tool, expecting that if students perceive that the tool requires no efforts (i.e., ease of use) this will imply they perceive that it assisted their task performance (i.e., usefulness).

Attitude offers information regarding the positive or negative feelings that the technology provokes in them (Wu and Chen, 2016). It has not been widely confirmed that perceived ease of use has a direct and positive impact on attitude regarding educational tools (Wu and Chen, 2016). Despite this fact, it seems reasonable that if students perceive the tool does not require efforts, they will have positive feelings concerning the technology.

Intention to use in the future is a significant outcome to evaluate in the TAM model, as it determines users' future continuance usage intentions. Saadé and Bahli (2005) concluded that perceived ease of use has a meaningful and positive impact on intention to use in another course the online learning system. Likewise, this research considers that students that feel that the VR Tour Creator tool is effortless they will be predisposed to use it in the future.

Finally, student engagement understood as a behavioural intention that comprehends a cognitive and an emotional dimension, has been measured in psychological terms of the effort and investment accomplished (Jung and Lee, 2018; Manwaring et al., 2017). It has been determined that perceived ease of use significantly and positively influences behavioural intention and cognitive engagement (Lin, 2009; Pallud, 2017). Precisely, it has been established that perceived ease of use has a positive and meaningful effect on student engagement (Bacca-Acosta and Avila-Garzón, 2021; Rahman et al., 2018). Hence, it is expected that if students perceive no efforts are requested using the VR Tour Creator tool, they will feel more engaged.

Based on the above discussion, although no existing study has undertaken research using the TAM model to evaluate a VR Tour Creator tool, it is postulated:

> H1. Perceived ease of use has a positive and significant effect on perceived usefulness (a), attitude toward using VR (b), intention to use (c) and student engagement (d).

The TAM model proposes that perceived of use is highly linked to perceived usefulness and that both aspects (i.e., constructs) have a positive and significant effect on users' behavioural intention (Visinescu et al., 2015). Also, Wu and Chen (2016) confirmed the impact of perceived usefulness on intention to continue using MOOCs. Therefore, it is expected that students that feel useful this VR Tour Creator tool will want to continue using it in the future.

In this context, satisfaction has been conceptualized as the acceptance of technology and the level of comfort a user has using it (Liaw and Huang,

2013). It has been established that there is an inverted U in the relationship between perceived usefulness and satisfaction (Osatuyi et al., 2020). Likely, students that consider the VR Tour Creator tool assists them in the task accomplishment (i.e., useful) they will be satisfied.

Therefore, the following hypotheses are proposed:

> H2. Perceived usefulness has a positive and significant effect on intention to use (a) and satisfaction (b).

Attitude has been defined as a factor that serves to evaluate users' predisposition towards the use of technology (Wu and Chen, 2016). It has been stated as a powerful predictor for usage intention in educational contexts (Dou et al., 2019; Wu and Chen, 2016). Taking into account these studies, it is reasonable to consider that students' attitude will influence their intention to use the VR Tour Creator tool. Thus, it is hypothesized:

> H3. Attitude toward using VR has a positive and significant effect on intention to use.

Student Engagement and Satisfaction

This research is interested on student engagement and satisfaction, as these features are particularly interesting regarding the objective of using VR Tour Creator tool for educational purposes so as to improve tourism professionals' qualification for the future of work. In this regard, student engagement defined as a multidimensional approach that entails cognitive and emotional aspects that requires users' mental investment to achieve the desired task (Jung and Lee, 2018; Lin, 2009) will likely influence users' attitude towards using the tool. Hence, it is suggested:

> H4. Student engagement has a positive and significant effect on attitude toward using VR.

The impact of satisfaction on continuance usage intention regarding e-learning environments, MOOCs and digital textbooks has been proved (Dağhan and Akkoyunlu, 2016; Joo et al., 2017, 2018). Based on these arguments, students that are satisfied with the VR Tour Creator tool will want to use it in the future. Hence, the following hypothesis is proposed:

> H5. Satisfaction has a positive and significant effect on intention to use.

Research Method

The model proposed in Figure 9.1 was tested in an empirical study in which students from two Tourism Master's degrees of two public universities located in Madrid, namely, Complutense University of Madrid and King

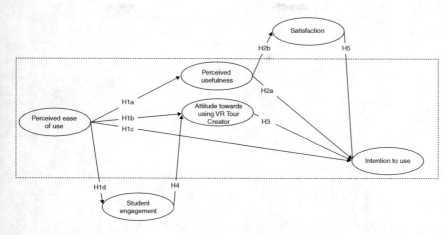

Figure 9.1 Proposed model.
Source: Researcher's own design.

Juan Carlos University, were asked to accomplish an assignment based on designing and creating a VR tour and subsequently voluntarily answer the questionnaire. This research approach is similar has been widely used by many scholars (i.e., Huang et al., 2012; Jung and Lee, 2018; McGovern et al., 2019; Recuero and Blasco, 2020; Visinescu et al., 2015).

Data Collection

The subjects for this research were postgraduate students enrolled in Tourism Master's degrees, precisely of students of Planning and Management of Tourist Destinations Master's Degree (14/22) of the Faculty of Commerce and Tourism of the Complutense University of Madrid and International Tourism Management Master's Degree (7/11) of the King Juan Carlos University, during the course 2020–2021 as part of the final task for the Positioning and Communication of Tourist Destinations and Cultural Heritage Management courses.

All students had to design and create, in groups of three or four persons, a VR tour using Google Tour Creator, a free tool that build immersive 360° tours. To ensure that the students completed correctly the task, they received concrete instructions. Thus, the assignment consisted of designing and creating a VR tour of maximum five minutes regarding cultural tourism resource or activity, following the support and assistance offered by the tool. The aim of this task was to prepare students to the future of work and offer them an immersive, memorable educational opportunity related to the communication aspects of both courses.

Once the assignment was accomplished, an email in form of invitation that contained a link to the online questionnaire was sent to students where they were requested to voluntarily answer it. Hence, this research adopted

Table 9.1 Profile of respondents (N = 21)

Characteristics		Frequency	Percentage (%)
Gender			
	Men	4	19
	Women	17	81
Age			
	20–25	15	71
	26–30	3	14
	30–35	3	14
Education			
	Master's Degree	20	95
	PhD Student	1	5
No of Times That You Have Used Google Tour Creator VR			
	2 to 4 times	5	24
	Once	16	76
Have You Used Any Other Platform to Create Virtual Reality?			
	No	21	100

Source: Researcher's own design.

purposeful sampling as other related studies (Chiao et al., 2018). Data was collected during the third wave of coronavirus pandemic in Spain, from February 2 to 8, 2021 and a total of 21 usable questionnaires were collected. The sample profile is shown in Table 9.1.

Measurement Model

This research adopted constructs from previous studies and all the items were rated on a seven-point Likert scale. The scale items of perceived usefulness and intention to use were based on Padilla-Meléndez, Rosa del Aguila-Obra, and Garrido-Moreno (2013). Perceived ease of use, attitude toward using VR, satisfaction and student engagement items were adopted from Pallud (2017), Wu and Chen (2016), Dağhan and Akkoyunlu, (2016) and Dieck, Jung and Rauschnabel (2018), respectively. Table 9.2 presents the measurement model and a descriptive analysis for all the items of the proposed model.

Data Analysis Process

SmartPLS (version 3.3.3) was used in this research to perform Partial Least Squares Structural Equation Modelling (PLS-SEM) analysis. PLS-SEM permits the statistical analysis based on a multivariate approach to examine

Table 9.2 Descriptive analysis

Construct/Associated Items	Mean	Standard Deviation
Perceived Usefulness (PUS)	5.667	0.891
Using this tool improves my performance for the task set in this course.[a]	5.810	1.139
Using this tool is useful to me for the task set in this course.[a]	5.476	1.052
Using this tool helps me learn effectively.	5.476	1.332
Using this tool makes it easier to carry out the task set in this course.		
Perceived Ease of Use (PEU)		
The tool was easy to use.	5.952	1.045
My interaction with this tool was clear and understandable.	5.952	1.045
I found it easy to get this tool to do what I wanted it to do.	5.524	1.180
Attitude towards Using VR Tour Creator (ATT)		
I believe that using this tool is a good idea.	6.095	0.811
I believe that using this tool is advisable.	6.048	0.785
I am satisfied using this tool.	6.000	0.617
Satisfaction (SAT)		
I am satisfied with the performance of the online learning through this tool.	5.952	0.785
I am pleased with the experience of using the online learning through this tool.	5.857	0.639
My decision to use the online learning through this tool was wise.	5.952	0.486
Intention to Use (INT)		
I plan to use this tool frequently during my next course.	4.619	1.588
Student Engagement (SEN)		
This experience has motivated me to find out more about this course.	5.952	1.253
This experience has motivated me to find out more about new forms of communication.	6.048	0.999
This experience has motivated me to participate in the activities organised by the online platform (Google).	5.857	0.888

Source: Researcher's own design.
[a] Dropped during the estimation of the measurement model.

each of the relationships between the variables in a conceptual model, regarding measurement and structural components (Rasoolimanesh et al., 2016). This technique was chosen as it is a nonparametric SEM method particularly recommendable when operationalizes with non-normal data and there are small sample sizes (Hair et al., 2014; Henseler et al., 2016; Sarstedt et al., 2011).

Analysis and Findings

Reliability and Validity Evaluation

The results of the measurement model's reliability and convergent validity tests are presented in Table 9.3. All loading factors were higher than the threshold of 0.7 for the indicator reliability which is considered adequate (Hair et al., 2011). Concerning construct reliability, the internal consistency indicators (Cronbach alpha coefficients) are above the recommended level of 0.70 (Hair et al., 2006). Likewise, composite reliability values show the shared variance among a set of observed items appraising a construct (Fornell and Larcker, 1981). All of these are higher than the recommended coefficient of 0.60 (Bagozzi and Yi, 1988) (Tables 9.4–9.6)

Table 9.3 Reliability and convergent validity of the final measurement model

		Standardised Loading	t-Value (Bootstrap)	CA	rho_A	CR	AVE
Attitude towards using VR Tour Creator	ATT1	0.795	3.804	0.735	0.735	0.851	0.65
	ATT2	0.888	8.976				
	ATT3	0.742	3.035				
Intention to use	INT1	1.000		1.000	1.000	1.000	1.00
Perceived ease of use	PEU1	0.893	5.634	0.893	0.935	0.933	0.82
	PEU2	0.942	8.950				
	PEU3	0.883	5.420				
Perceived usefulness	PUS3	0.928	8.350	0.883	0.943	0.943	0.89
	PUS4	0.962	12.691				
Satisfaction	SAT1	0.900	10.296	0.882	0.909	0.926	0.80
	SAT2	0.895	11.775				
	SAT3	0.899	7.090				
Student Engagement	SEN1	0.955	7.659	0.887	0.989	0.925	0.80
	SEN2	0.946	6.922				
	SEN3	0.783	4.552				

Source: Researcher's own design.
Note: All loadings are significant at $p < 0.01$ level. CA = Cronbach's *alpha*; CR = composite reliability; AVE = average variance extracted.

Table 9.4 Measurement model discriminant validity

Factor	1	2	3	4	5	6
1 Attitude towards using VR Tour Creator	0.811	0.831	0.411	0.727	0.593	0.3
2 Intention to use	0.710	1.000	0.054	0.236	0.564	0.2
3 Perceived ease of use	0.291	0.035	0.907	0.387	0.245	0.2
4 Perceived usefulness	0.596	0.238	0.373	0.945	0.368	0.2
5 Satisfaction	0.498	0.541	0.216	0.347	0.898	0.6
6 Student engagement	0.301	0.286	0.235	0.172	0.605	0.8

Source: Researcher's own design.
Note: The values on the diagonal are the square roots of the AVEs; the values below the diagonal are the variable correlation values; the values above the diagonal are the HTMT ratios.

Table 9.5 Evaluation of the estimated models

Concept	R^2
Attitude towards using VR Tour Creator	0.046
Intention to use	0.540
Perceived usefulness	0.094
Satisfaction	0.074

Source: Researcher's own design.

Table 9.6 Hypotheses testing

Hypothesis	Path	Standardised Path Coefficients		t-Value (Bootstrap)
1a	Perceived ease of use → perceived usefulness	0.226	*	1.652
1b	Perceived ease of use → attitude towards using VR Tour Creator	0.357		0.652
1c	Perceived ease of use → intention to use	0.195		0.778
1d	Perceived ease of use → student engagement	0.367		0.641
2a	Perceived usefulness → intention to use	0.199		1.321
2b	Perceived usefulness → satisfaction	0.172	**	2.014
3	Attitude towards using VR → intention to use	0.219	***	3.517
4	Student engagement → attitude towards using VR Tour Creator	0.142		0.457
5	Satisfaction → intention to use	0.197		1.431

Source: Researcher's own design
Note: ***$p < 0.01$; **$p < 0.05$; *$p < 0.10$.

Hypotheses Testing and Results

The results present that students' perceived ease of use of the VR Tour Creator tool has a positive and significant effect on their perceived usefulness (H1a; $\beta = 0.226$; $p < 0.1$), whereas it has no effect on their attitude toward using VR Tour Creator tool (H1b; $\beta = 0.357$), intention to use (H1c; $\beta = 0.195$), and student engagement (H1d; $\beta = 0.367$). Besides, perceived usefulness of the VR Tour Creator tool had no effect on intention to use (H2a; $\beta = 0.199$), but a positive and significant effect on satisfaction (H2b; $\beta = 0.172$; $p < 0.05$). Also, attitude toward using VR Tour Creator tool has a positive and significant effect on intention to use (H3; $\beta = 0.219$; $p < 0.01$). Finally, student engagement has no effect on their attitude toward using VR Tour Creator tool (H4; $\beta = 0.142$) and satisfaction has no effect on intention to use (H5; $\beta = 0.197$).

Interestingly only three hypotheses were found to be supported. Perceived ease of use has a positive and significant effect on perceived usefulness, as in other related educational scenarios (Chang et al., 2017; Padilla-Meléndez et al., 2013; Wu and Chen 2016). Also, perceived usefulness has a positive and significant effect on satisfaction, corroborating the idea of the existence of an inverted U in the relationship between perceived usefulness and satisfaction (Osatuyi et al., 2020). Finally, attitude towards using VR Tour Creator tool was found to have a significant and positive effect on intention to use, confirming prior results in educational environments (Dou et al., 2019; Wu and Chen, 2016). However, six hypotheses were not supported, revealing interesting and useful insight for future research and managerial insights.

Agenda: Suggestions for the Future

Education and tourism are both social activities that are determined by expectations. During the COVID-19 outbreak, plenty of educational initiatives have aroused so as to motivate students' e-learning process. These recent lockdowns have proved the need of adopting new forms and tools that qualify job-ready graduates for the post-COVID-19 world, which improve the soft and hard skills required in this new tech workforce (Recuero and Blasco, 2020). Despite the fact that is very significant to acknowledge tourism postgraduate students' perceptions concerning their performance with the creation of VR tours, no studies were found during the extensive literature review conducted.

Theoretical Contributions

This research advances knowledge regarding the adoption of VR Tour Creator tools in tourism university studies. Additionally, it evaluates a new technological advance in the context of the TAM model. Therefore, this study adds value to prior research related to the TAM model for several reasons.

First, this study extends the TAM model studies by empirically examining the direct effects: (1) perceived ease of use on student engagement; (2) student engagement on attitude toward using VR Tour Creator tool; (3) perceived usefulness on satisfaction; and (4) satisfaction on intention to use. Although it was reasonable to expect the relationships were found significant (Dağhan and Akkoyunlu, 2016; Joo et al., 2017, 2018; Jung and Lee, 2018; Lin, 2009), only the link between perceived usefulness and satisfaction was confirmed. Hence, the inverted U in this linkage was established (Osatuyi et al., 2020). Thus, this result confirms the contribution of this study adding satisfaction to complete the TAM model regarding e-learning tools.

Second, it was shown that just two out of the five hypotheses related to the TAM model were revealed as positive and significant. In this respect, it was determined that perceived ease of use has a positive and significant impact on perceived usefulness (Chang et al., 2017; Padilla-Meléndez et al., 2013; Wu and Chen, 2016); and that attitude toward using VR Tour Creator tool has a positive and significant effect on intention to use (Dou et al.,

2019; Wu and Chen, 2016). However, three hypotheses were not supported. Thus, perceived ease of use had no effect on attitude toward using VR Tour Creator tool, as in Wu and Chen's study (2016) of MOOCs. Besides, the six hypotheses rejected and the three supported in the proposed model expands the body of knowledge concerning the TAM model in the education sector.

Third, this research contributes to education and, precisely, to tourism education literature, by proposing and empirically testing a theoretical framework of VR tours and students' attitudes toward creating VR tours.

Managerial Implications

VR is becoming increasingly important among visitors, and, hence, for tourism professionals. This research raises awareness of the importance of qualifying tourism professionals in the use of innovative technological devices, which is slowly entering the education sector (McGovern et al., 2019).These last outbreaks due to COVID-19 sanitary crisis has proved the need of adopting VR e-learning tools that support tailored mentoring, and improve their hard and soft skills to join the current tech workforce. This exploratory research reveals it is crucial for the qualification of students to adopt technological approaches so as to encourage students learning process and it is expected to improve their academic performance (Ali et al., 2018). However, the findings of this research reveal that students' adoption of the VR Tour Creator tool based on the TAM model is weak, and thus, this suggests that improved tools have to be adopted such as computer-generated simulation of a 3D environments that are equipped with helmets, sensors and screens (Lee et al., 2019).

As VR device industry is expected to grow rapidly and hence, it will become cost effective (Rogers, 2020), there is a need to prepare tourism students for the fast-changing world. This research confirms that their attitude influences their intention to use this VR Tour Creator tool. Also, it demonstrates that if they perceive the tool is useful this will raise their satisfaction levels, which will in turn improve the learning system (Chiao et al., 2018). The assignment completed by the students entailed that they had to active learn at their own pace (i.e., remote learning) and design a tour guide which has improved the multidisciplinary approach of the STEAM-based curriculum design of their postgraduate studies with a non-traditional perspective of the academic program (MacDonald et al., 2020). Also, this task has developed their hard and soft skills (i.e., developing technological fluency and designing creative storytelling).

As suggested by Kim, Lee and Jung (2019) developers of VR tours could pay more attention on how to increase users' cognitive and affective responses, as these may lead to higher levels of attachment and behavioural intentions. This might be achieved introducing gamification components as it has been proved that these increase the interactivity within the tool (Lee et al., 2019), which will stimulate their emotions and thus, improve their engagement and learning outcomes (Shen et al., 2009).

Moreover, the use of immersive tools in tourism communication strategies is becoming increasingly popular as means to design digital experiences as well to educate visitors on preservation and cultural heritage (Bec et al., 2021). Thus, these interactive learning experiences entail real life training which improve their tourism professionals' qualification for the future of work as well as it transforms into agile the educational system for the new landscape of hybrid intelligence (Dellermann et al., 2019).

Limitations and Future Research Directions

Scholars are encouraged to consider the limitations of this research so as to improve the findings. First, this exploratory study has focused in a specific VR Tour Creator tool, and it would be interesting to advance knowledge by considering the interactivity that other tools that create VR tours may offer (Chiao et al., 2018).

Second, the approach of this research is based on the TAM model, but it would be revealing to examine performance and effort expectancy, social influence, facilitating conditions of the UTAUT model (Guo and Liu, 2013; Parameswaran et al., 2015) to extend the findings.

Third, as McGovern, Moreira, and Luna-Nevarez (2019) have stated as VR continues to spread in the education sector, it is needed to expand the sample of students could have led to bias, as the size is small. Therefore, scholars are prompted to replicate this study in different universities and studies (graduate, postgraduate, medicine, among others). Fourth, it could be interesting for future research to examine other variables such as curiosity and perceived enjoyment (Manis and Choi, 2019), as this would probably enrich the existing literature on this topic and influence students' active learning performance and engagement.

References

Abdullah, Fazil, Rupert Ward, and Ejaz Ahmed. 2016. "Investigating the influence of the most commonly used external variables of TAM on students' Perceived Ease of Use (PEOU) and Perceived Usefulness (PU) of e-portfolios." *Computers in Human Behavior* 63: 75–90. doi: 10.1016/j.chb.2016.05.014.

Ali, Zulqurnain, Bi Gongbing, and Aqsa Mehreen. 2018. "Understanding and predicting academic performance through cloud computing adoption: a perspective of technology acceptance model." *Journal of Computers in Education* 5: 297–327. doi: 10.1007/s40692-018-0114-0.

Al-Emran, Mostafa, Ibrahim Arpaci, and Said A. Salloum. 2020. "An empirical examination of continuous intention to use m-learning: an integrated model." *Education and Information Technologies* 5: 2899–2918. doi: 10.1007/s10639-019-10094-2.

Bacca-Acosta, Jorge, and Avila-Garzón. 2021. "Student engagement with mobile-based assessment systems: a survival analysis." *Journal of Computer Assisted Learning* 37 (1): 158–171. doi: 10.1111/jcal.12475.

Bagozzi, Richard P., and Youjae Yi. 1988. "On the evaluation of structural equation models." *Journal of the Academy of Marketing Science* 16: 74–94. doi: 10.1007/BF02723327.

Bec, Alexandra, Brent Moyle, Vikki Schaffer, and Ken Timms. 2021. "Virtual reality and mixed reality for second chance tourism." *Tourism Management* 83: 104256. doi: 10.1016/j.tourman.2020.104256.

Chiao, Huei-Ming, Yu-Li Chen, and Wei-Hsin Huang. 2018. "Examining the usability of an online virtual tour-guiding platform for cultural tourism education." *Journal of Hospitality, Leisure, Sports and Tourism Education* 23: 29–38. doi: 10.1016/j.jhlste.2018.05.002.

Chang, Ching-Ter, Jeyhun Hajiyev, and Chia-Rong Su. 2017. "Examining the students' behavioral intention to use elearning in Azerbaijan? The general extended technology acceptance model for e-learning approach." *Computers & Education* 111: 128–143. doi: 10.1016/j.compedu.2017.04.010.

Dağhan, Gokhan, and Bouket Akkoyunlu, B., 2016. "Modeling the continuance usage intention of online learning environments." *Computer Human Behaviour* 60: 198–211. doi: 10.1016/j.chb.2016.02.066.

Davis, Fred D. 1989. "Perceived usefulness, perceived ease of use, and user acceptance of information technology." *MIS Quarterly* 13(3): 319–340. *JSTOR*, www.jstor.org/stable/249008. Accessed 24 February 2021.

Davis, Fred D., and Viswanath Venkatesh. 1996. "A critical assessment of potential measurement biases in the technology acceptance model: three experiments." *International Journal of Human-Computer Studies* 45(1): 19–45. doi: 10.1006/ijhc.1996.0040.

Dellermann M.Sc., Dominik, Philipp Ebel, Matthias Söllner, and Jan Marco Leimeister. 2019. "Hybrid Intelligence." *Business & Information Systems Engineering* 61: 637–643. doi: 10.1007/s12599-019-00595-2.

Dieck, Claudia tom, Jung, Timothy Hyungsoo, and Philipp A. Rauschnabel. 2018. "Determining visitor engagement through augmented reality at science festivals: An experience economy perspective." *Computers in Human Behavior* 82: 44–53. doi:10.1016/j.chb.2017.12.043

Disztinger, Peter, Stephan Schlögl, and Aleksander Groth. 2017. "Technology acceptance of virtual reality for travel planning." In: Schegg R., Stangl B. (eds) *Information and Communication Technologies in Tourism 2017*. Springer, Cham. doi: 10.1007/978-3-319-51168-9_19.

Dou, Xinhua, Xiajing Zhu, Jason Q. Zhang, and Jie Wang. 2019. "Outcomes of entrepreneurship education in China: a customer experience management perspective." *Journal of Business Research* 103: 338–347. doi: 10.1016/j.jbusres.2019.01.058.

Huang, Yu Chih, Backman, Kenneth Frank, Backman, Sheila J., and Lan Lan Chang. 2015. "Exploring the implications of virtual reality technology in tourism marketing: An integrated research framework." *International Journal of Tourism Research* 18(2): 116–128. doi: 10.1002/jtr.2038.

Huang, Yueh-Min, Yong-Ming Huang, Shu-Hsien Huang, and Yen-Ting Lin. 2012. "A ubiquitous English vocabulary learning system: evidence of active/passive attitudes vs. usefulness/ease-of-use." *Computers & Education* 58: 73–282. doi: 10.1016/j.compedu.2011.08.008.

Gibson Alex, and Mary O'Rawe. 2018. "Virtual reality as a travel promotional tool: insights from a consumer travel fair." In: Jung T., tom Dieck M. (eds)

Augmented Reality and Virtual Reality. Progress in IS. Springer, Cham. doi: 10.1007/978-3-319-64027-3_7.

Guo, Feng, and Fengshan Liu. 2013. "A study on the factors influencing teachers' behaviour of internet teaching research." *International Journal of Continuing Engineering Education and Life-Long Learning* 23: 267–281. doi: 10.1504/IJCEELL.2013.055407.

Fornell, Claes, and David Larcker. 1981. "Structural equation models with unobservable variables and measurement error." *Journal of Marketing Research* 18: 39–50.

Hair, Joseph, William Black, Barry Babin, Rolph Anderson, and Ronald Tatham. 2006. *Multivariate Data Analysis.* Upper Saddle River, NJ: Pearson Prentice Hall.

Hair, Joseph F., G. Thomas M. Hult, Christian Ringle, and Marko Sarstedt. 2014. *A Primer on Partial Least Squares Structural Equation Modeling (PLS-SEM).* Los Angeles, CA: Sage.

Hair, Joseph F., Christian Ringle, and Marko Sarstedt. 2011. "PLS-SEM: indeed a silver bullet." *Journal of Marketing Theory and Practice* 19(2): 139–152. doi: 10.2753/MTP1069-6679190202.

Henseler, Jörg, Christian Ringle, and Marko Sarstedt. 2016. "Testing measurement invariance of composites using partial least squares." *International Marketing Review* 33(3): 405–431. doi: 10.1108/IMR-09-2014-0304.

Huang, Yu Chih, Kenneth Frank Backman, Sheila J. Backman, and Li Chang. 2016. "Exploring the implications of virtual reality technology in tourism marketing: an integrated research framework." *International Journal of Tourism Research* 18(2): 116–128. doi: 10.1002/jtr.2038.

Joo, Young Ju, Sunyoung Park, and Eui Kyoung Shin. 2017. "Students' expectation, satisfaction, and continuance intention to use digital textbooks." *Computers in Human Behavior* 69: 83–90. doi: 10.1016/j.chb.2016.12.025.

Joo, Young Ju, Hyo-Jeong So, and Nam Hee Kim. 2018. "Examination of relationships among students' self-determination, technology acceptance, satisfaction, and continuance intention to use K-MOOCs." *Computers & Education* 122: 260–272. doi: 10.1016/j.compedu.2018.01.003.

Jung, Yeonji, and Jeongmin Lee. 2018. "Learning engagement and persistence in massive open online courses (MOOCS)." *Computers & Education* 122: 9–22. doi: 10.1016/j.compedu.2018.02.013.

Kim, Myung Ja, Choong-Ki Lee, and Timothy Jung. 2019. "Exploring consumer behavior in virtual reality tourism using an extended stimulus-organism-response model." *Journal of Travel Research* 59(1): 69–89. doi: 10.1177/0047287518818915.

Lee, Jung Hyo, Jung Hun Kim, and Jae Young Choi. 2019. "The adoption of virtual reality devices: the technology acceptance model integrating enjoyment, social interaction, and strength of the social ties." *Telematics and Informatics* 39: 37–48. doi: 10.1016/j.tele.2018.12.006.

Liaw, Shu-Sheng, and Hsiu-Mei Huang. 2013. "Perceived satisfaction, perceived usefulness and interactive learning environments as predictors to self-regulation in e-learning environments." *Computers & Education* 60: 14–24. doi: 10.1016/j.compedu.2012.07.015.

Lin, Hsiu-Fen. 2009. "Examination of cognitive absorption influencing the intention to use a virtual community." *Behaviour & Information Technology* 28(5): 421–431. doi: 10.1080/01449290701662169.

MacDonald, Abbey, Kit Wise, Kate Tregloan, Wendy Fountain, Lousie Wallis, and Neil Holmstrom. 2020. "Designing STEAM education: fostering relationality through design-led disruption." *The International Journal of Art and Design Education* 39(1): 227–241. doi: 10.1111/jade.12258.

Manis, Kerry T., and Danny Choi. 2019. "The virtual reality hardware acceptance model (VR-HAM): extending and individuating the technology acceptance model (TAM) for virtual reality hardware." *Journal of Business Research* 100: 503–513. doi: 10.1016/j.jbusres.2018.10.021.

Manwaring, Kristine C., Ross Larsen, Charles R. Graham, Curtis R. Henrie, and Lisa R. Halverson. 2017. "Investigating student engagement in blended learning settings using experience sampling and structural equation modelling." *The Internet and Higher Education* 35: 21–33. doi: 10.1016/j.iheduc.2017.06.002.

Mathieson, Kieran. 1991. "Predicting user intentions: comparing the technology acceptance model with the theory of planned behavior." *Information System Research* 2: 173–191. doi: 10.1287/isre.2.3.173.

Moon, Ji-Won, and Young-Gul Kim. 2001. "Extending the TAM for a worldwide-web context." *Information & Management* 38(4): 217–230. doi: 10.1016/S0378-7206(00)00061-6.

McGovern, Enda, Gerardo Moreira, and Cuauhtemoc Luna-Nevarez. 2019. "An application of virtual reality in education: can this technology enhance the quality of students' learning experience?" *Journal of Education for Business* 95(7): 490–496. doi: 10.1080/08832323.2019.1703096.

Osatuyi, Babajide Hong Qin, Temidayo Osatuyi, and Ofir Turel. 2020. "When it comes to satisfaction ... it depends: an empirical examination of social commerce users." *Computers in Human Behavior* 111. doi: 10.1016/j.chb.2020.106413.

Padilla-Meléndez, Antonio, Ana Rosa del Aguila-Obra, and Aurora Garrido-Moreno. 2013. "Perceived playfulness, gender differences and technology acceptance model in a blended learning scenario." *Computers & Education* 63: 306–317. doi: 10.1016/j.compedu.2012.12.014.

Pallud, Jessie. 2017. "Impact of interactive technologies on stimulating learning experiences in a museum." *Information & Management* 54(4): 465–478. doi: 10.1016/j.im.2016.10.004.

Parameswaran, Srikanth, Rajiv Kishore, and Pu Li. 2015. "Within-study measurement invariance of the UTAUT instrument: an assessment with user technology engagement variables." *Information & Management* 52(3): 317–336. doi: 10.1016/j.im.2014.12.007.

Pham, Hiep-Hung, and Tien-Thi-Hanh Ho. 2020. "Toward a 'new normal' with e-learning in Vietnamese higher education during the post COVID-19 pandemic." *Higher Education Research & Development* 39(7): 1327–1331. doi: 10.1080/07294360.2020.1823945.

Rahman, Rafidah, Sabrina Ahmad, and Ummi Hashim. 2018. "The effectiveness of gamification technique for higher education students' engagement in polytechnic Muadzam Shah Pahang, Malaysia." *International Journal of Educational Technology in Higher Education* 15(1): 41. doi: 10.1186/s41239-018-0123-0.

Rasoolimanesh, S. Mostafa, José Luis Roldán, Mastura Jaafar, and T. Ramayah. 2016. "Factors influencing residents' perceptions toward tourism development: differences across rural and urban world heritage sites." *Journal of Travel Research* 56(6): 760–775. doi: 10.1177/0047287516662354.

Recuero-Virto, Nuria, and Maria Francisca Blasco López. 2020. "Lessons from lockdown: are students willing to repeat the experience of using interactive smartboards?" *International Journal of Emerging Technologies in Learning* 15(24): 255.

Roca, Juan Carlos, Chao-Min Chiu, and Francisco Jose Martínez. 2006. "Understanding e-learning continuance intention: an extension of the technology acceptance model." *International Journal of Human-Computer Studies* 64: 683–696. doi: 10.1016/j.ijhcs.2006.01.003.

Rogers, Steven L. 2020. "Cheap, accessible, and virtual experiences as tools for immersive study: a proof-of-concept study." *Research in Learning Technology* 28. doi: 10.25304/rlt.v28.2416.

Saadé, Raafat, and Bouchaib Bahli. 2005. "The impact of cognitive absorption on perceived usefulness and perceived ease of use in on-line learning: an extension of the technology acceptance model." *Information & Management* 42: 317–327. doi: 10.1016/j.im.2003.12.013.

Sagnier, Camille, Emilie Loup-Escande, Domitile Lourdeaux, Indira Thouvenin, and Gérard Valléry. 2020. "User acceptance of virtual reality: an extended technology acceptance model." *International Journal of Human–Computer Interaction* 36(11): 993–1007. doi: 10.1080/10447318.2019.1708612.

Sarstedt, Marko, Jörg Henseler, and Christian Ringle. 2011. "Multigroup analysis in partial least squares (PLS) path modeling: alternative methods and empirical results." *Advances in International Marketing* 22(1): 195–218. doi: 10.1108/S1474-7979(2011)0000022012.

Shen, Liping, Minjuan Wang, and Ruimin Shen. 2009. "Affective e-learning: using "emotional" data to improve learning in pervasive learning environment." *Journal of Educational Technology & Society* 12(2): 176–189.

Visinescu, Lucian L., Anna Sidorova, Mary C. Jones, and Victor R. Prybutok. 2015. "The influence of website dimensionality on customer experiences, perceptions and behavioral intentions: an exploration of 2D vs. 3D web design." *Information & Management* 52: 1–17. doi: 10.1016/j.im.2014.10.005.

Wu, Bing, and Xiaohui Chen. 2016. "Continuance intention to use MOOCs: integrating the technology acceptance model (TAM) and task technology fit (TTF) model." *Computers in Human Behavior* 67: 221–232. doi: 10.1016/j.chb.2016.10.028.

Part Four
Ethics and Responsibilities in Tourism Management Post COVID-19 Pandemic

10 Ethics and Responsibility in Tourism – the Impact of COVID-19

Harold Goodwin

Introduction

The COVID-19 pandemic has had significant consequences and potentially profound implications for the travel and tourism sector, and it will last for many years to come. The pandemic raises issues of ethics and responsibility and the practical challenges of travel bans, lockdowns, safety and trust in what may be a radically different new normal. Less than two years into the pandemic, cases and deaths are still rising, and the virus is still spreading and mutating. It is too early to define the impact of COVID-19 on tourism conclusively. Countries have appeared to gain the upper hand only to be hit by a second or third wave as new mutations emerge. As Dr Tedros Adhanom Ghebreyesus, Director-General, World Health Organization and Ursula von der Leyen, President of European Commission, amongst many others, have pointed out: "None of us will be safe until everyone is safe. Global access to coronavirus vaccines, tests and treatments for everyone who needs them, anywhere, is the only way out" (WHO, 2020). COVID-19 passes from person to person; we spread it. For an industry that moves people from one community to another, this has particular implications. It also creates risks for communities in the destinations and the places from which people travel and to which they will return. This chapter concludes with some reflections on what implications there may be for our willingness to tackle the challenges of climate change, biodiversity loss, poverty and inequality.

Ethics and Responsibility

Humanity, our common humanity, is tested by our willingness individually to wear a mask to protect others and collectively to provide aid through our governments for those with less developed economies and health services to fight the virus. The World Health Organization and many political leaders have reminded us that none of us will be safe until everyone is safe. As long as the virus is multiplying, it will mutate, and some of those mutations will be more infectious or cause more severe illness. The COVID-19 pandemic provides a salient example of the *tragedy of the commons* (Hardin, 1968)

DOI: 10.4324/9781003207467-15

where the costs borne by individuals and businesses in pursuit of the common good may exceed the perceived benefits to the individual or business. As a consequence of COVID-19 governments have, often reluctantly, imposed significant restrictions on freedom of movement, association and behaviour on individuals often denying personal contact within families. This has been necessary to ensure the common good. Governments have used the powers of the state to restrict personal freedoms, which would normally be unenforceable. There have been demonstrations against these denials of liberty in many countries. However, the regulations have in most places been complied with for the public good.

The COVID-19 pandemic presented a real and present danger to communities around the world. The responses to the pandemic varied between and within countries reflecting the diversity of humanity's cultures, preparedness to accept restrictions on individual freedoms, and the extent of economic development, which determines the adequacy of health services and the ability to sustain livelihoods during lockdowns. Public mask-wearing most effectively reduces transmission where the incidence of mask-wearing is high (Howard et al., 2021). The wearing of a mask protects others and the wearer. Initially, the efficacy of community mask-wearing to reduce the spread of respiratory infections was controversial, and there were some demonstrations against lockdowns and mask-wearing as an intolerable interference with individuals' freedom of choice, amounting to a denial of liberty. By early 2021 there was compelling evidence that community mask-wearing effectively reduced the spread of the virus, reducing the spread of infection and also protecting the wearer (Brooks & Butler, 2021). There is, therefore, a solid 'common good' argument for requiring the wearing of masks in public, to counter the risk of a *tragedy of the commons*. However, some remain unconvinced and refuse to wear a mask or be vaccinated. The ethics of the debates about enforcing the compulsory vaccination and wearing of masks where there is a clear public good is beyond the scope of this chapter. Save to say that travellers' perceptions of risk in destinations are likely in part to depend on the prevalence of public mask-wearing, which is culturally determined (Royo-Bordonada, García-López, Cortés, & Zaragoza, 2020).

Responsible Tourism

Responsibility is a highly nuanced word. It is about how we respond individually and collectively to the issues which we see around us. Do we respond willingly, decide this is something we should and can do something about and take responsibility or do we have responsibility imposed upon us by an employer or by legislation? In either case, we are accountable but in different ways. Responsibility is not spread evenly around society; we expect children to take less of it than adults – we expect more of those in positions of public office, those who are legally accountable and those who receive larger salaries because of the responsibility they carry. We admire those who take responsibility and make great personal efforts and sacrifices to tackle a particular injustice or issue. This is in the tradition of wanting to make a difference.

Sizoo (2010) edited a collection of papers about responsibility and culture, providing a set of references on the meaning of responsibility in a range of linguistic and cultural traditions. As Sizoo points out in her introduction, "the idea of responsibility does resound everywhere, although it is often expressed with more than one word, depending on the various relationships between people on between human beings and the non-human living world" (Sizoo, 2010, p. 21). The etymology of the word is from the Latin *responsabilis* and *respondere*, and it continues to carry the sense of obligation from the Latin along with the sense of moral purpose which resides in the idea of taking responsibility – of being amongst those – or the one – who does not look away or pass by on the other side.

The concepts of responsive, responsible and responsibility are different, and of course, language evolves, and meanings change over time. There are three core elements, the balance between them varying with languages and cultures. These three elements are the capacity, willingness or obligation to respond, closely related to empowerment. Respons-ability, the opportunity to take responsibility – to demonstrate our good character, to feel good about ourselves; the third element is imposed upon us, accountability, liability and blame.

Sustainable and responsible tourism are too often erroneously used together as though they have a shared meaning. The concepts are related but fundamentally different. Too often, sustainable and sustainability are used only in the abstract sense. Inoperative, their use is little more than greenwashing. Responsibility requires that we say what we are doing to make tourism better and transparent about what we achieve. Sustainability is the ambition. Responsible Tourism is about what we do as destinations, producers and consumers to realise the aspiration. Responsible action is required to achieve sustainability.

The COVID-19 epidemic and then the pandemic presented an issue that constituted an immediate threat to health, with a significant risk of hospitalisation, invasive and traumatic treatment and death. Businesses, governments and individuals were faced with a threat that required them to take responsibility to ensure the safety of their travellers and guests, their employees and communities. This was a public health emergency that required a response and one where, as test and trace geared up, failure to operate to rigorous protocols would be exposed.

Responsible Tourism has a number of antecedents in Krippendorf's thinking about the future of holiday making (Krippendorf, 1987), the UN-WTO (2020a)'s Global Code of Ethics, and in the campaign for more ethical forms of outbound tourism from the UK in the 1990s. Research undertaken with the Association of Independent Tour Operators demonstrated that a claim to be ethical was too big to be credible; some would expect the product to be vegan, exclude flying, and avoid operating in countries with unacceptable human rights practices. Responsible Tourism emerged from discussions with outbound tour operators as an approach where businesses could choose the issues which were important to their clients or in the destinations in which they operated; issues that they could effectively address and report on the difference they were making (see Goodwin, 2011). It was immediately evident that COVID-19 was just such an issue, both for clients and for local communities and their governments

The COVID-19 pandemic presented an issue that could not be ignored. Not taking responsibility would be seen by clients, communities and governments as irresponsible. As the pandemic spread and its impacts deepened, hospitalisations and deaths mounted, fear rose, and governments acted. The pandemic hit travel, hospitality and attractions hard through lockdowns and travel bans as governments fought to reduce the spread of the virus to save lives and protect health services, which even in rich countries, were threatened with being overwhelmed. The virus compelled businesses and governments in originating markets and destinations to take responsibility.

The ceasing of domestic and international travel starkly revealed the impacts of tourism on local economies and natural and cultural environments. There were reports of fish and swans in the canals in Venice, although many of these reports about Venice, and other honeypots, overstated the scale of the silver lining brought by the pandemic.[1] As destinations and domestic source markets moved in and out of lockdowns, rural and coastal areas, in particular, experienced unwelcome levels of visitation with littering, trampling, overcrowding and wild toileting, negative impacts with no compensating gain.[2]

Overtourism resulted from businesses and destinations paying little more than lip service to sustainability over many years. Overtourism crept upon communities in destinations and on travellers as each year the quality of life in the area or the quality of the experience deteriorated. The abrupt ceasing of tourism revealed the extent of the changes tourism has brought. The pandemic has contributed to revealing the scale of tourism's impacts, positive and negative, whether post-pandemic more will be done to tackle it remains uncertain. There is some evidence that travellers and holidaymakers are in the context of the pandemic aspiring to travel more sustainably.

Booking.com commissioned research conducted among a sample of adults who had travelled for business or leisure in the previous 12 months, and who were planning to travel in the next 12 months (if/once travel restrictions were lifted). In total, 20,934 respondents across 28 countries were polled in July 2020. A total of 53% said that they were looking for more sustainable ways to travel, to avoid travelling during peak season (51%), overcrowding (48%) and overly busy tourist attractions (63%). More than half (53%) of global travellers said that they were willing to reduce their waste and recycle their plastic when travelling. Agreement with the statement, *I want to travel more sustainably because COVID-19 has opened my eyes to humans' impact on the environment*, ranged from 74% in Colombia to 27% in the Netherlands. Agreement with *I expect the travel industry to offer more sustainable travel options*, ranged from 86% in Colombia to 47% in Denmark (Booking.com, 2020).

The Boston Consulting Group surveyed more than 3,000 people across eight countries in May 2020 and found that in the wake of the pandemic, people were more, not less, concerned about the environmental challenges and reported that they were more committed to changing their own behaviour to advance sustainability. 70% of respondents said they were more aware now than before COVID-19 that human activity threatens the climate and that degradation of the environment, in turn, threatens humans. More than two-thirds of respondents think that economic recovery plans should make environmental issues a priority. 40% reported that they intended to adopt more sustainable practices in the future (Boston Consulting Group, 2020).

IBM surveyed 14,000 consumers in nine countries. Not surprisingly, the survey found significant variations between countries, only 51% of US consumers surveyed said addressing climate change was very, or extremely important to them, compared to 73% of respondents from all other countries. On average 54% of the consumers, IBM surveyed, said that they were willing to pay a premium for sustainable and/or environmentally responsible brands (IBM, 2021).

Amid the global pandemic, survey evidence supported the emerging consensus that consumer attitudes and aspirations were changing. The pandemic appeared to have acted as a catalyst, accelerating changes in the consumer marketplace, which were already evident. Only with the benefit of hindsight shall we be able to determine to what extent the pandemic permanently changed attitudes to sustainability and whether or not that resulted in the anticipated step-change in production and consumption.

Incidence of Epidemics and Pandemics

The travel and tourism sector was not alone in being ill-prepared for the COVID-19 pandemic, but it was at the heart of it. There follows a review of the risks of further epidemics and pandemics, necessary to understand the importance of taking responsibility and being prepared for other similar events. The World Economic Forum published a list of the ten countries with the highest level of pandemic preparedness headed by the US and the UK (World Economic Forum, n.d.). A year later, a paper in Global Health pointed out that: "Vietnam is ranked 50th in Global Health Security Index overall scores, 59th in Joint External Evaluations scores, and 104th in universal health coverage but so far has been one of the more successful countries in containing the coronavirus" (Crosby, Dieleman, Kiernan, & Bollyky, 2020, p. 2020). It is reasonable and fair to describe the level of pandemic planning beyond a few countries with recent experience of epidemics as lamentable and irresponsible.

The last global pandemic was the influenza virus which emerged in America in the wake of world war one and became known as Spanish flu. America had military censorship, Spain was neutral and without censorship, so Spain got the blame. New infectious diseases are often associated with foreign nationals and foreign countries. As Hoppe has pointed out: "Intentional or not, an effect of this naming convention is to communicate a causal relationship between foreign populations and the spread of infectious disease, potentially promoting irrational fear and stigma" (Hoppe, 2018, p. 1462). The ethical and political reasons, the World Health Organization has urged public health officials to generate and disseminate accurate and non-stigmatizing epidemic names to the public.

COVID-19 was originally named after China, and there were subsequently Brazilian, Kent and Indian variants of concern. Prior to COVID-19, all four pandemics of the 20th century were given colloquial names: Spanish flu, 1918–1920 (50 million estimated dead); Asian flu, 1957–1958 (2 million estimated dead); Hong Kong flu, 1968–1969 (1 million estimated dead) and AIDS, termed initially "gay-related immune deficiency" (1981–present; 30 million estimated dead). Hoppe (2018) concluded that efforts to be "more scientifically accurate" resulted in "their incomprehensibility render[ing] them a failure."

Academics and scientists debate the effectiveness of efforts to curtail epidemics by clamping down on global travel, although they may delay the spread and arrival (Cooper, Pitman, Edmunds, & Gay, 2006). However, restrictions on travel are to be expected when countries impose lockdowns and movement restrictions to hamper the spread of disease. An IpsosMORI poll in the UK in May 2021 found 70% net support for stopping people entering the UK from countries with higher levels of COVID-19 infections; 57% for requiring all those returning from abroad to quarantine in hotels; and 54% for stopping people from entering the country from any other country (IPSOS MORI, 2021).

The first confirmed COVID-19 case in Italy was reported on January 31, 2020, when two Chinese tourists in Rome tested positive for the virus. Clusters of cases were later detected in Lombardy and Veneto, and by the beginning of March, the virus had spread to all regions of Italy. However, the National Institute of Health (ISS) reported that water from Milan and Turin showed genetic COVID-19 virus traces on 18 December (La Rosa et al., 2021). Testing wastewater may emerge as one of the most effective means of identifying the presence of viruses.

Parmet and Rothstein, in a prescient paper published in November 2018 to marl the centenary of the influenza pandemic of 1918–1920, a year before the emergence of COVID-19 in December 2019, identified hubris, isolationism and distrust as leading threats to global public health. Reminding us that our technology (genomics, vaccines, antibiotics and mechanical ventilators) "remains woefully ineffective in preventing influenza" and that many millions live in poverty without access to modern sanitation and healthcare, conditions that "support the rapid spread of infectious diseases." Isolationism is ineffective too. "Airplane travel facilitates the rapid spread of pathogens, and even faster communication technology enables the spread of fear and misinformation." They expressed concern too about the dangers of living in an era of political polarisation, arguing that as a result of "fake news, and tribal politics, trust in the media, government officials, and even science is fading." Leading to "the public's failure to trust the guidance offered by public health officials may well make a bad situation worse." Reviewing the papers they characterised the centenary collection as "a sobering reminder of the dangers of pandemics and the inadequacies of our planning and response" (Parmet & Rothstein, 2018, p. 1435). Prescient indeed.

The Global Preparedness Monitoring Board (GPMB) was established in response to the recommendations of the UN Secretary General's Global Health Crises Task Force in 2017 under the auspices of the World Health Organization and the World Bank Group. In September 2020, the GPMB published *A World in Disorder*, warning that the world cannot afford to be unprepared again when the next pandemic hits. The GPMB called for responsible leadership, engaged citizenship, strong and agile systems for health security; sustained investment; and robust global governance for preparedness (Board, 2019).

The GPMB had published *A World at Risk*, in September 2019 before the emergence of COVID-19, although it was clearly already circulating (Board, 2019). They explained that

> Vulnerability is heightened by an increase in outbreaks occurring in complex humanitarian emergencies, as well as a novel convergence of ecological, political, economic and social trends including population growth, increased urbanization, a globally integrated economy, widespread and faster travel, conflict, migration and climate change.
>
> Between 2011 and 2018, WHO tracked 1483 epidemic events in 172 countries. Epidemic-prone diseases such as influenza, Severe Acute Respiratory Syndrome (SARS), Middle East Respiratory Syndrome (MERS), Ebola, Zika, plague, Yellow Fever and others, are harbingers of a new era of high-impact, potentially fast-spreading outbreaks that are more frequently detected and increasingly difficult to manage.
>
> (Board, 2019, p. n.d.)

Naicker (2011) in a paper in *Archives of Clinical Microbiology* in 2011, reported that approximately 60% of emerging human pathogens are zoonoses, a consequence of the human-animal interface and that climate change, pathogen adaptation and animal migration drive their emergence. "Travel, tourism and trade are the major human factors impacting the epidemiology of zoonotic diseases." In a special edition of the *Institute for Laboratory Animal Research (ILAR) Journal* in 2017, Aguirre points out that the

> fundamental human threats to biodiversity include overexploitation of species, habitat destruction, and exotic species introduction (referred as the "evil trio"), and have led to ecosystem disruptions causing alteration of disease transmission patterns. Adding pathogen pollution, global toxification, and global environmental change linked to climate (the "savage sextet") compound the pervasive biodiversity loss.
>
> Every year we have novel viruses spilling over from wildlife to humans or domestic animals in unexpected ways. Highly pathogenic H5N1 avian influenza surprised many epidemiologists' rules by jumping from chickens straight to humans, calling world attention to a potential pandemic with the H1N1 outbreak in Mexico.
>
> (Aguirre, 2017)

Our governments were ill-prepared for COVID-19 – it would be unwise to regard it as a once in a century occurrence. Countries which had recent experience of dealing with epidemics were significantly better prepared and able to contain COVID-19. The travel and tourism sector must recognise that epidemics and pandemics are now likely to be part of the new normal and that when there are lockdowns, restrictions on free movement domestically and internationally are very likely, if not inevitable.

In 2017, the World Health Organization estimated that 290,000 to 650,000 people worldwide die of respiratory diseases linked to seasonal flu each year (WHO, 2017). We have vaccinations and treatments, and we have learnt to live with it. New variants arise each year, annual vaccination is required. Vaccinations and treatments help us to control the impact of the virus and to reduce its death toll. We may in time, be able to manage it as we do influenza. Murray and Piot in a paper published in March 2021 conclude that "the public and health systems need to plan for the possibility that COVID-19 will persist and become a recurrent seasonal disease" (Murray & Piot, 2021, p. 1249).

Travel Bans and Lockdowns

As COVID-19 is spread by social contact, travel and tourism, domestically and internationally, will inevitably be subject during epidemics to restrictions within countries and across borders. To enable travel and tourism a range of domestic and international travel and tourism methods have emerged, including corridors, bubbles, and vaccine passports.

There is a patchwork of regulations, requirements for test and vaccinations. The traveller's journey is fragmented and complex, from home to the airport or train by car, taxi or public transport, through check-in, security and the departure lounge to the aircraft and then through immigration, baggage reclaim, car, taxi or public transport to the accommodation. There are plenty of opportunities along the passenger journey to contract the virus. If the hotel, B&B or guest house is COVID secure what of local cafes, bars and restaurants, museums, galleries attractions and the beaches. And what of residents and other tourists? Will they be social distancing and wearing masks?

Fiji, along with many other tourism-dependent destinations, recognises that the entire population needs to take responsibility for COVID security:

> From the moment a traveller steps onto the plane and onto our shores, from the transport that picks them up from the airport, to the restaurants where they eat, or the handicrafts or tour trips that they do to villages, all will need to have protocols in place to ensure the safety of our visitors, our communities and the survival of the industry.
>
> But this is not just something for the tourism industry the entire population must be engaged in promoting and enacting protocols that discourage the spread of the virus. A single outbreak could end future opportunities for tourism pathways with other countries.
>
> (Penjueli, 2020)

Vaccinated, tested and judged fit to travel, the traveller may face further tests on arrival and again departing to travel home. Travellers and holidaymakers will perceive risk differently in a rapidly evolving situation at home and abroad. How significant is the risk of being denied boarding, trapped abroad and needing to pay for accommodation, or being forced to quarantine on arriving home, perhaps in a hotel at great expense? In February 2021, there were nearly 40,000 Australians stuck overseas because of government caps on international arrivals, transit-country restrictions and expensive and cancelled flights (McAdam, 2021). Travel has become significantly riskier.

Safety, Trust and Certification

Safety and trust are the new currencies of travel, but in a fragmented industry, with any trip involving numerous businesses and fellow consumers from multiple places delivering a safe environment is very challenging. The pandemic has revealed the contribution of travel for leisure, business, and work to the spread of viruses and demonstrated the danger of dependency on tourism for livelihoods. Governments worldwide have sought to protect their citizens and health services by closing borders and imposing a quarantine on those arriving from areas with higher rates of COVID-19 infections. While there is optimism that vaccines will be found to contain the virus and more effective treatments to reduce the impact of further waves of disease will be developed, it is not yet possible to determine with certainty the new normal.

The industry needs to evolve to thrive in a world where trust and safety are again an issue. The UN World Tourism Organization has worked with member states to create an International Code for the Protection of Tourists, a set of principles calling for a common global approach to assist tourists and "to find a fair and equitable balance between what is desirable and what is achievable." The code asserts the "duty of public authorities and tourism service providers to provide assistance to tourists in emergency situations" and the "responsibility of tourists to either acquaint themselves or to follow the information provided by the tourism service provider" (UNWTO, 2021, p. n.d.).

The World Travel and Tourism Council (WTTC) developed "meaningful action plans that optimise sector-wide recovery efforts." Protocols "with insights & toolkits for interaction & implementation to ensure that people are, and feel, safe." However, the WTTC, clearly stated: "our members, and the sector cannot guarantee 100% safety." They created the *SafeTravels Stamp*, to be used by destinations and businesses that had adopted and implemented the protocols. Use of the Stamp was "based upon an accurate and honest conclusion" that the organisation is fully compliant with the relevant protocols. WTTC explicitly denies any responsibility for assessing initial or continued compliance with the protocols (WTTC, n.d.). It amounts to self-certification.

Reputation is important to businesses, and most will take COVID security and guest and employee safety seriously, the *#SafeTravels Stamp* is no guarantee. However highly, the traveller rates the hotel's commitment to cleanliness and guest safety; they still have to reach the check-in desk, leave the hotel to mix with locals and other visitors, and then make the journey home. COVID-19 is a risk at all stages in the journey. Until travellers can be sure that their vaccination protects them from all variants of COVID-19, risk will be a significant determinant of travel choices, and there will always be the risk of a new variant of concern. Depending on the prevalence of COVID in the source market, whether domestic or international, host populations will similarly be concerned about what viruses visitors may be bringing with them.

Our Relationship with Nature

Over the last 50 years, there has been a slow realisation that the challenges of climate change and biodiversity represent serious threats to life and prosperity. The COVID-19 pandemic presented as a real and present danger at a global scale, as cases mounted, the hospitals filled, and the dead were buried or burned. The International Federation of Red Cross and Red Crescent Societies (IFRC) in their World Disasters Report 2020 point out that "…extreme weather- and climate-related disasters have killed more than 410,000 people in the past ten years" and that a "…further 1.7 billion people around the world were affected by climate- and weather-related disasters during the past decade – many injured, left homeless or without livelihoods" (International Federation of Red Cross and Red Crescent Societies, 2021, p. 21). They caution that these figures are underestimates given poor data collection in many countries and challenges over attribution in food crises.

We have 'known' since 1972 that although we see ourselves as having dominion over nature and our planet, which we can exploit for our benefit, individually and collectively. Since we first saw those Apollo photographs of Earth in 1968, we have known that our planet is finite. It is not infinite. We have not, yet, accepted the implications and learnt to live within the planetary boundaries. Urgent action is required to tackle the connected global threats of climate change and biodiversity loss, and mounting inequality. We have had decades of procrastination and prevarication. This is now the critical decade, we have delayed action for decades, refusing to adopt the precautionary principle and paid no more than lip service to sustainability.

The Declaration of the first United Nations Conference on the Human Environment in 1972 recognised that for "...the purpose of attaining freedom in the world of nature, man must use knowledge to build, in collaboration with nature, a better environment." And that this would "...demand the acceptance of responsibility by citizens and communities and by enterprises and institutions at every level, all sharing equitably in common efforts. Individuals in all walks of life as well as organizations in many fields, by their values and the sum of their actions, will shape the world environment of the future" (Handl, 2012, p. 3). The 1972 Declaration recognised both the challenge and man's responsibility to shape our world's environment. The Declaration suggests that citizens and communities, enterprises and institutions must accept responsibility, but there is no mention of governments. Looking back now, and as we recognise the scale of the sustainability challenges we face, this is perhaps surprising. From the 1950s, the thinking of neoliberals like Hayek became more influential, market solutions and consumer choice were increasingly the preferred approaches to dealing with issues. Citizens were redefined as consumers, tax and regulation were anathemas. The influence of Keynesianism and the post-war consensus declined, neoliberalism has become the new consensus (Hay, 2018).

In the Judaeo-Christian tradition, nature is perceived by many as for the benefit of man, for us to use to enable our societies to grow without limit. In Genesis 1:28 God speaks to us, "Be fruitful and multiply, and fill the earth and subdue it; and have dominion over the fish of the sea and over the birds of the air and over every living thing that moves upon the earth." Kay (1989) in a paper demonstrates that the Bible's most persistent environmental message is that God confers human dominion over nature to righteous or faithful people, whereas God punishes transgressors with natural disasters. We shall come back to this shortly. It is not necessary to subscribe to the view that COVID-19 is a punishment from God to accept that the pandemic is a reminder that we are in nature and vulnerable to it.

It is widely accepted that tourism is at least a tenth of global GDP, 10% of global consumption. Since the middle of the 20th century, tourism has grown inexorably and more rapidly than the global economy. In January 2020, the UNWTO characterised tourism as "a leading and resilient economic sector" (UNWTO, 2020b). Shortly afterwards, it quickly became obvious that tourism was going to be hard hit by the pandemic.

William Anders's "Earthrise," taken from Apollo 8 on Christmas Eve 1968 revealed spaceship Earth and became a symbol of the environmentalist movement but it did not change humanity's perception of a world of infinite possibilities and limitless growth. An expectation of limitless growth continues to characterise our thinking about the future. The Club of Rome financed an interdisciplinary team led by Dennis Meadows at Massachusetts Institute of Technology, which used a computer simulation to determine the Limits to Growth. Published in 1972, the report was widely criticised for suggesting that population growth and material consumption needed to be limited.[3]

Individuals and businesses acting alone cannot slow or counter these threats. As with COVID-19, climate change and biodiversity loss are 'tragedy of the commons' issues. The benefits I enjoy from activities that result in climate change and biodiversity loss are greater, generally much greater, than the negative impacts I will experience from the consequences. The benefit accrues to me, while the damage is shared by all; it is the same for businesses. The negative effects are shared by everyone so that it makes sense for individual businesses to continue exploiting and polluting the global commons. Their competitors will; they may be disadvantaged if they don't.

In most but not all countries, governments imposed lockdowns to tackle COVID-19 for the 'common good', recognising that the pandemic, without restrictions on individual freedoms, could kill many more and that health services might be overwhelmed. However, in many societies, there have been protests against mask-wearing and social distancing. Action to secure the common good will be opposed by some and often by many.

Similarly, efforts to reduce greenhouse gas emissions are opposed or ignored. Climate change and the pandemic are both examples of the *tragedy of the commons*. The cost to the individual or the organisation of taking responsibility and taking effective action is greater than the negative impacts felt by the individual or organisation at least in the short term. In February 2021 the European Commission adopted a new EU strategy on adaptation to climate change, setting out the pathway to prepare for the unavoidable impacts of climate change (European Commission, 2021). Vice-President Frans Timmermans presenting the EU's action plan on climate change, drawing on the experience of the COVID-19 pandemic, said "There is no vaccine against the climate crisis, but we can still fight it and prepare for its unavoidable effects" (The Brussels Times, 2021), a point that has become a meme.

The Future, Living with COVID-19

In an article published in Nature in February 2021, two academics from the Scripps Research Institute in California called for an alternative approach to pandemic preparedness and investment in the development of a vaccine based on broadly neutralizing bodies. Burton and Topol "call for an investment now in basic research leading to the stockpiling of broadly effective vaccines." They explain why this should be a priority: "As we've seen for influenza, one virus strain can cause more deaths than a world war and result in trillions of dollars of economic damage. Surely, global governments that together spend US$2 trillion a year on defence can find a few hundred million dollars to stop the next pandemic?" (Burton & Topol, 2021, p. n.d.).

For the future of travel and tourism, we need the world to be much better equipped to deal with pandemics as they emerge. Those countries with recent experience of epidemic diseases have generally been more successful than those which have not. We have learnt to live with and manage influenza; hopefully, we will learn to live with and manage COVID-19 too. The development of broad-based vaccines is likely critical to maintaining the open borders essential to our industry. Otherwise, we may face uncertainty with periodic panic, lockdowns and forced quarantine as a regular hazard for travellers and holidaymakers.

As we have seen the WHO has reminded us that no one is safe until everyone is safe. The COVAX initiative, a joint endeavour between WHO, Gavi, and the Coalition for Epidemic Preparedness Innovations, aims to ensure that the COVID-19 vaccines are equitably distributed around the world. In 2021 demand for the vaccines will far exceed supply this year and there were growing concerns that poorer countries would be left behind. Even if everything goes according to plan, countries relying on COVAX alone cannot expect to vaccinate more than 20% of their population (Burki, 2021).

Governments around the world moved centre stage in addressing the pandemic. Governments invested in new plants to make the vaccines and removing many liberties in liberal democracies, generating an anti-vax libertarian backlash fuelled by conspiracy theories strong enough in the US to result in the storming of the Capitol. The good news is that governments took responsibility for tackling COVID, understanding that the urgency, scale and complexity of the problem meant that it could not be left to the market. The competence of governments has been tested, and many were found wanting. The challenge of climate change is also characterised by scale and complexity. But, it is not seen as a clear and present danger; it is not seen as urgent. Scientists and economists have been telling us for years that there is a growing problem and that the later we address it, the more difficult and costly it will be.

COVID-19 reminded residents of what their place was like before tourism and raised awareness of both negative and positive impacts. Destinations had a holiday from tourism. Overtourism crept up on destinations and it was accepted. While most destinations in 2021 were in the survival phase some were already looking to build back better and to use tourism rather than to be used by it.

Travel and tourism will need to learn to deliver business and leisure travel in a world where COVID-19, and its variants, will pose a health risk for tourists and destination residents alike. COVID-19 and other zoonotic viruses rely on human to human transmission. As long as there are areas of the world where the virus is rampant, there will be a risk that new more virulent and dangerous variants will occur and be spread by travel – domestic and international, and there may be more zoonotic epidemics in the future. Businesses and governments need to be prepared for the next epidemic, not to be prepared is irresponsible.

Notes

1 See for example www.afar.com/magazine/clear-water-in-venice-means-the-return-of-wildlife.
2 There are many examples of local paper reports of this in Responsible Tourism News https://responsibletourismpartnership.org/blog/.
3 See for example Peter Passell, Marc Roberts and Leonard Ross (1972) The Limits to Growth, April 2, 1972, Section BR, Page 1, https://www.nytimes.com/1972/04/02/archives/the-limits-to-growth-a-report-for-the-club-of-romes-project-on-the.html.

References

Aguirre, A. A. (2017). Changing patterns of emerging zoonotic diseases in wildlife, domestic animals, and humans linked to biodiversity loss and globalization. *ILAR Journal, 58*(3), 315–318.

Board, G. P. M. (2019). *A world at risk.* Geneva: World Health Organization and the World Bank.

Booking.com. (2020). Impact awakening: the rise of responsible travel. Retrieved from www.booking.com/articles/impact-awakening-the-rise-of-responsible-travel.html.

Boston Consulting Group. (2020). The pandemic is heightening environmental awareness. Retrieved from https://www.bcg.com/en-gb/publications/2020/pandemic-is-heightening-environmental-awareness.

Brooks, J. T., & Butler, J. C. (2021). Effectiveness of mask wearing to control community spread of SARS-CoV-2. *Jama, 325*(10), 998–999.

Burki, T. K. (2021). Challenges in the rollout of COVID-19 vaccines worldwide. *The Lancet Respiratory Medicine, 9*(4), e42–e43.

Burton, D. R., & Topol, E. J. (2021). Variant-proof vaccines—invest now for the next pandemic. Nature Publishing Group, Retrieved from https://www.nature.com/articles/d41586-021-00340-4 [Accessed on 15 June, 2021].

Cooper, B. S., Pitman, R. J., Edmunds, W. J., & Gay, N. J. (2006). Delaying the international spread of pandemic influenza. *PLoS Med, 3*(6), e212.

Crosby, S., Dieleman, J., Kiernan, S., & Bollyky, T. (2020). All bets are off for measuring pandemic preparedness. *Think Global Health, 30,* 2020.

European Commission. (2021). EU adaptation strategy. Retrieved from https://ec.europa.eu/clima/policies/adaptation/what_en.

Goodwin, H. (2011). *Taking responsibility for tourism.* Goodfellow Publishers Limited, Woodeaton.

Handl, G. (2012). Declaration of the United Nations conference on the human environment (Stockholm Declaration), 1972 and the Rio Declaration on Environment and Development, 1992. *United Nations Audiovisual Library of International Law, 11,* n.d.
Hardin, G. (1968). The tragedy of the commons. *Science, 162*(3859), 1243–1248.
Hay, C. (2018). The "crisis" of keynesianism and the rise of neoliberalism in Britain: an ideational institutionalist approach. In J. L. Campbell & O. K. Pedersen (Eds.), *The rise of neoliberalism and institutional analysis* (pp. 193–218). Princeton, NJ: Princeton University Press.
Hoppe, T. (2018). "Spanish flu": when infectious disease names blur origins and stigmatize those infected. *American Journal of Public Health, 108*(11), 1462–1464.
Howard, J., Huang, A., Li, Z., Tufekci, Z., Zdimal, V., van der Westhuizen, H.-M., … Rimoin, A. W. (2021). An evidence review of face masks against COVID-19. *Proceedings of the National Academy of Sciences, 118*(4), e2014564118. doi:10.1073/pnas.2014564118.
IBM. (2021). IBM study: COVID-19 pandemic impacted 9 in 10 surveyed consumers' views on sustainability. Retrieved from https://newsroom.ibm.com/2021-04-22-IBM-Study-COVID-19-Pandemic-Impacted-9-in-10-Surveyed-Consumers-Views-on-Sustainability.
International Federation of Red Cross and Red Crescent Societies. (2021). World disasters report. Retrieved from https://media.ifrc.org/ifrc/world-disaster-report-2020/.
IPSOS MORI. (2021). Majority of Britons are concerned about COVID-19 variants coming to the UK and support 2021 holiday ban to prevent. Retrieved from https://www.ipsos.com/ipsos-mori/en-uk/majority-britons-are-concerned-about-COVID-19-variants-coming-uk-and-support-2021-holiday-ban.
Kay, J. (1989). Human dominion over nature in the Hebrew Bible. *Annals of the Association of American Geographers, 79*(2), 214–232.
Krippendorf, J. (1987). *Holiday makers*. Oxford, UK: Heinemann.
La Rosa, G., Mancini, P., Ferraro, G. B., Veneri, C., Iaconelli, M., Bonadonna, L., … Suffredini, E. (2021). SARS-CoV-2 has been circulating in northern Italy since December 2019: evidence from environmental monitoring. *Science of the Total Environment, 750,* 141711.
McAdam, J. (2021). Should Aussies stranded overseas go to the United Nations for help to get home? Retrieved from https://theconversation.com/should-aussies-stranded-overseas-go-to-the-united-nations-for-help-to-get-home-154372.
Murray, C. J., & Piot, P. (2021). The potential future of the COVID-19 pandemic: will SARS-CoV-2 become a recurrent seasonal infection? *Jama, 325*(13), 1249–1250.
Naicker, P. R. (2011). The impact of climate change and other factors on zoonotic diseases. *Archives of Clinical Microbiology, 2*(2), 1–6.
Parmet, W. E., & Rothstein, M. A. (2018). The 1918 influenza pandemic: lessons learned and not—introduction to the special section. *American Journal of Public Health, 108*(11), 1435–1436. doi:10.2105/ajph.2018.304695.
Penjueli, M. (2020). Reset tourism in the age of pandemics. *The Fiji Times*. Retrieved from https://www.fijitimes.com/reset-tourism-in-the-age-of-pandemics/.
Royo-Bordonada, M. A., García-López, F. J., Cortés, F., & Zaragoza, G. A. (2020). Face masks in the general healthy population. Scientific and ethical issues. *Gaceta Sanitaria*. doi:10.1016/j.gaceta.2020.08.003.
Sizoo, E. (Ed.) (2010). *Responsibility and cultures of the world: dialogue around a collective challenge*: Bern: Peter Lang.

The Brussels Times. (2021). 'There is no vaccine against the climate crisis': EU adopts new strategy on climate change. *The Brussels Times*. Retrieved from https://www.brusselstimes.com/news/eu-affairs/156788/to-late-for-prevention-new-eu-strategy-on-adaptation-to-climate-change/.

UNWTO. (2020a). Global code of ethics. Retrieved from https://www.unwto.org/global-code-of-ethics-for-tourism.

UNWTO. (2020b). International tourism growth continues to outpace the global economy. Retrieved from https://www.unwto.org/international-tourism-growth-continues-to-outpace-the-economy.

UNWTO. (2021). International code for the protection of tourists Madrid [Press release]. Retrieved from unwto.org/news/new-international-code-to-provide-greater-legal-protection-for-tourists.

WHO. (2017). Up to 650 000 people die of respiratory diseases linked to seasonal flu each year. Retrieved from https://www.who.int/news/item/13-12-2017-up-to-650-000-people-die-of-respiratory-diseases-linked-to-seasonal-flu-each-year.

WHO. (2020). A global pandemic requires a world effort to end it – none of us will be safe until everyone is safe. Retrieved from https://www.who.int/news-room/commentaries/detail/a-global-pandemic-requires-a-world-effort-to-end-it-none-of-us-will-be-safe-until-everyone-is-safe.

World Economic Forum. (n.d.). These are the top 10 countries for pandemic preparedness. Retrieved from https://www.weforum.org/agenda/2019/11/countries-preparedness-pandemics.

WTTC. (n.d.). Safe travels stamp terms & conditions. Retrieved from https://wttc.org/SafeTravels-Stamp-Terms-Conditions.

11 The Importance of Tourism Security and Safety after COVID-19

Özgür Yayla, Ali Solunoğlu and Hüseyin Keleş

Introduction

International travel activities, due to the flexibility of tourism demand, may be interrupted because of a number of reasons such as natural disasters (Rossello et al., 2020), economic depression (Okumus & Karamustafa, 2005; Gunter & Smeral, 2016), wars between countries (Smith, 1998) or epidemics (Blake & Thea Sinclair, 2003; McKercher & Chon, 2004).

Despite the important economic, social and cultural impacts of tourism for countries, the events that may endanger safety of tourists create major problems in terms of the sector (Sönmez & Graefe, 1998). The September 11 terrorist attack in America, the SARS disease and the tsunami disasters that hit South Asia in the 21st century can be considered as obstacles to international travel. In recent years, such diseases, disasters or terrorist attacks have made the importance of security concerns in tourism sector to be felt more. COVID-19, which affected the world in 2019 and was officially announced as a pandemic by the World Health Organization (WHO) on March 12, 2020, has restricted touristic trips and made destination security much more effective limited travels (Sigala, 2020).

Tourism demand is particularly sensitive to health and safety issues (Blake & Thea Sinclair, 2003). Throughout human history, a number of infectious diseases such as HIV, Ebola, H1N1, and H5N1 have emerged. These diseases that are seen on the regional basis can be observed in wider areas with the development of technology and people's traveling to far places from where they live.

The effective role of tourism in the spread of these infectious diseases negatively affects the Destination Management Organizations (DMO) and the plans of the businesses serving in the destinations. As for the COVID-19 pandemic, on the other hand, it is described as an unprecedented crisis for the tourism sector (Bahar & Çelik İlal, 2020). The increasing concerns of tourists about health risks and the security measures implemented by destinations are effective in the holiday destination decision-making processes of touristic consumers (Enders & Sandler, 1991). The corona virus, which emerged in Wuhan city of China and affected the whole world, has created

DOI: 10.4324/9781003207467-16

serious difficulties for the tourism sector (Winston, 2020), and with the pandemic in question, the new normal concept has started to be used frequently in people's daily life (Serra & Leong, 2020). The concept of new normal means the necessary routines that start with the loosening of the restrictions (WTTC, 2020).

In this context, the new normalization process covers the elements such as safe distance, personal hygiene, contactless payment and so on. The new normalization has brought a number of changes and measures in tourism sector, as well. From this point of view, the study has examined, along with the COVID-19 pandemic, the security element, the importance of which is felt more than ever in tourism sector. According to Maslow's Hierarchy of Needs Theory, the need for security, which must be met right after physiological needs, besides affecting every stage of life has a determining role in terms of people's touristic trips. It is very difficult to realize tourism activities and provide tourist satisfaction in an unsafe destination because the success or failure of a destination depends on its ability to create a safe environment for the tourists visiting it (Milman et al., 1999). In addition to this, ensuring security in tourism destinations plays a direct role in the formation processes of destination image (Sudigdo et al., 2019).

The study has been completed by making use of secondary data as a result of a comprehensive literature review. In this context, the concept of destination security in tourism has been examined and the effect of destination security on tourism demand has been explained, as well. Besides, the effects of the pandemic on tourism and the security practices of the destinations have been evaluated. As a result of the study, a number of suggestions have been presented to academicians working in the literature, sector representatives and destination management organizations.

Literature Review

Destination Security in Tourism

Maslow's Hierarchy of Needs Theory is one of the most frequently used theories in social sciences although there are some studies that examine it with a critical point of view (Tikkanen, 2007). According to Maslow, all the needs that must be satisfied are ranked hierarchically and it is not correct to talk about another need without fulfilling the former one. The desire of people to get rid of fear and anxiety and to eliminate self-threatening elements, which takes place immediately after physiological needs such as eating and sleeping, is considered as the need for security. Although security or being safe means that the body of the individual is free from external threats and safe, it actually carries a much wider content and it means that health, work, family, personal resources, property, morals, values and even the society in which we live is safe as well (Maslow, 1943). In societies security is generally related to situations consisting human rights, economy, military threats, environment, epidemics and a number of crimes (Baldwin, 1997). When tourism is examined in terms of security, it can be associated with the fear and various other threats experienced by the tourists as a natural result of leaving their places of residence and staying away from their homes for a certain period of time (WTO, 1997; Sönmez & Graefe, 1998; Fuchs & Reichel, 2006).

Security is one of the most important factors for visitors in touristic destinations. In other words, the tourists not only consider the factors of attraction in the destination they want to go, but also the security factors, as well (Seçilmiş, 2009). At some certain times, countries may warn their own citizens about unsafe regions. For this reason, the security issue in tourism sector has already become an important factor as a result of the pandemic problem throughout the world.

When tourist behavior is examined, there are findings in the literature regarding the importance of security measures and elimination of the threats that pose a risk for tourists while deciding to travel to a specific destination (Moven & Minor, 1998). The risk factors that threaten the safety of the destination can be categorized as physical, financial, performance and social risks (Schiffman & Kanuk, 1994; Moven & Minor, 1998; Mitchell, 1999). Physical risk involves the risks that the tourist consumer is physically harmed. The risk caused by tourist injuries or infectious diseases is examined with regards to physical risk. While the risks such as loss of money value are evaluated at the category financial risk, the failure of the purchased service to meet the expectations signifies performance risk. Besides, the fear that the product or service purchased in the destinations will not match the reference groups defines the social risk (Fuchs & Reichel, 2006).

Since it is not possible to completely eliminate the risks in the destinations, it can be said that prior knowledge of the destination through risk assessment will reduce the perceived risk of the tourist (Tsaur et al., 1997). The concept of perceived risk, which is frequently used in studies on consumer research in the literature, is defined as the consumer's perception of both uncertainty and the magnitude of possible negative consequences (Curras-Peres et al., 2017). In addition, studies provide evidence that businesses operating in the service sector such as tourism carry more risks than businesses producing concrete products (Murray & Schlacter, 1990). Concerning the subject, Sönmez and Graefe (1998) identified ten different risks in total, as equipment, financial, health, physical, political problems, psychological, satisfaction, social, terrorism and time risks, in their study to identify risk factors that could threaten security in touristic destinations. Tsaur, Tzeng and Wang (1997), on the other hand, in a similar study, examined the risk factors that threaten the destination security in two different categories as physical and equipment risks. Roehl and Fesenmaier (1992) evaluated the risks perceived by tourists in three different groups as physical risk, vacation risk and destination risk. Similarly, Pennington-Gray and Schroeder (2013) measured the perceptions of international travelers towards destination safety and obtained seven different risk groups as crime, infectious disease, physical, equipment failure, weather, cultural barriers, and political crises.

Throughout human history, different risks have come into prominence in every period. For example, with the September 11 attacks, terrorism is shown as one of the more serious threats in terms of touristic destinations than other threats. From this point on, the perceived travel risk is specific to that period (Seabra et al., 2013). In other words, tourists pay more attention to the actual risk of that period than other threats in their destination selection (Chua et al., 2021). Although different threats come into prominence periodically, health risk during travel has been one of the most important issues by tourists (Jonas et al., 2011). As a matter of fact, the nature of the danger or risk for tourists can vary according to personality types (Carr, 2001). On the other hand, tourists with different characteristics on issues such as health or contagious disease are expected to show a common behavior (Jonas et al., 2011). However, the issue of health is considered important not only by the tourists but also by the local people living in the destinations they travel to (Wilks, 2006).

Tourism, which has an important place in the economies of countries, constantly fluctuates in terms of demand due to its fragile structure that can be easily affected by the abstraction and negative situations in the product (Williams & Baláž, 2013). For this reason, a negative event that may occur in a destination causes a decrease in demand, while positive developments in the region (image enhancement, increased awareness for tourism, development of alternative tourism types, etc.) increase the demand. Within this context, destination management organizations, local governments or policy makers have emphasized the security factor, which is one of the most important indicators in the formation of demand (Mansfeld & Pizam, 2006).

Pandemic and Tourism

Crises are natural events that can be encountered in tourism. Many destinations are affected by natural and human-induced crises. Over the years, resistance and mitigation tactics and strategies have been developed in response to such situations (Ritchie & Jiang, 2019). However, it was observed that the effects of SARS, Ebola and H1N1 epidemics, which were encountered, starting from late 90s throughout the world, on tourism were mainly felt in local regions where these viruses emerged. What's more, these epidemics could be limited before affecting the whole world.

The difference of COVID-19 from these epidemics is that it has turned into a global health crisis and the financial crisis triggered by this situation has been continuing (Fotiadis et al., 2021). This fundamental difference has affected many sub-sectors of the tourism industry (Gossling et al., 2020) and caused the industry to shut down for months. Travel bans and closure of country borders have resulted in serious economic losses. The United Nations World Tourism Organization (UNWTO) 2020 predicted a decrease in international tourist mobility between 20% and 30% (approximately $300 to $450 billion) (WTO, 2020). Yang et al. (2020) have developed a dynamic stochastic general equilibrium (DSGE) model so as to determine the impacts of the pandemic on tourism sector. The relevant model shows that with the increase in the number of COVID-19 cases, the health risks have increased and then the demand for tourism has dramatically decreased (Yang et al., 2020).

The economic shocks of the pandemic have affected all the industries worldwide. However, some industries have been able to maintain their activities by adapting to digital platforms (Mehrolia et al., 2020). As for the tourism industry, it is one of the main sectors that have been most adversely affected by this epidemic. Due to widespread travel restrictions and business closures in many countries, the tourism industry has caused some socio-economic damages that are difficult-to-compensate.

It is seen that the number of corona virus cases have exceeded 140 million worldwide, and deaths reported due to infection have reached 3 million (https://www.worldometers.info/coronavirus/). In the process following the increasing health risk and falling tourist demand, it has been stated that temporary workplace closures and job losses in tourism sector have reached 50 million on the global scale (World Travel and Tourism Council, 2020). Undoubtedly, pandemics and epidemics have a transformative impact on the environment and societies. Infectious diseases are considered to be the main cause of people's getting sick, deaths and the increase of subsequent social anxiety (Hall et al., 2020). Because the increasing population, high urbanization rate, facilitation of global shopping, changing consumption habits, and rapid consumption of biological diversity facilitate the emergence and spread of different diseases by causing people to come into contact with animal pathogens more closely (Myers et al., 2013; Mossoun et al., 2015). For this reason, it is very important to examine the transformative effects of modern pandemics on societies and to evaluate the findings for future crises.

The Effects of COVID-19 on Tourism Sector

COVID-19 has created conditions affecting the lives of all countries and people around the world, and has arguably pushed political, economic and socio-behavioral changes in societies on an unprecedented scale in the modern era (Baum & Hai, 2020). The COVID-19 pandemic has been one of the most influential and tragic epidemics of modern times. While the travel and tourism industry are critical for transporting disease and disease vectors (Browne et al., 2016), pandemics appear to allow limited intervention methods other than medical drugs, such as quarantine and border control. Chinazzi et al. (2020) emphasized that air travel and especially mega-ship voyages are the main reasons behind the rapid and global spread of the pandemic. The fact that there are scientific findings that the possibility of virus transmission during airline transportation, which has an important place in destination transportation, increases by 20% (Browne et al., 2016), reveals the correctness of many governments in imposing prohibitions on national and international travel. These prohibitions have triggered the economic effects (Assaf & Scuderi, 2020, Hu et al., 2021) and caused the closure of tourism sector, which is dependent on global mobility, by dramatically reducing the revenues of the sector.

All human movements suddenly stopped due to COVID-19 (Sheller, 2020). The concept of social distance has entered the dictionary among daily routines in a way that contrasts with the tourism and travel literature (Long, 2020). Article 7 of the Global Tourism Ethics of the World Tourism Organization contains the following statements: "A universal right of discovering and harnessing the planet's resources by direct and personal access through tourism" (WTO, 1999). Due to the pandemic, the right to education, transportation and tourism has been seriously affected. Due to COVID-19, Shengen has today left its place to stricter borders than before, which was expressing the limitlessness between EU countries before. Because of, social distance restrictions, many people have headed towards eco-tourism, in a sense, towards nature. The interest has increased again to the destinations that are less known or visited by people. In this way, there has been a correct flow in the train known as "slow tourism", where tourists enjoy the travel, not the destination (Benjamin et al., 2020).

The Security Measures Taken in Tourism on the Global-Scale after COVID-19

The COVID-19 virus spreading from the epicenter of the Wuhan region should be considered as a turning point. For the service industry, the year 2020 could be the trigger for the start of the new normal. Destinations that are complaining about excessive tourism understanding due to the inability of the previously existing tourism system to bear the capacity are now afraid that the complex system they have established, like the spider web, remains idle or completely collapses due to insufficient tourism concerns.

Tourism is full of dreams of escaping the banality of everyday life and relating to otherness (Salazar, 2012). In addition, Larsen and Guiver (2013) stated that as the journey itself becomes important in order to experience difference and 'get away from everything', people need a distance where travel is functional. One of the most likely consequences of this crisis is concluding that nearby destinations are the best routes (Diaz-Soria, 2017). Although it is described as an economic crisis, COVID-19 is actually a health crisis. In this sense, the route close to home is considered the most reliable route in terms of health (Lew, 2020).

Considering the measures taken on a global scale after COVID-19, the first measure is to close the borders; reduce or even stop air, land and sea transportation unless it is necessary. Measures have been taken like closing schools / universities and non-essential businesses / businesses, canceling or postponing events (e.g. major conferences and trade fairs, concerts and festivals, political debates and elections, sports seasons and summer Olympics) (Gössling et al., 2020).

The corona virus can be spread by talking, coughing, and sneezing. In order to prevent this situation, people started to isolate themselves and use mask and obey distancing rules, however, with health concerns; travel restrictions, online education, meetings and organizations have become widespread. Increasing cleaning costs, together with the regulations on capacity reduction (customer acceptance condition far below the maximum occupancy due to social distance) significantly affected the profitability of the sector and it was predicted that this situation could increase the prices (Assaf & Scuderi, 2020).

In addition, in the tourism market, pricing inequality has emerged with the decrease in demand and increased production costs in many tourism enterprises. It has revealed dozens of responsibility aspects for tourism enterprises, such as accommodation, ventilation, personnel hygiene, sanitation practices, renewal of air conditioning installations, restriction of the use of buffet and beverage machines, table layout, quarantine application and control of employee health (UNWTO, 2020).

Conclusion

The global world thesis, which tourism has long supported, has opened the door to a disaster whose dimensions are yet unpredictable. Due to the almost abolition of the borders between countries, it is seen that the masses traveling for touristic and different purposes are unprepared for corona virus and similar epidemics. All countries have taken similar measures with regards to corona virus measures. At this point, it is thought that the possibility of success is directly related to the socio-cultural structures of societies. Within the scope of corona virus measures, social distance, hygiene and mask measures are the most primitive but partially successful methods of avoiding the virus. More effort and practice than these are required for the tourism sector to regain its current economic potential. It is especially important to accelerate and popularize vaccination practices. Vaccine studies should be supported, and procurement and applications should be implemented quickly.

In terms of tourism, COVID-19 has been a painful experience for such situations that are possible to happen in the future. For this reason, for future pandemics, tourism businesses can provide technology-oriented services, develop a correct understanding of boutique business, distribute financial risk by making market diversification, making smaller investments frequently, reallocating the trust and risk perception of tourists in the travel and service industry. In addition, it is recommended that governments should increase the grants they offer, restrict the construction of new businesses in medium-term periods in order to prevent the formation of idle capacity, and offer visas and incentives that facilitate the travel of people who have produced antibodies by overcoming the disease.

References

Assaf, A., & Scuderi, R. (2020). COVID-19 and the recovery of the tourism industry. *Tourism Economics*, 26(5), 731–733. http://doi:10.1177/1354816620933712.

Bahar, O., & Çelik İlal, N. (2020). Coronavirüsün (Covid-19) turizm sektörü üzerindeki ekonomik etkileri. *International Journal of Social Sciences and Education Research*, 6(1), 125–139. https://doi.org/10.24289/ijsser.728121.

Baldwin, D. A. (1997). The concept of security. *Review of International Studies*, 23, 5–26. https://www.jstor.org/stable/20097464.

Baum, T., & Hai, N. T. T. (2020). Hospitality, tourism, human rights and the impact of COVID-19. *International Journal of Contemporary Hospitality Management*, 32(7), 2397–2407. https://10.1108/IJCHM-03-2020-0242.

Benjamin, S., Dillette, A., & Alderman, D. H. (2020). "We can't return to normal": committing to tourism equity in the post-pandemic age. *Tourism Geographies*, 22(3), 476–483. https://doi.org/10.1080/14616688.2020.1759130.

Blake, A., & Thea Sinclair, M. (2003). Tourism crisis management: US response to September 11. *Annals of Tourism Research*, 30, 813–832. https://doi.org/10.1016/S0160-7383(03)00056-2.

Browne, A., St-Onge Ahmad, S., Beck, C. R., & Nguyen-Van-Tam, J. S. (2016). The roles of transportation and transportation hubs in the propagation of influenza and coronaviruses: a systematic review. *Journal of Travel Medicine*, 23(1), tav002. https://doi.org/10.1093/jtm/tav002.

Carr, N. (2001). An exploratory study of gendered differences in young tourists' perception of danger within London. *Tourism Management*, 22, 565–570. https://doi.org/10.1016/S0261-5177(01)00014-0.

Chinazzi, M., Davis, J., Ajelli, M., Gioannini, C., Litvinova, M., Merler, S., Pastore y Piontti, A., Mu, K., Rossi, L., Sun, K., Viboud, C., Xiong, X., Yu, H., Halloran, E., Longini Jr, I., & Vespignani, A. (2020). The effect of travel restrictions on the spread of the 2019 novel coronavirus (COVID-19) outbreak. *Science*, 368(6489), 395–400. https://doi.org/10.1126/science.aba9757.

Chua, B. L., Al-Ansi, A., Lee, M. J., & Han, H. (2021). Impact of health risk perception on avoidance of international travel in the wake of a pandemic. *Current Issues in Tourism*, 24(7), 985–1002. https://doi.org/10.1080/13683500.2020.1829570.

Curras-Peres, R., Ruiz, C., Sanches-Garcia, I., & Sanz, S. (2017). Determinants of customer retention in virtual environments. The role of perceived risk in a tourism services context. *Spanish Journal of Marketing-ESIC*, 21, 131–145. https://doi.org/10.1016/j.sjme.2017.07.002.

Diaz-Soria, I. (2017). Being a tourist as a chosen experience in a proximity destination. *Tourism Geographies*, 19(1), 96–117. https://10.1080/14616688.2016.1214976.

Enders, W., & Sandler, T. (1991). Causality between transnational terrorism and tourism: The case of Spain. *Terrorism*, 14(1), 49–58. https://doi.org/10.1080/10576109108435856.

Fotiadis, A., Polyzos, S., & Huan, T. C. T. (2021). The good, the bad and the ugly on COVID-19 tourism recovery. *Annals of Tourism Research*, 87, 1–14. https://doi.org/10.1016/j.annals.2020.103117.

Fuchs, G., & Reichel, A. (2006). Tourist destination risk perception: the case of Israel. *Journal of Hospitality & Leisure Marketing*, 14(2), 83–108. https://doi.org/10.1300/J150v14n02_06.

Gössling, S., Scott, D., & Hall, C. M. (2020). Pandemics, tourism, and global change: a rapid assessment of Covid-19. *Journal of Sustainable Tourism*, 1–6. https://doi.org/10.1080/09669582.2020.1758708.

Gunter, U., & Smeral, E. (2016). The decline of tourism income elasticities in a global context. *Tourism Economics*, 22(3), 466–483. https://doi.org/10.5367/te.2014.0431.

Hall, C. M., Scott, D., & Gössling, S. (2020). Pandemics, transformations and tourism: be careful what you wish for. *Tourism Geographies*, 22(3), 577–598. https://10.1080/14616688.2020.1759131.

Hu, X., Yan, H., Casey, T., & Wu, C. H. (2021). Creating a safe haven during the crisis: how organizations can achieve deep compliance with COVID-19 safety measures in the hospitality industry. *International Journal of Hospitality Management*, 92, 102662. https://doi.org/10.1016/j.ijhm.2020.102662.

Jonas, A., Mansfeld, Y., Paz, S., & Potasman, I. (2011). Determinants of health risk perception among low-risk-taking tourists traveling to developing countries. *Journal of Travel Research*, 50(1), 87–99. https://doi.org/10.1177/0047287509355323.

Larsen, G. R., & Guiver, J. W. (2013). Understanding tourists' perceptions of distance: a key to reducing the environmental impacts of tourism mobility. *Journal of Sustainable Tourism*, 21(7), 968–981. https://doi.org/10.1080/09669582.2013.819878.

Lew, A. (2020). How to create a better post-COVID-19 world. *Medium*, 21 February 2021. https://medium.com/@alanalew/creating-a-better-post-covid-19-world-36b2b3e8a7ae.

Long, N. (2020). From social distancing to social containment: reimagining sociality for the coronavirus pandemic. *Medicine Anthropology Theory*, 7(2), 247–260. https://doi.org/10.17157/mat.7.2.791.

Mansfeld, Y., & Pizam, A. (2006). Toward a theory of tourism security. In Y. Mansfeld, & A. Pizam (Eds.), *Tourism, Security and Safety: From Theory to Practice*. Elsevier, Butterworth-Heinemann. https://booksite.elsevier.com/samplechapters/9780750678988/9780750678797.PDF (accessed 12 March 2021).

Maslow, A. H. (1943). A theory of human motivation. *Psychological Review*, 50(4), 370–396, 376–380. http://citeseerx.ist.psu.edu/viewdoc/download?doi=10.1.1.318.2317&rep=rep1&type=pdf (accessed 19 March 2021).

McKercher, B., & Chon, K. (2004). The over-reaction to SARS and the collapse of Asian tourism. *Annals of Tourism Research*, 31(3), 716–719. http://dx.doi.org/10.1016/j.annals.2003.11.002.

Mehrolia, S., Alagarsamy, S., & Solaikutty, V. M. (2020). Customers response to online food delivery services during COVID-19 outbreak using binary logistic regression. *International Journal of Consumer Studies*, 45(3), 396–408. https://doi.org/10.1111/ijcs.12630.

Milman, A., Jones, F., & Bach, S. (1999). The impact of security devices on tourists' perceived safety: the central Florida example. *Journal of Hospitality and Tourism Research*, 23(4), 371–386. https://doi.org/10.1177/109634809902300403.

Mitchell, V. W. (1999). Consumer perceived risk: conceptualisation and models. *European Journal of Marketing*, 33(2), 163–195. https://doi.org/10.2753/JEC1086-4415130402.

Mossoun, A., Pauly, M., Akoua-Koffi, C., Couacy-Hymann, E., Leendertz, S. A. J., Anoh, A. E., Gnoukpoho, A. H., Leendertz, F. H., & Schubert, G. (2015). Contact to non-human primates and risk factors for zoonotic disease emergence in the Taï region, Côte d'Ivoire. *EcoHealth*, 12(4), 580–591. https://doi.org/10.1007/s10393-015-1056-x.

Moven, J., & Minor, M. (1998). *Consumer Behavior*. Englewood Cliffs, NJ: Prentice-Hall. https://www.worldcat.org/title/consumer-behavior/oclc/36485784.

Murray, K. B., & Schlacter, J. L. (1990). The impact of services versus goods on consumers' assessment of perceived risk and variability. *Journal of the Academy of Marketing Science*, 18(1), 51–65. https://doi.org/10.1177/009207039001800105.

Myers, S. S., Gaffikin, L., Golden, C. D., Ostfeld, R. S., Redford, K. H., Ricketts, T. H., Turner, W. R., & Osofsky, S. A. (2013). Human health impacts of ecosystem alteration. *Proceedings of the National Academy of Sciences of the United States of America*, 110(47), 18753–18760. https://doi.org/10.1073/pnas.1218656110.

Okumus, F., & Karamustafa, K. (2005). Impact of an economic crisis: evidence from Turkey. *Annals of Tourism Research*, 32(4), 942–961. http://dx.doi.org/10.1016/j.annals.2005.04.001.

Pennington-Gray, L., & Schroeder, A. (2013). International tourist's perceptions of safety & security: the role of social media. *Matkailututkimus*, 9(1), 7–20. http://dx.doi.org/10.1177/0047287514528284.

Ritchie, B. W., & Jiang, Y. (2019). A review of research on tourism risk, crisis, and disaster management. *Annals of Tourism Research*, 79, 1–6. https://doi.org/10.1016/j.annals.2019.102812.

Roehl, W. S., & Fesenmaier, D. R. (1992). Risk perceptions and pleasure travel: an exploratory analysis. *Journal of Travel Research*, 30(4), 17–26. https://doi.org/10.1177/004728759203000403.

Rossello, J, Becken, S., & Santana-Gallego, M. (2020). The effects of natural disasters on international tourism: a global analysis. *Tourism Management*, 79, 1–10. https://doi.org/10.1016/j.tourman.2020.104080.

Salazar, N. B. (2012). Tourism imaginaries: a conceptual approach. *Annals of Tourism Research*, 39(2), 863–882. https://doi.org/10.1016/j.annals.2011.10.004.

Schiffman, L. G., & Kanuk, L. L. (1994). *Consumer Behavior*. Englewood, Cliffs, NJ: Prentice-Hall. https://www.worldcat.org/title/consumer-behavior/oclc/29182396.

Seabra, C., Dolnicar, S., Abrantes, J. L., & Kastenholz, E. (2013). Heterogeneity in risk and safety perceptions of international tourists. *Tourism Management*, 36, 502–510. https://doi.org/10.1016/j.tourman.2012.09.008.

Seçilmiş, C. (2009). Turistlerin kişisel değişkenlerinin güvenlik algılamalarındaki rolü. *Elektronik Sosyal Bilimler Dergisi*, 8(30), 152–166. https://dergipark.org.tr/en/pub/esosder/issue/6144/82468.

Serra, A., & Leong, C. (2020). *Here's What Travelling Could Be Like after COVID-19*. World Economic Forum, Global Agenda. Retrieved from https://www.weforum.org/agenda/2020/05/this-is-what-travelling-will-be-like-after-covid-19/ (accessed 03 February 2021).

Sheller, M. (2020). Some thoughts on what comes after a mobility shock. Critical Automobility Studies Lab. Accessed at: https://cas.ihs.ac.at/some-thoughts-on-what-comes-after-a-mobility-shock/ (accessed 2 April 2021).

Sigala, M. (2020). Tourism and COVID-19: impacts and implications for advancing and resetting industry and research. *Journal of Business Research*, 117, 312–321. https://doi.org/10.1016/j.jbusres.2020.06.015.

Smith, V. L. (1998). War and tourism: an American ethnography. *Annals of Tourism Research*, 25(1), 202–227. https://doi.org/10.1016/S0160-7383(97)00086-8.
Sönmez, S., & Graefe, A. R. (1998). Influence of terrorism risk on foreign tourism decisions. *Annals of Tourism Research*, 25(1), 112–144. https://doi.org/10.1016/S0160-7383(97)00072-8.
Sudigdo, A., Khalifa, G. S. A., & Abuelhassan, E. A. (2019). Driving Islamic attributes, destination security guarantee & destination image to predict tourists' decision to visit Jakarta. *International Journal on Recent Trends in Business and Tourism*, 3(1), 59–65. https://ejournal.lucp.net/index.php/ijrtbt/article/view/115.
Tikkanen, I. (2007). Maslow's hierarchy and food tourism in Finland: five cases. *British Food Journal*, 109(9), 721–734. https://doi.org/10.1108/00070700710780698.
Tsaur, S. H., Tzeng, G. H., & Wang, K. C. (1997). Evaluating tourist risks from fuzzy perspectives. *Annals of Tourism Research*, 24(4), 796–812. https://doi.org/10.1016/S0160-7383(97)00059-5.
UNWTO. (2020). Tourism and covid-19. Online at https://www.unwto.org/tourism-covid-19 (last accessed 13 April 2021).
Wilks, J. (2006). Current issues in tourist health, safety and security. In J. Wilks, D. Pendergast, & P. Laggat (Eds.), *Tourism in Turbulent Times: Towards Safe Experiences for Visitors* (pp. 3–18). Elsevier. https://www.ncbi.nlm.nih.gov/pmc/articles/PMC7155716/.
Williams, A. M., & Baláž, V. (2013). Tourism, risk tolerance and competences: travel organization and tourism hazards. *Tourism Management*, 35, 209–221. http://dx.doi.org/10.1016/j.tourman.2012.07.00.
Winston, A. (2020). Is the COVID-19 outbreak a black swan or the new normal? *MIT Sloan Management Review*, March 16. Retrieved from https://sloanreview.mit.edu/article/is-the-covid-19-outbreak-a-black-swan-or-the-new-normal/ (accessed 10 February 2021).
World Tourism Organization (WTO). (1997). *Tourist Safety and Security: Practical Measures for Destinations* (2nd ed.). Madrid: World Tourism Organization. https://www.unwto.org/archive/global/publication/tourist-safety-and-security-practical-measures-destinations (accessed 08 April 2021).
World Tourism Organization (WTO). (1999). Global code of ethics for tourism [resolution a/RES/406(XIII)]. Thirteenth WTO General Assembly, Santiago, Chile, September 27–October 1.
World Travel and Tourism Council (WTTC). (2020). Coronavirus puts up to 50 million travel and tourism jobs at risk. Skift. https://skift.com/2020/03/13/coronavirus-puts-50-million-tourism-jobs-at-risk-says-wttc-report/.
Yang, Y., Zhang, H., & Chen, X. (2020). Coronavirus pandemic and tourism: dynamic stochastic general equilibrium modeling of infectious disease outbreak. *Annals of Tourism Research*. https://doi.org/10.1016/j.annals.2020.102913.

12 Defining Responsibilities of Tourists in the Post-COVID-19 Period

Anila Thomas

Introduction

Many businesses have been severely harmed as a result of the novel coronavirus, but tourism remains one of the most affected. Tourism, a revolution that has helped tourists travel billions of miles since its inception, now allows one to remain dormant and quarantine oneself. The loss cannot be quantified because data changes as rapidly as the virus spreads. If the lockdown and pandemic continue for many months, the World Travel and Tourism Council (News Article | World Travel & Tourism Council (WTTC), 24/04/2020) and the trade body representing large global travel firms predict a global loss of US$2.1 trillion in sales and 75 million jobs (Gössling, Scott, & Hall, 2020). And as the planet struggles from these losses, there is still hope that the tourism industry will recover. In reality, several tourism companies and institutes have already begun preparing for a rumored Post-COVID-19 period. The WTO has implemented transportation restrictions, ensured visitor safety, and contributed to tourism development (Barkas, Honeck, & Rubio, 2020). This pandemic case has had certain environmental benefits in terms of reducing pollution levels, and the chlorination of water bodies as a result of climate change has reduced the unfavorable environmental conditions as they have changed. Tourism has seen rapid growth and integration over the last seven decades, being one of the world's largest and fastest developing sectors. Over time, more destinations have been opened and integrated into the development of tourism, rendering modern tourism a critical driver of socioeconomic transformation. Tourism has long been regarded as an important form of international trade. It is one of the main revenue streams and the number one export group for many developing countries, offering much-needed employment and opportunities for advancement. In the management and promotion of tourist sites, there are many responsibilities and tasks. They are led in different ways and in various locations, but are broadly classified as national, regional, or local. The national strategy, in general, offers a basis for more ideological functions, while the state level is concerned with operational practices.

DOI: 10.4324/9781003207467-17

The coronavirus outbreak, officially known as COVID-19 (Rabadan, 2020), has quickly spread around the world since the first case was discovered in December 2019 (Horton, 2021). Prior to the lockdown in Wuhan, China, COVID-19 expanded quickly both throughout China and internationally, following the course of networking and extremely high passenger numbers. The epicenter from Wuhan rapidly spread to Iran, then Italy, and then the rest of Europe, preceded by incredibly bigger outbreaks in the United States, Brazil, and other countries in the Americas (Koley, & Dhole, 2020). Every country has made significant strides to prevent further spread of COVID-19 and lower the number of fatalities. COVID-19 has had an undeniable effect on the world economy. Almost all businesses and economies are negatively impacted by COVID-19. Even, the tourism sector has been particularly hard hit by the latest pandemic.

Interestingly, for some time now the optimistic trajectory of tourism has been sluggish and tentative, with some limitations on travel beginning to rise in a few countries, some restoring foreign flights, and reopening some domestically and interregional. Domestic tourism is projected to recover faster than foreign travel during the peri-pandemic time, with improvements such as more trips taken closer to home, bookings made closer to trip departure times, an inclination for car travel, and a growth in the use of car rentals (Borko, Greets, & Wang, 2020). Despite the fact that travel could be on the rise, customers' worries about the dangers associated with travel remain. There continues to be a gradual and sporadic turnaround and analysts advice against improvements in the business processes expected in the future to succeed. In this unpredictable tourism environment, learning and interpreting overseas travelers' post-pandemic habits is important for any destination professional and researcher in the international tourism industry. This study focuses on the post-pandemic safer destination preference activities of foreign travelers since no previous analysis has examined and forecast their post-pandemic safer destination selection mechanism. Numerous studies by tourism, social psychology, and consumer behavior researchers agree that examining the fundamental reasons that contributed to travelers' specific motivations, taking into account purposive (social and interpersonal) and nonvolitional components, giving appropriate perspectives into travelers' decision-making mechanism for a destination/product/service/brand.

It is critical for the tourism industry to instill prudent practices in order to reduce negative growth outcomes while promoting constructive ones. As a result of this, the idea of responsible tourism has gained global adhesion, emerging as a key industry force. The central idea of Responsible Tourism is to make tourism more sustainable (O'Rourke, & Koščak, 2019); it is more about how we can promote sustainable development for the good of cities and vacation destinations through tourism. Responsible tourism is concerned with "leveraging tourism to build a better place to rest and an outstanding place to visit" (Bricker, Black, & Cottrell, 2013).

In a responsible tourism situation, all involved parties at a destination must accept responsibility for the consequences of their decisions. Feruzi suggested using the word "ethical tourism" to refer to all types of tourism that are more socially and environmentally conscious (Feruzi, 2012).

Various Responsibilities of Tourists/Travelers towards the Destinations Visited

A tourist to the destination has many obligations and personal traits, and these responsibilities are often multi-faceted and complex, with many parameters and ratios. Moving forward with traditional conceptions of duty is context-dependent, and it may be the moral obligation of destinations to inform and guide tourists accordingly. The adverse effects of tourism have a significant influence on the societal distinctiveness, which has a constructive stimulus on tourists' sense of obligation (Budeanu, 2005). Besides that, disseminating knowledge about the benefits of tourism is sufficient to instill a sense of responsibility in tourists, which is essential for encouraging positive behavior. There are a variety of practical implications for addressing tourists' sense of duty, including the tourists' understanding of negative impacts on tourism, enhancing the efficacy and usability of facts on the impact of tourism, and campaigning for tourists' behavior and mindset to improve things for the better in holiday spots (Goodwin, 2020a, Responsible Tourism is about the Experience). Like one might expect, the popularity of a tourist attraction, or hospitality industry as a whole, is as much dependent on the visitors as it is on the people in charge of providing their services. After COVID-19, both sides would need to take on a lot of liability. Tourists must be as concerned with their welfare as the rest of the population. According to studies on stakeholder roles in responsible tourism, all players must accept responsibility for the consequences of their decisions (Herremans, 2006). Considering the perspectives of other players in the responsible tourism situation is a proposed approach in the current study to resolve certain problems in recognizing stakeholder obligations.

Responsible tourism is important for providing improved holiday experiences for visitors and enhanced market prospects for entrepreneurs in the tourism industry by outlining the tourists' ethical obligations in three major types of issues: fiscal, socio-cultural, and environmental (Goodwin, 2011). Furthermore, responsible tourism contributes to a higher quality of life for local communities through increased socioeconomic benefits and better use of limited natural resources (Mathew, & Sreejesh, 2017). Latest studies in the field of responsible tourism have exposed the idea that all interested stakeholders have a role to play in the creation of a responsible destination (Byrd, 2007). There seems to be an increase in the number of socially responsible travelers. When people are searching for unique experiences, they are looking for ways to acquaint themselves in a location's history and nature. Throughout the pandemic, stakeholders, including visitors, demonstrated high levels of commitment, solidarity, and rational intervention.

Methodology

Keeping in mind the purpose and nature of the research problem, this research paper employs techniques involving qualitative (substantive) aspects to determine empirical assimilation across several theoretical perspectives or literary sources. The paper focuses on conceptual research techniques for revising existing tourist responsibilities in context of the present pandemic situation. The structural evaluation will also help to summarize and integrate the existing responsibilities of tourists, as well as outline the conceptual domain of new modalities to be followed by tourists. This paper is presented in a theoretical framework that will aid in recognizing and comprehending the key issues that arise in the consumer's / tourist's responsibility to provide a better experience. The extensive and comprehensive review of the current literature in this field has provided a base for the study and extant knowledge towards theoretical thinking and conceptual-based research. This paper emphasizes on findings from an elaborate evaluation of experiences of tourists to build up a consociate tourism environment with regard to the consequences of the changing travel patterns and resource availability.

The author used a descriptive research design in this data study to ascertain the underlying patterns of the research objectives. This is because descriptive research methods make an in-depth analysis of each variable before making conclusions, as it was not sure about the validity of the existing pandemic condition. This method has also helped to investigate the background of the research problem and provided the required information needed to carry out additional research.

During the present study, the researcher has used Purposive (Selective) sampling, as this technique relies on the judgment of the researcher in choosing whom to approach to contribute their views on the topic of study. The researcher has implicitly chosen a "representative" sample and precisely approached those respondents with to suit the required criteria or characteristics. In qualitative research, purposeful sampling is frequently used to identify and select information-rich cases related to the research problem (Palinkas, Horwitz, Green, Wisdom, Duan, & Hoagwood, 2015).

There were mainly two reasons behind in the selection of Purposive (Selective) sampling in order to collect the data. First, the lack of knowledge of the intensity of current pandemic situation among the citizens as it is a first-time tragic experience to many. Second, due to the pandemic situation, extensive travel was not advisable and there was lack of opportunity for the researcher to contact the respondents personally because of restricted traveling while gathering the data. The sample was framed from a group of respondents who have travelled extensively. There were no age limits insisted to the sample group, with an intention to collect the views from people of all ages in order to understand their viewpoints better.

The target population for this study was travelers. An online survey questionnaire created and was distributed to a sample of individuals of at least

18 years of age. A total of 138 questionnaires were distributed. Of that, 12 questionnaires were omitted owing to incomplete data. The final data set comprises a total of 126 usable questionnaires. Data was collected over the month of December 2020 during lockdowns and border closures in most of the countries.

The questionnaire comprised of questions to measure traveler's intentions / expectations / changing patterns during their travel domestically and internationally for business or leisure. The questionnaire includes different sections like profile, traveling habits of the participant, perception about growth of domestic tourism, various sectors affected by COVID-19 pandemic, perception about sustainability and accountability in practices, integrating and strengthening travelers' expectations during post-COVID-19 period and peri-pandemic travel experiences/responsibilities.

The secondary data were gathered by reviewing papers, statistical documents, newspaper articles, World Health Organization statistics, government data, and web-based materials related to the severity of COVID-19 on the tourism sector. Interview transcripts from research respondents or other identifiable writings that reflect subjectively on the study's topic are examples of qualitative data. The researcher has used Thematic analysis to analyze the collected data as it is a good approach to research which supports to find out to a certain extent about people's views, opinions, knowledge, experiences or values from a set of qualitative data, including interview transcripts or survey responses. Table 12.1 illustrates the various codes and its respective themes to analyze the collected data.

Table 12.1 Different codes and its identified themes

Codes	Theme
• Uncertainty of travel patterns • In accordance to expert opinions	Uncertainty
• Changing life patterns • Dislike toward restricted movements • Apprehension of government regulatory system	Mistrust of the conventional directive principles
• Inappropriate evidences • Misinterpretation of acquaintance • Prejudiced sources	Distortion
• Less crowded • Peer/family Recommendation in destination selection	Destination – choice
• Experience local/ethnic lifestyles/culture and traditions • Strengthen local economy • The intention to safeguard local resources	Socio-economic reflections
• Increased anxiety level and concern of family • Vigilant about the wellbeing and health conditions	Physical/psychological attributes

Results/Findings of the Study

The review of sources ideates that anxiety level of tourists/travelers were at its height in the initial stages of the pandemic outbreak; the struggle to cope with the challenges of the socio-economic anarchy was really an unfamiliar experience and the socio-cultural environment were affected with isolation and social distancing. Respondents were given the questionnaire and requested to give their Reponses.

Review of Pre-pandemic Travel Experiences/Responsibilities

Travel demand declined dramatically after the COVID-19 epidemic began, and the possible effect of COVID-19 on various facilities required by travelers tends to be a vital topic of discussion. As a result, it will be stimulating to explore the role and responsibilities of travelers in the aftermath of the coronavirus pandemic. Because of the pandemic, people have become more concerned with sanitation, cleanliness, and hygiene (Huremović, 2019). During the COVID-19 pandemic, the airline industry took a cautious strategy in order to increase safe operation, including extended gateway ventilation, onboard and disembarkation policies, improved aircraft disinfection, and pre-flight monitoring such as temperature tests and COVID-19 checking (Table 12.2).

Changing Travel Patterns during the COVID-19 Pandemic

Owing to the extent and impact of the tourism industry on economies, as well as the prevalence of COVID-19, tourist destinations are the most impacted by the pandemic. Flights were grounded, neighborhoods came to a halt, trains ceased operations, and nearly all public transportation ceased operations, while hotels, stores, bars, and restaurants practically closed their doors. Broad restrictions on all modes of transportation have resulted in an immeasurable financial downturn in the majority of the world's nations, whether they have been directly impacted by the outbreak or would be directly affected by its induced effects.

This Table 12.2 clearly shows that the pandemic has had an effect on nearly all aspects of tourism. However, travel style ($n = 48$) and tourist events ($n = 37$) were the most affected aspects, followed by accommodation ($n = 27$), locale ($n = 21$), and infrastructure ($n = 14$). The immediate effect on the hospitality industry is a significant decline in guests, occupancy levels, and a drop-in average daily rate (ADR) and Revenue Per Available Room (RevPAR) (Rodríguez-Antón, & Alonso-Almeida, 2020). Such short-term effects, such as work losses, operational shifts, and service reductions, hinder the hospitality industry's revival. In the coming years, uncertainties in extra revenues, delayed future expansion plans, or complications in loan repayments will hasten the return to a normal life (Table 12.3).

Table 12.2 Peri-pandemic travel experiences/responsibilities

Phases of Destination Visit	Peri-Pandemic Travel Experiences/Responsibilities					
	Destination – Choice/ Demand/Appealing	Travel Arrangements	Stay/Lodging/Food Services	Healthcare/Precautionary Measures	Socio-economic Reflections	Physical/Psychological Attributes
Pre-visit plans	* Less crowded Natural attractions * Local/regional/ domestic destinations * Peer/family Recommendation in destination selection	* Self-centered plans * Avoid group travel facilities * Last minute bookings/ reservations * Prefer to be dropped by own vehicles/extra care to be taken in case arranging public transport	* Carry necessary utensils, cutleries, food packets/ sachets, etc. * Prefer to carry home-made food while traveling to destinations	* Health check-up/ vaccination certificate * Carry medical kit: sanitizer (spray & gel), masks, required medicines, first-aid medicines, etc. * Ensure the luggage to be clean and disinfected and sanitize the suitcases covers, chains, locks, etc.	* High fares due to last minute bookings * Loss of money due to unexpected cancellations * Spend more time learning and finding about the socio-cultural aspects	* Increased anxiety level and concern of family/relatives/ friends/colleagues * Self-discipline and mind management * The willingness to sacrifice comfort and the desire to travel * The acceptance not to travel too far
During the journey/ at the destination	* Exposure to unexplored destinations on the way * Avoid crowded environment * Experience local/ agri/rural set up	* Avoid traveling with more passengers * Small vehicles, with proper safety measures, are preferred during road journey * More popularity for self-driven/ rent-a-vehicle concept	* Be cautious and attentive to the protocols while entering the place of stay * Sanitize hands before touching the items kept inside the room	* Avoid usage of paper documents * Use of E-sources transactions	* Encourage online payment * Promote local/ desi products/ support to cottage industries * Experience local/ethnic lifestyles/ culture and traditions	* Experience a dissimilar anxiety level while traveling with fellow passengers

	* Extra-cautious regarding flight/land transport journeys * Touchless travel/maintain social distancing * Wear mask throughout the journey period	* Be careful while having local food/visiting local restaurants	* Ensure the surrounding areas of seating to be clean and disinfected and sanitize the surfaces before touching	* Strengthen local economy * The intention to safeguard local resources * The desire to protect the cultural and natural heritage of the visited areas	* Tourism phobia – the fear, aversion or social rejection that local citizens feel towards tourists * Discernment * Always vigilant about the wellbeing and health conditions
Post-visit modalities	* Sharing experience with peer/family and recommend in destination selection * Social media promotion of destination visited	* Prefer to be received by own vehicles/extra care to be taken in case arranging public transport * Try to avoid the assistance of people in transporting luggage	* Be cautious and attentive to the protocols while entering home * Sanitize hands before touching the items kept inside home * Be careful while preparing and having food * Advised to wear mask inside home and try to be isolated for minimum three days	* Ensure the luggage to be clean and disinfected and sanitize the suitcases covers, chains, locks, etc. * If required, undergo health check-up while returning from the journey * Follow the guidelines and protocols regarding healthcare/clinical hygiene and other Precautionary measures	* Difficulties due to last minute bookings of return journey * Loss of money due to unexpected cancellation of flights * Reassure to have online payment for return travel * Be careful while dealing with cash payments/avoid cash transactions	* Encounter a differing anxiety level while interacting with family and fellow-beings * Always watchful about the wellbeing and health conditions

Source: Author's observations and findings of the study.

198   Anila Thomas

Table 12.3 Various sectors affected by COVID-19 pandemic

Sectors Affected by COVID-19

		Responses N	Responses %	Percentage of Cases
Sectors affected by COVID-19[a]	Locale	21	14.3	26.3
	Travel mode	48	32.7	60.0
	Accommodation	27	18.4	33.8
	Infrastructure and amenities	14	9.5	17.5
	Tourist activities	37	25.2	46.3
Total		147	100.0	183.8

Source: Author's observations and findings of the study.
a Dichotomy group tabulated at value 1.

Recognizing improvements in human movement during the early stages of the COVID-19 pandemic is critical for evaluating the effects of travel controls intended to limit disease transmission. Due to the closing of national borders, an increase in inbound traffic was noted around the globe, meaning that inland holiday travel could have played a greater role in mobility improvements than imminent travel restrictions. The studies revealed no evidence of significant improvements in the transportation network, and the changes that were found were only transient and did not result in systemic reorganization of the transportation network.

To control the spread of COVID-19, several countries have adopted international travel regulatory mechanisms. During recent outbreaks of two associated diseases, Severe Acute Respiratory Syndrome (SARS) and Middle East Respiratory Syndrome (MERS), several countries performed relatively the same travel related control steps (Cheshmehzangi, 2020). Air travel would be a new experience in the coming years, which is a point of concern for most travelers.

Several restrictions and protocols are now in force to ensure a smooth flight journey:

- In airports and on flights, social distance is used to minimize the possibility of physical touch. Passengers are currently advised to maintain a social gap even from security personnel. Throughout the terminal, there would be a social distancing. On flights, you will also be allowed to sit one seat apart to allow for extra room. Owing to social distancing, there could also be a restricted number of seats available at the airport.
- Masks must be worn on both flights and within airports.
- Check-ins over the internet would be welcomed.
- Time slots would be used for arrival at the airport in order to prevent long lines when inside the airport purchasing tickets or boarding the train.

- Improved sanitization. More hand-washing prompts and pop-up hand sanitization stations are possible.
- Foodservice options can be restricted across flights in order to reduce interaction between staff and customers.
- While entering or departing an airport, temperature scans or thermal imaging cameras might be used. Passenger's temperature may be taken at the airport as part of intensified passenger medical evaluation.

Generally speaking, travel related safety measures can help to restrict epidemic dissemination around country boundaries. Transnational transit limits are significantly more effective than entry points screening. Screening is expected to be more successful when combined with other interventions such as quarantine and observation. We found hardly any details on travel related quarantine as a specific measure, as well as no data on risks or harmful consequences.

It would be much more crucial in the aftermath of COVID-19. Although wide traveling will be among the last aspects of regular society to rebound from the 2020 Coronavirus pandemic, domestic tourism will be among the first to show signs of it (Table 12.4).

The table shows that the majority of people (*n* = 46) expect domestic tourism to increase in the post-COVID-19 timeframe. The standard deviation of 0.879 indicates that people's opinions on the growth of domestic tourism after the pandemic are not widely varied. The customer base has changed from foreign travelers to those looking for vacations closer to home; lower risk vacation options. Exploring one's own "backyard" is a common activity these days, with people visiting areas close to their home city and engaging with their own local community (Mathur, 2020, Domestic tourism to recover before international ... leisure tourism will rebound faster than business travel). Families, in particular, would want to get good value for their capital.

When we traverse this modern age, we realize that hygiene and healthcare can play a critical role. Spending time in rented accommodation would be

Table 12.4 Perception about growth of domestic tourism

Perception about Growth of Domestic Tourism

		Frequency	Percent	Valid Percent	Cumulative Percent	Standard Deviation
Valid	Strongly disagree	2	2.5	2.5	2.5	0.879
	Disagree	4	5.0	5.0	7.5	
	Neutral	28	35.0	35.0	42.5	
	Agree	35	43.8	43.8	86.3	
	Strongly agree	11	13.8	13.8	100.0	
	Total	80	100.0	100.0		

Source: Author's observations and findings of the study.

the most challenging, if not the most worrying, experience for a tourist. We cannot just walk into some hotel on a vacation or go on a tour with no plans. In reality, planning and booking are critical right now. The hospitality sector will address this issue in a range of methods:

- Investigating the most properly sanitized and suitable accommodation for visitors to stay in. A comprehensive modification after a customer has left the hotel is crucial. Before making any choices, look at the hotel's ratings.
- Reserve a room in advance because, in this post-COVID-19 period, pre-reservation of lodging will be crucial.
- Ensuring proper contact between the visitor and the hoteliers. Until making a reservation, inspect the hotel's hygiene and sanitation facilities.
- Do not linger in a location that has been confirmed to have a high risk of COVID-19 infection.
- Stay away from the hotel's public rooms. For example, public pools, gyms, and so on.
- Ensuring that no one occupies the tourist's room unless specifically instructed to do so by the client.
- Maintaining an acceptable distance from others, including hotel workers.
- Touch less payment is just as critical in this pretext as contact less booking.
- It is not recommended that tourists use eateries if they want to eat food brought from outside.

Another of the main issues for the post-COVID-19 protocols is to ensure the safety of visitors. There will be many policies and rules that the hospitality industry must obey in the post-COVID-19 period, but visitors bear just as much obligation for any outbreak as hoteliers.

To prevent contamination, it is recommended that the tourist disinfect his or her hands several times a day, or even immediately after making close contact with some known or unknown individual (Abale, & Charak, 2020). It is essential that each individual wash his or her hands with soap and water at least once a day for at least 20 seconds. They are often reminded to keep a sanitizer on hand at all times and to avoid touching any unsanitary objects in public. You can, for example, come into contact with baggage trolley handles, self-service check-in displays, and security trays when traveling through an airport.

When going outside, use a face mask to prevent touching your face, mouth, or eyes. When you cough or sneeze, cover your mouth and nose with a towel or your forearm. When taking long walks, do wear a face mask and keep a respectful distance from other people.

Health care professionals will offer a variety of resources to support and maintain the most properly sanitized and infection-free atmosphere possible, but they will not always be capable of protecting each person. One must exercise the same caution as they did during the COVID-19 period. Each tourist has to follow certain responsibilities while traveling to destinations (Goodwin, 2020b, Cape Town Declaration on Responsible Tourism):

- Maintain vigilance in the surroundings.
- If not absolutely necessary, do not touch any unknown or common surface areas.
- Avoid using bathroom facilities.
- As often as possible, change your clothes and take a shower after each outing.
- Should not litter.
- Keep a spacing of five feet.

Most people are aware that COVID-19 pandemic is an airborne illness (Parikh, Desai, & Parikh, 2020). Since our main goal is to minimize the chances of contamination and avoid a second outbreak of coronavirus pandemic, it is required that one wears a mask beforehand. So, while traveling between destinations, or if a tourist is spending time in a public area while on vacation, wear a face mask. The face mask should cover your mouth and nose, but it should also allow you to breathe.

Social distance between people is a significant aspect that will almost certainly determine the world's future. Stop crowds and confined spaces wherever possible. It is still advised that you stay at least two meters away from people from other households (or one meter, if other precautions are taken). Doing activities outside should make you feel more at ease. Temperature testing, socially distanced encounters, and the need to wear suitable face coverings are all steps that establishments should implement (Abale, & Charak, 2020). Some would use online scheduling services to limit the number of people who may come any one time. We will continue to enjoy travel after COVID-19, but it has given us pause to reflect on our obligations as we travel.

Tourists' Responsibilities in Rebuilding Destination during and Post-COVID-19 Period

Although several research works on pandemics (Ebola, MERS-CoV, SARS) have been published, there is a dearth of literature that explores the variables that affect tourists' travel evasion behavior as a result of COVID-19. This research would fill the void by identifying the reasons that cause tourists to avoid traveling in response to COVID-19. The tourism industry has suffered greatly as a result of the outbreak of the coronavirus disease (COVID-19). In this volatile tourism environment, every destination practitioner and researcher in the international tourism industry must observe and understand post-pandemic behaviors of international travelers. The primary goal of this study is to build a theoretical structure that explains tourists' post-pandemic obligations in reinforcing their decision-making for safer destinations.

Almost all types of tourism should endeavor for greater sustainability through inner transparency. Obtaining environmental sustainability is a continuous process that necessitates constant follow up of impacts (economic, social, and environmental) in order to capitalize on incentives and adapt to issues as they emerge, as well as advise prospective regulatory frameworks (Smith, 2020).

However, for two respondents, the table explicitly shows that, with the exception of two, nearly all study participants called for sustainability and openness as intrinsic principles in the destination planning process. Though development is expected to undergo ups and down, better accessibility for destinations, technical advances, and increased awareness for more balanced and equitable growth are expected to radically change the face of tourism by 2040 (OECD, 2018).

The augmented growth of agricultural/rural tourism demonstrates the role of such a type of tourism towards enhancing the dignity and lifestyle of people who live in rural areas. This same aspect of sustainability of rural tourism destinations helps to achieve a number of goals, including the protection of local traditions and community identity, the conservation of the environment resources and natural "ecosystems" (Petrović, Vujko, Gajić, Vuković, Radovanović, Jovanović, & Vuković, 2018), the long-term growth of the regional livelihoods, and the long-term development of the tourism industry. Strive to operate towards achieving a balanced and dynamic rural economy by developing understanding leadership and vision of policy makers in fields that they consider to be in danger for tourism and dependence on them.

Table 12.5 shows that the majority of respondents (n = 69) believe that implementing activities that support the concept of sustainable rural tourism growth is also a pressing need. The standard deviation of 0.708 indicates that the majority of respondents agree on the activities that are needed. Tourists are drawn to rural areas because they can meet their needs for vacations, recreation, adventure vacations, and learning about country life (Table 12.6).

Table 12.5 Perception about sustainability and accountability in practices

Perception about Sustainability and Accountability in Practices

		Frequency	%	Valid Percent	Cumulative Percent	Standard Deviation
Valid	No	2	2.5	2.5	2.5	0.157
	Yes	78	97.5	97.5	100.0	
	Total	80	100.0	100.0		

Source: Author's observations and findings of the study.

Table 12.6 Adopting practices for the sustainability of rural tourism

Adopting Practices for the Sustainability of Rural Tourism

		Frequency	Percent	Valid Percent	Cumulative Percent	Standard Deviation
Valid	Strongly disagree	0	0	0	0	0.708
	Disagree	1	1.3	1.3	1.3	
	Neutral	20	25.0	25.0	26.3	
	Agree	43	53.8	53.8	80.0	
	Strongly agree	16	20.0	20.0	100.0	
	Total	80	100.0	100.0		

Source: Author's observations and findings of the study.

It is indeed vital for integrating and strengthening travelers' expectations of COVID-19, and it's been reinforced by the inclusion of depressive symptoms. We can assume that, during and Post-COVID-19, spending time in a remote area surrounded by nature, eating organic plant crops in renewable energy environments (Agarwal, 2020, Domestic tourism: silver lining in the post-COVID world – KPMG India), will be an unquestionable choice over the usual options of a comfy voyage, for three reasons:

- Tourists will become more vigilant about their own wellbeing and will avoid highly urbanized tourism areas.
- After a long period of home confinement, it would be preferable to reconcile with nature while simultaneously attempting to contribute back to society by choosing local travel choices.
- Small is the new powerful experience. Travelers would choose uniqueness over commodification, giving a lift to amazingly natural and experiential destinations.

Any traveler could perhaps take guidance on potential hazards in their chosen destinations, as well as take measures to protect their health and lessen the probability of transmitting disease. They will safeguard their health and minimize the risk of injuries or sickness by planning ahead of time, getting proper preparation, and taking every precaution. While the health system and the travel industry may have a plethora of data and helpful advice, it is the responsibility of the traveler to verify information, consider risks, and take the necessary precautions to protect their health while traveling. Specialists in the wellness and hospitality industries will be equipped to supply travelers with a lot of resources and advice to help them avoid health hazards while traveling. Travelers, on the other hand, are responsible for their own health and well-being while on the trip and back, as well as preventing the transmission of infectious agents to others (World Health Organization (WHO), 28/04/2020, Travel precautions).

According to World Health Organization (2020), the main responsibilities of the traveler include:

- the travel choices;
- recognizing and recognizing the potential risks;
- obtaining medical advice in advance;
- agreeing with recommended vaccinations and all necessary medication and safety precautions;
- diligent planning before departure;
- carrying a medical kit and knowing its use;
- obtaining insurance coverage;
- ensuring health precautions
- securing a physician's endorsement on all prescribed drugs, syringes, etc. being carried;
- the protection and well-being of accompanied children;
- measures to avoid spreading any infectious disease to anyone before and after travel;
- full disclosure to a medical professional of any illness on return, including specifics on all recent travel.

Health practitioners focus their instructions, such as those for vaccinations and other medications, on an individual risk assessment for each traveler. This takes into account the person's risk of developing a disease as well as the intensity of the disease. The healthcare counselor will take into account the traveler's pre-travel health status, destination(s), length and purpose of travel, mode of transportation, accommodation and food safety conditions, and destructive behavior while flying. The evidence required to make a risk analysis is collected by an in-depth interview with the traveler. A review or protocol may assist in the collection and documentation of all relevant data. Since vaccines are often administered at several locations, the traveler should be provided with a personal record of the vaccinations acquired (patient-retained record), which should include, for example, intramuscular administration of rabies vaccine.

Eventually, this hardly matters until and unless countries work together to ensure that health needs are met while tourism will recover in a timely manner. In this regard, some countries with traditional coronavirus caseloads and case-control protocols (e.g., scanning and monitoring vs. quarantine periods) are considering the possibility of extending travel "corridors" or "bubbles" as a first venture toward establishing new markets in their countries to foreign tourism (Senanayake, 2021).

Mitigative Measures

The study offers very first overview of the destination's management to mitigate the effects of COVID-19, allowing for a detailed investigation of the procedures and strategies that were successful during the virus epidemic. There is a framework for government policy analysts and practitioners, especially in the areas of crisis management and destination resilience to overcome the issues caused by COVID-19 outbreak (Sharma, Thomas, & Paul, 2021). The findings merit further investigation into how the updated travel rebuilding process promotes risk management and the rebuilding of a tourism industry in a disaster setting, in comparison to other national programs. When a visitor visits a destination, whether national or regional, it is critical to stick to and embrace environmental values such as:

- **Using energy in a sustainable manner**
  The protection and fair use of resources – natural, social, and cultural – is critical and makes good business sense in the long run.
- **Reducing waste and overconsumption**
  Reducing overconsumption and pollution saves money on the costs of repairing long-term environmental degradation and improves tourist efficiency.
- **Protecting natural habitats**
  Sustaining and promoting physical, social, and ethnic identity is suitable for efficient social sustainability and helps to create a solid base for the sector.
- **Incorporating tourism into planning**
  Tourism growth that is incorporated into a national and local strategic planning system and conducts environmental impact evaluations improves tourism's long-term viability.
- **Assisting urban markets**
  Tourism that promotes a diverse variety of local economic operations while accounting for environmental costs and values both preserves these economies and prevents environmental harm.
- **Involvement of community organizations**
  Local people's complete engagement in the tourism sector not only benefits them and the region as a whole, but it also improves the quality of the tourism experience.
- **Collaboration with investors and the general public**
  To collaborate and resolve potential conflicts of interest, the tourism industry and local governments, organizations, and agencies must communicate.
- **Workforce training**
  Staff preparation that incorporates sustainable tourism into job activities, as well as personnel recruiting at all levels, increases the efficiency of the tourism product.
- **Responsible business marketing**
  Tourism marketing that offers complete and responsible knowledge to visitors raises appreciation for the natural, social, and cultural conditions of destination areas and improves consumer loyalty.

- **Conducting investigation and research**
  Continuous market study and reporting using efficient data collection and analysis are needed to help solve challenges and support destinations, the industry, and customers.
- **Encourage local economy**
  By choosing to eat in local shops, buying locally manufactured souvenirs and items, exploring local markets, and hiring a local tour guide... perfectly variety of living local! This way, one will be certain that the money is going back into the community and to the individuals who are welcoming everyone, rather than some anonymous business organization.
- **Visit unexplored and untapped locations**
  Yet another significant truth is that when people visiting towns, there are obvious sights to see, but consider the elusive treasures that can be discovered off the tourist trail.

Post-COVID-19 would be a period experienced at a distant land surrounded by nature for the adventurous traveler who prefers realistic vacation over other types of tourist activities for the reasons: first, visitors will be even more concerned with their own wellbeing and will disregard popular tourist destinations as a precaution. Second, they would like to live in a more environment conscious and sparsely inhabited location. After all, the COVID-19 pandemic has opened many visitors' eyes. Third, after being locked up in the house for far too long, a more logical move would be to reconnect with nature, which, combined with the commitment to providing back to society by choosing local in their tourist experiences, would be a more natural choice. Finally, tourists would always choose uniqueness to intensified commodification, boosting the popularity of tropical and experiential destinations.

Conclusion

Based on various aspects identified as part of the observations and discussions, the virus spread across the boundaries of different countries following the outbreak in Wuhan. The virus spreads at various rates across different nations, based on a variety of variables such as group cultural and behavioral reactions, population density, and so on. As a result of this trend, countries' preparedness and reactions to the crisis have varied significantly.

COVID-19 is perhaps the worst global epidemic of this century in terms of size and intensity (MacKenzie, 2020), resulting in the greatest multitude fatalities, with the majority of deaths registered in high-income countries. Amid the growing border controls and travel bans, it spread rapidly across the world through air travel. Travel sanctions, on the other hand, postponed the importation and thereby limited the size of the epidemic. Due to the high fatality rate, tackling COVID-19 would necessitate an all-government and all-society solution.

COVID-19 is reshaping the traveler's attitudes and perceptions; more associated to an intimately acquainted, stable, trustworthy, and even low-risk destination. Tourism companies and destinations are already adapting domestic and regional holidays, and with intensive training and preparation, and recreational activities, these companies will reign supreme in the near term. Proactive coordination would be essential for increasing demand. While the long-term impact of these changes remains unpredictable, the travel and tourism industry have a rare opportunity to revisit and refresh existing market models in collaboration with local communities and with regard for its most precious commodity, its inhabitants (Darbari, Ritwija, World Economic Forum (24/08/2020). Travel and tourism after COVID-19: perspectives for South Asia).

The pandemic situation provides an impetus to consider tourism's sustainability (Cawthorn, Kennaugh, & Ferreira, 2021). Tourism is at a transition point, and the policies put in motion now will affect tourism in the future. Governments must understand the crisis's long-term ramifications when capitalizing on digitalization, embracing the low-carbon transition, and fostering the institutional change needed to create a bigger, more competitive, and robust tourism industry.

References

Abale, M., & Charak, K. S. (2020). *Covid-19: The Preventive Protocol for Educational Institutions*. EduPedia Publications Pvt. Ltd.

Agarwal, V. (2020). Domestic tourism: silver lining in the post-Covid world – KPMG India. Retrieved December 12, 2020, from https://home.kpmg/in/en/blogs/home/posts/2020/05/domestic-tourism-silver-lining-in-the-post-covid-world.html.

Barkas, P., Honeck, D., & Rubio, E. (2020). *International Trade in Travel and Tourism Services: Economic Impact and Policy Responses during the COVID-19 Crisis* (No. ERSD-2020-11). WTO Staff Working Paper.

Borko, S., Greets, W., & Wang, H. (2020). *The Travel Industry Turned Upside Down: Insights, Analysis, and Actions for Travel Executives*. McKinsey and Company Skift Research.

Bricker, K. S., Black, R., & Cottrell, S. (Eds.). (2013). *Sustainable Tourism & the Millennium Development Goals: Effecting Positive Change*. Jones & Bartlett Publishers.

Budeanu, A. (2005). Impacts and responsibilities for sustainable tourism: a tour operator's perspective. *Journal of Cleaner Production, 13*(2), 89–97.

Byrd, E. T. (2007), Stakeholders in sustainable tourism development and their roles: applying stakeholder theory to sustainable tourism development. *Tourism Review, 62*(2), 6–13.

Cawthorn, D. M., Kennaugh, A., & Ferreira, S. M. (2021). The future of sustainability in the context of COVID-19. *Ambio, 50*(4), 812–821.

Cheshmehzangi, A. (2020). *The City in Need*. Springer Singapore.

Darbari, R., & World Economic Forum. (2020). Travel and tourism after COVID-19: perspectives for South Asia. Retrieved December 27, 2020, from https://www.weforum.org/agenda/2020/08/travel-and-tourism-recovery-south-asia-covid19-pandemic-economy-india-nepal-bhutan-sri-lanka/.

Feruzi, J. K. (2012). *An Evaluation of Responsible Tourism Practices in the Tanzanian Tourism Industry* (Doctoral dissertation, Cape Peninsula University of Technology).

Goodwin, H. (2011). *Taking Responsibility for Tourism* (p. 256). Goodfellow Publishers Limited.

Goodwin, H. (2020a). Responsible tourism is about the experience. Retrieved December 20, 2020, from https://haroldgoodwin.info/responsible-tourism-is-about-the-experience/.

Goodwin, H. (2020b). Cape town declaration on responsible tourism. Retrieved December 18, 2020, from https://www.printfriendly.com/p/g/ZMbz2e.

Gössling, S., Scott, D., & Hall, C. M. (2020). Pandemics, tourism and global change: a rapid assessment of COVID-19. *Journal of Sustainable Tourism, 29*(1), 1–20.

Herremans, I. M. (2006). *Cases in Sustainable Tourism: An Experiential Approach to Making Decisions.* Psychology Press.

Horton, R. (2021). *The COVID-19 Catastrophe: What's Gone Wrong and How to Stop It Happening Again.* John Wiley & Sons.

Huremović, D. (Ed.). (2019). *Psychiatry of Pandemics: A Mental Health Response to Infection Outbreak.* Springer.

Koley, T. K., & Dhole, M. (2020). *The COVID-19 Pandemic: The Deadly Coronavirus Outbreak.* Routledge India.

MacKenzie, D. (2020). Covid-19 goes global. *New Scientist, 245*(3271), 7.

Mathew, P. V., & Sreejesh, S. (2017). Impact of responsible tourism on destination sustainability and quality of life of community in tourism destinations. *Journal of Hospitality and Tourism Management, 31,* 83–89.

Mathur, S. (2020). Domestic tourism to recover before international ... leisure tourism will rebound faster than business travel. Retrieved December 27, 2020, from https://timesofindia.indiatimes.com/blogs/return-of-the-native/domestic-tourism-to-recover-before-international-leisure-tourism-will-rebound-faster-than-business-travel/.

News Article | World Travel & Tourism Council (WTTC). (2020). Retrieved December 8, 2020, from https://wttc.org/News-Article/WTTC-now-estimates-over-100-million-jobs-losses-in-the-Travel-&-Tourism-sector-and-alerts-G20-countries-to-the-scale-of-the-crisis.

O'Rourke, T., & Koščak, M. (Eds.). (2019). *Ethical and Responsible Tourism: Managing Sustainability in Local Tourism Destinations.* Routledge.

OECD (2018). "Analysing megatrends to better shape the future of tourism", OECD Tourism Papers, No. 2018/02, OECD Publishing, Paris, https://doi.org/10.1787/d465eb68-en.

Palinkas, L. A., Horwitz, S. M., Green, C. A., Wisdom, J. P., Duan, N., & Hoagwood, K. (2015). Purposeful sampling for qualitative data collection and analysis in mixed method implementation research. *Administration and Policy in Mental Health and Mental Health Services Research, 42*(5), 533–544.

Parikh, S., Desai, M., & Parikh, R. (2020). *The Coronavirus: What You Need to Know about the Global Pandemic.* Penguin eBury Press

Petrović, M. D., Vujko, A., Gajić, T., Vuković, D. B., Radovanović, M., Jovanović, J. M., & Vuković, N. (2018). Tourism as an approach to sustainable rural development in post-socialist countries: a comparative study of Serbia and Slovenia. *Sustainability, 10*(1), 54.

Rabadan, R. (2020). *Understanding Coronavirus.* Cambridge University Press.

Rodríguez-Antón, J. M., & Alonso-Almeida, M. D. M. (2020). COVID-19 impacts and recovery strategies: the case of the hospitality industry in Spain. *Sustainability*, *12*(20), 8599.

Senanayake, U. J. (2021). Threats and opportunities of the COVID 19 on tourism industry in Sri Lanka and South Asian region. *International Journal of Hospitality & Tourism Management*, *5*(1), 15.

Sharma, G. D., Thomas, A., & Paul, J. (2021). Reviving tourism industry post-COVID-19: a resilience-based framework. *Tourism management perspectives*, *37*, 100786.

Smith, F. (2020). *Environmental Sustainability: Practical Global Applications*. CRC Press.

World Health Organization. (2020). *Water, Sanitation, Hygiene, and Waste Management for the COVID-19 Virus: Interim Guidance, 23 April 2020* (No. WHO/2019-nCoV/IPC_WASH/2020.3). World Health Organization.

World Health Organization. (2020). Travel precautions. Retrieved January 12, 2020, from https://www.who.int/westernpacific/news/q-a-detail/travel-precautions.

13 Applied Ethics in Post-COVID-19 Destination Management

Jordi Arcos-Pumarola, Marta Conill-Tetuà and Núria Guitart-Casalderrey

Introduction

The World Health Organization declared a global pandemic alert in March 2020 due to COVID-19, which started at the end of 2019 (World Health Organization, 2021). Since then, it has generated an economic crisis in multiple sectors. The tourism and hospitality sector has been one of the worst affected, due to restrictions on mobility and requirements for social distancing deployed in many countries to control the disease's spread (Anguera-Torrell et al., 2020).

In this new scenario, governments' strategies for the reactivation of tourism consumption have focused on three main areas, according to Collins-Kreiner and Ram (2020). First, there has been a focus on mitigating the impact of the pandemic by, for instance, protecting the most vulnerable groups, supporting the liquidity of companies, reviewing taxes and regulations impacting tourism, and including tourism in emergency economic packages. Second, governments have concentrated on the stimulation and acceleration of the recovery by fostering tourism investment, regulative aid, and recovery programs, as well as providing training in new skills. Finally, some efforts have been made to prepare the sector for possible future crises. These actions are aimed at securing the sector's structure and vitality by supporting companies and job continuity.

Alongside government action, the sector has strived to ensure tourists' safety as individuals and strengthen their confidence in the destination. This has been done by complying with sanitary protections measures, implementing protocols, and collaborating with certifying entities in the security field. These actions aim to build trust among tourists, eliminate contagion among clients and staff, and reinforce tourism businesses' brand (Rodríguez-Antón and Alonso-Almeida 2020). Additionally, these measures help to stabilize the tourism sector and enhance its resilience should it face similar situations in the future. Nevertheless, the influence of border control measures, introduced to decrease the rate of the disease's exportation (Wells et al., 2020) poses ongoing challenges to the future of the tourism industry, since international tourism flows are deeply affected by total or partial border

DOI: 10.4324/9781003207467-18

lockdowns and other measures, such as testing visitors (before departure or upon arrival) and quarantine (UNWTO, 2020). The constant changes in these measures around the world, in reaction to changing health data in individual countries, means that tourists have been reluctant to make travel plans. In this context, the tourism industry has been asking for less restrictive measures that permit travelling while controlling the spread of disease: for instance, the testing on arrival of tourists who want to enter a destination.

Nevertheless, the use of health resources such as tests in order to restart the tourism industry is not free from ethical issues, especially in countries where health resources for the local population are scarce. The following chapter will focus on this debate, emphasizing the new insights into the tourism industry that arise from adopting an applied-ethics approach. As Lew et al. (2020) state, the situation that COVID-19 has produced in the tourism industry created an opportunity to rethink how the sector should operate once it is restarted. In this vein, we will present the applied ethics perspective as vital to allowing a fairer and more sustainable restoration of the tourism industry.

In the following sections, we will highlight various cases where PCR (polymerase chain reaction) tests and other health resources have been made available for visitors in order to revitalize the tourism industry. Then, we will clarify the various arguments for and against this approach from an ethical point of view. This reflection will help us shed light on the various conceptions of tourism that are behind the arguments. Finally, we will highlight the need to adopt a holistic perspective when dealing with ethical dilemmas in tourism, due to the complexity of the phenomenon (Fennell, 2015).

Using Health Resources to Foster the Tourism Industry

COVID-19 has highlighted – and in many cases, broadened – the differences that exist in some destinations between citizens and visitors, to an extent that in some cases could be considered ethically questionable. For example, Turkey welcomes tourists and lets them visit its main attractions and stay in hotels without providing any test results or undergoing quarantine upon arrival. However, its own citizens are obliged to stay at home: Istanbul has a curfew from 9 pm to 5 am, and those who break the rules are fined. None of these restrictions or fines applies to foreign tourists who can visit and wander the city freely. Such decisions are not only implemented by countries such as Turkey, but recommended in the European Draft Report on Establishing an EU Strategy for Sustainable Tourism, which announced that "the imposition of new restrictions, in the event of adverse developments in epidemiological conditions, should not include travellers that are already in the destination" (Committee on Transport and Tourism, 2020).

Even if these exceptions can be argued from an economic point of view (avoiding job losses or guaranteeing local income, for instance), they are debatable from both health and the ethical perspectives. Indeed, in many places, residents are starting to feel this situation is unfair. A *New York Times* article on the situation in Istanbul highlights voices such as Tulin Polat's, a waitress who has been laid off due to lockdown measures: "I'm happy for tourists to visit my country, but when hospitals are full, and people are dying, this is not an appropriate time to be adventurous" (Yeginsu, 2020). This highlights one of the key questions facing the industry: is tourism valid when hospitals are strained to breaking point, resources are limited, and citizens' rights, such as mobility, are restricted?

The containment of COVID-19 is particularly difficult in a globalized world, international mobility being one of the main factors contributing to the pandemic's spread (Kubota et al., 2020). The limitation of cross-border mobility is a useful measure to contain the pandemic in an era of hypermobility (Urry, 2013), mainly because it helps avoid exporting cases from significantly affected territories (Kraemer et al., 2020). This was why most countries completely closed their borders during the spring of 2020 (UNWTO, 2020). Nevertheless, given the significant role tourism plays in national economies, travel restrictions have been progressively eased to revitalize the tourism industry (Seyfi et al., 2020). Thus, by the beginning of May, most countries began to reopen their borders but still imposed some limitations.

In most countries, visitors have been required to follow social distancing and hygienic measures such as wearing masks in public (depending on the country, this might mean everywhere, or only in indoor spaces such as museums, monuments, and so on). Meanwhile, restaurants have been required to limit capacity and sometimes their schedules, in cases where curfews apply, as well as adapt to rules that only permit outdoor dining. Moreover, entry to destinations has also been subject to various restrictions following the partial opening of borders. These include destination-specific travel restrictions to COVID-19 hotspots, the request of a negative PCR test certificate upon or after arrival, quarantine upon arrival, registration through "passenger locator forms" to facilitate track-and-trace measures, among others (UNWTO, 2020).

For the purpose of this chapter, we will focus on countries that requested negative PCR tests when travelling. Certification might be required at various stages of travel: the tourist might be required to submit a negative result certificate on arrive, or required to undergo a test at the destination's airport, or be tested after a period of self-isolation/quarantine. These three models for using PCR tests, all designed to foster international tourism while trying to avoid importing infected individuals, have very different impacts from the tourist's point of view. The first – having to present a negative PCR certificate – requires the tourist to pay for a test, increasing the preparation time and cost of travelling. On the contrary, the second option, testing upon arrival at the airport, makes it simpler to prepare for travel and, if the result is negative, the tourist is free to enjoy the destination. The third option, a negative PCR result after quarantine, makes it extremely difficult to travel and undermines the destination's attractiveness, since the visitor must spend part of their trip in self-isolation, locked down in an enclosed space.

Considering this, it seems clear that testing international tourists upon arrival is the most attractive option to boost the tourism industry while containing the pandemic's spread. However, the way this policy is applied can lead to some very strong debates within a country. Below we consider some examples from Southern Europe.

In Spain, the response has taken on several different forms as different Autonomous Communities have tried to set their own specific requirements for international tourism arrivals, mostly aimed at easing restrictions and supporting the tourism industry. This approach not only risks overruling national regulations but can also potentially lead to grievances between regions with unequal approaches.

For instance, the local government of the Canary Islands decided in August to pay the medical costs of any tourists that contracted COVID-19 during their vacation on the islands. This policy aimed to restart tourism and restore the destination's attractiveness. The cost of covering the claims was expected to reach €450,000, from which €100,000 were obtained from the Governing Council of the Canary Islands in the form of a loan to the public company Promotur.[1] More recently, the Andalusian Autonomous Community approved, through the Vice-President of the Board and the Tourism Council, free medical insurance for international tourists who stay at regulated accommodation establishments, covering any medical, surgical and hospitalization expenditure in addition to repatriation or extension of stay due to mandatory quarantines (Martínez, 2021).

Portugal's tourism authority, in agreement with RNA Seguros de Assistência, implemented a similar system just as international borders were beginning to reopen, which covered all medical, pharmaceutical and hospital expenses associated with COVID-19.

These various approaches to implementing free COVID-19 health insurance for tourists seem to provide supporting evidence for the need to respond to the demands of the sector by reactivating the hotelier sector, differentiating destinations' offer, and regaining confidence of tourists by reinforcing the region's image as a safe travel destination. Indeed, these initiatives have proven effective for the recovery of the tourism industry: in the Canary Islands, bookings rose by 31.6% after the health insurance policy went public (Fenton and Penza, 2020). However, the controversy of such measures centre on whether government funds should be used to finance international tourists' private healthcare instead of being used to safeguard the population, their ability to access resources, and the integrity of the health system.

Another controversy emerged when the Canary Islands autonomous president admitted, in November 2020, that he was considering accepting the quicker but less reliable antigen tests for visitors arriving in the archipelago. This controversial proposal, supported by Tenerife's Hospital de la Candelaria and published in the Canary Islands Decree 87/2020 of December 9, 2020, meant that the perimeter closure of the Autonomous Community[2] conflicted with the General Directorate of Public Health Resolution of November 11, 2020 regarding the sanitary controls to be carried out at all points of entry from Spain,[3] which required a PCR or Transcription-Mediated Amplification (TMA) test for all foreign passengers arriving by sea and air.

Another controversial proposal was discussed by the Balearic government and the Association of Hoteliers back in May 2020. Although the tourism minister and the regional minister supported the strategy of testing at the point of origin, recommending that travellers have tests in advance, they discussed paying for PRC for international visitor's tests to guarantee that they were carried out. This measure has now been included in the high season recovery plan "Ibiza Reinicia 2021", which expects to spend from €7 million to €80 million to conduct a total of 800,000 PCR tests on travellers arriving from March 2021 (Tur, 2021).

When it comes to the objective of stimulating the tourism market, funding testing upon arrival seems a reasonable measure. However, and depending on the context in each country, it can also raise a number of ethical dilemmas, particularly with regard to the extraordinary and sustained demands COVID-19 has placed on public health systems all around the world, and the resultant need to ration health resources and reflect carefully on how to allocate them fairly (Emanuel et al., 2020). Spain is no exception: its health system has suffered severe shortages of resources, including to personal protective equipment (PPE) and tests (Deusdad, 2020).

Taking this context into account, in the following sections, we will contrast the ethical arguments for and against testing tourists on arrival, to seek an ethical approach to this controversy that could also be applied to other tourism policies.

Reflecting on the Use of Health Resources to Foster the Tourism Industry from an Ethical Approach

Legitimizing the Funding of Testing upon Arrival: The Consequentialist Approach

The reasoning underlying the various policies mentioned above arises from a consequentialist approach. Consequentialism includes various theories that, despite their divergences, all put the focus of moral judgement on the consequences of actions (Sinnot-Armstrong, 2019). From this perspective, an action is right when it produces a desirable outcome (Lovelock and Lovelock, 2006).

In terms of the case study of this chapter, prioritising the testing of tourists can be justified in terms of producing positive wellbeing outcomes due to the expected economic benefits derived from tourist expenditure. In this sense, using PCR tests that are property of the country on visitors is justified because this will contribute to the common good by supporting the economy and avoiding probable unemployment and the closure of businesses involved in tourism and related economic sectors. This position is exemplified by the approach of governments such as that of the Balearic Islands, whose Councillor for Economic Model, Tourism and Labour, Iago Negueruela, declared, after meeting with hoteliers, that testing foreign and Spanish tourists on arrival was necessary to reactivate tourism and should be established as soon as possible, especially before the Easter season (Santana, 2020). Moreover, policies that permit the recovery of the tourism industry and promote international tourism flows may decrease the pandemic's overall impact on national budgets, allowing a potential increase in public spending on the healthcare system to the benefit of the local population.

The potential positive economic outcomes of these measures may seem obvious and, in a non-scarcity context, their implementation is reasonable. This situation is well illustrated by Iceland, where anyone who wants to be tested for coronavirus can, even if they do not display symptoms. This decision enabled 5% of the total population to be tested by April 2, 2020, long before they considered reopening international borders. By 25 November, 55% of the total population had been tested (Scudellari, 2020). In this favourable resource management context, Iceland's Ministry of Finance and Economic Affairs sought to revive the tourism sector for intervals, from June to August (2020) and December to January (2021), by facilitating free double screening arrangements for visitors: upon arrival and after a five-day compulsory quarantine.

However, in situations where local residents and healthcare workers struggle to access essential services such as testing, the diversion of vital resources to visitors can be ethically controversial. The following section will present three different arguments that clash with the consequentialist approach.

Counter-Arguments against the Consequentialist Approach

The Justice Argument

Distributive justice is concerned with the distribution of benefits and burdens. To decide on this distribution, concepts such as equality, priority, sufficiency and desert are applied (Vallentyne, 2007). The desert approach to distributive justice stresses that people should get what they deserve. One of the dimensions taken into account when defining what people deserve is the notion of contribution. For example, the individual's contribution to society may be a relevant factor in their right to claim benefits (Lamm and Schwinger, 1980).

As Tedmanson et al. (2013) state, tourism is an industry that may raise issues of injustice, since it involves people from different places, potentially introducing unequal relations of power and a different gaze to the territory. Mostly, such questions have been related to particular tourism typologies. For instance, when ethically confronting the phenomenon of medical tourism, the concept of distributive justice is placed under the spotlight, because visitors seeking medical treatment can have a negative impact on the distribution of health resources and fair access to medical treatment within the local population (Lovelock and Lovelock, 2006).

Applying this approach to our case study forces us to question whether the use of tests to exclusively support one economic sector might negatively affect the local population's medical access, that is, their access to a primary good. In this sense, the allocation of limited resources to foster tourism can be understood as unjust in two different senses.

First, tests are set aside for visitors to the residents' detriment. Mass testing and monitoring to identify infected individuals in the population is essential to control the spread of COVID-19 (Binnicker, 2020). When tests are diverted to boost the tourism sector, tracking the local population becomes harder, and this policy can thus lead to more restrictive measures being imposed on the local population. Many would argue that supporting tourism by using scarce national resources, while at the same time restricting residents' free movement and social interactions, is unfair. It is especially unfair if residents are forced to respond to the lack of health resources by adapting their daily lives to additional restrictions imposed by the local government. Usually, such restrictions are focused on residents' spare time, while work-related activities are, as far as possible, protected to avoid an economic crisis that could worsen the situation. In terms of distributive justice, if residents perceive that they are sacrificing their personal freedoms for the common good, while resources that could ultimately reduce the limits on their freedom are instead being used to attract visitors who can enjoy their free time as they please, then people's sense of distributive justice might decrease, affecting not only their quality of life but their perception of the tourism sector (Su et al., 2019).

Against this point of view, it could be contended that moral deserts do not represent a suitable basis for distributing resources within a society. Different theories of justice support this argument, some of them broadly recognized, such as Rawl's theory of justice, which distinguishes between moral deserts and legitimate expectations (Rawls, 1971). Through this distinction, Rawls aims to separate the idea of justice from the traditional conception that understands it as a reward for good behaviour, that is, as a fair return for virtue, talent, or individual effort (O'Neill, 2014). Instead, he proposes the notion of legitimate expectations, understood as the legitimate claims that individuals are entitled to when they take part in just arrangements in a just society. He illustrates this distinction through the example of a championship match in which the losing team has played better than the winning one. The first deserved the victory but is not entitled to claim the championship. This example shows that what we should expect from society is not always linked to what we morally expect, but is defined through social and public arrangements and institutions.

This could problematize the presented argument we used to start this section, which highlighted the use of the desert dimension of justice to justify the claim that health resources should be allocated to residents and not used for encouraging tourism. According to that argument, the residents' contributions to "flattening the curve" of COVID-19 infections by sacrificing their rights to free movement makes them morally deserving of prioritization for health resources. However, as O'Neill (2014) affirms, legitimate expectations provide us with a theoretical framework to adapt the desert approach to the social and public sphere. In this sense, even when we cannot affirm that their individual contribution to the common good makes citizens morally deserving of receiving health resources, their status as citizens entitles them to claim access. This is particularly relevant in the case of Spain, which has signed international treaties that defend health as a fundamental right (Lema Tomé, 2014). Thus, a distributive justice approach to resource allocation must take into consideration the existing social agreements and what resources citizens are legitimately able to expect from their society.

Second, beyond the desert dimension of justice, this policy may also affect the equality approach to justice, from two different perspectives. The consequentialist approach presented in the previous section can be criticized for generating unequal access to resources between visitors and residents who might not be allowed to travel, or decide not to travel because they do not wish to be responsible for spreading the virus, or who cannot afford to travel. Residents who remain within the destination for any of these three reasons are bound to a territory that hinders their access to the health system in order to receive individuals who can travel.

This policy also promotes inequality between territories of the same state. For example, when tourism activity is one of the factors determining the distribution of tests, territories without a consolidated tourism infrastructure may receive fewer tests than would be the case were other factors prioritised. Thus, the consequentialist approach includes the tourism industry in the distributive justice debate while making it an actor in distributing health resources (Jamal and Camargo, 2014). As a result, the consequentialist argument tips the scales in the debate between health and the economy, typically in favour of the latter.

Undermining Tourism as a Social Practice

Beyond the idea of justice, it is necessary to reflect on the effects on the tourism phenomenon. The arguments for implementing free testing or healthcare for tourists' approach tourism principally from an economic point of view. Following Sandel's (2012) thoughts on the effects of marketization on society, an ethical approach should question whether this policy, which is based on a mercantilist approach to tourism, might be crowding out other ways of comprehending tourism and whether it represents a devaluation of tourism as a social practice. The primacy of economic interpretations of social activities can potentially produce what Sandel calls the "skyboxification" of life, by which he means the social division that commercialism introduces in a community (Sandel, 2012).

Sandel's reflections on the effects of marketization were developed from the context of the members of a single society. Nevertheless, our case study and, concretely, the equality argument presented in the previous section permit us to develop a similar line of reasoning. In this vein, the unequal treatment of visitors and residents may undermine the quality of a destination's tourism activity. This is because tourism is not merely an economic activity, but also a social activity that people undertake to fulfil social, subjective or cultural yearnings (Donaire, 2008). In other words, tourism requires the presence of otherness, as the understanding of tourism as a quest for authenticity reveals (MacCannell, 1999), an authenticity that are based on the existence of spaces for social encounters and experiences. Managing tourism without paying attention to this other facet undermines its essence as a social practice.

Reflecting on the consequences of that, it seems conceivable that the unequal treatment of residents and visitors may lead residents to resent tourism activity during the pandemic. Beyond this fact tourist represents a potential vector for spreading the disease; this is especially likely if tourists are treated as an advantaged social group, displacing residents in terms of resource allocation. This might lead to the social rejection of visitors and, as a result, to an unwelcoming atmosphere that harms the tourism experience.

This view is also relevant in contexts where, even before the COVID-19 pandemic, the tourism industry had to address critics and social perceptions of its impacts (Guitart-Casalderrey et al., 2018). Some cities that have based their economy on the third sector have seen an urgent need to address rising conflict between citizens and visitors, over issues such as access to certain public services; the use of public spaces, monuments or attractions; or overcrowded public transportation. In particular, many destinations are experiencing an increasing sense among citizens that their cities have become primarily tourist destinations and all developments have been in favour of tourism, with little or no regard for the needs of those who live and work there.

Discussion and Conclusion: Rethinking the Consequentialist Perspective

The complex system formed by present destinations, and the complicated situation faced by many destinations during the pandemic mean that the tourism industry interacts with and plays a role in debates beyond the limits of the sector, such as access to health systems and the allocation of health resources. To tackle the dilemmas arising from this context, tourism academics cannot depart from a restricted industry perspective. In this vein, the last section showed that adding an ethical dimension to our perspectives on the complex issues surrounding tourism in a pandemic enriches our discussion of the consequences of tourism policies. The process has shown that successful application of ethics to real contexts does not rely on finding a perfect theory. Rather, it involves considering various ethical theories that can heighten our understanding of the situation, permitting us to make better choices (Román, 2016).

Considering our case study and adopting an ethical approach, the above discussions have revealed several concerns that need to be taken into account when managing tourism in a pandemic. Local societies are essential actors in tourism activities, not only in a practical sense – in that they sustain the industry with their workforce and inhabitants' lives are influenced by the positive and negative impacts of tourism – but also in a more existential way, because societies give sense to territories. Therefore, tourism policies must not treat the industry as an isolated agent but bear in mind the role of local communities and how they are treated. This is the perspective that Rastegar et al. (2021) embrace when adopting the notion of justice to rethink the framework for guaranteeing a responsible and just recovery of the tourism industry after the COVID-19 pandemic.

The COVID-19 crisis has drawn attention to – and provoked or worsened – global problems that are common in various spheres of society, including in popular tourist destinations. Nowadays, responsible tourism theories conceptualize locals and visitors as citizens as permanent or *temporary citizens* respectively (Goodwin, 2019). This designation, citizenship, implies rights, but also duties, to everyone who bears it. In this regard, it engenders responsibilities and also a sense of community, a key requirement for fostering the individual's contribution to the common good. From this perspective, several dilemmas arise. For instance, there is the question of whether it is appropriate to travel when mobility is restricted, especially when the permanent residents of the destination must remain at home or have restricted mobility within their city or country. Is travelling and having access to medical resources therefore a privilege? Is it ethical to prioritize tourists' health to maintain a particular type of economy when hospitals are at risk of being overwhelmed dealing with the disease?

The various arguments presented in the previous sections may shed light on these questions and offer new insights to policymakers. The concept of justice and the holistic understanding of tourism as a social practice go beyond simplistic consequentialist arguments and highlight the possible mid-range and long-term results of our decisions. In the presented case, the call for free tests for tourists reinforces tourism as an industry alienated from society. This perspective may also incite resentment and lead to an atmosphere of exclusion, especially if residents feel unrecognized by a government that emphasizes the distinction between them and the visitors, by ensuring the latter are given priority over scarce and desirable resources. This holds true in contexts beyond the one considered in this chapter: the issues analysed here resonate strongly with other challenges raised in the literature regarding the coexistence of tourists and residents in popular destinations.

Bringing these arguments to light provides an opportunity to address further dilemmas arising from the reactivation of the tourism sector from an applied theoretical approach. For instance, the ethics perspective allows us to address future challenges for the tourism sector, such as how to use vaccine passports as a way to facilitate a gradual return to the free movement of tourists while avoiding the risk of discriminatory consequences that might otherwise arrive when tourists from wealthy countries travel to less wealthy countries with weakened health systems. To conclude, we argue that to enhance the coexistence of tourists and residents, destination managers must consider this conceptual approach when designing tourism policies. In this sense, the concept of tourist as a temporary resident and not just a customer should be reconsidered to ensure fairness between both groups, easing the destination's inclusion and social sustainability.

Notes

1 Promotur is the Canary Islands' Tourist Board. Further information on this public company can be viewed at: https://turismodeislascanarias.com/en/.
2 This decree, published by the Canarias Official Gazette, can be viewed at: http://www.gobiernodecanarias.org/boc/2020/252/001.html.
3 This resolution, published by the Spanish Official State Gazette, can be viewed at: https://www.boe.es/boe/dias/2020/11/12/pdfs/BOE-A-2020-14049.pdf.

References

Anguera-Torrell, Oriol, Juan Pedro Aznar-Alarcón, and Jordi Vives-Perez. 2020. "COVID-19: Hotel Industry Response to the Pandemic Evolution and to the Public Sector Economic Measures." *Tourism Recreation Research*: 1–10. https://doi.org/10.1080/02508281.2020.1826225.

Binnicker, Matthew J. 2020. "Emergence of a Novel Coronavirus Disease (COVID-19) and the Importance of Diagnostic Testing: Why Partnership between Clinical Laboratories, Public Health Agencies, and Industry Is Essential to Control the Outbreak." *Clinical Chemistry* 666: 664–66. https://doi.org/10.1093/clinchem/hvaa071.

Collins-Kreiner, Noga, and Yael Ram. 2020. "National Tourism Strategies during the Covid-19 Pandemic." *Annals of Tourism Research*, January. https://doi.org/10.1016/j.annals.2020.103076.

Committee on Transport and Tourism. 2020. "Draft Report on Establishing an EU Strategy for Sustainable Tourism (2020/2038(INI))."

Deusdad, Blanca. 2020. "COVID-19 and Care Homes and Nursing Homes Crisis in Spain: Ageism and Scarcity of Resources." *Research on Ageing and Social Policy* 8 (2020): 142–68. https://doi.org/10.17583/rasp.2020.5598.

Donaire, José Antonio. 2008. *Turisme Cultural. Entre l'experiència i El Ritual*. Bellcaire d'Empordà: Edicions Vitel·la.

Emanuel, Ezekiel J., Govind Persad, Ross Upshur, Beatriz Thome, Michael Parker, Aaron Glickman, Cathy Zhang, Connor Boyle, Maxwell Smith, and James P. Phillips. 2020. "Fair Allocation of Scarce Medical Resources in the Time of Covid-19." *New England Journal of Medicine* 382 (21): 2049–55. https://doi.org/10.1056/nejmsb2005114.

Fennell, David A. 2015. "Education for Sustainability in Tourism." In *Education for Sustainability in Tourism: A Handbook of Processes, Resources and Strategies*, edited by Dianne Dredge, 75–90. https://doi.org/10.1007/978-3-662-47470-9.

Fenton, Rosaleen, and Natalia Penza. 2020. "Canary Islands to Cover Costs If Brits Catch Coronavirus on Holiday." *The Mirror*, 6 August 2020. https://www.mirror.co.uk/travel/news/canary-islands-cover-costs-holidaymakers-22480658.

Goodwin, Harold. 2019. "Managing Tourism in Barcelona." *Institute of Place Management, Manchester Metropolitan University* 1 (2019): 1–39. http://ajuntament.barcelona.cat/turisme/en/presentation.

Guitart-Casalderrey, Nuria, Jessica Alcalde Garcia, Anna Pitarch Mach, and Óscar Vallvé Fernández. 2018. "De La Turismofobia a La Convivencia Turística: El Caso de Barcelona. Análisis Comparativo Con Ámsterdam y Berlín." *ARA: Revista de Investigación En Turismo* 8 (2): 25–34. http://revistes.ub.edu/index.php/ara/article/view/21980/28461.

Jamal, T., and B. A. Camargo. 2014. "Sustainable Tourism, Justice and an Ethic of Care: Toward the Just Destination." *Journal of Sustainable Tourism* 22 (1): 11–30. https://doi.org/10.1080/09669582.2013.786084.

Kraemer, Moritz U. G., Chia Hung Yang, Bernardo Gutierrez, Chieh Hsi Wu, Brennan Klein, David M. Pigott, Louis du Plessis, et al. 2020. "The Effect of Human Mobility and Control Measures on the COVID-19 Epidemic in China." *MedRxiv* 497 (May): 493–97. https://doi.org/10.1101/2020.03.02.20026708.

Kubota, Yasuhiro, Takayuki Shiono, Buntarou Kusumoto, and Junichi Fujinuma. 2020. "Multiple Drivers of the COVID-19 Spread: The Roles of Climate, International Mobility, and Region-Specific Conditions." *PLoS ONE* 15 (9 September): 1–15. https://doi.org/10.1371/journal.pone.0239385.

Lamm, Helmut, and Thomas Schwinger. 1980. "Norms Concerning Distributive Justice: Are Needs Taken into Consideration in Allocation Decisions? Auth." *Social Psychology Quarterly* 43 (4): 425–29.

Lema Tomé, Margarita. 2014. "Health Care Reform in Spain: The Situation of Undocumented Immigrant Population." *Eunomía* 5: 95–115.

Lew, Alan A., Joseph M. Cheer, Michael Haywood, Patrick Brouder, and Noel B. Salazar. 2020. "Visions of Travel and Tourism after the Global COVID-19 Transformation of 2020." *Tourism Geographies* 22 (3): 455–66. https://doi.org/10.1080/14616688.2020.1770326.

Lovelock, Brent, and Kirsten Lovelock. 2006. *The Ethics of Tourism*. New York: Routledge. https://doi.org/10.1017/CBO9781107415324.004.

MacCannell, Dean. 1999. *The Tourist: A New Theory of the Leisure Class*. Berkeley: University of California Press.

Martínez, Pilar. 2021. "Los Turistas Extranjeros Que Viajen a Andalucía Tienen Ya Un Seguro Gratis Por Covid-19." *Diario Sur*, 2021. https://www.diariosur.es/turismo/seguro-coronavirus-extranjeros-andalucia-20210107191130-nt.html.

O'Neill, Martin. 2014. "Legitimate Expectations." In *The Rawls Lexicon*, edited by D. Reidy, and J. Mandle. Cambridge University Press. https://doi.org/10.5040/9781509925360.ch-005.

Rastegar, Raymond, Freya Higgins-Desbiolles, and Lisa Ruhanen. 2021. "COVID-19 and a Justice Framework to Guide Tourism Recovery." *Annals of Tourism Research*. In press. https://doi.org/10.1016/j.annals.2021.103161.

Rawls, John. 1971. *A Theory of Justice*. Harvard University Press. https://doi.org/10.2307/j.ctt22nmdb8.12.

Rodríguez-Antón, José Miguel, and María Del Mar Alonso-Almeida. 2020. "COVID-19 Impacts and Recovery Strategies: The Case of the Hospitality Industry in Spain." *Sustainability (Switzerland)* 12 (20): 1–17. https://doi.org/10.3390/su12208599.

Román, Begoña. 2016. *Ética de Los Servicios Sociales*. Barcelona: Herder.

Sandel, Michael J. 2012. *What Money Can't Buy. The Moral Limits of Markets*. London: Penguin.

Santana, Mayka. 2020. "Baleares Realizará Test Rápidos de COVID a Los Turistas." 2020. https://www.hosteltur.com/140367_baleares-contempla-poder-a-hacer-test-rapidos-de-covid-a-los-turistas.html.

Scudellari, Megan. 2020. "How Iceland Hammered COVID with Science." *Nature* 587 (7835): 536–39. https://doi.org/10.1038/d41586-020-03284-3.

Seyfi, Siamak, C. Michael Hall, and Bardia Shabani. 2020. "COVID-19 and International Travel Restrictions: The Geopolitics of Health and Tourism." *Tourism Geographies*: 1–17. https://doi.org/10.1080/14616688.2020.1833972.

Sinnot-Armstrong, Walter. 2019. "Consequentialism." 2019. https://plato.stanford.edu/archives/sum2019/entries/consequentialism/.

Su, Lujun, Songshan (Sam) Huang, and Mehran Nejati. 2019. "Perceived Justice, Community Support, Community Identity and Residents' Quality of Life: Testing an Integrative Model." *Journal of Hospitality and Tourism Management* 41 (August): 1–11. https://doi.org/10.1016/j.jhtm.2019.08.004.

Tedmanson, Deirdre, Freya Higgins-desbiolles, and Kyle Powys Whyte. 2013. "Tourism and Environmental Justice." In *Just Leisure*, edited by K. Schwab, and D. Dustin. Urbana: Sagamore.

Tur, Joan. 2021. "El PSOE Dice Que El Plan 'Ibiza Reinicia 2021' Es 'Inviable' Sin El Visto Bueno de Otras Instituciones." SER. 2021. https://cadenaser.com/emisora/2021/01/06/radio_ibiza/1609932024_353903.html.

UNWTO. 2020. "Covid-19 Related Travel Restrictions a Global Review for Tourism." *World Tourism Organization*, September, 1– 40. https://webunwto.s3.eu-west-1.amazonaws.com/s3fs-public/2020-09/200909-travel-restrictions.pdf

Urry, J. 2013. "Mobility and Proximity." *Sotsiologicheskie Issledovaniya* 36 (2): 3–14.

Vallentyne, Peter. 2007. "Distributive Justice." In *A Companion to Contemporary Political Philosophy*, edited by R. Goodin, P. Pettit, and T. Pogge, 548–62. Oxford: Blackwell Publishing.

Wells, Chad R., Pratha Sah, Seyed M. Moghadas, Abhishek Pandey, Affan Shoukat, and Yaning Wang. 2020. "Impact of International Travel and Border Control Measures on the Global Spread of the Novel 2019 Coronavirus Outbreak" 117 (13). https://doi.org/10.1073/pnas.2002616117.

World Health Organization. 2021. "Timeline: WHO's COVID-19 Response." 2021. https://www.who.int/emergencies/diseases/novel-coronavirus-2019/interactive-timeline#!.

Yeginsu, Ceylan. 2020. "Istanbul Is Locking Down. But Not If You're a Tourist." *The New York Times*, 8 December 2020. https://www.nytimes.com/2020/12/08/travel/istanbul-tourists-curfew.html?smid=wa-share.

Part Five
COVID-19 and Tourism Governance

14 Impact of COVID-19 Pandemic on the Tourism Industry in Sri Lanka

The Dilemmas of Industry Sustainability

R. S. S. W Arachchi and W. K. A. C Gnanapala

Introduction

The effect of COVID-19 global pandemic to the tourism industry caused the complete shutdown of tourism operations not only in Sri Lanka but also in the global context. The world economy is now at a very crisis situation and the economists are telling that the crisis situation likely to remain this way until at least the last quarter of this year. However, WHO has predicted the pandemic remain in even 2021. The remedial measures are taken by many countries to recover the tourism supply chain over the coming months. Even though the tourism supply chains come to the normal operations again, demand-side recovery will take more time, given the interlinked consequences of the economic and health crises, and the progressive lifting of travel restrictions. Therefore, the negative consequences of the COVID-19 epidemic on tourism industry may be more severe than the expected level. The Sri Lankan Government and the industry professionals are taking various measures to take the industry into normality and maintain the sustainability of tourism businesses. The government is in a challenging situation to develop resilience strategies to overcome the devastating impacts faced by the tourism in Sri Lanka.

Purpose and the Significance of the Research

Main objectives of this paper are, first, to identify the impact of COVID-19 pandemic on the tourism industry in the world and second, to identify the sustainability issues faced by the tourism operators in Sri Lanka. Further, the study addresses the resilience strategies required by the industry to sustain their business during and post-pandemic situation. This review is really important for policy makers and planners as well as industry operators to plan the continuation of business in future. Further, success stories of the Sri Lankan tourism sector can be used by the other countries in their context while avoiding the negative impacts caused by the COVID-19.

DOI: 10.4324/9781003207467-20

Methodology

The study was carried out using different methods. It employed qualitative methodology. First, a desk review was done to identify the impact COVID-19 pandemic on tourism industry using different data sources. Then, the semi structured interviews were held with the officials of the Sri Lanka Tourism and Development Authority (SLTDA), travel agents, hoteliers, industry associates to identify the true effect of the pandemic and the resilience strategies expected by them for the sustainable business.

Findings

The findings revealed that the industry is severely affected and currently around 12,000 tourists are blocked in the country. Some tourism operations are temporarily and permanently closed down and moving towards other businesses. The government is eagerly waiting with the financial motives to reopen the airport and bring tourists back to the country. The industry is trying to function their operations with the domestic and foreign markets especially the hoteliers. All the income sources of the country have been blocked. The country is facing a severe financial crisis and they think tourism as the panacea for its all ill. The tourism and hospitality sector is facing the challenges of regaining the business position and sustainability, engaging with employees and stakeholders, building a proper tourism resilience plan, transforming tourism and hospitality spaces to suit COVID-19 lifestyle. However, it will not be easy in short run in the pandemic affected economies and societies and, therefore, it need to use resilience strategies effectively.

Implications

First, it is necessary to assess the affected parties and give guidance, financial and other supports immediately to retain them in the industry. Further, the authorities need to use short, medium and long-term resilient strategies effectively to ensure the sustainable tourism development in the post-COVID-19 pandemic. The tourism hospitality sector has to transform the business as suitable to the expectations of the tourists under new normal. However, it is a more challenging task for the industry. Therefore, it is necessary to have more independent, transparent and collective works effectively.

The COVID-19 pandemic has created a huge impact of the livelihood of the global citizens who mainly depend on tourism. Due to the fast spreading of the corona virus the airports, cities, and countries are closed or lock downed. Further, millions of people were in quarantine with hundreds of travels bans in place. COVID-19 has brought the global tourism industry to a grinding halt. COVID-19 is an unprecedented crisis; therefore, the destination management organization does not have any previous experiences and even they cannot imagine what kinds of strategies would be used to overcome the devastating situation. This pandemic has impacted different tourism regions in the world in various scales. Mostly tourism generating regions were heavily affected such as Europe, North and South American regions and China and Southeast Asian countries. Due to these impacts, as a South Asian Country as well as world number one tourism destination in 2020 Sri Lanka is facing a huge challenge of continuing the tourism industry sustainability.

Sri Lanka has identified tourism as one of the key development strategies of its local economy. The industry has been growing rapidly since 2009 after ending the terrorism problem of the country in the same year and the total tourist arrivals has exceeded 2.3 million in 2018. Tourism represents the 3rd largest income earner of the country, during last few years, and therefore, government wishes to become tourism as the main income earner. The country has taken much effort to promote the tourism industry though developing new products, source markets and other strategies. The industry was well prepared to welcome he tourists and satisfy them to meet their business objectives. However, the industry operation was come to a stop point, the industry faced a lot of big crisis and survival strategies are needed.

The tourism industry in Sri Lanka is totally collapsed, the cities are lockdown, airports are closed, and many travel restrictions. Since the situation has happened in the middle part of the holiday season, the tourists were in resorts while having round tours. Since the virus is attacking and spreading very fast in other country, the government suddenly decided to close down airport and the same time made travel restrictions to control the spreading of the deadly virus. At the same time impose the curfew covering Whole Island to control the mobility of citizens. The tourist started to leave the country, but they faced many difficulties to rearrange the return journey since most of the air ports were totally closed down.

Those who come through travel agents and other parties took the responsibility and facilitate their stay in the country safely. However, the majority of tourists has arrived to country as FIT arranging their own travel, also they are budget conscious, has faced so difficulties to plan their stay and departure since there is no responsible parties to facilitate their travel arrangements. The government also has intervened to handle the crisis situation; however, it was very tuff since everyone is in shock and conflicted situations. The informal accommodation and transport providers were very much reluctant to have their services for tourists. On the other hand, the majority of the tourists are not fluent in English and the local community English knowledge also very poor and therefore the situation became further complicated.

Tourism businesses are seasonal and other parts of the years it is just surviving, therefore the, business organizations are waiting the tourist's season to have sufficient businesses to manage other parts of the year. Due to the sudden cancellation of the bookings the travel agents, hoteliers, etc. faced a crisis situation. The businesses suddenly came to the zero without having a time to think about their survival strategies. At the same time the government imposed the curfew and shut down some cities asking the organizations to allow their workers to work from home. As a result of that, the business organizations faced big about survival. They suddenly decided the lay off their temporary, contact based employees and trainees to reduce the operational cost and further some of the small and medium scale travel agents and hotelier's temporary closedown their business even to reduce their overhead costs and potential losses. Therefore, the COVID-19 is an unprecedented crisis that has the potential to unravel all we once knew about, among others, social inequality, environmental sustainability and host-guest encounters. Indeed, it has shocked the very core of global tourism.

Based on the above background the main objectives of this paper are, first, to identify the effect of COVID-19 pandemic on the tourism industry in the world and second, to identify the possible resilience strategies to overcome this devastating situation faced by the tourism industry in Sri Lanka. Finally, the paper considers how the COVID-19 pandemic may change society, the economy, and tourism in Sri Lanka, and how to address more sustainable post-pandemic tourism sector, as soon as the virus is under control.

Literature Review

Global Impact of COVID-19 Pandemic in Tourism Sector

The COVID-19 pandemic is currently having a widespread effect on the global economy. There has been a steep plunge in financial markets and the resulting of growth and income declining, wealth depletion, disruption of global supply chains in manufacturing and retails such as the drop in energy prices and production due to reduced consumption and decreased international trade for investment and intermediate goods, mostly created by China and other dominant countries. It is obvious fact that the world must prepare for the COVID-19 pandemic led 2020 and 2021 Global Recession (Silva, 2020).

The major players of the global economy such as China, U.S.A., India and other European countries are directly and seriously affected by the pandemic and the stability of the global economy and its development is mainly depending on these economic giants. The full scale and density of the damage of Coronavirus still with no clear estimation as businesses and consumers are still cutting back on their spending. The business decline results in drops at all the share markets in the world. Though the COVID-19 pandemic affects all the industries and markets of all the countries, the tourism sector is the worst affected among them. The world Travel and Tourism Council has projected the COVID-19 pandemic could cut 50 million jobs worldwide in the travel and tourism sector and Asia expected to be the worst affected tourism region (World Economic Forum, 2020). Further, WTTC expected it could take more than 10 months to recover once the outbreak is over. However, COVID-19 pandemic is badly affected the Global GDP due to the vulnerable situation. Due to the non-availability of vaccine so far to prevent the disease and limited medical interventions available to treat it, most of the countries responded with various forms of interventions such as, including lockdown, social distancing, travel ban, closure of schools/universities, closure of airports, ports and non-essential businesses/workplaces, cancelling or postponing events (i.e. major conferences and tradeshows, concerts and festivals, sports seasons and the summer Olympics), and bans on gatherings of people over certain numbers. Within countries, the virus affected virtually all parts of the hospitality value chain. The impact of cancelled events, closed accommodations, and shut down attractions became immediately felt in other parts of the supply chain, such as catering, input suppliers, SME's and other indirect services (Gossling et al., 2020). Due to these interventions, all the countries had to stop all the tourism related activities. It was immediately affected national economies, including tourism systems.

The world tourism industry has faced various crises in various forms previously. Since tourism industry is sensitive to external factors, it will have an immediate influence of any crisis. Industry has faced many crises time to time such as global terrorism, natural disasters, wars, diseases, riots and global economic crisis. However, these disasters or crisis could not stop total operations of the tourism in the world. They were affected to a country or a tourism region in the world. Most of the time, the tourism sector was able to recover speedily after these disasters. But the impact of COVID-19 pandemic to the tourism sector is totally different from that in earlier crisis.

The last time total tourism operations in the world was cancelled due to the impact of World War II from 1939 to 1945. Thereafter, this is the first time all tourism systems in the world were stopped. "Can Tourism rebound as previous crisis?" This is the general discussion going on at the moment. Though the industry is optimistic on it, the evidence of the impact shows that the recovery period of tourism after this pandemic will be longer than previous incidents. Due to this pandemic tourism revenue is permanently lost because unsold capacity – for instance in accommodation – cannot be marketed in subsequent years, with corresponding implications for employment in the sector (Gossling et al., 2020).

The tourism industry accounts for 10% of the world's GDP and jobs. According to WTTC, 50 million jobs that could be lost, around 30 million would be in Asia, 7 million in Europe, 5 million in the Americas and the rest in other continents (World Economic Forum, 2020). Further, the equivalent to a loss of three months of global travel in 2020 could lead to a corresponding reduction in jobs of between 12% and 14%. In addition, United Nations World Tourism Organization (UNWTO) estimates a drop of 30% international tourist arrivals compared to 2019. It is a huge loss tourism receipt (UNWTO, 2020).

COVID-19 is not as contagious as measles and not as likely to kill an infected person as Ebola, but people can start shedding the virus several days in advance of symptoms (Bai et al., 2020). Fast spreading nature of this pandemic has created a situation of social distancing to avoid contagious. As a result, industry like tourism that is based on human interaction, interpersonal relationship and human movement has to be halted. Further, social distancing mainly reduces the capacity of hospitality operations and transportation operations.

Bans on public gatherings and closure of public places, affect tourist activities and limit the hosting of events, meetings and conferences. Therefore, travel restrictions spread out and global tourism has slowed down significantly. Since travel and tourism are critical for carrying disease and disease vectors, pandemics have major impacts on tourism (Browne et al., 2016).

The capacity for a destination to respond to pandemics depends on the stages of a disaster.

Destinations and industry may learn from prior pandemic or other disaster experiences and adapt accordingly (Hall & Prayag, 2020). In case of analyzing various alternative forms of tourism, there are highly affected tourism forms such as Senior Tourism (Grey Tourism), VFR Tourism (Visiting Friends and Relatives), Sports and Event Tourism (Liu et al., 2020). These forms cannot be recovered until a vaccine is developed because of high vulnerability to COVID-19. When the current scenario is analyzed, it is clear that the pandemic declines economic growth, the world will be poorer because of the increase unemployment ratio and collapse of economy. Therefore, strong rebound in the tourism economy is needed with a strategic effort to transform it toward sustainability.

Sustainable Recovery Planning for COVID-19

After considering the current scenario of COVID-19 pandemic in the world, it is essential to address the relevant challenges adequately with most suitable structural and implementing agencies and their processes. This should be carried through a Public-Private and People Partnership with multi-level participations. Getting the constructive and continuous contribution of all stakeholders is a must. A clear understanding of the special needs and requirements of the affected and non-affected sectors of the economy is decisively essential. Globally integrated trade, technology and training strategies are very important here and they should be successfully addressed to face the Global Recession, otherwise it could be more painful experience for all countries at different degrees and severities.

During this type of pandemic, business operations are initially facing the four major issues ('4R's), namely (1) Regaining their business operation; (2) Re-employing their staff members back; (3) Redeveloping the business relationship with their suppliers of all kinds of supply chain and (4) Reaching their regular customers (Ceylon Digest, 2020). In this scenario, a proper integrated approach is needed with the key stakeholders in the Tourism Industry. However, Survival can be tough for small- and medium-sized operators, which constitute a large part of the tourism business. Since the industry largely dependent on tourists, the sustainability of surviving is not easy. The closures and change in market demand bring about uncertainty. It is time to think about opportunistic moves. It is time to think about resilience. The industry should identify the capacity to cope with the unexpected and be capable of identifying alternatives.

Before coming to industry recovery, epidemic should be under control. The government must develop a proper social protection and health care system and health regulations to face the post-pandemic time. The prevailing capacity gaps of major responsible organizations and current resource base of the heath sector should be filled. It will build resilience to future threats and challenges. It provides the confidence to tourism stakeholders to back into their business again. To regain the business position, Industry establishments need subsidized loans, relief of loan recovery period, favorable tax reforms. Then only industry can focus on a sustainable recovery (Hallegatte and Hammar, 2020). Some countries such as China, Cambodia, and Thailand have already started of giving concessions to uplift the tourism sector.

In a recovery process, First Attention must be focused on the households hit by drastically reduced incomes, especially those with exposed occupations in the tourism sector (e.g., tourism, hotels or restaurants, tour guides). When the background is built, next step is to get the positive impacts of COVID-19 pandemic and implement them in the tourism sector. For example, as a result of this outbreak, industry identified the importance of distance business operations reducing unnecessary air travel, more usage and adaptation of technology for meetings and conferences. This can be a new phase for business tourists and MICE Tourism. Furthermore, Domestic tourism will play a major role as a short term solution. It will be the short term behavior of the consumers too. Further, tourism has highlighted the need to consider the zero-carbon imperative in combination with destination models seeking to reduce leakage, and to better capture and distribute tourism value (Hall, 2009; Gossling et al., 2016). In addition, for a sustainable recovery, understanding of consumer demand and behavior of post-pandemic period is vital. In the case of China, the first country to go through the various stages of the COVID-19 pandemic, McKinsey and Company (2020) found consumers were regaining confidence, and interestingly, a greater interest in environmentally friendly products. Therefore, in future tourism industry will be more focused on alternative forms such as eco-tourism, nature based tourism, agro tourism, homestay tourism etc. These tourism forms will be more focusing with nature and society. This will be an opportunity for world tourism sector to reconsider a transformation of the global tourism system more aligned to the SDGs. The control of the pandemic and regaining the tourism industry position depends on how countries are dealing with the crisis and smart way of escaping from the corona crisis. Local tourism should be encouraged for destinations with the help of good package prices while developing and accessing the international tourism with the strategy of promoting tours with the safest options. Further, industry should take actions to provide a job security for tourism sector employees. Companies can reduce expenses and explore incomes through innovative marketing and create new products and services. There should be a staff retention strategy. The key is to keep surviving.

Methodology

The study was carried out using qualitative methodology and employed qualitative data collection techniques. The semi structured interviews were held with travel agents, hoteliers, government offices and officials in industry associations etc. Interview checklist was prepared and used to get the opinions from them. In addition to that a desk review was carried out to identify the response of government, academic, organizational and media publications. The data obtained from secondary data sources such as journals, newspapers, interviews, web articles were analyzed to develop the discussion.

Results and Discussion

Addressing the Dilemmas of Sustainability

Sustainable Recovery of the Tourism Business

Many Destination Management Companies (DMCs) are prioritizing their first attention on strengthening the domestic tourism. It is the initial step of recovering after this crisis is over. There, they are expecting to promote excursions in the beginning. Then, they have to move for short distance and long distance travelling and tour packages within the country. The main purpose of this is to give confidence for domestic tourists on normalcy. Industry should provide more promotional packages to attract the customers while adding safety measures or guidelines. This will be a great opportunity for the domestic tourism sector to focus on it and give more benefits to the community through alternative forms of tourism such as eco-tourism, agro tourism, home stay tourism, wellness tourism and rural tourism.

Further, DMCs can identify new potential regional tourist generating countries and promote them rather than depending on China and India. This will become a good step by step initiation rather than directly focusing on international tourist market as a whole.

All the tourism and hospitality service providers have to familiarize with disease preventive and controlled methods to maintain the health and safety standards of both guests and employees. Hence, it is really important for all the stakeholders including Sri Lanka Tourism Development Authority and Tourism and Aviation Ministry to follow the guidelines given by the health officials.

Rebuilding Consumer Trust and Regional Corporation

When we are welcoming tourists, need to have comprehensive sector reopening strategy aimed towards building trust among tourists. The government should put tourists into a strict safety and hygiene standards to ensure the safety of both tourists as well as locals. If locals are not accepting the tourists, then it will create another issue of social conflict. Therefore, considering both aspects are essential. In addition, as a region, South Asian countries should be get-together and discuss the impact the impact of the pandemic on the travel and tourism industry and the measures that need to be adopted to support recovery efforts. Recently, initial discussion was started. There it is essential to pay our attention on inter regional tourism promotion, more favorable fiscal conditions for the development of the industry, possibility of establishing protocols for opening airports, hotels and tourist attractions sites.

Engaging with Employees and Other Stakeholders

The mass unemployment caused by the rapid shutdown of Sri Lankan economy is a serious issue in the travel and tourism sector. The COVID-19 pandemic crisis badly affected to lower paid, casual, part-time employees and trainees in the industry. Majority of them lost their jobs and positions. Not only the lower level employees' also permanent and top level staff also had to face a cut down of their salary and other fringe benefits, by March 26, 2020, 90% of member businesses had temporarily laid off staff, with 78% of businesses reducing at least three quarters of the workforce. This has caused an uncertainty about the job security among the tourism and hospitality sector employees. Some of them are frustrated and thinking of leaving the industry too. This is a serious issue faced by the industry. As per the discussion had with top level SLTDA authorities, they are now working with the private sector to protect the employees in the industry. It is a good move from Sri Lankan tourism point of view. Though the industry has taken temporary decision to lay off their staff, industry should not allow their employees to suffer due to that action. Hence, when the situation is back to normal, they must have a program to get the service of laid off employees to the companies. It is not ethical to give a hard time to the employees who provided good service to the sector when it was running smoothly. Therefore, companies must take actions to protect the job security of them in this pandemic situation. Though the industry can't give benefits like earlier, they must keep the employees while motivating them to stay with them. If they do not protect the employees, there will be a big crisis in future, when they want to find human resources. Then no one will come to the industry in future. Thus it is essential to give a confidence to the all types of employees that they are looking after in this situation by the government as well as their company. Hence, staff retention strategy should be implemented. This is already being done in Thailand. Travel companies in Thailand have now reduced working hours and salary at 10%–25% for a period of four to six months. But they did not ask the employees to leave. They have explained the situation and asked them to stay with them till the industry regains the position. The sustainability of the business is the most important aspect in the tourism sector. This industry is vulnerable to various issues than other industries. However, every time industry survived with the support of the stakeholders. Therefore, the sustainability will depend on clear, transparent and timely communications with all the stakeholders while creating a platform to reshape the business and to secure ongoing support from customers, employees, suppliers, creditors, investors and regulatory authorities.

Task of Building Resilience

It is important to have a resilience plan for better management of future situations like COVID pandemic. It will sustain the economic prosperity and living standards of the people. Tourism industry also needs that kind of plan to face the challenge of COVID-19 as well as future pandemic situations. Hence government should have an integrated plan with the support of industry organizations to develop a resilience plan for tourism. Tourism Industry stakeholders should identify the issues faced by them due to this crisis and develop a contingency plan to build resilience and better respond to future crises. The lessons learned from this situation are very important to put the business in correct track. Tourism industry should think about the related diversification of their business. The tourism sector should engage with other sectors and develop integration to the business such as plantation sector, retailing business, agriculture, transportation. In this situation, Central government financial support, tax concessions, favorable policies are essential to rebuild the industry within a short period of time. From employees point of view, companies should come with new working practices such as introducing flexi-time work, work from home methods, actions to provide a safe and healthy working environment, health and safety protections measures. Most importantly, strong administration of the government and the discipline of people in the country are essential to face future pandemic like this. Here after, Sri Lankan people have to follow strict health regulations and guidelines that they were not used to it earlier. On the other hand, COVID-19 will be an opportunity for the people and the industry to correct their wrong practices and move for more sustainable actions. As a developing nation, it is vital to be proactive and should develop well-focused disaster management and resilience building strategies for future development endeavors of the country, without underestimating the possible future disasters. Further, the country must set up large-scale surveillance systems with a strong virus contact tracing while supporting public-health sector with more facilities. It will give more confidence for tourists and the community to start their normal life.

Transforming Tourism and Hospitality Spaces to Suit COVID-19 Lifestyle

With the emergence of COVID-19, tourism and hospitality sector has to learn new lessons or buzz words such as demand for social distancing, self-discipline, resilience strategies, and health safety. When the situation is back to normal, one of the major challenges faced by the industry is social distancing. The industry will have to continue the business practicing it within their establishments. Otherwise the sustainability of the business is questionable. The tourism and Hospitality business is based on the social interaction. Therefore, the industry must think about the transforming tourism and hospitality spaces to suit COVID-19 lifestyle. Since customers are well aware of the healthy aspects now than earlier, their attitudes, behaviors and lifestyles will be changed. They will search and question about healthy practices, when they come to tourism or hospitality establishments. Hence, the industry should prepare to face it. Since the industry is working on a built environment, it is a challenge to keep social distancing and space. Therefore, the operators have to go with new space planning or creating new space within the existing space. Re-arrangement of furniture layout, removing additional furniture and equipment to avoid blockages and give more space, introducing new affordable furniture in order to achieve social distancing, expansion of public spacing should be concerned here. There, they have to consider the number of people that can be accommodated in the place, cost and time, aesthetic value of the premises, adherence to the rules and regulations. If the business can do the structural or designing change as per the requirements of healthy living standards, it can be a good sales and marketing strategy to promote post-COVID-19 era. Tourists will more think about private space when they travel and stay. It will be a demanding factor for tourists when they visit travel industries and hotels. In addition, tourists will more concern on cleanliness in the premises and minimum touching of the surfaces. Then we have to expect the introduction of more robotics and new technology in future to minimize the human touch. The Sri Lankan tourism and hospitality sector should adjust the business based on this situation to sustain the future business. These changes can be important to attract more high-end tourists. These changes can be done in different scale. It depends on the business type. There are many small and medium scale entrepreneurs and different forms of accommodations in Sri Lanka. They should more concern about the space and expansion rather than integration of technology. There is no requirement to integrate everything to the business. The industry should identify the customer base and change their business. For example, rural area tourism and hospitality business can market the nature, fresh air, healthy meals and the remote environment; they have more space than city and suburbs area. This kind of adoptability is really needed in sustainable tourism businesses in future. It will be the strategy to focus for the tourism marketers in Sri Lanka.

Conclusion

Currently, many countries in the world are facing the second and third waves of the pandemic. Further, new versions of the virus have emerged from the UK and it has started to spread to other countries too, thus starting the operations of tourism industry again in dire state. Estimation of the consequences of COVID-19 for the global tourism industry is essential, when facing the crisis in 2021. Though some vaccinations were developed to as a solution, it is fundamentally unclear how the pandemic will develop until the end of 2021, and how travel restrictions and massive job losses will impact tourist demand. Therefore, the industry has to get ready with the resilience strategies to face this situation. The implications of the correct government policies are essential for the future of the tourism industry. Some of the essential suggestions and policy decisions can be mentioned as follows.

The government should pay attention on local tourism first. It is important to develop a policy to encourage local tourism and promotion. It is critical to restart the tourism economy at local, national and perhaps limited international scales (e.g., regional level). Opening of airports and air travel with the guidance of health officials and strict health safety measurements are needed here. The Sri Lankan government has taken some initiatives with the opening of the airport from January 2021 and starting international tourism in a small scale. In addition, the role of domestic tourism in the recovery and the longer-term transformation to more resilient destinations should be concerned. However, the domestic tourism should be started under a COVID-19 controlled environment.

Industry should follow the guidelines given by the Ministry of Health and World Health Organization. All the tourism and hospitality service providers must adapt controlled methods for the health and safety of both in-house guests and employees. Not only in the hospitality sector, also in the airlines, office premises, land transportation, shopping and other recreational activities are needed to be operated with proper health guidelines to avoid the risk of COVID-19. The authorities have to introduce new guidelines on how to run the tourism and hospitality ventures while avoiding the health risks.

An appropriate analysis of post-COVID-19 tourists' behavior is really essential. In future, there will be more online transactions, online reservations, Virtual Reality (VR) promotions, Artificial Intelligence (AI), mobile apps than earlier. Hence, the authorities and industry officials should take necessary steps to upgrade their systems. Sri Lanka should develop new strategies to position the country globally with the strong promotional campaign that can lead the country to new era.

Acknowledgment

We, acknowledge the work declared in this paper is original and no part of this has been copied or taken from other sources without necessary permissions. Further this abstract or manuscript has not been published in anywhere in any form of publication and not presently under consideration of publication anywhere in form of publication. Further, we thank all the resource persons in the SLTDA and industry for providing their thoughts on this review.

Declaration of Interest Statement

The authors declare that they have no known competing financial interests or personal relationships that could have appeared to influence the work reported in this paper.

References

Bai, Y., Yao, L., Wei, T., Tian, F., Jin, D.-Y., Chen, L., & Wang, M. (2020). Presumed asymptomatic carrier transmission of COVID-19. *JAMA*, 323(14), 406.

Browne, A., St-Onge Ahmad, S., Beck, C. R., & Nguyen-Van-Tam, J. S. (2016). The roles of transportation and transportation hubs in the propagation of influenza and coronaviruses: a systematic review. *Journal of Travel Medicine*, 23(1), tav002.

Ceylon Digest. (2020). Can Sri Lanka be the next best in our region? Controlling of global disaster: coronavirus COVID 19. Retrieved April 28, 2020 from https://www.ceylondigest.com/can-sri-lanka-be-the-next-best-in-our-region-controlling-of-global-disaster-coronavirus-covid-19/.

Gossling, S., Ring, A., Dwyer, L., Andersson, A. C., & Hall, C. M. (2016). Optimizing or maximizing growth? A challenge for sustainable tourism. *Journal of Sustainable Tourism*, 24(4), 527–548.

Gossling, S., Scott, D., & Hall, C. M. (2020). Pandemics, tourism and global change: a rapid assessment of COVID-19, *Journal of Sustainable Tourism*, 29(1): 1–20. doi:10.1080/09669582.2020.1758708.

Hall, C. M. (2009). Degrowing tourism: decroissance, sustainable consumption and steady-state tourism. *Anatolia*, 20(1), 46–61.

Hall, C. M., & Prayag, G. (2020). Earthquakes and tourism: impacts, responses and resilience – an introduction. In C. M. Hall, & G. Prayag (Eds.), *Tourism and Earthquakes*. Channel View 2021: 1–35. https://doi.org/10.21832/9781845417871-004

Hallegatte, S., & Hammer, S. (2020). Thinking ahead: for a sustainable recovery from COVID-19 (Coronavirus). Retrieved April 28, 2020 from https://blogs.worldbank.org/climatechange/thinking-ahead-sustainable-recovery-covid-19-coronavirus.

Liu, C., Zhou, Q., Li, Y., Garner, L. V., Watkins, S. P., Carter, L. J., Smoot, J., Gregg, A. C., Daniels, A. D., Jervey, S., & Albaiu, D. (2020). Research and development on therapeutic agents and vaccines for COVID-19 and related human coronavirus diseases. *ACS Central Science*, 6(3), 315–331.

McKinsey & Company. (2020). Cautiously optimistic: Chinese consumer behaviour post-COVID-19. Retrieved April 29, 2020, from https://www.mckinsey.com/business-functions/marketing-and-sales/our-insights/global-surveys-ofconsumer-sentiment-during-the-coronavirus-crisis.

Silva, D. A. C. (2020). Lessons from global best practices to make Sri Lanka more resilient. Retrieved April 27, 2020 from http://www.dailynews.lk/2020/03/26/finance/215202/lessons-global-best-practices-make-sri-lanka-more-resilient.

UNWTO (2020). Retrieved May 12, 2020 from https://www.unwto.org/impact-assessment-of-the-covid-19-outbreak-on-international-tourism

World Economic Forum. (2020). This is how coronavirus could affect the travel and tourism industry. Retrieved April 27, 2020 from https://www.weforum.org/agenda/2020/03/world-travel-coronavirus-covid19-jobs-pandemic-tourism-aviation.

15 Managing Events Tourism Sustainability Post-COVID-19

Exploring the New Realities

Priyakrushna Mohanty, Pinaz Tiwari and Nimit Chowdhary

Introduction

Events, in general, are deep-rooted in the culture of any place and exist in several *avatars* that distinguish themselves in terms of size, nature, scope, attendance, and professionalism (Bouchon et al., 2017). Irrespective of one's region, religion, caste, creed, colour, and ideologies followed, everyone participates in events celebrating the tradition, culture, customs, and rituals of their own or others (Yeoman et al., 2012). As an integrated part of the tourism industry, events have been applauded for their ability to create positive economic and touristic outcomes both for the host and tourists. Events tourism, in particular, is known to provide employment opportunities and economic benefits to the host community while facilitating tourists a chance to experience the unique culture of the destination (Getz, 2005, 2008). In the tourism systems, events tourism plays a critical role of being both push and pull factor i.e. they induce (*push*) the tourists to visit a particular destination to experience their culture and also attract (*pull*) tourists from tourist generating regions to visit a particular destination (Getz and Page, 2016). Facts like these rightfully justify the vibrant niche events tourism has created for itself and the extraordinary growth that it has achieved since the 1990s. Especially in the last decade, tourist service provides and travel agents have been specializing in the organization and management of events backed by the growing interest shown by the contemporary tourists who place greater importance in experiencing the culture than just visiting it for the touristic attraction (Maguire and Hanrahan, 2017). So, the importance of events tourism in this modern-day world is more than what meets the eye. However, this critical industry has gone on its knees since the outbreak of perhaps the biggest pandemic mankind has ever seen i.e. the COVID-19 disease.

Severe acute respiratory syndrome coronavirus 2 (SARS CoV-2) or more commonly known as the COVID-19 disease has emerged as the *worst* pandemic the world has seen in last the 100 years (Rosenthal, 2020). The multi-faceted impacts of this deadly disease are so severe that it has brought the whole world to a standstill (de España, 2020). With almost all economic activities halted to contain the spread of the virus, the world is crippling

DOI: 10.4324/9781003207467-21

in terms of economy and society as a whole. Consequently, if there is one industry that has been the hardest hit, it is the tourism industry (UNWTO, 2020). The impacts of this disease on the tourism industry is said to be unprecedented and unparalleled affecting both the demand and supply side (UNWTO, 2020). By the advent of 2021, the international tourist arrivals had reduced by 86% in comparison to January 2020 risking the jobs of about 100 million people employed in the tourism industry (UNWTO, 2021). Subsequently, Events tourism which is also considered one of the fastest-growing forms of tourism was also devastated by the COVID-19 disease. As events involve the gathering of the people, it was one of the first sectors to take the wrath of the disease. With stringent measures like lockdown and social distancing, most of the events were either cancelled or postponed after the outbreak of the pandemic.

Though vaccinations for this disease have been released, their effectiveness is not full-proofed. Also, the distribution of these vaccines and medicines is expected to take a substantial amount of time during which the second wave of the COVID-19 disease has hit various countries like India, Brazil, and the UK with greater force. All these facts refer to a point that COVID-19 is here to stay (Phillips, 2021) and so, it would be only wise for mankind to restart all activities on a safer scale and with all protocols in place. Keeping this in the backdrop, the tourism industry is also shifting gears for a strong and sustainable recovery under the leadership of UNWTO, the governing agency of tourism worldwide (UNWTO, 2020). Like the other forms of tourism, events will also eventually rebound to their course, but it is almost certain that events of the future will never be the same (Mohanty et al., 2020a). Many new trends and guidelines will come into the limelight and they will put the events tourism industry on the tracks of recovery. Apart from recovery, many experts have beheld this pandemic as a prospect to offer a novel direction to the tourism (and events tourism) sector by swotting its entire system while working towards the sustainability objective (Brouder, 2020). Discarding the unsustainable and reinforcing the sustainable practices of the past will play a major role in this regard (Ioannides and Gyimóthy, 2020). Also, many new ways that promote sustainability will evolve as we progress and become a part of our day to day lives. Just like the impact of this disease, the future of events tourism is also unprecedented and so a thorough enquiry of the scenario will assist in better estimation of the future. Keeping this in mind, the current chapter deals with two major objectives. For the first objective, the authors have tried to envisage the various facets of events tourism sustainability pre and during COVID-19. Second, the emergent trends and practices which have the potential to shape the future of events tourism will be depicted through a framework. Given the novelty and ever changing nature of the disease academic works have hardly delved upon this particular issue of events tourism sustainability in the context of COVID-19.

Sustainability of Events Tourism: Reopening the Debate

The sustainability debate in the context of events tourism is not a new phenomenon. Since the staggering growth of events tourism in the 1990s, the sustainability debate also simultaneously took shape backed by the cautionary works of Fayos-Solá (1998); Fredline, Faulkner, and Tourism (1998); Harris, Jago, Allen, and Huyskens (2000). However, these works were mostly scattered and did not concentrate on the sustainability aspect as their primary objective. Over the next decade (2001–2010), the events tourism scholarship experienced an upsurge for the sustainability debate with collaborative works like O'Sullivan and Jackson (2002); Raj and Musgrave (2009); Sherwood, Jago, and Deery (2004) raising questions over the sustainability of events. Subsequently, in the last decade (2011–2020), the debate only intensified and became a part of the mainstream debate. While the works published during this period concerning the sustainability of events tourism are in plenty, the book by Holmes, Hughes, Mair, and Carlsen (2015) and articles of Mair and Laing (2013); Okech (2011); Negruşa, Toader, Rus, and Cosma (2016) are considered landmarks in the field. The rise in the number of the available literature is also a significant indicator for the intensifying sustainability debate in the events tourism discourse. A basic search on Google Scholar with keywords "Events tourism" AND "Sustainability" shows only 26 results for the period 1991–2000. However, the same search query fetches about 353 and 2,190 results considering the 2001–2010 and 2011–2020 periods, respectively. This existing literature brings many issues about the sustainability of the events tourism industry which will be briefly touched upon in the next sub-section.

Over the last three decades, the sustainability of the events industry has been a huge question mark from all the triple bottom lines (economic, socio-cultural, and environmental) of sustainability. On the economic front, events have been blamed for providing benefits only in the short-run (Spilling, 1996), creating large scale economic leakages (Diedering and Kwiatkowski, 2015), misusing tax payer's money (Hall, 2012; Mules and Faulkner, 1996), and halting local economic activities vendors (Daniels et al., 2004). From the socio-cultural angle, events have been held responsible for commodification and staged authenticity, disruption in the quality of life of residents, increasing health disorders, prostitution, sexual assault, and inducing crime and vandalism in the host community (Mohanty et al., 2020b). Similarly, events have been under the radar of various practitioners and academicians for their negative impacts on the environment in the form of pollution, higher carbon emission, depletion of local resources, and not following green practices for earning higher profits (Getz, 2009). Apart from these challenges, Mohanty, Singhania and Hasana (2020b) also associate infrastructural problems such as overcrowding, congestion, traffic jams, and encouraging of crowding out effect to the events tourism industry.

Any industry which gathers a swift momentum without being considerate towards the triple bottom lines of sustainability is deemed to be vulnerable in the long run and such is the case of events tourism. Considering the above, the COVID-19 disease has not only negatively impacted the events industry but also has refuelled the sustainability debate in the doctrine of tourism and events. Further, the higher vulnerability of the tourism and events industry has made this debate more intense. Therefore, pertinent issues of sustainable events tourism in the light of the COVID-19 pandemic demand due consideration.

This devastating situation has exposed the severe vulnerabilities of the events tourism industry. By default, industries like events and tourism are much more susceptible to any internal or external disturbances i.e. any small incident can percolate to a huge negative bearing on the industry (Barbhuiya and Chatterjee, 2020; Mohanty et al., 2020a). Events also suffer from the innate disadvantage of having the capability to become a super-spreader for the infectious disease (Kumar et al., 2020). Scholars like Higgins-Desbiolles (2020) have viewed this pandemic much more devastating for specific sections (mostly the ones at the bottom) of the society which brings the issues of social and ecological justice into the sustainability debate. In the context of events tourism, this issue has alleviated significance. Events tourism is infamous for providing very little return to the local community while making the corporates richer. During and post COVID-19, it is the local community which will be suffering more because, for an attendee of an event, a cancelled event does not make much of a difference, but for the organizers of it causes a tragedy. Due to many such reasons, COVID-19 disease has made the events tourism sustainability debate much more complex. However, it has also given a bright chance to restart the whole industry with a sustainability approach. The upcoming section will deal with the emergent themes and trends that will or have the potential to shape the future of events in a sustainable way.

Future of Events Post COVID-19: A Sustainable Approach

The pandemic has disrupted social norms and activities for an infinite period. As the number of cases is upsurging in different parts of the world despite the regulation of movement and vaccine drives, the business operations require a fresh perspective to deal with the situation. Tourism is one such sector that is reconsidering its operational strategies to remain robust amidst the global health crisis. Coherently, the events sub-sector is also re-designing its strategies, and attempting to adapt to the changing social norms for long-term viability. Davies (2020) raised concerns that events, especially festivals may likely become 'exclusive' or a larger proportion of small-scale organisations would enter the new sharing economy after the pandemic. Even though the pandemic impacted the sector financially and otherwise, Luonila and Kinnunen (2019) found that festival managers consider erratic economic situations as an 'opportunity'. Nevertheless, the perceptions of attendees and organisers tend to differ in different situations and needs to be comprehended. Despite being a topic of discussion, Seraphin (2021) reported a dearth of studies on events tourism and COVID-19 in top-rated tourism journals. Moreover, as the pandemic has allowed tourism and its sub-sectors to re-establish the pillars of sustainability (Chang et al., 2020), this section proposes sustainable strategies that would help the event tourism business to re-establish itself efficiently.

Re-designing Physical Spaces

Managing events, especially within the ambit of COVID-19 new norms, social distancing will be widely prevalent in the future. In the case of physical events, re-designing the spaces to accommodate the crowd with the social distancing norms is a prerequisite of a successful event. In the pre-COVID phase, crowd management at events and destinations were widely discussed in academia (Dichter and Guevera Manzo, 2017). However, as COVID-19 has given a new direction to the global tourism sector to re-establish the pillars of sustainable tourism development (Romagosa, 2020), resilience in strategizing events is vital. Thus, to adopt a sustainable approach in event tourism, destination management organisation should reconsider the physical distancing aspects while re-designing the spaces to accommodate and manage the crowd.

Virtual Events

As the pandemic hit the conventional ways of organising events, event management companies are adopting alternate solutions in the form of virtual events to remain robust. It is considered an innovative measure to combat the impact of COVID-19 on business operations (Bartis et al., 2021). Virtual or online events are organised and hosted on electronic platforms, and attendees can attend the event using technological tools. Several start-up organisations are venturing into this emerging business segment such as Hopin which defines itself as a "virtual venue". Virtual events are cost-effective and allow global interaction among individuals on a single platform. It eradicates the need of travelling through the air which otherwise would have contributed to carbon emissions, consequently triggering the issue of global warming. Virtual events are financially sustainable for the event management companies, and attendees, and environmentally sustainable for the society at large. Menezes et al. (2020) also suggested adding the 'environmental sustainability' dimension in the ServQual model for evaluating events.

Hybrid Events

Hybrid Events implies combining the virtual and physical elements of an event. These events provide a greater opportunity for the event organisers to follow the official norm or guidelines laid by the government on the restricted gathering (Bartis et al., 2021), and use technological platforms to invite a larger audience. Hybrid events are attendee-centric as people who want to enjoy the live experience can attend the event, and vice-versa. Certainly, the safety of the attendees and participants is a prerequisite in hybrid events during the pandemic. Therefore, hybrid events are physically sustainable, financially viable, and attendee-centric in terms of offering a better experience.

ICT in Events Planning and Management

Information Communication and Technology will play a crucial role in planning and managing events worldwide. Irrespective of the size of an event, incorporating technology will bring out the sustainability aspects. At the pre-event stage, technological tools can be integrated into the booking of tickets, maintain time slots, and planning the physical spaces. Gajjar and Parmar (2020) stressed the need for effective communication to the attendees before organising a live event about the precautions to be taken, things to carry, and impromptu changes in the schedule. From the management perspective, using e-marketing solutions, and social media platforms connect potential audience (pre-event stage) and help in increasing attendance during an event (Luonila and Kinnunen, 2019).

The Bio Bubble Events

The tourist bubble or travel bubble concept is emerging around the globe after the outbreak of COVID-19. The travel bubble is an agreement between two countries to open their borders for each other while restricting travel movements with other countries. Likewise, the notion of bio bubble is significantly growing in mega-events such as in the Indian Premier League. The bio-secure bubble is providing a secure environment by permitting officials, authorised individuals, and support staff to enter protected areas (e.g., Hotel, lobby, training session, transportation) after testing COVID-19 negative. It was implemented successfully by the Board of Control for Cricket in India (BCCI) in 2020. The emerging notion of the bio-secure bubble will be successful in conducting mega-events, especially sports tourism would resurrect with similar initiatives without incurring losses. Furthermore, as the safety of support staff and participants are crucial amidst COVID-19 (Maditinos et al., 2020), the implementation of a bio-secure bubble will ensure safety by preventing infected people to attend the event. The step will also lead to lesser financial burdens to the events organisations as the changes are minimal.

Certifications and Labels

Reassurance in the post-COVID-19 times will be a prerequisite to attract visitors and revive the events sector. Amongst the varied measures undertaken by destination and event management organisations, introducing COVID safe labels and health certifications are increasingly becoming important to restart the operations successfully. Compliance with the COVID-19 safety guidelines, and health and hygiene measures would encourage visitors, and combat risk perceptions while travelling or staying at a destination. Seraphin (2021) highlighted the need to develop and adopt health certifications so that consumers perceive the services positively. Some organisations have embraced the certification approach in the tourism and hospitality industry. For example, the "SG Clean" quality mark launched by Singapore aims to raise the hygiene standards of tourism businesses such as hotels, restaurants, tourist attractions, and MICE venues (Eagan, 2020). Likewise, the Accor group of hotels partnered with Bureau Veritas has launched the "ALLSAFE" initiative to certify safety and hygiene measures. It is a collaborated program among industry experts, and people from academic fields (Accor Group, 2020). Within the destination context, Portugal launched a label titled "Clean & Safe" which distinguished tour operators that guarantees compliance with COVID-19 safety guidelines (Eagan, 2020).

Mutual Aid Events

Amidst COVID-19, tourism sub-sectors realised the potential of wide-scale networking and collaboration as a key to revive. Mair (2020) devised that societies being based on mutual aid i.e., building networks to protect the vulnerable groups/individuals and extend support within the communities. As the pandemic raised people's consciousness to assist the vulnerable segment of the society, financially or otherwise, growth in the number of smaller community events is evident. Such events (virtually) are operated by communities where 'enjoying the art' is the primary motivation of both attendees and participants (Davies, 2020). These are affordable community events, and the earnings from the show go directly into the pockets of the community which operates the event. It is, therefore, a step towards ensuring socio-economic sustainability through events among vulnerable groups during the crisis.

Demarketing Events

Demarketing manoeuvres the market in numbers and consciously aim to influence the demand for a product through various deliberate strategies (Tiwari et al., 2020). This technique was widely used at tourist destinations where tourism harmed the environment (Armstrong and Kern, 2011) or heritage sites (Soliman, 2010). Demarketing an event could be a new norm for better management and ensuring sustainability. Even though more visitors at an event would mean more profits for the event organisers, Medway et al. (2010) highlighted that implementation of demarketing strategies at places is sustainable by ensuring lesser but regular supply and leads to better visitor management.

Based on the size of the event, financial and operational capabilities of the event organiser, an event manager may choose the alternative solution presented in Figure 15.1. These alternatives embrace the sustainability approach in organising and managing an event.

Conclusion

In the current scenario, the unpredicted global health crisis is impacting all the sectors and has created a situation of economic crisis. The catastrophic impact is evident in the tourism, hospitality, and event sector all over the world. Eventually, the road to recovery for tourism and its sub-sectors

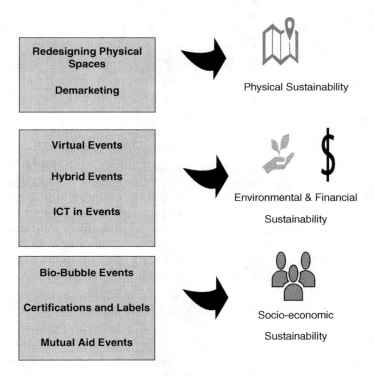

Figure 15.1 A sustainable approach for managing events in the post-COVID-19 phase.
Source: Authors' own work.

requires significant transitions to regain the economic performance while curtailing the spread of the infectious disease. Events tourism is one of the fastest-growing sub-sectors which is severely affected by the COVID-19. It acted as both a push and pull factor for visitors, and created a sustainable livelihood for the local community and organizers. However, the outbreak of the pandemic, restricted movement of people, and frequent lockdowns in several cities and countries have resulted in large-scale cancellations of the events. This has left the event tourism sector in a state of indistinctiveness, and uncertainty concerning the future is pre-dominant among the stakeholders.

As the discourses on re-establishing the pillars of sustainability in tourism have re-surfaced in both academics and the industry, the chapter proposed a set of sustainable strategies for the event tourism sector. These include the use of technology in planning and managing events, hybrid and virtual events, creating bio-bubble at the location of events, obtaining certification and labels to mitigate the risk perceptions among visitors, re-designing the physical spaces as per new COVID-19 norms to manage crowd, adopting demarketing strategies, and opting for mutual-aid events to help the vulnerable people in the society. These alternatives would help achieve financial sustainability for the stakeholders involved, physical and environmental sustainability at the destination, and socio-economic sustainability for the local community. The incremental adoption of the proposed measures would help event tourism to revive, and create resilience in the post-COVID-19 phase. Moreover, the chapter supports the discussion provided by Ziakas and Getz (2021). The authors exemplify the reinforcement of a holistic perspective for creating sustainable development in the events tourism sector.

As the physical events are facing an existential crisis amidst the pandemic (Ho and Sia, 2020), unquestionably, the post-COVID-19 phase requires the event management companies and event organizers to ensure the safety of visitors, and the working staff. This needs to be achieved along with recovering the losses made in the past few months. Thus, recovering the losses, and re-discovering the business practices would be a challenging task for the event sector if it follows the conventional ideas of business operations. In the contemporary world, it is crucial to initiate creativity in promotional campaigns, offering flexible services (hybrid/virtual events), and leveraging the cancellation policies. These strategies would help the events business to attract visitors, and thus, achieving long-term sustainability. Even though the recovery of the events business is dependent on factors such as the government policies concerning social gatherings, people's confidence in attending mega-events, motivations of attending the events, and the successful drives of vaccinations, the event management organisations need to understand the specific demands and issues of the target audience. In the same backdrop, data analytics would aid the sector in speedy and sustainable recovery from the crisis.

References

Accor Group. (2020, May 15). *ALL Safe and Well*. Retrieved from https://www.allsafeandwell.com/.

Armstrong, E. K., & Kern, C. L. (2011). Demarketing manages visitor demand in the Blue Mountains National Park. *Journal of Ecotourism*, *10*(1), 21–37. https://doi.org/10.1080/14724040903427393.

Barbhuiya, M. R., & Chatterjee, D. J. T. M. P. (2020). Vulnerability and resilience of the tourism sector in India: effects of natural disasters and internal conflict. *Tourism Management Perspectives*, *33*, 100616. https://doi.org/10.1016/j.tmp.2019.100616

Bartis, H., Hufkie, B., & Moraladi, M. (2021). The economic impact of the COVID-19 pandemic on the business events sub-sector in South Africa: mitigation strategies and innovations. *African Journal of Hospitality, Tourism and Leisure*, *10*(1), 102–114. https://doi.org/10.46222/ajhtl.19770720-89.

Bouchon, F., Hussain, K., & Konar, R. (2017). Event management education and event industry: a case of Malaysia. *MOJEM: Malaysian Online Journal of Educational Management*, *3*(1), 1–17.

Brouder, P. (2020). Reset redux: possible evolutionary pathways towards the transformation of tourism in a COVID-19 world. *Tourism Geographies*, *22*(3), 484-490. https://doi.org/10.1080/14616688.2020.1760928.

Chang, C. L., McAleer, M., & Ramos, V. (2020). A charter for sustainable tourism after COVID-19. *Sustainability (Switzerland)*, *12*(9), 10–13. https://doi.org/10.3390/su12093671.

Daniels, M. J., Backman, K. F., & Backman, S. J. (2004). Supplementing event economic impact results with perspectives from host community business and opinion leaders. *Event Management*, *8*(3), 117–125.

Davies, K. (2020). Festivals post Covid-19. *Leisure Sciences*, *43*(1–2), 184–189. https://doi.org/10.1080/01490400.2020.1774000.

de España, B. J. E. B. (2020). Reference macroeconomic scenarios for the Spanish economy after Covid-19. *Economic Bulletin*, (2), 1–32. https://ideas.repec.org/a/bde/journl/y2020i06daan10.html.

Dichter, A., & Guevera Manzo, G. (2017). *Managing Overcrowding in Tourism Destinations* (p. 64). https://www.wttc.org/-/media/files/reports/policy-research/coping-with-success---managingovercrowding-in-tourism-destinations-2017.pdf?la=en.

Diedering, M., & Kwiatkowski, G. (2015). Economic impact of events and festivals on host regions-methods in practice & potential sources of bias. *Polish Journal of Sport and Tourism*, *22*(4), 247–252.

Eagan, K. (2020, May 11). *Encouraging Travellers with Labels and Health Certifications*. Retrieved April 15, 2021, from Tourism Review News: https://www.tourismreview.com/companiesencouraging-travelers-with-certifications-news11525.

Fayos-Solá, E. (1998). The impact of mega events. *Annals of Tourism Research*, *25*(1), 241–245. https://doi.org/10.1016/S0160-7383(97)00083-2.

Fredline, E., Faulkner, B. J. F. M., & Tourism, E. (1998). Resident reactions to a major tourist event: the Gold Coast Indy car race. *Festival Management & Event Tourism*, *5*(4), 185–205.

Gajjar, A. M., & Parmar, B. J. (2020). The impact of Covid 19 on event management industry in India. *Global Journal of Management and Business Research: Real Estate, Event and Tourism Management*, *20*(2), 76–79. https://doi.org/10.46501/ijmtst060617.

Getz, D. (2005). *Event Management and Event Tourism*. New York: Cognizant Communication Corporation.

Getz, D. (2008). Event tourism: definition, evolution, and research. *Tourism Management*, 29(3), 403–428.

Getz, D. (2009). Policy for sustainable and responsible festivals and events: institutionalization of a new paradigm. *Journal of Policy Research in Tourism, Leisure and Events*, 1(1), 61–78.

Getz, D., & Page, S. J. (2016). Progress and prospects for event tourism research. *Tourism management*, 52, 593–631.

Hall, C. M. (2012). Sustainable mega-events: beyond the myth of balanced approaches to mega-event sustainability. *Event Management*, 16(2), 119–131.

Harris, R., Jago, L., Allen, J., & Huyskens, M. (2000). Towards an Australian event research agenda: first steps. *Event Management*, 6(4), 213–221.

Higgins-Desbiolles, F. (2020). Socialising tourism for social and ecological justice after COVID-19. *Tourism Geographies*, 22(3), 610–623.

Ho, J. M., & Sia, J. K. M. (2020). Embracing an uncertain future: COVID-19 and MICE in Malaysia. *Local Development & Society*, 1(2), 190–204. https://doi.org/10.1080/26883597.2020.1818533.

Holmes, K., Hughes, M., Mair, J., & Carlsen, J. (2015). *Events and Sustainability*: Routledge.

Ioannides, D., & Gyimóthy, S. (2020). The COVID-19 crisis as an opportunity for escaping the unsustainable global tourism path. *Tourism Geographies, 22*(3), 624–632. https://doi.org/10.1080/14616688.2020.1763445.

Kumar, S., Jha, S., & Rai, S.K. (2020). Significance of super spreader events in COVID-19. *Indian Journal of Public Health, 64*(6), 139. https://doi.org/10.4103/ijph.IJPH_495_20.

Luonila, M., & Kinnunen, M. (2019). Future of the arts festivals: do the views of managers and attendees match? *International Journal of Event and Festival Management*, 11(1), 105–126. https://doi.org/10.1108/IJEFM-04-2019-0028.

Maditinos, Z., Vassiliadis, C., Tzavlopoulos, Y., & Vassiliadis, S. A. (2020). Sports events and the COVID-19 pandemic: assessing runners' intentions for future participation in running events–evidence from Greece. *Tourism Recreation Research*, 1–12. https://doi.org/10.1080/02508281.2020.1847422.

Maguire, K., & Hanrahan, J. (2017). Assessing the economic impact of event management in Ireland: a local authority planning perspective. *Event Management*, 21(3), 333–346.

Mair, S. (2020, March 30). *What Will the World Be Like after Coronavirus? Four Possible Futures*. Retrieved April 10, 2021, from The Conversation: https://theconversation.com/what-will-theworld-be-like-after-coronavirus-four-possible-futures134085?utm_medium=email&utm_campaign=Latest.

Mair, J., & Laing, J. H. (2013). Encouraging pro-environmental behaviour: the role of sustainability-focused events. *Journal of Sustainable Tourism*, 21(8), 1113–1128.

Medway, D., Warnaby, G., & Dharni, S. (2010). Demarketing places: rationales and strategies. *Journal of Marketing Management*, 27(1–2), 124–142. https://doi.org/10.1080/02672571003719096.

Menezes, A., Lima, R. M., Aquere, A. L., & Amorim, M. (2020). An adaptation of ServQual for events evaluation: an environmental sustainability add on. *Sustainability (Switzerland)*, 12(18). https://doi.org/10.3390/SU12187408.

Mohanty, P., Dhoundiyal, H., & Choudhury, R. (2020a). Events tourism in the eye of the COVID-19 storm: impacts and implications. In S. Arora, & A. Sharma (Eds.), *Event Tourism in Asian Countries: Challenges and Prospects* (pp. 74–114). Apple Academic Press.

Mohanty, P., Singhania, O., & Hasana, U. (2020b). Mega-events tourism and sustainability: a critique. In S. Arora, & A. Sharma (Eds.), *Event Tourism in Asian Countries: Challenges and Prospects* (1st ed., 219–234). Apple Academic Press.

Mules, T., & Faulkner, B. (1996). An economic perspective on special events. *Tourism economics*, *2*(2), 107–117.

Okech, R.N. (2011), Promoting sustainable festival events tourism: a case study of Lamu Kenya. *Worldwide Hospitality and Tourism Themes*, *3*(3), 193–202. https://doi.org/10.1108/17554211111142158.

Negruşa, A. L., Toader, V., Rus, R. V., & Cosma, S. A. (2016). Study of perceptions on cultural events' *Sustainability*, *8*(12), 1269.

O'Sullivan, D., & Jackson, M. J. (2002). Festival tourism: a contributor to sustainable local economic development? *Journal of Sustainable Tourism*, *10*(4), 325–342.

Phillips, N. (2021). The coronavirus is here to stay-here's what that means. *Nature*, *590*(7846), 382–384.

Raj, R., & Musgrave, J. (2009). *Event Management and Sustainability*: Cabi.

Romagosa, F. (2020). The COVID-19 crisis: opportunities for sustainable and proximity tourism. *Tourism Geographies*, 1–5. https://doi.org/10.1080/14616688.2020.1763447.

Rosenthal, M. (2020). Fauci: COVID-19 Worst Pandemic in 100 Years. Retrieved from https://www.idse.net/Covid-19/Article/10-20/Fauci--COVID-19-Worst-Pandemic-in-100-Years/60937.

Seraphin, H. (2021). COVID-19: an opportunity to review existing grounded theories in event studies. *Journal of Convention and Event Tourism*, *22*(1), 3–35. https://doi.org/10.1080/15470148.2020.1776657.

Sherwood, P., Jago, L., & Deery, M. (2004). *Sustainability Reporting: An Application for the Evaluation of Special Events*. Paper presented at the CAUTHE: Creating Tourism Knowledge.

Soliman, D. M. (2010). Managing visitors via demarketing in the Egyptian World Heritage site: Giza pyramids. *Journal of Association of Arab Universities for Tourism and Hospitality*, *7*(1), 15–20.

Spilling, O. R. (1996). Mega event as strategy for regional development the case of the 1994 Lillehammer Winter Olympics. *Entrepreneurship & Regional Development*, *8*(4), 321–344.

Tiwari, P., Kainthola, S., & Chowdhary, N. R. (2020). Demarketing: a marketing framework for overtourism. In *Handbook of Research on Impacts, Challenges, and Policy Responses to Overtourism* (pp. 94–114). IGI Global Edition. https://doi.org/10.4018/978-1-7998-2224-0.ch006.

UNWTO. (2020). UNWTO Launches Global Guidelines to Restart Tourism. Retrieved from https://www.unwto.org/news/unwto-launches-global-guidelines-to-restart-tourism.

UNWTO. (2021). International Tourism and COVID-19. Retrieved from https://www.unwto.org/international-tourism-and-covid-19.

Yeoman, I., Robertson, M., Ali-Knight, J., Drummond, S., & McMahon-Beattie, U. (2012). Introduction. In I. Yeoman, M. Robertson, J. Ali-Knight, S. Drummond, & U. McMahon-Beattie (Eds.), *Festival and Events Management* (pp. xix–xxi). New York: Routledge.

Ziakas, V., & Getz, D. (2021). Event portfolio management: an emerging transdisciplinary field of theory and praxis. *Tourism Management*, *83*(April 2020), 104233. https://doi.org/10.1016/j.tourman.2020.104233.

16 The Impact of COVID-19 Pandemic on Small Tourism Enterprises in Pakistan

Kalsoom B. and Mehtab Alam

Introduction

The COVID-19 pandemic has slanted the driving tourism enterprises in the recent setback. These small business enterprises are sized and covered under a limited investment. The specificity of the impacts sited on the businesses are varied (Imache et al., 2012; Cil and Turkan, 2013; Dhewanto et al., 2020). The wide-ranging influence of the disease is relative and the measures to safeguard through the social distancing are effective. There is reflection of the attraction due to the impacts of the pandemic which drive small businesses to contest with appalling state of affairs. The commencement of the pandemic provides the researchers to check progressively the impacts on tourism (Tsai and Chen, 2010). These individuals develop a difference in their research aim and their object of examination to remind the world about devastation in tourism sector (Di Domenico and Miller, 2012). The stakeholders are concerted towards the hotel business lapse during the lockdown while some interested on small sized tourism enterprises (SMTEs) to be recovered and reused through a planned step by step actions.

To understand the impacts there are various types of enterprises serving in a same mode of operation, following the local's response and tourists visiting to that sites. A STE is defined as the micro sized enterprises which are distinct while containing 1–9 employees and small enterprises by 10–49 employees. It involves cluster of STEs stakeholders that are drowned by pandemic, including the venders, operators, residents in small houses nearby the tourism enterprises (STE). The small tourism enterprises near tour sites are actively involved in tourism and their income depends on all these activities (Kwok and Koh, 2020; Shao et al., 2020). The brief argument on the loss of the businesses may demand for a handsome amount of critical response to the event of coronavirus (Akbulayev et al. (2020); Arturas et al. (2015); Higgins-Desbiolles (2020a, b); Karaś and Kozioł (2015); Liu et al. (2018); Nhamo et al. (2020); Rogerson and Rogerson (2020); Saikia (2020); Sofrankova et al. (2017); Spencer (2010); Thomas and Wood (2015); Yamano et al. (2020). The event of pandemic has put thousands of low earning jobs at risk, which were normal and used to earn a striking amount of money for

DOI: 10.4324/9781003207467-22

meeting their needs. In addition to this, risks developed during the time are the unavailable food services and accommodation of those daily wage workers (Imache et al., 2012; Cil and Turkan, 2013; Dhewanto et al., 2020). Their vulnerable condition varies to the extension of the lockdown and implementation for social distancing measures, in the world and especially covering the developing states.

Amid the unindustrialized states, Pakistan represents as the state facing with hardest conditions it faced during the COVID-19. It reminds sudden falls in the producing of those small businesses and tourism enterprises (Kwok and Koh, 2020; Shao et al., 2021). Underlying these factors, the paper uncovered the appalling conditions of individuals associated with the small tourism enterprises. The interviews conducted from these owners and relevant stakeholders provide a key insight into the damages caused by pandemic. The categories of the impacted stakeholders are included the women in view of their job and economic growth, tourist guides, small shelters and hotel management, trip operators, work areas and sellers around the destinations (King et al., 2014; Koziol et al., 2017; Regent et al., 2019).

Literature Review

Small Tourism Enterprises Studies and Impact

Contemplating the small tourism enterprises STEs, the paper incorporates various studies through the evaluation in terms of their method, subject and main results about tourism loss during COVID-19 (Tippett et al., 2020). As a consequence, the authors yield a comprehensive review of the on the enterprises. They provide an agenda for impacts recovery in the small sized tourism enterprises. Providing to the tourism enterprise factors it is entail that there is no uncertainty regarding tourism enterprises their dominance in the tourism sector (Higgins-Desbiolles, 2020b). The researchers inquired the sample of the European tourism industry which is at the same acceleration of disjointed consequences.

The pandemic distortion resulted in wreck enterprise situation (Kaushal and Srivastava, 2020). It stops production following the selling an indistinguishable tourism products or services in a high marketplace. Those are the assorted customers (Carr, 2020; Hadi and Supardi, 2020; Higgins, 2020). According to these authors are no more available where the single SMTEs could provide on average jobs for six employees. Certainly, the factors lead to the values that restricted even large or the micro sized enterprises to sustain in the tourism market (Keul, 2014; Rahmanov et al., 2020). Proving further explanation, the studies contain an illustration of Austria which is one of the most important tourism destinations worldwide. However, it is facing 90% shut of all tourism enterprises (Kyrylov et al., 2020; Williams, 2020). To analyze recent STEs trend, one can classify some major global trends. These include the multiculturalization and globalization of the tourism features. The shorter

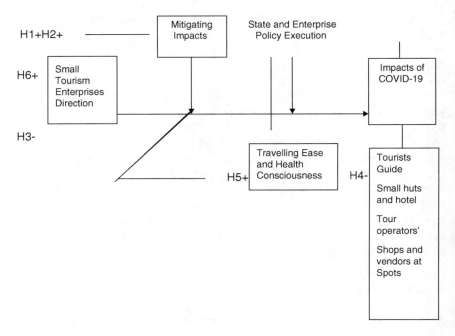

Figure 16.1 Conceptual framework.
Source: Authors' development.

but intensified stays on those destinations, selling of multi-optional products and enhancing travel experience is needed query of the current times. Traveling becomes a health quality consciousness issue for every single individual travelling to respective destination (Brouder et al., 2020). This proposes:

Entrepreneur's Response to COVID-19

Contrary to awful situation, authors provided that some smart entrepreneurs are trying to redesigned their enterprises. Over their product compendium as well as in terms of tourism management these entrepreneurs are struggling with low-slung skills (Lu et al., 2020; Nugroho and Negara, 2020). Several entrepreneur attempts are in precise nature that provides small tourism entrepreneurs, to be inundated with the changes on the demand side of COVID-19 by searching for a hybrid customer. Such entrepreneur behavior is completely diversified and brings travelling in action. Subsequently, owners/managers of tourism enterprises are forcing to pursue clearly for distinctive tactics (Boori et al., 2015; Effendi et al., 2020; Ioannides and Gyimóthy, 2020; Napierała et al., 2020; Salehnia et al., 2020). Concerning the growth of new products and services while facing wreck impacts on tourism provides enterprise to see a difference with global tourism firms or those running SMTEs (Jacobsen and Tiyce, 2014; Matiza, 2020). These SMTs are classically known as international hotel chains, which are managed similar to invite tourists. During the COVID-19, enterprises with cosmopolitan firms in manufacturing were trying to counter the effects through one-man or one-woman initiative.

Reassessing STEs with Smart Strategies

This shows a smart strategy (Kumar, 2020; Parks et al., 2020). There is need for the different enterprise management knowledge which may be responsible for catering the deficit of SMTEs. This provides tourism/hotel business branded by a hyper attraction for travelers (Lu et al., 2020; Nugroho and Negara, 2020). The hotel industry is appropriate with the cases, licenses and patent registration comparison to the tourism business, but both are inter-linked with each other (Shen et al., 2020). The dominance of small businesses in the shape of enterprises displays shortcomings as impacts of COVID-19 limit the profit margins and product development. The short and smart units' employ recovery of the lost business to reinvest in enterprise marketing, and development of product (Ateljevic, 2020; BAYAT, 2020; Bin et al., 2020; Shafi et al., 2020). Research and studies show that enterprises-sized are unwilling in terms of cooperation from government bodies. The traveler's freedom of choice regarding visit to specific destinations provides entrepreneurs to advance economies of scope. The variations in increasing product and services provides an overweighting impact of COVID-19 on the enterprises (Bieloborodova and Bessonova, 2020; Mohanty et al., 2020). Hence, the role of SMTEs unfolds the diverse perspectives of countering the pandemic and sustaining the tourism activities (Armstrong, 2012; Gustavsson and Larsson, 2020; Uğur and Akbıyık, 2020).

Methodology

Data and Sample Collection

Research studies provide for a deteriorating situation as obtained from the following researches conducted in various areas. These included the impacts on STEs that were previously based on continuous functioning of tourism areas. The arrival of the travelers from domestic to national and subsequently on the global destinations is measured through the incorporation of international journals, and related data bases about the information of small and tourism enterprises (Imache et al., 2012; Cil and Turkan, 2013; Dhewanto et al., 2020). The critical assessments have a considerable role in protecting the sampling for the data collection of the 25 members of STEs. The research is focusing on the small and tourism enterprises with impacts on the key areas that include Northern areas and local small enterprises such as small shops, local transportations, small huts and venders near tourists' sites (Imache et al., 2012; Boori et al., 2015; Dhewanto et al., 2020; Ioannides and Gyimóthy, 2020). As provided in the various international journals of tourism management and those related with the enterprises, the interviews are conducted through a standard sampling. The provided impacts on the available studies available offer an overview of impacts research in assessing the enterprises.

The important scientific journals are part of the concentrated impacts or enterprises. This available information is scanned while incorporating the last few years for this research, while maintaining the latest developments in the enterprise businesses around the globe (Ateljevic, 2020; BAYAT, 2020; Bin et al., 2020). There are secondary studies that have no theoretical impacts method, following the entrepreneurial design where the sampling is implied as an intangible process to see the impacts of pandemic (Lebe et al., 2014). The international entrepreneurship journal used the small businesses within the volumes of data that unfolded the consistency of impact on the small businesses. These journals subsidized for the consideration of sampling more than 25 are in void with the results not meeting the international standards of the research (Boori et al., 2015; Effendi et al., 2020; Napierała et al., 2020; Salehnia et al., 2020). The researchers reviewed total of one hundred and seventy-three relevant papers for selecting the sample to respond the queries.

The semi-structure interviews of the selected individuals based on their expertise on the enterprise business and the relevant functions on the destinations of areas including the Nathiagali, Donga Gali, Main Murree, Kashmir Point, Lower Topa and Ayubia. These destinations in the northern areas of Pakistan are evaluated and the questionnaire was handover to the experts. Unlike the quantitative overview of the literature the research focused on impacts faced by enterprises through the interviews (Effendi et al., 2020; Napierała et al., 2020; Salehnia et al., 2020). After receiving the response, the procedure of the subject, was to align sample and method with the main results. Further the individuals having participated in the process of opinion giving and developing themes through their responses are detailed as 04 participants from each destination including Kashmir Point, Lower Topa and Ayubia while others from Donga Gali, Nathiagali, and main area of the Murree.

Response Measurement Procedures

The questions for the respondent while viewing the economic impacts of COVID-19 and it includes the shutting enterprises and the opportunities for their recovery. Each stakeholder impacted by COVID-19 is incorporated with their key profession and negative situation faced by them. The responsibility of government and key tourism organization is widely discussed at the disposal of questions developed accordingly. The research considered measurement of the responses through the questionnaire developed according to the level of impact on each tourism enterprises (Tsai and Chen, 2010). The discussion during the interview with participants involves in charge of the enterprises in each area, workers with those head of the STEs, local representative and the officials of tourism department.

Percentage for each of them is as follows: 12% of local representatives, 48% of enterprises, while remaining 40% are from the tourism department. Those having background of local representatives have education around graduation (Hadi and Carr, 2020; Supardi, 2020). On the other side, officials and the in charge of the enterprises have little formal education. The normal average pertaining to all of the respondents reflects a significant educational status. However, the experience varies to most of them for in charge and officials.

The representatives of local residents represent more as an observer than as an enterprise manager. There are 68% male members with 32% are female representatives of the enterprises business. The entrance of the travelers in the areas and destinations is significant but not up to the mark as most of them during the interview session remain disappeared from the destinations and enterprises location. The participants received the inform consent format copy to explain the reasons and recovery ratio of loss faced by STEs. The copy of the consent form is with the participant as it reflects their single identification towards their role in this research. Those individuals who were served through the online business maintain their record and send copies back through the Google forms. Between the ages of 25–45 there are 06 members of in charge of the small and tourism enterprises. Other participants are aged at 20–28, 30–45 and in charge are 40–50 years of age. The dominance of questions was influencing the accurate responses; those were scrutinized through the development of themes. The issues of enterprise assessment are transformed through the transcription of the meaning and single unit explanation towards the title of the research. The small business firms in the Northern areas of Nathiagali, Donga Gali, Main Murree, Kashmir Point, Lower Topa and Ayubia provide diverse response to the interviewer.

Data Analysis Techniques

A semi-structured interview was conducted with the participants to see the impacts of COVID-19 on small tourism enterprises (Tsai and Chen, 2010). The loss of the business, following those enterprises and the impacts on each of the individual along with their profession is well incorporated in the development of techniques. The codified issues of small tourism enterprises are share with the respondents. The response, observation and the techniques implied for the analysis of collected data is through themes and transcription of the opinions from the original language to the explanation and understanding of the perception about small tourism enterprises (Carr, 2020; Hadi and Supardi, 2020).

258 Kalsoom B. and Mehtab Alam

The effects for many are influencing current business and others stress for the asked questions to be explained. As a facilitator the questions presented before the respondent are explained well to determine the level of response. The recording of the interviews was progressed owing to the permission of each individual containing 20–250 minutes for each respondent. The qualitative thematic analysis is the unsurpassed technique employed after the transcription of each record or the available response (Jacobsen and Tiyce, 2014; Matiza, 2020). The patterns of analysis prove efficient as various studies contain such qualitative techniques to see the impacts on small businesses and daily wage earning as in the case of small tourism enterprises in this study. The identification of the analytical patterns becomes apparent from the responses as well as through the unfolding of various concepts related to enterprises. The participants are approached through the original language commonly speaks at the desire enterprises and destinations of tourism (Table 16.1).

The assessments through the quality data analysis provide a key insight into the aspects of degradation of businesses on the destinations and key tourism spots. Each question asked from the participants involved an issue that is currently faced by them. Further the tourism promotion and future impacts of the COVID-19 are effectively discussed by using the participants' reviews over the crisis. The development of the theme and the maintenance of codes along with sub-heading are to identify the analysis of the opinion and observations received through the questions.

Results and Discussion

An important development is accumulated through the research on the impacts of COVID-19 on small tourism enterprises. The transcription of

Table 16.1 Qualitative Data Analysis

Questions	Meaning Unit	Category	Theme
How you realize the lasting impacts of COVID-19 on STE?	Unable to cope with COVID-19 impacts	Isolated destinations	Non-availability of the customers
How are the opportunities of selling a product on destinations?	There are no opportunities of vending	Empty tourism marketplace	Closure of shops
What are the expectations of tour operators for guiding travelers?	Travelling operations are padlocked	Tour operators	No earning
Which condition demonstrates the existence of occupation?	Premature necessity of business survival	Small tourism enterprise	Unfilled tourism places

Source: Authors' development.

the responses provides an insight into the factors contributing for certain themes (Kwok and Koh, 2020; Shao et al., 2021). Among those are the three major results that reflect a sedative picture of the small tourism enterprises and the acceptability of those factors that may restore the capacity of vendors, tour guides, supervising staff of small huts and hotel, travel operators, shops and small business individuals on the destinations.

Theme I

Considering the first theme, the acceptability and perception about the loss of important business movement are major concerns of small traders. Respondents with 40% of the opinion focused on the loss that may not be able to recover as soon as it is commonly observed (Jacobsen and Tiyce, 2014; Matiza, 2020). There is illustration of remaining 60% that they are accepting the natural cause and devastation, however remedial measures for them is not possible because of nothing is left with them out of that earning. The demonstration of the fear regarding the future constraints on the lock down and social distancing measures may disturb the already aggravated situation of small tourism enterprises.

Theme II

The second theme emerged out of the response and systematic analysis of the retreating is the individual impacts of COVID-19 on each stakeholder connected with the small tourism enterprises (Kyrylov et al., 2020; Williams, 2020). These include the STEs guide, small huts and hotel, tour operators, shops and venders. The percentage counted for the each of them is follows as; vendors with 14%, shops with 45%, tour operators with 50% small huts and hotels have 40% and same is the case with tourists' guides having 56% impact of COVID-19 on their business. The entire percentage accumulated as the central figures where each product, process and behavior is devastated. The impacts of the COVID-19 on the small tourism enterprises varied for the third major theme developed out of the discussion. It reflects through observations and through the secondary studies that the capacity of enterprises is compromise to sustain in a grim stretch period of pandemic.

Theme III

These stakeholders have difficulties in renewing this strategy as they begin to grow due their initial success during the short period providing reopening of the travelling destinations. The loss of the larger business may get retrieval as stakeholders have the stronger inexpensive gravity of the understanding about COVID-19 season. SME may able to develop new strategic measures to disperse those impacts on the enterprises with a positive response. The latest investment on the recapturing of SMEs origination, involvement and strategic attention requires the inter-firm cooperation (Kyrylov et al., 2020; Williams, 2020). These are positively related to export traveling behavior for those tourists who make a visit to their peace-driven destinations. The process, product and the vendors' services may stimulate the enterprises in the Northern region of Pakistan to remain active and sustainable. The comparison of small tourism enterprises with the other sectors shows same results of deficits. Non-availability of hotel and catering services press for the impacts and paves way for the practices and the development of enterprise association. The study stress for the providing of specific education and training to enterprises owners in order to be benefited for the common vendors and daily wagers.

Theme IV

The demonstration of the encouragement reflects the development of deeper and wider culture on each destination. STEs growth performance sum up that original product and the simulation of employment for daily wages along with the enhancement in sales is incremental during the season of COVID-19. This may be increase with the lifting of lockdown and social distancing measures those may be soften by the government can allow the STEs owner to be informed and well knitted with the latest development in their business. The focused remains on the provisions of services from the tourists' guides, fellow vendors or those workers at the hotel shaped small huts available on the destinations. The services clearance and the impacts on in enterprises during the one and half year are non-reversible.

Further inquiry and discussion on the tourism and in particular the huts/hotels attached with the small tourism enterprises may contribute for the key determinants and firm performance in small tourism services (Kwok and Koh, 2020; Shao et al., 2021). New products, stalls, sales and related services of the employees not able to advance the quality as limitations and impacts of the virus are distorting. Significantly these are faster than those tourism firms that do not introduce new products during the crisis times. The impacts studies agreed out for enterprises in tourism that reports of satisfactory responses are scanned with zero progress shown during the pandemic.

Conclusion and Recommendations

In brief, the study explores the impacts of COVID-19 on the small tourism enterprises in Pakistan while focusing on the northern areas of Pakistan. The areas considered for the research incorporated the destinations of Nathiagali, Donga Gali, Main Murree, Kashmir Point, Lower Topa and Ayubia. These are unvarying visiting themes of tourism activities; those are never reflecting an unfilled place during the winter as well as summer season (Armstrong, 2012; Gustavsson and Larsson, 2020; Uğur and Akbıyık, 2020).

The opening of these spots facilitates stakeholders like the tourists' guide, small huts and hotel, tour operators, shops and venders to generate revenue and to sustain their life. However, the impacts of the COVID-19 have confounded the areas through health security measures of lockdown and maintaining of social distancing. The pandemic has put thousands of low earning jobs at risk, which were normal and used to earn a striking amount of money for meeting their needs. In addition to this, risks developed during the time are the unavailable food services and accommodation of those daily wage workers (Imache et al., 2012; Cil and Turkan, 2013; Dhewanto et al., 2020). Their vulnerable condition varies to the extension of the lockdown and implementation for social distancing measures.

There is the factor for common individuals who are not aware of restricting themselves at home without earning a penny for their survival. The compromise on their survival may vary but it does not imply on all serving workers with a single and demanding family needs. Further the impacts seem considerable for the extended interest of business both in the smaller and larger context. Unlike this study most of the impact research considers the tourism manufacturing businesses or those destinations where the frequent movement of travelling is in progress. The determinants of the impacts and their relationship to the small tourism enterprises performance contributed for the deficit in earning and jobs attaining positions. Qualitative review of the study enhances an agreement that is needed for overseeing the positive influences and growth of enterprises for each stakeholder. This provides and extension to the requirement of entrepreneurial alignment with current market direction. For example, an online system of inviting or attracting tourists to the sites is an attribute of a highly professional worker.

The strain through the cultural values with capital through the external support among the same tourism guides may counter the impacts of COVID-19 (Kwok and Koh, 2020; Shao et al., 2021). The interaction with international tourism enterprises specifically the small individuals may result in a new idea of curbing the negative influence of pandemic. However, there is dilemma, which is the darker side of the enterprises in developing countries like Pakistan, that these ignore barriers influencing negative perception or contribution to the business. Same is the case with STEs which are facing with problems in terms of project based working or relevant resources. For such situations there are many small tourism entrepreneurs those occasionally apply some changes to their business in crisis. Here the comparison is not about the small tourism businesses other forms of trading but about the survival of those vendors, tour guides and key workers.

It is observed that only minor differences look as the pandemic consequences on small businesses from the service business appear to be highly relevant for tourism. There is need of following the tourism values for the trendsetter's small enterprises (Armstrong, 2012; Gustavsson and Larsson, 2020; Uğur and Akbıyık, 2020). Adoption of a strategic approach as a permanent process of enterprise of tourism may sustain the research. An example to such degree of pandemic impacts on small sized hotel enterprises in Pakistan is to assess the condition of loss. To mitigate that distortion, the small entrepreneurs may focus on the innovative style, and through the services and products of digital sites (Akbulayev et al., 2020). A significant element for success of enterprises during crisis situation is through the tourism origin which may be in any form of its existence. Empowering the enterprises especially STEs is also the responsibility of the state for countries as Pakistan to uplift the life of common workers earn on the daily basis (Carr, 2020; Hadi and Supardi, 2020; Higgins, 2020). Skills learning and training of these poor small business owners may provide them to earn their wages in diverse manner. Developing personal characteristics in a single entrepreneur contribute for exploration of tourism activities in Northern Areas. This is not a limited factor instead it provides an extensive opportunity for the state to follow the pandemic instructions by World Health Organization. At the same time, it retreats a smart lockdown strategy for tourists to get out of their homes paving way for jobs and business opportunities to the daily wagers.

Future Research Directions

The studies consider for the tourism management and especially those areas which are fragile in the wake of COVID-19 may extend their scope to the other parts or regions in Pakistan. The dimensions and resources emerge from the broad consensus or review of literature exists on the relevancy of the extended small profession (Carr, 2020; Hadi and Supardi, 2020; Higgins, 2020). Consequently, the inordinate and mainstream tourism based experiential studies concentrate on exploring resources inside the destinations or the areas of traveling business. For future research based on the fact mentioned above there are certain research gaps existing in small tourism businesses. These maybe the area of research, following the fulfilling customer or tourists needs. The presence of services and businesses in an innovative style may result in receiving a positive response from the customers. Further, the understanding of the research regarding the impacts of any crisis is important to be part of future research.

Similarly, the forthcoming research may examine the reasons for fail countering the impacts of COVID-19 on small tourism enterprises (Hadi and Supardi, 2020). The collection of information for the next stage research may also be extended though the broader statistical records. Despite the presence of certain limitations of the paper like the exhaustive literature review or limited resources to meet the relevant results, but the originality of the paper is distinctive. The study is technically able to convey the painful conditions of the workers, entrepreneurs, daily-wagers, workers and the tourist guides in a better and systematic way (Uğur and Akbıyık, 2020). This shows the demonstration that impacts of crisis are rare, for STEs it is focusing on the business side of the services those should be enhanced. From the northern region of Pakistan, this research may vary and may be extended to the other side where national destinations are part of the forthcoming study. Lack of diversity or the cultural touch in the systematic procedures is in dire need of understanding to rise the business activities at the larger scale.

An important observation noted during the research is unavailability of stress for business concentrations in the selected regions which is a major flaw for the common individual to survive during pandemic. These crisis situations have no reality unless these are reflected by the amplified records and databases present in the digital libraries (Effendi et al., 2020; Napierała et al., 2020). A single stakeholder may consider for each research paper to highlight the sufferings of affected persons. Other issues or the limitations for further discovery of issues with the small tourism enterprises are the extension of favoring the qualitative and quantitative methods under a single approach. This is to receive more profound results and realities with assorted sentiments. Studies for the STEs present with insufficient experiments (Effendi et al., 2020; Napierała et al., 2020). It should be encouraged through the placement of emphasis on enterprise side and to attain the current marketing objectives. Inter-connecting the networks is significant for the researchers to build a comprehensive learning on impacts of crisis situation on the happenings of small tourism initiatives.

References

Akbulayev, N., Guliyeva, N., and Aslanova, G. (2020). Economic analysis of tourism enterprise solvency and the possibility of bankruptcy: the case of the Thomas Cook Group. *African Journal of Hospitality, Tourism and Leisure*, 9(2), 1–12.

Armstrong, R. (2012). An analysis of the conditions for success of community-based tourism enterprises. *ICRT Occasional Paper*, (OP21), 1–52.

Arturas, S., Jasinskas, E., and Svagzdiene, B. (2015). Risk assessment models in the tourism sector. *Amfiteatru Economic Journal*, 17(39), 836–846.

Ateljevic, I. (2020). Transforming the (tourism) world for good and (re) generating the potential 'new normal'. *Tourism Geographies*, 22(3), 467–475.

BAYAT, G. (2020). The effects of COVID-19 on the tourism sector and hotel businesses: the case of Marmaris. *Igdir University Journal of Social Sciences*, 23, 628–630e.

Bieloborodova, M., and Bessonova, S. (2020). External environment transformation of Ukraine's tourist enterprises during the crisis. *European Journal of Management Issues*, 28(3), 72–80.

Bin, Z., Weihua, Z., and Jinming, C. (2020). Bio-statistical analysis on the enterprise dynamic management in the COVID-19 pandemic. *Journal of Endocrinology and Metabolism Research*, 1(1), 1–19.

Boori, M. S., Voženílek, V., and Choudhary, K. (2015). Land use/cover disturbance due to tourism in Jeseníky Mountain, Czech Republic: a remote sensing and GIS based approach. *The Egyptian Journal of Remote Sensing and Space Science*, 18(1), 17–26.

Brouder, P., Teoh, S., Salazar, N. B., Mostafanezhad, M., Pung, J. M., Lapointe, D.,... and Clausen, H. B. (2020). Reflections and discussions: tourism matters in the new normal post COVID-19. *Tourism Geographies*, 22(3), 735–746.

Carr, A. (2020). COVID-19, indigenous peoples and tourism: a view from New Zealand. *Tourism Geographies, 22*(3), 491–502.

Cil, I., and Turkan, Y. S. (2013). An ANP-based assessment model for lean enterprise transformation. *The International Journal of Advanced Manufacturing Technology, 64*(5–8), 1113–1130.

Dhewanto, W., Nazmuzzaman, E., and Fauzan, T. R. (2020). Cross-countries' policies comparison of supporting tourism enterprises-sized enterprises during Covid-19 pandemic. In *ECIE 2020 16th European Conference on Impacts and Entrepreneurship* (p. 218). Academic Conferences limited.

Di Domenico, M., and Miller, G. (2012). Farming and tourism enterprise: experiential authenticity in the diversification of independent small-scale family farming. *Tourism Management, 33*(2), 285–294.

Effendi, M. I., Sugandini, D., and Istanto, Y. (2020). Social media adoption in enterprises impacted by COVID-19: the TOE model. *The Journal of Asian Finance, Economics, and Business, 7*(11), 915–925.

Gustavsson, S., and Larsson, S. (2020). Marketing Innovation for SMEs during COVID-19 Pandemic: A case study of the hospitality industry in Norrbotten (Dissertation). Retrieved from http://urn.kb.se/resolve?urn=urn:nbn:se:ltu:diva-79426.

Hadi, S., and Supardi, S. (2020). Revitalization strategy for tourism enterprises after Corona virus disease pandemic (covid-19) in Yogyakarta. *Journal of Xi'an University of Architecture & Technology, 12*, 4068–4076.

Higgins-Desbiolles, F. (2020a). Socialising tourism for social and ecological justice after COVID-19. *Tourism Geographies, 22*, 1–14.

Higgins-Desbiolles, F. (2020b). The "war over tourism": challenges to sustainable tourism in the tourism academy after COVID-19. *Journal of Sustainable Tourism, 29*(4), 551–569.

Imache, R., Izza, S., and Ahmed-Nacer, M. (2012). An enterprise information system agility assessment model. *Computer Science and Information Systems, 9*(1), 107–133.

Ioannides, D., and Gyimóthy, S. (2020). The COVID-19 crisis as an opportunity for escaping the unsustainable global tourism path. *Tourism Geographies, 22*(3), 624–632.

Jacobsen, D., and Tiyce, M. (2014). *Aboriginal and Torres Strait Islander Tourism Enterprise Approaches to Creating Value for Visitors in Remote Australia*. Retrieved from: http://www.crc-rep.com.au/resource/CR003_AboriginalTorresStraitIslanderTourismEnterprisesCreatingValue.pdf. Available from, http://www.nintione.com.au/publication/crc-rep-0280 (Accessed: the 01st December, 2020).

Karaś, A., and Kozioł, L. (2015). The concept of the tourism enterprise impacts analysis. *EkonomiczneProblemyTurystyki, 32*, 19–29.

Kaushal, V., and Srivastava, S. (2020). Hospitality and tourism industry amid COVID-19 pandemic: perspectives on challenges and learnings from India. *International Journal of Hospitality Management, 92*, 102707.

Keul, A. (2014). Tourism neoliberalism and the swamp as enterprise. *Area, 46*(3), 235–241.

King, B. E., Breen, J., and Whitelaw, P. A. (2014). Hungry for growth? Tourism enterprises-sized tourism enterprise (SMTE) business ambitions, knowledge acquisition and industry engagement. *International Journal of Tourism Research, 16*(3), 272–281.

Koziol, L., Wojtowicz, A., and Karaś, A. (2017). The concept of the innovative tourism enterprises assessment capability. In V. Katsoni, A. Upadhya, and A. Stratigea (Eds.), *Tourism, Culture and Heritage in a Smart Economy* (pp. 159–172). Cham: Springer.

Kumar, V. (2020). Indian tourism industry and COVID-19: present scenario. *Journal of Tourism and Hospitality Education*, *10*, 179–185.

Kwok, A. O., and Koh, S. G. (2020). COVID-19 and extended reality (XR). *Current Issues in Tourism*. https://doi.org/10.1080/13683500.2020.1798896.

Kyrylov, Y., Hranovska, V., Boiko, V., Kwilinski, A., and Boiko, L. (2020). International tourism development in the context of increasing globalization risks: on the example of Ukraine's integration into the global tourism industry. *Journal of Risk and Financial Management*, *13*(12), 303.

Lebe, S. S., Mulej, M., Štrukelj, T., and Šuligoj, M. (2014). Holism and social responsibility for tourism enterprise governance, *Kybernetes, 43*(3/4), 394–412. https://doi.org/10.1108/K-07-2013-0159.

Liu, Y. L., Ho, L. M., and Liu, F. (2018). The brand management evaluation indicators model of agri-tourism farms: a core competence perspective. *Open Access Library Journal*, *5*(8), 1–9.

Lu, Y., Wu, J., Peng, J., and Lu, L. (2020). The perceived impact of the Covid-19 epidemic: evidence from a sample of 4807 enterprises in Sichuan Province, China. *Environmental Hazards*, *19*(4), 323–340.

Matiza, T. (2020). Post-COVID-19 crisis travel behaviour: towards mitigating the effects of perceived risk. *Journal of Tourism Futures*. https://doi.org/10.1108/JTF-04-2020-0063.

Mohanty, P., Dhoundiyal, H., and Choudhury, R. (2020). Events tourism in the eye of the COVID-19 storm: impacts and implications. *Event Tourism in Asian Countries: Challenges and Prospects* (1st ed.). Florida, USA: Apple Academic Press.

Napierała, T., Leśniewska-Napierała, K., and Burski, R. (2020). Impact of geographic distribution of COVID-19 cases on hotels' performances: case of polish cities. *Sustainability*, *12*(11), 4697.

Nhamo, G., Dube, K., and Chikodzi, D. (2020). Tourism economic stimulus packages as a response to COVID-19. In *Counting the Cost of COVID-19 on the Global Tourism Industry* (pp. 353–374). Cham: Springer.

Nugroho, Y., and Negara, S. D. (2020). *COVID-19's Impact on Micro, Small, & Medium Enterprises and Tourism in Indonesia*. ISEAS Yusof Ishak Institute. http://hdl.handle.net/11540/12673.

Parks, T., Chatsuwan, M., and Pillai, S. (2020). *Enduring the Pandemic: Surveys of the Impact of COVID-19 on the Livelihoods of Thai People*. The Asia Foundation. http://hdl.handle.net/11540/12528. Keywords.

Rahmanov, F., Aliyeva, R., Rosokhata, A. S., and Letunovska, N. Y. (2020). Tourism management in Azerbaijan under sustainable development: impact of COVID-19. *Marketing and Management of Innovations*, *3*, 195–207.

Regent, T. M., Glinkina, O. V., Ganina, S. A., Markova, O. V., and Kozhina, V. O. (2019). Improvement of strategic management of a tourism enterprise in the international market. *Journal of Environmental Management and Tourism*, *10*(2), 427–431.

Rogerson, C. M., and Rogerson, J. M. (2020). COVID-19 tourism impacts in South Africa: government and industry responses. *GeoJournal of Tourism and Geosites*, *31*(3), 1083–1091.

Saikia, R. (2020). Developing sustainable tourism post COVID 19: challenges for the tourism enterprises. *CLIO An Annual Interdisciplinary Journal of History*, *6*(10), 298–308.

Salehnia, N., Zabihi, S. M. G., and Safarzaei, K. (2020). *The impact of COVID-19 Pandemic on Tourism Industry: A Statistical Review in European Countries*. 10.6084/m9.figshare.14528886.v2.

Shafi, M., Liu, J., and Ren, W. (2020). Impact of COVID-19 pandemic on micro, small, and medium-sized Enterprises operating in Pakistan. *Research in Globalization*, *2*, 100018.

Shao, Y., Hu, Z., Luo, M., Huo, T., and Zhao, Q. (2021). What is the policy focus for tourism recovery after the outbreak of COVID-19? A co-word analysis. *Current Issues in Tourism*, *24*(7), 899–904.

Shen, H., Fu, M., Pan, H., Yu, Z., and Chen, Y. (2020). The impact of the COVID-19 pandemic on firm performance. *Emerging Markets Finance and Trade*, *56*(10), 2213–2230.

Sofrankova, B., Kiselakova, D., and Matkova, S. (2017). Analysis of tourism enterprise performance evaluation by enterprise performance model. In *4th International Multidisciplinary Scientific Conference on Social Sciences and Arts Sgem 2017* (pp. 753–762). Bulgaria.

Spencer, D. M. (2010). Facilitating public participation in tourism planning on American Indian reservations: a case study involving the Nominal Group Technique. *Tourism Management*, *31*(5), 684–690.

Thomas, R., and Wood, E. (2015). The absorptive capacity of tourism organisations. *Annals of Tourism Research*, *54*, 84–99.

Tippett, A. W., Yttredal, E. R., and Strand, Ø. (2020). *Ecolabelling for Tourism Enterprises: What, Why and How*. Retrieved from: https://www.waddenseaworldheritage.org/sites/default/files/2020_Ecolabel%20report.pdf (Accessed: the 1st December, 2020).

Tsai, C. H., and Chen, C. W. (2010). An earthquake disaster management mechanism based on risk assessment information for the tourism industry-a case study from the island of Taiwan. *Tourism Management*, *31*(4), 470–481.

Uğur, N. G., and Akbıyık, A. (2020). Impacts of COVID-19 on global tourism industry: a cross-regional comparison. *Tourism Management Perspectives*, *36*, 100744.

Williams, C. C. (2020). Impacts of the coronavirus pandemic on Europe's tourism industry: addressing tourism enterprises and workers in the undeclared economy. *International Journal of Tourism Research*. https://doi.org/10.1002/jtr.2395.

Yamano, T., Pradhananga, M., Schipani, S., Samson, J. N., Quiao, L., Leuangkhamsing, S., and Maddawin, A. (2020). The impact of COVID-19 on tourism enterprises in the Lao People's Democratic Republic: an initial assessment. http://dx.doi.org/10.22617/BRF200187-2.

17 Perspectives in the Strategic Management of Destinations in the Post-COVID Period

Dália Liberato, Beatriz Limbado, Bruno Sousa and Pedro Liberato

Introduction

According to Lee and Chen (2020), it is widely recognized that the most important sector in a country's economic development path is travel and leisure. The growth of the tourism industry has been phenomenal, becoming one of the most competitive sectors, and this competition is increased as destinations seek to attract tourists. In this sense, Castro et al. (2020) state that the tourism industry plays a crucial role in the economy, since, with its substantial growth in recent years, this economic activity is also responsible for boosting the global economy. In fact, according to 2019 data, this industry has been responsible for 10.3% of the global Gross Domestic Product (GDP) and has supported the lives of about 330 million people, outpacing the growth of the global economy for the ninth consecutive year (WTTC, 2020).

According to Niewiadomski (2020), the outbreak of COVID-19 in China in January 2020 was initially seen as a local problem, however, the spread of the virus to other parts of the world in February and March 2020 gave rise to a global crisis of unprecedented scale and nature. In fact, Ioannides and Gyimóthy (2020) also indicate that since the emergence of COVID-19, the rapid spread of the pandemic has caused global havoc. As a result of this situation, Araujo et al. (2020) explain that governments have adopted containment measures in order to control the spread and avoid the collapse of the healthcare system due to an eventual increase in the number of infected. The pandemic caused by COVID-19 is a once-in-a-lifetime experience, since there has never been a recorded event in modern human history that has affected the entire population of the planet to the same degree as the new coronavirus, this is because, this pandemic is the culmination of a series of evolutionary changes that brought together elements that did not exist before this moment (Galvani et al., 2020).

According to Chinazzi et al. (2020), COVID-19 differs from previous pandemics by having a longer incubation period and fewer noticeable symptoms, which facilitates its spread. After the outbreak in Wuhan, the new coronavirus was confirmed to spread globally through international travelers

DOI: 10.4324/9781003207467-23

(Adongo et al., 2021). In this sense, Hall et al. (2020) explain that nowadays urban centers are more interconnected than ever, as a result of the connectivity of air, rail, sea and road transport, which implies that a passenger, and likewise a disease, can travel from one urban center to the other side of the world in a single day. In this perspective, Prideaux et al. (2020) add that COVID-19 has spread through air, land and sea travel used by the tourism industry, resulting in a large-scale disruption of domestic and international tourism flows and consequently causing an unparalleled crisis for the global tourism industry. In fact, COVID-19 disrupted the global tourism industry in 2020 (Ma et al., 2020), and it is possible to add, that this pandemic interrupted global mobility on an unprecedented scale, causing the mechanisms of tourism to be severely disrupted (Ioannides & Gyimóthy, 2020). When the world stopped, so did tourism, a sector that not only accounts for more than 10% of global GDP, but for one in ten jobs on the planet and one in four new jobs created globally in the last five years (WTTC, 2020).

By February 2020, global air transport was already carrying the virus to every continent, and by mid-March it was already affecting 146 countries (Gössling et al., 2020), mainly due to tourist movements, which promoted the spread of the epidemic (Shao et al., 2020).

In this context, Shao et al. (2020) show that numerous tourism recovery-related policies have been issued to guide the operation of tourism enterprises and suppress the spread of COVID-19. It is also noted by Farzanegan et al. (2020) that the negative impacts of COVID-19 are not only limited to the loss of human lives, but also include short- and long-term social, economic, and political effects. Countries have closed borders, limited the movement of citizens, and even confined them in quarantine for weeks inside their own homes (Donthu & Gustafsson, 2020). In fact, according to Cave and Dredge (2020), the preventive measures concerning COVID-19, including travel bans, border crossing restrictions, blockades and physical distancing, have created instability for social, economic and political life, but also, for the ecological well-being of the planet. Initially, with the absence of the vaccine and limited medical interventions available to prevent the new coronavirus, most countries responded with various forms of non-pharmaceutical interventions, including isolation (home, voluntary or mandatory quarantine); social distancing (vulnerable or entire populations); closure of schools, universities, businesses and non-essential workplaces; cancellation or postponement of events such as large conferences and fairs, concerts and festivals, political debates and elections or sporting events (Gössling et al., 2020).

Finally, Wen et al. (2020) state that COVID-19 has already been shown to exert crippling effects on the economy, including in travel and tourism. According to Higgins-Desbiolles (2020), COVID-19 has the potential to transform the tourism industry as well as the context in which it operates. In the same perspective, Ma et al. (2020) state that this pandemic resulted in negative impacts, not only on the economy, but also on the physical and mental health of the population, since the anguish caused by the virus and the lack of social interaction caused a great emotional pressure on society.

The targets of this research are the entities of the tourism and hospitality sector that are located in the Northern Region of Portugal. To cover the destination in its entirety and, verifying that this region is divided into eight subregional units (Alto Minho, Cávado, Ave, Metropolitan Area of Porto, Alto Tâmega, Tâmega e Sousa, Douro, and Terras de Trás-os-Montes), this study chose to conduct interviews in all NUT III (subregional units), thus building the population with 13 organizations. The sampling technique used in this research is theoretical sampling, which consists of identifying those who have the greatest capacity to help answer the intended objectives.

The Crisis in Tourism and Factors Determining Demand

The World Tourism Organization (UNWTO, 2020) declared tourism as one of the most affected sectors by COVID-19 and Abbaspour et al. (2020) stated that this outbreak presented unprecedented challenges to tourism due to the global nature of its pandemic effect.

Indeed, Yang et al. (2020) demonstrated that outbreaks of infectious diseases (including COVID-19) impede tourism growth due to the industry's dependence on human mobility. Since March 2020, the pandemic caused by COVID-19 has been causing economic damage globally (Pan et al., 2021), and unlike recent epidemic outbreaks, e.g., SARS, Ebola, and H1N1, the coronavirus remains the world's deadliest outbreak, accompanied by a global health crisis, financial crisis, and economic slowdown, known as the COVID-19 recession (Fotiadis et al., 2021).

National administrations have quickly realized that ease of travel is the main factor that helps the spread of COVID-19, resulting in the closure of national borders, the disruption of cross-border movement of people, and the suspension of international transportation (Niewiadomski, 2020). On the other hand, Hall et al. (2020) report that social distancing requirements reduce the capacity of hospitality operations, such as catering and accommodation. This finding has led to the closure of borders, travel has been banned, social activities have been reduced, and people have been directed to stay in their homes (Higgins-Desbiolles, 2020). As a result, the restriction of non-essential services, travel movements and the closure of places where social distancing is not possible, made tourism a victim of the pandemic caused by COVID-19 (Lapointe, 2020). In the same context, the spread of COVID-19 and associated travel bans, and movements have infiltrated almost every aspect of daily life, threatening to paralyze the tourism and hospitality industry (accommodation services have stopped and restaurants have closed) (Wen et al., 2020). Sectors in tourism, hospitality, and events were hampered by government efforts to reduce and control the pandemic (Higgins-Desbiolles, 2020), as, with the flow of tourists disrupted, a portion of businesses focused on tourism services sharply reduced the number of customers (Lapointe, 2020). In this regard, Niewiadomski (2020) states that the closure of hotels, restaurants, entertainment centers, and various tourist attractions has brought the entire tourism and travel industry to a standstill.

In addition, air transportation, accommodation facilities, travel agencies, tourist attractions, and restaurant facilities were hit unevenly; supply chains were severely disrupted; the entire workforce was laid off; and some businesses were able to focus on addressing emerging opportunities (Cave & Dredge, 2020), yet museums, hotels, and restaurants closed, beaches and ski slopes found themselves empty, and events of all sizes were postponed or canceled, thus showing that the economic effects, especially in localities or countries that rely heavily on tourism arrivals, were catastrophic (Ioannides & Gyimóthy, 2020).

Thus, Higgins-Desbiolles (2020) argues that the pandemic crisis of COVID-19 was devastating for its impacts on travel and tourism, as well as the affiliated hospitality, arts, and events sectors. Indeed, as shown by Gössling et al. (2020), international, regional, and local travel restrictions immediately affected national economies, including tourism systems, i.e., international travel, domestic tourism, day visits, and various segments such as air transportation, cruises, public transportation, accommodation, catering, conventions, festivals, meetings, or sporting events.

The Organization for Economic Cooperation and Development (OECD) estimates an 80% drop in international tourism by 2020, and while domestic tourism has resumed, not all destinations or businesses have benefited equally (Guerreiro, 2020). All destinations showed declines in arrivals between 51% and 85% and about one in three destinations saw declines between 70% and 79% (ETC, 2021). Montenegro (−85%), Cyprus (−84%) and Romania (−83%) were the hardest hit, having been affected by a strong dependence on international markets; Spain (−77%), where tourism represents 12% of the country's GDP, suffered from the loss of demand from major markets (UK, Germany, France, Netherlands, and Italy); tourist arrivals in Portugal, Serbia, Malta, and Hungary (showing drops of 75%) also fell (ETC, 2021).

Significant decreases in destination arrivals and business such as tourist travel, number of visitors at tourist attractions, and occupancy rate in hotel units are some of the adverse impacts of disease outbreaks (Adongo et al., 2021). According to Lew et al. (2020), the widespread crisis surrounding the outbreak of the pandemic revealed the fragility and unsustainable nature of the current global economic system, in which travel and tourism play a crucial role, and it was largely due to international tourism and business travel that the new coronavirus spread so rapidly across the planet. Consequently, tourism is one of the economic sectors most affected by country-imposed travel blocks and restrictions (Lew et al., 2020).

From this perspective, the sector remains in survival mode, and potentially faces a period of cycles adjusted to the situation of COVID-19, delaying its recovery (Guerreiro, 2020). Until the beginning of COVID-19, few people within the communities had realized how dependent they were on tourism, until this sector had completely stagnated (Haywood, 2020). For Niewiadomski (2020) tourism as we knew it no longer exists.

Tourism has been aggressively hit with millions of jobs at risk, this being considered one of the most labor-intensive sectors of the economy (UNWTO, 2020). Because of the global health crisis caused by COVID-19, Araujo et al. (2020) state that companies are readjusting and many workers in this sector have been laid off, some have had their contracts suspended and others are at risk, not considering the indirect jobs that have also been halved.

In fact, Donthu and Gustafsson (2020) mention that the sectors that have seen the largest increases in unemployment are those of a hedonic nature and that require the physical presence of the customer, such as hospitality, tourism or entertainment, since the demand for such services no longer exists. Employees in the tourism industry face steep drops in income, with dramatic changes in both their professional and personal lives, and the panic caused by the threat of the spread of this virus and the associated uncertainties has caused anxiety and frustration (Mao et al., 2020).

Thus, COVID-19 had a significant impact on the workforce in this sector, causing the loss of more than 121 million jobs (WTTC, 2020), 18.4 million of which were in Europe (WTTC, 2020).

The hospitality industry was undoubtedly one of the hardest hit sectors by the pandemic, as decreased demand meant that many hotel units remained closed for most of 2020 (ETC, 2021). Some tourists were temporarily forced to be stranded due to the outbreak of COVID-19, which may cause anxiety and panic (Chen et al., 2020). Thus, Chen et al. (2020) confirm that hotels have provided in-room delivery services and scheduled staff to care for guests' physical conditions, thus creating a sense of home, and numerous lodging establishments in China have also provided their space for healthcare professionals or medical observation, and some resorts have even been converted into rest and rehabilitation facilities for healthcare professionals (Mao et al., 2020).

For Gössling et al. (2020), with restaurant closures in most countries and the expectation that social distancing will continue to be a strategy in the fight against COVID-19, it is important to note that restaurant units may face recovery difficulties, essentially because they are characterized by limited liquidity and low profit margins, and takeaway is an operational alternative, when possible, for restaurants to remain open, which requires fewer employees.

Also, according to Hall et al. (2020), while the most extreme measures involve the closure of operations to avoid social contact, the prohibition of public meetings and the closure of public places affect tourism activities, but also limit events, meetings, and conferences. In this context, Donthu and Gustafsson (2020) mention that exhibitions, conferences, events, and cultural establishments, such as galleries and museums, have been abruptly canceled. Indeed, actions such as closing tourist spots, public cultural sites (e.g., museums and art galleries), and recreational areas (e.g., movie theaters), have been considered efficient approaches to prevent COVID-19 cross-infection caused by travel and leisure activities (Chen et al., 2020).

Hall et al. (2020) state that travel restrictions have been widely enacted in response to COVID-19. However, travel is a requirement for tourism activity, and any factor that prevents travel can have a profound impact on the tourism industry (Yeh, 2020).

Airlines have suffered large financial losses and wish to resume international routes (Buckley, 2020), as the impact of COVID-19 on sectors of the tourism industry that rely heavily on-air travel is devastating (Gallego & Font, 2020), and this virus has been highly damaging to tourism, forcing travel companies to lay off employees and shut down temporarily, if not forever (Benjamin et al., 2020).

From a medium-term analysis perspective, tourism companies quickly introduced response measures, such as terminating the travel contract and providing a full refund to tourists, in order to effectively deal with tourism complaints and disputes caused by COVID-19 (Chen et al., 2020), and many refunds had to be issued across the tourism industry due to the strong and extensive COVID-19 infections, which reduced the perceived safety to travel among consumers in general (Mao et al., 2020).

Likewise, and according to Renaud (2020), destinations began to refuse to receive cruise ships that were still at sea when the virus began to spread rapidly, so most countries closed their borders to non-essential transit and, as a result, the industry ceased to operate while waiting for public health stabilization. In fact, Farzanegan et al. (2020) explain that cruise tourism has exacerbated the situation, as the disease has spread through thousands of cruise ship passengers and crew members since the beginning of the pandemic caused by COVID-19. In early 2020, the shares of the three largest cruise companies that together hold over 80% of the world market (Royal Caribbean Cruise Lines, CCL and Norwegian Cruise Line) fell by an average of 84.2% in 62 days between January 17 and March 18 (Renaud, 2020). Therefore, the incidence of several outbreaks on cruise ships during the pandemic caused by COVID-19, illustrates the vulnerability and weakness of these voyages (Pan et al., 2021).

Gössling et al. (2020) show that as most countries aspire to avoid a number of positive cases of COVID-19 exceeding hospital capacity, social distancing will remain an important strategy to limit the speed of the pandemic, this involves restricting all forms of events with a high number of participants, including concerts, meetings, conferences, sports or large family gatherings (e.g. weddings).

According to Donthu and Gustafsson (2020), the current COVID-19 outbreak has had severe economic consequences worldwide, leading to dramatic changes in the way businesses act and consumers behave. Because of the observed changes, online communication, entertainment, and shopping, have experienced unprecedented growth (Donthu & Gustafsson, 2020).

In this sense, Jiménez-Barreto et al. (2021) state that as the world adjusts to COVID-19, progressively recover tourists' mobility, and reopen hotel and tourism facilities, in this new reality, managers need to (re)understand tourists' beliefs and the main factors that drive consumption in hospitality. Indeed, people who face constant constraints in their daily activities, also change their behaviors regarding tourism and travel (ETC, 2021).

In fact, regarding consumers' monthly travel searches in 2020, greater than any other global region, Europe exhibited contradictory behavior (WTTC & McKinsey & Company, 2021). In fact, the increase in consistent searches in the second quarter was followed by a decrease of similar magnitude in the third quarter, with a decrease in these searches becoming evident with an increase in positive Covid-19 cases (WTTC & McKinsey & Company, 2021).

However, the consumer response in terms of reduced travel is not just about increased infection rates, but also government responses, especially in Europe where there are strict restrictions on travel (ETC, 2021). Consumers mostly avoid international travel due to health issues and movement restrictions, thus giving rise to growth in domestic travel in the year 2020 (ETC, 2021).

Regarding the market segments, adventure tourism was the one that registered the highest increase in searches in early 2020 and, the one that felt a smaller decrease in searches, compared to the same periods in 2019 (WTTC & McKinsey & Company, 2021). On the other hand, cultural tourism started the year in line with what was seen in 2019 and, throughout the year was always accentuating the level of decrease in searches (WTTC & McKinsey & Company, 2021). Sun and beach and family tourism started 2020 with an increase in searches, year-on-year, but with the advent of the pandemic they quickly turned negative, with losses between 30% and 40%, and urban tourism showed a similar behavior until September (WTTC & McKinsey & Company, 2021). In fact, between September and November, when there was insistent talk of progress on the availability of a vaccine, some optimism was unleashed, along with the approach of the Christmas season, even though Europe was already facing the second wave of the pandemic (WTTC & McKinsey & Company, 2021).

Hotel facilities, according to Jiménez-Barreto et al. (2021), in many countries were forced to close due to the restrictions imposed during the pandemic, thus there is an inherent need to communicate how they deal with the new coronavirus in order to motivate guests to visit in the future. However, Jiménez-Barreto et al. (2021) state that, the lack of knowledge on how to persuasively communicate about hotel units' cleanliness programs for COVID-19, may challenge the survival of this industry.

In addition, over 2020, air travel and lodging bookings were found to have recovered slightly from the initial shock and stabilized around a slight upward trend (WTTC & McKinsey & Company, 2021). Hotel occupancy was not as hard hit as air travel bookings, suggesting that there will have been substitution from air travel to other modes of transportation (WTTC & McKinsey & Company, 2021). Thus, concerns about the mutation of the new coronavirus significantly influence the already weakened tourism demand in many important markets, including those in Europe, and therefore the beginning of 2021 is certainly a challenge for the European airline industry (ETC, 2021).

COVID-19 Influence on Tourism Sub-sectors

The value of this research, with a qualitative methodology, lies in the ability to provide different perspectives (Lanka et al., 2021) by providing in-depth insight, but with an interpretive and subjective approach (Barnham, 2015). Through qualitative data, it is possible to preserve the chronological flow, understand the events that led to the consequences, and obtain fruitful explanations; thus having an evident quality when they are more likely to reveal unexpected discoveries and new integrations helps researchers go beyond initial conceptions and create or revise conceptual frameworks (Miles et al., 2014).

In this sense, the collection of information in this research was based on a semi-structured interview with 14 open-ended questions. In fact, compared to closed interviews, semi-structured interviews can employ a better use of the information collected, allowing more room to follow up on any perspectives considered important by the interviewee, and the interviewer has a greater opportunity to become visible as a participant, rather than hiding behind a pre-defined interview script (Denzin & Lincoln, 2018). On the other hand, compared to open-ended interviews, in semi-structured interviews, the interviewer has more relevance in focusing the conversation on questions that he or she considers important in relation to the research topic (Denzin & Lincoln, 2018) (Table 17.1).

The interviews are intended for *stakeholder of* the destination and entrepreneurs of the sector in the destination, which constitute the sample of the study, because it is considered that these are the actors with the greatest knowledge of the difficulties facing the COVID-19, as well as the practices adopted, and future strategies implemented. In effect, the interview begins with the identification of the areas of the tourism and hospitality sector most affected by COVID-19, which allows them to be grouped according to their designation. Another aspect to consider is the impact of the pandemic overall, analyzing the periods referring to the different phases of containment and deconfinement that were imposed at a national level.

In identifying the main changes caused by the pandemic, it is essential to know the change in the typology of summer demand, organizing the participants' answers by market segments. In addition, it is also important to question which products or services have ceased and started to be demanded, as well as, if there was creation of new tourism products or services. In this scope, the data analysis and processing are divided by categories and by

Table 17.1 Theoretical background of the interview guide

Interview Questions	Theoretical Foundation
Objective 1: Define the Most Affected Sector Areas in the Northern Region of Portugal	
Which areas were most affected by COVID-19?	Donthu and Gustafsson (2020); Adongo et al. (2021); Gössling et al. (2020); Higgins-Desbiolles (2020); Cave and Dredge (2020); Lew et al. (2020); Hall et al. (2020).
How were they affected during the different stages of confinement?	Donthu and Gustafsson (2020); Lew et al. (2020); Hall et al. (2020); Ioannides and Gyimóthy (2020); INE (2020).
Objective 2: To Identify the Main Changes Brought about by COVID-19 in the Northern Region of Portugal	
How has the summer changed the typology of demand?	Hall et al. (2020); Haywood (2020); Travel BI (2020); INE (2021).
Which tourism products or services are no longer in demand?	Adongo et al. (2021); Quintero et al. (2020); Ioannides and Gyimóthy (2020); Donthu and Gustafsson (2020); Lapointe (2020).
What is the reason why they are no longer wanted?	Donthu and Gustafsson (2020); Gössling et al. (2020); Lapointe (2020); Hall et al. (2020).
In what way were new tourism products or services designed?	Ioannides and Gyimóthy (2020); Rowen (2020).
What justifies the alternatives created?	Benjamin et al. (2020); Rowen (2020).
What tourism products or services began to be in demand?	Lew et al. (2020); Guerreiro (2020); Quintero et al. (2020); Niewiadomski (2020).
Why are these the new tourism products or services?	Chen et al. (2020); Hall et al. (2020); Romagosa (2020).
Objective 3: To Identify the Practices Adopted by Organizations in the Fight against COVID-19 in the Northern Region of Portugal	
How has the destination and the tourism offer prepared itself for the new tourism products and services demanded by the demand?	Araujo et al. (2020); Hall et al. (2020); Gössling et al. (2020); Pan et al. (2021); Chen et al. (2020); Jiménez-Barreto et al. (2021).
How were the new products and services improved to reach new markets?	WTTC (2020); Sigala (2020); Quintero et al. (2020); Chen et al. (2020).
In what ways, in the different stages of confinement, was there time to learn about new communication strategies?	WTTC (2020); Araujo et al. (2020); Sigala (2020); Gössling et al. (2020); Chen et al. (2020).
Goal 4: Define the Strategies Implemented in the Future Post COVID-19, in the Northern Region of Portugal	
In what ways did the opening-closing experiences serve to learn about new communication strategies?	Prideaux et al. (2020); Jiménez-Barreto et al. (2021).
What are the prospects for the tourism sector: medium and long term?	Araujo et al. (2020); Higgins-Desbiolles (2020); Hall et al. (2020); Lew et al. (2020); Prideaux et al. (2020); Ioannides and Gyimóthy (2020); Brouder (2020).

the reasons that justify the choice for those tourism products or services. To identify the practices adopted by organizations in the fight against COVID-19, the questions are related to the preparation of the destination and the tourism offer, the improvement of tourism products and services, and the learning of new communication strategies. In this context, the data collected can be grouped according to the actions, initiatives, and strategies listed. Finally, to define the strategies implemented for the future, questions are asked concerning the new communication strategies, which are grouped according to the practices indicated, and what are the prospects for the tourism and hospitality sector, in the short, medium, and long term.

COVID-19 affected all areas of tourism transversally, completely interrupting some activities. Having been considered as one of the sectors most affected by the pandemic, in this context the most recurrently mentioned areas were hotels, restaurants and tourist entertainment (see Table 17.2).

In the references to hospitality, there is a disagreement of opinions regarding the impact of COVID-19. While some participants referred to this area as one of the most affected by the pandemic, since several establishments closed, with a sharp drop in turnover and very low occupancy rates. On the other hand, compared to the other areas of tourism mentioned, two of the interviewees, curiously from the same region, considered it to be the least affected area, because it did not work exclusively for tourists and had many people with accommodation contracts, which meant that they ended up staying open. In fact, despite everything, the hotel industry was not forced to close during the confinement phases, but many establishments decided to close.

About the restaurant area, there is general agreement that these establishments were severely affected and showed very sharp falls, despite the existence of financial support and alternatives. However, due to the existing alternatives and possibilities, such as the takeaway service, in some perspectives, despite the undeniable impact, restaurants were not the area most affected by COVID'19, having been affected at a lower level and probably less than hotels. Continuously, there are the tourist entertainment companies because they are activities that take place face-to-face. In this context, the response from the interviewees was unanimous in relation to the marked negative impact on these organizations, which almost disappeared for 1 year, practically did not work, and are still so to the present day. Although we have observed some companies that have managed to reinvent themselves into micro-groups, and have been active, they have not had the turnover levels that could be expected. In fact, with the restrictions imposed by the Government in Portugal, they were even prevented from carrying out activities with groups and, consequently, had to suspend their activity. In addition, other areas highlighted by the participants, although less recurrent, were event organization companies, cultural spaces, tour guide activities, transportation, and travel agencies. All these areas were mentioned as having an almost total reduction in their activity.

Table 17.2 Areas most affected by COVID-19

Subcategories	Interview Evidence
General	COVID-19 affected the entire sector transversally, completely halting some activities. Tourism had very negative consequences, which are still being felt today, and was one of the sectors that really suffered the most from the consequences of the pandemic, as well as everything that revolves around the tourism dynamic.
Hospitality	In the first three months of 2021, in the lodging sector, occupancy rates were around 5% and 8%, not exceeding 10%. And this was also the reality this past year. Of the most affected areas in tourism, the hotel industry had very significant drops, in some cases around 90%.
Restoration	The restaurant business, was severely affected, but has found other possibilities and alternatives, such as the takeaway service.
Touristic animation	Initially, they could carry out activities with a certain number of people per group. But later, they were even prevented from carrying out these activities, when the restriction of a maximum limit of two people in outdoor physical activity was imposed. The tourist entertainment companies, in this last year, should only have been active for four months.
Tourist guide	The tour guide business was greatly affected by the fact that the groups were reduced and by all the constraints of this business. The guide business had a zero turnover, and there was a brutal reduction in organized tourism, which is still going on today.
Events	The main area affected was events because it always includes some crowds of people. The traditional festivals that were previously held at this destination no longer exist at all.
Cultural spaces	There has been a significant drop in the cultural part, especially in urban centers, since it encompasses activities that take place indoors, and in general people have preferred to avoid these situations and opt for the outdoors.
Transportation	All areas that involve the transportation of people, whether by air, land, sea, or river. The planes were grounded, and everything stopped, because we were forced to stay at home, and tourism is an activity that depends on the dynamics and the movement of people.
Travel agencies	They registered in the region activity drops of 95%.

In relation to events, due to the need for large groups and the existence of crowds of people, these businesses were affected almost 100%, as well as all related services. Regarding cultural spaces, due to the obligation to close, and because they are characterized by activities that take place indoors, visitors preferred to opt for outdoor activities. Finally, due to the imposed restrictions and circulation limitations, all areas involving the transportation of people were mentioned since tourism is an activity that depends on the dynamics and movement of people. It is also important to highlight the reference to travel agencies, which were strongly affected and had a 95% drop in business.

Since March 2020, there has been a major reduction across the board in the tourism sector and all associated services. This was mainly due to the restrictions imposed in the country in the fight against the pandemic, which led to the closure of establishments and the reduction of tourism activities. The new tourist profile, afraid of getting infected with COVID-19, opted for accommodations where it was not necessary to share common spaces with others. All services of direct contact with the customer had to be rethought in terms of logistics, from accompanying the guest to the room and carrying his suitcase to all the associated services, such as wine tasting or sightseeing. In addition, the ban on commercial aviation has meant a reduction in tourist services at destinations, such as accommodation (see Table 17.3).

Through the answers of the participants during the interviews, it is possible to state that the impact of the pandemic was different in each of the areas and inconstant throughout the year 2020. In fact, tourism was affected in different phases and in several dimensions, being that in the mandatory confinement phases, the impact was 100% and all organizations showed sharp breaks. In this sense, the periods highlighted corresponded to the confinement and deconfinement phases referred to in the literature review (see Table 17.4).

To identify the main changes brought about by COVID-19, the interviewees were firstly asked about the modification of the typology of demand in the summer of 2020. The main changes identified were the increase of the domestic market, the decrease of the foreign market, and the modification of the profile and behavior of the tourist (see Table 17.5).

With the increase of domestic tourism, a new paradigm and a new visitor has emerged, with different motivations, who wants to value and rediscover the territory, who values the outdoor spaces and activities, hiking trails, spas, health, and wellness tourism. In addition, this new visitor seeks a tourist offer that guarantees hygiene and safety in the face of the pandemic, and prefers to travel with cohabitant groups, smaller and more restricted groups, rather than large groups and organized trips.

Strategies in Tourism Destination Management

Considering the tourism sector, no new tourism products or services have emerged. What was verified, was the adaptation of what already existed before, or the adoption of new business strategies. This need for adaptation and reinvention was a factor that all participants in the study emphasized throughout the interviews, even if in different questions (see Table 17.6).

The main justification for this need was due to the adaptation to the change in demand, that is, to the new tourist profile that was mentioned before. But also, in bringing added value to the experience of the visit, to meet new markets.

Table 17.3 Tourism products and services with decreasing demand

Subcategories		Interview Evidence
Tourism products and services	Hotel units	Classic hotels suffered the most. People were afraid of anything that shared space, and therefore didn't want to go to hotels or lodging that had common spaces, which hotels can't escape.
	Tourism entertainment and organized tourism	Guided tours for groups are no longer in demand, and the activities themselves are no longer available. There is a clear reduction in tourist entertainment services, tour guide services, and organized tours between regions. Companies have had to readapt, create new services and work with smaller groups. Everything that was organized groups, were reduced to groups of 5–6 people, causing a reduction in what is operating at these levels.
	Events	The large events segment used to have significant demand, and now has no demand. Summer festivals, traditional festivals and markets, and handicraft shows have been banned by the government and no longer exist or are being held with restrictions.
	Urban tourism	The big cities were the most affected because people avoided these destinations. City breaks were clearly very affected in cities like Porto and Braga. While Porto had maximum occupancy rates of 15%, the low-density territories, i.e., the inland locations, had occupancy rates in the summer of 90% and 95%.
	Health and wellness tourism	There was a sharp decline in products associated with health and spas. Wellness services, like massages and gyms, had to close, and even if the client wanted to use them, the regulations didn't allow it.
Reasons why they are no longer wanted	Health and safety reasons	The main reasons were undoubtedly the health issues and the demand for safety that the pandemic caused. People are very worried about these pandemic issues and are retracting a lot, whether it's going out to lunch or dinner, or traveling. If the feeling of insecurity persists, there is going to be this drop in demand, whether for services or for goods associated with tourism.
	Circulation limitations	The limitations on movement have meant that many people can no longer leave their municipalities and, as a result, no longer go to spend weekends or a few days in other territories. It is obvious to the international tourist that airplanes can no longer circulate in the airspace, people can no longer circulate between international territories.

Table 17.4 Evidence on the impact on different phases of confinement

Subcategories	Interview Evidence
Initial confinement	The first phase, in March 2020, was the worst moment, because people, institutions, businesspeople themselves, didn't know how to communicate, and didn't know how to adapt. The sector was affected in terms of the loss of business that was predicted. When there was the progressive closure, starting in other destinations, accommodation units had to cancel everything that was planned and organized, while all other activities simply had to close.
Beginning of deconfinement	During the phased reopening, different regions of Portugal had different rules and regulations to follow, which became complicated for businesses and for tourism. When we went ahead with the deconfinement plan, in late May, early June, there was a reopening, and companies were adapting, training, and adopting procedures to ensure safety and customer confidence.
Peak deconfinement	The impact was general and transversal throughout the year 2020. Although in the high season, i.e., July and August, the months ended up being very interesting for low density territories, but the drops during the rest of the year were quite sharp. In the summer, in June, July and August, with the reopening of the establishments, there was indeed some tourism demand, very focused on the national market and on the local market. But nothing to overcome the negative consequences of what had been happening.
Second confinement	The activity went down significantly starting in September, October and November. These are always months where activity drops, even without a pandemic, due to seasonality in the tourism market. With the pandemic, many tourist activities returned to zero revenue. November, and especially December, were also periods of huge losses in terms of economic profitability.

It is observed a growing preference for nature tourism and rural tourism as well as experiences in these territories. Effectively, these territories had accommodation units with an occupancy rate of almost 100%: the choice for accommodation typologies in rural areas, with the possibility of experiences, such as horseback riding, hiking trails and swimming pool, spaces where they could socialize as a family, without the interference of third parties, outside their family nucleus. Another aspect to consider is the preference for destinations with lower population density, which focuses on inland destinations and more remote places, such as villages and river beaches, i.e., much more secluded places. The destinations with lower population density, benefited from this feature in this pandemic period, and that was previously seen as a weakness in terms of tourism.

Table 17.5 Summary of evidence on modification of the typology of demand

Subcategories	Interview Evidence
National market	In terms of demand, it was the domestic market that was holding tourism [...], but this market is not enough for the existing tourism supply in Portugal, since it is a country that is prepared with an offer to receive millions of visitors. This territory observed a growing demand, especially from people of the national territory since the borders were physically closed.
Proximity market	The Spanish market, represented about 12% of tourists last summer. Regarding the local market, with the closing of the borders, the visit of these tourists to Portugal was severely compromised.
International market	As for the external markets, there was a drop in the number of tourists. In terms of nationalities, the long-distance tourists (Brazil, America, Canada, Australia, Japan) were lost. There was also a significant reduction in the European markets, which even though some tourists showed up, was incomparable to the data registered in previous years (England, France, Germany, Switzerland).
Tourist profile	A different tourist, who wants to get to know his country better, who looks for authenticity and genuineness of the places, who gives more importance to hiking, cycling, and nature. [...] that looks for genuine products, that wants to know well the regional gastronomy, the wine, and wants to be able to buy endogenous products locally. [...] wanting to have their meals in safer places as far as the lodging units are concerned. [...] who will opt for short-term visits. The motivations for traveling have become different [...] the search for more outdoor spaces and activities, hiking trails, spas, health and wellness tourism, offers that guarantee safety and hygiene.
Market segmentation	The demand that used to come from large groups and the travel agency organization has almost disappeared, and there are now smaller and more restricted groups. The segmentation that has emerged is not even comparable with the profile or the market of previous years, which presented several age groups and several nationalities. The family segment, which had been lost in the global massification, and the overnight stay profile that fitted into cohabitant groups, were revisited concepts.

There was also a big bet on digital media, and on the adaptation of services that could happen at a distance: the organization of wine tastings online, or the realization of virtual tourist visits to any part of the world, or even, the simple possibility of purchasing products or tourist services online. In this way, the digital medium will continue to be greatly enhanced, evidencing itself as a growing trend.

Table 17.6 Evidence to the future perspectives for the tourism sector

Subcategories		Interview Evidence
General perspective		The destination Portugal may be vulnerable in the short term, but in the medium and long term will be back to assert itself and will compete for the top places as a destination worldwide, due to the good infrastructures, entrepreneurs, and qualified employees in the several tourism areas. It is extraordinary the way Portugal develops and communicates tourism, but also, the quality of the infrastructures and the present accessibilities. Portugal assumes all the factors to ensure and perspective a bright future regarding tourism.
Short-term		The expectation is that the summer of 2021 will be similar to 2020, mostly with domestic tourism. However, some increases are also expected in neighboring markets, such as Spain, France, and Germany, if pandemic numbers remain stable. 2021 will continue in the preference for rural areas, and there is a very particular criterion here that is the summer, and destinations with sun and beach, even without the foreign market, continue to be a highly desired motivation (between July and September).
Medium-term	Positive perspectives	The medium-term expectations are that it will be a good summer; the pandemic situation will calm down; free movement will be possible; international travel will be allowed to recover, resulting in the arrival of tourists who previously spent their vacations in Portugal, as well as those who seek nature tourism and tourism in rural areas.
	Negative perspectives	In 2022, we will continue to suffer, because at the vaccination level, not everything will be solved yet, and if it is in Portugal, it won't be in the rest of the world. In the medium term, until 2024, there will still be the stigma of the past, the fear of groups and crowded spaces.
Long term	Market segmentation	If we can succeed, for two more summers, in keeping national tourism, building loyalty, creating a good image, and that these national tourists who visit us leave here with a good perception of the destination. We can extend this trend of staying in the territory in the medium and long term.
	Transport	Another trend that could happen in the near future is the increase in tourism based on car circulation, such as self-owned cars or motorhomes. This will increase this year and could be a trend in the coming years.
	Sustainable tourism	In the long term, these sustainability practices of eco-sustainability, sustainable tourism, ecotourism experience tourism, and creative tourism are here to stay.

Conclusion

Regarding the definition of the most affected areas in the sector, despite the impact having occurred in different dimensions, among all the interviewees eight distinct areas were considered: hospitality, restaurants, tourist entertainment, tour guide activity, events, cultural spaces, transportation, and travel agencies.

First, the areas of hospitality, restaurants, and events, are all in line with what is stated by Gössling et al. (2020) in the literature review. The impact on events is also justified by Rowen (2020). Continuously, the consideration of cultural spaces, agree with Donthu and Gustafsson (2020) and Chen et al. (2020). Other areas highlighted in the interviews were tourism entertainment, tour guide activity, and travel agencies. Finally, tourism transport, was little mentioned by the participants, but several authors such as Prideaux et al. (2020), Hall et al. (2020), Buckley (2020), Benjamin et al. (2020) Renaud (2020) and Pan et al. (2021), mentioned air and cruise transport as the most affected.

Regarding the identification of the main changes caused by COVID-19 in the Northern Region, the analysis of the demand typology was carried out, in terms of the modification of tourism products and services demand, and the creation of new tourism products and services.

In the demand typology, the main changes identified were the increase of the domestic market, the decrease of the foreign market, and the modification of the tourist profile and behavior. In this sense, through the data made available by TravelBI and the National Institute of Statistics (INE), it is possible to verify that in fact, there was an increase in the domestic market and a pronounced decrease in the foreign market in 2020, in this region. Regarding the change in consumer profile and behavior, the conclusions drawn by the interviews regarding the market segmentation, mostly family, were supported by WTTC & McKinsey & Company (2021).

The tourism products and activities that were no longer in demand were hotels, tourism entertainment and organized tourism, events, urban tourism, and health and wellness tourism. Regarding hotels, through the statistical data made available by INE, it is possible to verify the marked decrease in overnight stays in hotel units in 2020. Furthermore, there are no specific data on the absence of demand for events in the Northern Region, however, it was one of the areas considered to be most affected by Gössling et al. (2020) and Rowen (2020), worldwide. Continuously, the accentuated decrease in urban tourism in this region is in line with the study developed by WTTC & McKinsey & Company (2021). Within the same theme, the main reasons for this change were health and safety reasons, and traffic limitations, motivations that are also mentioned by Haywood (2020) and present in the data presented by INE and European Tourism Council (ETC).

In addition, the participants in this study did not identify any new tourism product or service, but referred to adaptations in the existing business models, namely, in the restaurants with takeaway, in the outdoor tourism activities, in the use of digital media for the provision of services. In this sense, the prevalence for takeaway is in agreement with Gössling et al. (2020), and Araujo et al. (2020) also explains the digital transformation of the tourism sector. Thus, the main reasons were adaptation to changing demand and the need to bring added value to the experience.

Finally, according to the interviewees, the products and activities that started to be more in demand due to the pandemic were nature and rural tourism, as well as destinations with lower population density. In this context, the main motivations for this demand were security issues and the rediscovery of the country. Thus, security issues are in line with the data presented by the ETC.

According to the strategies adopted by the organizations, we highlight, in planning the destination and the tourism supply present in the North Region, the initiatives of the Regional Entities, the implementation of security measures and the adaptation of products and services. In addition, in the improvement of tourism products and services is also referred to the Clean & Safe seal, an initiative of the Tourism of Portugal, national Destination Management Organization (DMO). In communication strategies, the role of the regional DMO and Turismo de Portugal is again highlighted, as well as strategies in the digital environment.

Regarding the implementation of security measures in organizations, it is a strategy that meets the information requested by INE, TravelBI and General Direction of Health (DGS). In addition, the World Travel & Tourism Council (WTTC) refers to the initiative created by the Clean & Safe seal, which was adopted by companies and the important role of Tourism of Portugal. Finally, the strategies in the digital environment, are evidenced by Chen et al. (2020) and the WTTC.

The future strategies for the sector and for the region are the valorization of the destination and the attraction of human resources. Furthermore, the future perspectives for the tourism sector were analyzed in the short, medium, and long term. In the long term, the prevalence of segmentation of the national market, transportation within the scope of automobile circulation, and sustainable tourism stand out.

The outlook for ecological and sustainable tourism fits the vision of Prideaux et al. (2020), Sesini et al. (2020), Niewiadomski (2020), Booking.com (2020), Higgins-Desbiolles (2020) and Hall et al. (2020). It is also mentioned by Booking.com (2020), the trend of avoiding public and collective transportation. Furthermore, according to Buckley (2020) and Booking.com (2020), domestic tourism will prevail at an early stage.

References

Abbaspour, F., Soltani, S., & Tham, A. (2020). Medical tourism for COVID-19 post-crisis recovery? *Anatolia, 32*(1), 140–143.
Adongo, C. A., Amenumey, E. K., Kumi-Kyereme, A., & Dubé, E. (2021). Beyond fragmentary: A proposed measure for travel vaccination concerns. *Tourism Management, 83*, 104–180.

Araujo, E. J. S., Melchán, J. A. S., Bermejo, B. R., & Río, J. J. L. D. (2020). Comportamiento del sector turístico colombiano durante la pandemia, una luz al final del camino: ¿Lamentación o llamado a la acción? *Revista Ibérica de Sistemas e Tecnologias de Informação, E36*, 295–308.

Barnham, C. (2015). Quantitative and qualitative research. *International Journal of Market Research, 57*(6), 837–854.

Benjamin, S., Dillette, A., & Alderman, D. H. (2020). We can't return to normal: Committing to tourism equity in the post-pandemic age. *Tourism Geographies, 22*(3), 476–483.

Booking.com. (2020). *The Future of Travel*. https://travelbi.turismodeportugal.pt/pt-pt/Paginas/futuro-das-viagens-por-booking.aspx.

Brouder, P. (2020). Reset redux: Possible evolutionary pathways towards the transformation of tourism in a COVID-19 world. *Tourism Geographies, 22*(3), 484–490.

Buckley, R. (2020). Pandemic travel restrictions provide a test of net ecological effects of ecotourism and new research opportunities. *Journal of Travel Research*, 1–3. https://doi.org/10.1177/0047287520947812.

Castro, D., Robalinho, J., Bessa, L., Ramalho, M., & Au-Yong-Oliveira, M. (2020). Soluções para o impacto do turismo nas alterações climáticas. *Revista Ibérica de Sistemas e Tecnologias de Informação, E36*, 114–126.

Cave, J., & Dredge, D. (2020). Regenerative tourism needs diverse economic practices. *Tourism Geographies, 22*(3), 503–513. https://doi.org/10.1080/14616688.2020.1768434.

Chen, H., Huang, X., & Li, Z. (2020). A content analysis of Chinese news coverage on COVID-19 and tourism. *Current Issues in Tourism*. https://doi.org/10.1080/13683500.2020.1763269.

Chinazzi, M., Davis, J. T., Ajelli, M., Gioannini, C., Litvinova, M., Merler, S., Piontti, A. P., Mu, K., Rossi, L., Sun, K., Viboud, C., Xiong, X., Yu, H., Halloran, M. E., Longini Jr., I. M., & Vespignani, A. (2020). The effect of travel restrictions on the spread of the 2019 novel coronavirus (COVID-19) outbreak. *Science, 368*(6489), 395–400. https://doi.org/10.1126/science.aba9757.

Denzin, N. K., & Lincoln, Y. S. (2018). *The SAGE Handbook of Qualitative Research* (Fifth Edition). SAGE Publications, Inc. https://us.sagepub.com/en-us/nam/the-sage-handbook-of-qualitative-research/book242504#description.

Donthu, N., & Gustafsson, A. (2020). Effects of COVID-19 on business and research. *Journal of Business Research, 117*, 284–289.

ETC. (2021). *European Tourism: Trends & Prospects (Q4/2020)*. https://etc-corporate.org/uploads/2021/02/ETC-Quarterly-Report-Q4-2020_Public-1.pdf.

Farzanegan, M. R., Gholipour, H. F., Feizi, M., Nunkoo, R., & Andargoli, A. E. (2020). International tourism and outbreak of Coronavirus (COVID-19): A cross-country analysis. *Journal of Travel Research, 60*(3), 687–692.

Fotiadis, A., Polyzos, S., & Huan, T.-C. T. C. (2021). The good, the bad and the ugly on COVID-19 tourism recovery. *Annals of Tourism Research, 87*, 103–117. https://doi.org/10.1016/j.annals.2020.103117.

Gallego, I., & Font, X. (2020). Changes in air passenger demand as a result of the COVID-19 crisis: Using Big Data to inform tourism policy. *Journal of Sustainable Tourism, 29*(9), 1470–1489. https://doi.org/10.1080/09669582.2020.1773476.

Galvani, A., Lew, A. A., & Perez, M. S. (2020). COVID-19 is expanding global consciousness and the sustainability of travel and tourism. *Tourism Geographies, 22*(3), 567–576. https://doi.org/10.1080/14616688.2020.1760924.

Gössling, S., Scott, D., & Hall, C. M. (2020). Pandemics, tourism and global change: A rapid assessment of COVID-19. *Journal of Sustainable Tourism, 29*(1), 1–20. https://doi.org/10.1080/09669582.2020.1758708.

Guerreiro, S. (2020). *Rebuilding Tourism: An OECD Perspective.* https://travelbi.turismodeportugal.pt/pt-pt/Paginas/Rebuilding-Tourism-An-OECD-Perspective.aspx.

Hall, C. M., Scott, D., & Gössling, S. (2020). Pandemics, transformations and tourism: Be careful what you wish for. *Tourism Geographies, 22*(3), 577–598.

Haywood, K. M. (2020). A post COVID-19 future: Tourism re-imagined and re-enabled. *Tourism Geographies, 22*(3), 599–609.

Higgins-Desbiolles, F. (2020). The «war over tourism»: Challenges to sustainable tourism in the tourism academy after COVID-19. *Journal of Sustainable Tourism, 29*(4), 551–569. https://doi.org/10.1080/09669582.2020.1803334.

INE. (2020). *Mobilidade da População ao Nível Regional no Contexto da Pandemia COVID-19.* Instituto Nacional de Estatística. https://www.ine.pt/xportal/xmain?xpid=INE&xpgid=ine_destaques&DESTAQUESdest_boui=465143606&DESTAQUESmodo=2&xlang=pt.

INE. (2021). *Hóspedes (N.º) nos estabelecimentos de alojamento turístico por Localização geográfica (NUTS -2013) e Tipo (alojamento turístico).* Instituto Nacional de Estatística. https://www.ine.pt/xportal/xmain?xpid=INE&xpgid=ine_indicadores&indOcorrCod=0009812&contexto=bd&selTab=tab2.

Ioannides, D., & Gyimóthy, S. (2020). The COVID-19 crisis as an opportunity for escaping the unsustainable global tourism path. *Tourism Geographies, 22*(3), 624–632.

Jiménez-Barreto, J., Loureiro, S., Braun, E., Sthapit, E., & Zenker, S. (2021). Use numbers not words! communicating hotels' cleaning programs for COVID-19 from the brand perspective. *International Journal of Hospitality Management, 94*, 102–872.

Lanka, E., Lanka, S., Rostron, A., & Singh, P. (2021). Why we need qualitative research in management studies. *Journal of Contemporary Administration, 25*(2), 1–7.

Lapointe, D. (2020). Reconnecting tourism after COVID-19: The paradox of alterity in tourism areas. *Tourism Geographies, 22*(3), 633–638.

Lee, C.-C., & Chen, M.-P. (2020). Do country risks matter for tourism development? International evidence. *Journal of Travel Research.* https://doi.org/10.1177/0047287520954539.

Lew, A. A., Cheer, J. M., Haywood, M., Brouder, P., & Salazar, N. B. (2020). Visions of travel and tourism after the global COVID-19 transformation of 2020. *Tourism Geographies, 22*(3), 455–466.

Ma, S., Zhao, X., Gong, Y., & Wengel, Y. (2020). Proposing «healing tourism» as a post-COVID-19 tourism product. *Anatolia, 32*(1), 136–139.

Mao, Y., He, J., Morrison, A. M., & Coca-Stefaniak, J. A. (2020). Effects of tourism CSR on employee psychological capital in the COVID-19 crisis: From the perspective of conservation of resources theory. *Current Issues in Tourism,* 1–19. https://doi.org/10.1080/13683500.2020.1770706.

Miles, M. B., Huberman, A. M., & Saldaña, J. (2014). *Qualitative Data Analysis: A Methods Sourcebook* (3ª edição). SAGE Publications, Inc.

Niewiadomski, P. (2020). COVID-19: From temporary de-globalisation to a re-discovery of tourism? *Tourism Geographies, 22*(3), 651–656.

Pan, T., Shu, F., Kitterlin-Lynch, M., & Beckman, E. (2021). Perceptions of cruise travel during the COVID-19 pandemic: Market recovery strategies for cruise businesses in North America. *Tourism Management, 85*, 104–275.

Prideaux, B., Thompson, M., & Pabel, A. (2020). Lessons from COVID-19 can prepare global tourism for the economic transformation needed to combat climate change. *Tourism Geographies, 22*(3), 667–678.

Quintero, F. Á. L., Coello, E. A. C., Rodríguez, N. R. H., Calderón, M. G. M., & Saltos, J. E. S. (2020). *Gestión del Comportamiento del Consumidor Turístico* (Primera Edición). Área de Innovación y Desarrollo, S.L. https://doi.org/10.17993/EcoOrgyCso.2020.62.

Renaud, L. (2020). Reconsidering global mobility—Distancing from mass cruise tourism in the aftermath of COVID-19. *Tourism Geographies, 22*(3), 679–689.

Romagosa, F. (2020). The COVID-19 crisis: Opportunities for sustainable and proximity tourism. *Tourism Geographies, 22*(3), 690–694.

Rowen, I. (2020). The transformational festival as a subversive toolbox for a transformed tourism: Lessons from burning man for a COVID-19 world. *Tourism Geographies, 22*(3), 695–702.

Sesini, G., Castiglioni, C., & Lozza, E. (2020). New trends and patterns in sustainable consumption: A systematic review and research agenda. *Sustainability, 12*(15), 1–23.

Shao, Y., Hu, Z., Luo, M., Huo, T., & Zhao, Q. (2020). What is the policy focus for tourism recovery after the outbreak of COVID-19? A co-word analysis. *Current Issues in Tourism, 24*(7), 899–904.

Sigala, M. (2020). Tourism and COVID-19: Impacts and implications for advancing and resetting industry and research. *Journal of Business Research, 117*, 312–321.

Travel BI. (2020). *Perfil do Mercado em Portugal*. Travel BI – smarter decisions. http://travelbi.turismodeportugal.pt/pt-pt/Mercados/Paginas/pt.aspx.

UNWTO. (2020). *Impact Assessment of the COVID-19 Outbreak on International Tourism*. https://www.unwto.org/impact-assessment-of-the-covid-19-outbreak-on-international-tourism.

Wen, J., Wang, W., Kozak, M., Liu, X., & Hou, H. (2020). Many brains are better than one: The importance of interdisciplinary studies on COVID-19 in and beyond tourism. *Tourism Recreation Research, 46*(2), 310–313.

WTTC. (2020). *To Recovery & Beyond: The Future of Travel & Tourism in the Wake of COVID-19*. https://wttc.org/Research/To-Recovery-Beyond.

WTTC, & McKinsey & Company. (2021). *Evolução das pesquisas de viagens em 2020 e o impacto da Covid-19*. Travel BI – smarter decisions. http://travelbi.turismodeportugal.pt/pt-pt/Paginas/evolucao-das-pesquisas-de-viagens-em-2020-e-o-impacto-da-Covid-19.aspx.

Yang, Y., Zhang, H., & Chen, X. (2020). Coronavirus pandemic and tourism: Dynamic stochastic general equilibrium modeling of infectious disease outbreak. *Annals of Tourism Research, 83*, 102–913.

Yeh, S.-S. (2020). Tourism recovery strategy against COVID-19 pandemic. *Tourism Recreation Research, 46*(2), 188–194.

Index

Note: **Bold** page numbers refer to tables and *italic* page numbers refer to figures.

Abiose, Adejumoke 2
Acar, Y. 21
Accelerated Mobile Pages (AMP) 2, 93
Aguirre, A. A. 169–170
Allen, J. 241
Anders, William 174
anti-tourism 128
Araujo, E. J. S. 267, 271, 284
Arcos-Pumarola, Jordi 3
Arora, S. 2
Arpaci, Ibrahim 146
Artificial Intelligence (AI) 65–66, 94, 101, 236
Autonomous Communities, health resources 213, 214
axiology 133–135

Bahar, O. 22
Bahli, Bouchaib 147
behavior-guided spatial structure and layout, Geopark: closed space 51, *52*; open space 51, *51*; semi-closed space 51, *52*; spaces types 50; upgrades *52*
Benjamin, S. 283
Berjozkina, Galina 2
bio bubble events 244, 247
Biswas, Rajiv 24
Black Death pandemic 9
Blažević, B. 116
blogging 2, 93, 98, 99
Bosnić, I. 112, 116
Boston Consulting Group 167
Bouket Akkoyunlu, B. 150
Buckley, R. 283, 284
Budke, C. 22
business clients: advantages 82–83; demarketing strategies 84; green hotel policies 83; guests strategies 83–84; room rates 83

Çalışkan, Gürkan 2
Carlsen, J. 241
Castro, D. 267
Cave, J. 268
CEIR *see* Center for Exhibition Industry Research (CEIR)
Çelik İlal, N. 22
Cellan-Jones, R. 94
Center for Exhibition Industry Research (CEIR) 64
certifications and labels, sustainability 245
Chen, H. 271, 283, 284
Chen, M.-P. 267
Chen, Xiaohui 146, 147, 150, 155
Chigora, Farai 2
Chinazzi, M. 183, 267
Chowdhary, Nimit 3
cleaning/sanitizing and longer stays 80–81
Collins-Kreiner, Noga 210
Conill-Tetuà, Marta 3
Connell, Joanne 130, 132
consequentialist approach: discriminatory consequences 220; funding 214–215; health systems 218–219; justice argument 215–217; medical resources 219
corporate values 95
Cosma, S. A. 241
critical content analysis 136

Dağhan, Gokhan 150
Davies, K. 242

Deery, M. 241
demand and supply: chain 11–14; economy 9; GDP 11; global tourism industry growth 10, *10*; implication, local tourism industry 8; meat contamination 7; non-pharmaceutical interventions 7; OECD 10; SIDs 11; SMEs 11; social consumption 13; WTTC 10
demarketing 81–82; business clients 84; strategies 1; sustainability, events tourism 245–246; types 82; *see also* marketing/demarketing strategies, hotel operation
destination branding 117; definition 110; financial and socio-economic goals 111; management 112; stakeholders 111, 112
destination management, post-COVID period 278, 280–281, **282**
Destination Management Companies (DMCs) 232
destination management organizations (DMOs) 179, 284; co-creating initiatives 116–117; digital transformation 117; marketing activities 111–112; objectives 111; ownership 112; stakeholders 112, 116
destination rebranding strategies, sustainable tourism recovery 115–117
Dieck, Claudia tom 150
distributive justice 215, 217
domestic tourism 64, 67, 191, 194, 199, **199,** 236, 284
Donohoe, Holly 40
Donthu, N. 271, 272, 283
Dredge, D. 132, 133, 268
Drinking Water Festival 47
dynamic stochastic general equilibrium (DSGE) model 183

Ebola virus 9
ecotourism continuum, wellness tourism 40–41, *41*
Edelheim, Johan R. 3
EDM *see* External Destination Marketing (EDM)
education and research, tourism studies 1
Edwards, Rem B. 135
e-learning process 154
Ell, Laura 2
Al-Emran, Mostafa 146

environmental, tourists' ethical obligations 192
EQF *see* European Qualifications Framework (EQF)
ETC *see* European Tourism Council (ETC)
ethical issues, social media marketing 1
ethical tourism digital and social media marketing: 4IR 93, 94; AI 94, 101; corporate storytelling 100; decision making 94, 95, *95*; individual tourism organisational behaviour 96; Internet-of-Things 94; predictive, post Covid-19 97–99; quality of 93; teleology 96
ethics and responsibility: bans and lockdowns 170–171; climate change 174; epidemics and pandemics incidence 167–170; humanity 163; IFRC 172; Judaeo-Christian tradition 173; living with COVID-19 174–176; public mask-wearing 164; regulations 164; responsible tourism 164–167; safety and trust 171–172; self-certification 172; UNWTO 173–174; WTTC 172
European Draft Report, health resources 211
European Qualifications Framework (EQF) 130
European Tourism Council (ETC) 283, 284
European tourism industry 253
events tourism: organization and management 239; sustainability 240 (*see also* sustainability, events tourism); vaccinations 240
External Destination Marketing (EDM) 111

Farzanegan, M. R. 268, 272
Faulkner, B. J. F. M. 241
Fayos-Solá, E. 241
female business travelers 85–86
Fesenmaier, D. R. 181
fiscal, tourists' ethical obligations 192
501Y.V2 variant, South Africa 8
Fourth Industrial Revolution (4IR) 93, 94
Fredline, E. 241

Gajjar, A. M. 244
Garanti, Zanete 2
Gardiner, Sarah 40

Garling, C. 94
Garrido-Moreno, Aurora 150
general demarketing 82
Getz, D. 247
Ghebreyesus, Tedros Adhanom 163
global economy 228
Global market development 61
Global Preparedness Monitoring Board (GPMB) 169
global tourism industry growth 10, *10*
Global Wellness Institute (GWI) 39
Goodwin, H. 3
Gössling, S. 22, 33, 117, 270, 271, 272, 283, 284
Graefe, A. R. 181
green hotel policies 86; business clients 83
gross domestic product (GDP) 11, 267
Guitart-Casalderrey, Núria 3
Guiver, J. W. 184
Gustafsson, A. 271, 272, 283
Guterres, Antonio 109
Gyimóthy, S. 267

H1N1 swine flu 9
Hall, C. M. 22, 268, 269, 271, 272, 283, 284
Harris, R. 241
Hartman, Robert S. 134, 135
Hasana, U. 241
Haywood, K. M. 283
healing gardens, wellness tourism: behavior-guided spatial structure and layout 50–52, *51–52*; behaviors, tourist source and demands 48–50, **48–50**; educators in 54; environmental elements integration 52–53; Heilongjiang, China *43*, 43–47, *45, 46*; local resident health 54; microstimulation 41; multidisciplinary wellness team 53; physical planning and design 42; plants selection and optimization 52; post-secondary education 54; resources development 47; single tourism products 47; target markets destinations 55; tourist service facilities 48; users requirements 42; wellbeing promotion 42
health insurance policy 213
health resources: Autonomous Communities 213, 214; certification 212; consequentialist approach (*see* consequentialist approach); European Draft Report 211; health insurance policy 213; international mobility 212; passenger locator forms 212; PCR tests 212–214; social practice 217–218
Heilongjiang, China, wellness tourism 38; by foreign nationals **48,** 48–49; health benefits, warm and cold mineral springs 45–46; province 43, *43*; tourist source market 49–50, **49–50**; volcanic folk cultural resources 47; volcanic resources 44–45; Wudalianchi UNESCO Global Geopark 44, *45, 46*
Higgins-Desbiolles, F. 54, 242, 268, 270, 284
higher education (HE): Nordic types 130, **131**; *see also* tourism higher education (THE)
Holmes, K. 241
Holy Water Festival 47
Hoppe, T. 168
hospitality customers: accommodation business 33; international flights 19; Kenyan government 22; Malaysian tourism industry 21; monthly tourist numbers 19, *20*; monthly tourist rates 19, *20*; national flights 19; thematic analysis process 33; tourist rates by region 19, *20*; Turkey statistics 22–32; WTO 19, 21, *21*
hospitality industry: accommodation 58; AI 65–66; characteristics 59, *60*; COVID-19 uncertainty 63–64; domestic tourism 64, 67; food and beverages 58; metrics dimensions, pre and post COVID-19 64, **65**; Ministry of Tourism 60; pre–coronavirus 61–62; rebound back campaign 65; recreation 58; robotics technology 66; service and satisfaction 59–60; sustainable tourism 65, *66*; UNWTO 62
hospitality spaces, Sri Lanka tourism 235–236
Hughes, M. 241
Huyskens, M. 241
hybrid events 244
hygiene-oriented services 33–34

Indigenous-inspired spa tourism 40
individual tourism organisational behaviour 96
Information Communication and Technology (ICT) 244

Index

interdisciplinary partnerships 37
Internal Development Role (IDD) 111–112
International Federation of Red Cross and Red Crescent Societies (IFRC) 172
international flights 19, 63
International Halal Tourism Association (IHATO) 25
International Monetary Fund (IMF) 24
Internet-of-Things 94
Ioannides, D. 267

Jackson, M. J. 241
Jago, L. 241
Jamal, T. 22
Janowski, Ingo 40
Jiménez-Barreto, J. 273
Jung, Timothy Hyungsoo 150, 155

Karim, W. 21, 33
Katemliadis, Iordanis 2
Keleş, Hüseyin 3
Kim, Jung Hun 155
Kinnunen, M. 243
Kock, F. 118
Kotler, Philip 81–82
Krippendorf, J. 165
KwaZulu-Natal province, COVID-19 lockdown 14
Kwek, Anna 40

Laing, J. H. 241
Larsen, G. R. 184
Lee, C.-C. 267
Lee, Jung Hyo 155
Levy, Sidney 81–82
Lew, A. A. 211, 270
Leyen, Ursula von der 163
liability risks 74
Liberato, Dália 3
Liberato, Pedro 3
Limbado, Beatriz 3
Luna-Nevarez, Cuauhtemoc 156
Luonila, M. 243

Ma, S. 268
Magalhães, Maria José 2
Mair, J. 241
Majeed, Salman 42
Malaysian tourism industry 21
marketing/demarketing strategies, hotel operation 1, *88*; advantages 74; business clients 82–84; cleaning/sanitizing and longer stays 80–81; economic activity reduction 73; female business travelers 85–86; green hotel policies 86; housecleaners risk 87; limitations 87; operational cost 75; single room cost 75–79, **79**, *79*; social distancing 74
Marques, Susana 2
Marriot International India Pvt Ltd 60
Martin, Said 41
Maslow's Hierarchy of Needs Theory 180
MAXQDA program 2
McGovern, Enda 156
McMurtry, John 134
Medway, D. 246
Meetings, Incentives, Conventions and Exhibitions (MICE) industry 64, 231
Menezes, A. 243
Mensah, I. 60–61
Micro-Vlogging 2, 93, 97–98
Middle East Respiratory Syndrome (MERS) 198
Ministry of Tourism 60
Mohanty, P. 3, 241
Moreira, Gerardo 156
Morgan, Nigel 59
Morse, Joshua W. 39
Mphahlele, M. 14
multidisciplinary wellness team 53
Murray, C. J. 170
Musgrave, J. 241
mutual aid events 245

Naicker, P. R. 169
national flights 19, 63
National Institute of Health (ISS) 168
Navarrete, Pinos 37, 39–40
Needham, Roger 40
Negruşa, A. L. 241
Nelson, Andrew 116
Nepal, S. K. 55
Nicola, M. 21, 33
Niewiadomski, P. 267, 270, 271, 284
Nyagadza, B. 2

Oberoi Group of Hotels 60
Okech, R. N. 241
O'Neill, Martin 217
Organization for Economic Cooperation and Development (OECD) 10, 24, 270
ostensive demarketing 82
O'Sullivan, D. 241

Overall Destination Management (ODM) 112
overtourism 166, 175
Ozone disinfection systems 81

Padilla-Meléndez, Antonio 150
Page, Stephen J. 130, 132
Pakistan, STEs *see* small tourism enterprises (STEs)
Pallud, Jessie 150
Pamukçu, Hüseyin 2
Pan, T. 283
Parmar, B. J. 244
Parmet, W. E. 168
Parrish, D. 66
Partial Least Squares Structural Equation Modelling (PLS-SEM) analysis 150–151
Patel, Prahlad Singh 67
Patrick, Hosea 2
Pennington-Gray, L. 181
perceived ease of use 146, 147
perceived risk 181
perceived usefulness (PUS) 146–148
Peršić, M. 116
Personal Protective Equipment (PPE) 80
Piot, P. 170
Planet Happiness methodology 54
polymerase chain reaction (PCR) tests 212–214
post COVID-19 period 127; academic system 135; axiology and values 133–135; codes and themes 194, **194**; confinement phases 278, **280**; contamination prevention 200; crippling effects 268; critical content analysis 136; data selection and collection 135–136; demand 269–274, **281**; destination management 278, 280–281, **282**; destinations 201; domestic tourism 191, 194, 199, **199**; foundational philosophies 133; GDP 267; hospitality sector 200; mitigative measures 204–206; pandemic outbreak stages 195; Purposive sampling 193; representative sample 193; research context 129–130, **131**; research problem 128–129; research questions 129; research significance 129; responsibilities 192, 193; restrictions and protocols 198–199; rural tourism 202, **203**; social distance 201; socioeconomic transformation 190; stakeholders responsibility 1; sustainability and accountability 202, **202**; THE 130, 132–133, **137**, 137–138, **138, 139,** 140; tourism products and services 278, **279**; tourism sub-sectors 274, **275,** 276–278, **277, 279–281**; tourists' responsibilities 201–204; transnational transit limits 199; traveler responsibilities 204; travel patterns 195, **196–197**; uncertainties 195, **198**; values-rich components 136–137; WTO 190
Poulin, Daniel 40
pre-pandemic travel experiences/responsibilities 195
Presenza, Angelo 111
Prideaux, B. 268, 283
Pritchard, Annette 59
Public-Private and People Partnership 230
Public–Private-Partnerships (PPPs) 61
Purposive sampling 193
PUS *see* perceived usefulness (PUS)

Raj, R. 241
Ram, Yael 210
Ramkissoon, Haywantee 42
Rastegar, Raymond 219
Rauschnabel, Philipp A. 150
Rawls, John 216
reaching, business operations 230
rebranding strategies, sustainable tourism 1
Recuero-Virto, Nuria 3
redeveloping, business operations 230
re-employing, business operations 230
regaining, business operations 230
relativism 128
Renaud, L. 272, 283
reputational risks 74
Richter, F. 10
risk management strategy 80
robotics technology 66
Roehl, W. S. 181
Rosa del Aguila-Obra, Ana 150
Rothstein, M. A. 168
Rowen, I. 283
rural tourism 202, **203**
Rus, R. V. 241

Saadé, Raafat 147
Salloum, Said A. 146
Sánchez, M. M. 22
Sandel, Michael J. 217–218
sanitizing process 80

satisfaction 147, 148
Schroeder, A. 181
Scott, D. 22
SCPRT *see* South Carolina Dept. of Parks, Recreation & Tourism (SCPRT)
security and safety: after COVID-19 184–185; COVID-19 effects 183–184; destination 180–182; Maslow's Hierarchy of Needs Theory 180; normalization process 180; pandemic and tourism 182–183; tourism demand 179
selective demarketing 82
self-isolation 39
Seraphin, H. 243, 245
service industry *see* hospitality industry
ServQual model 243
Sesini, G. 284
severe acute respiratory syndrome (SARS) 9, 19, 198
severe acute respiratory syndrome coronavirus 2 (SARS CoV-2) 7, 8, 127, 239
Shao, Y. 268
Sharma, Anukrati 2
Shaw, Gareth 37, 39–40
Sheller, M. 59
Sherwood, P. 241
SIDs *see* Small Island Developing States (SIDs)
Simonite, T. 94
Singhania, O. 241
single room cost: CDC guidelines 76; direct revenue 75; guest capacity 78, *79*; guests per room 77; indirect revenue 75; maximum rate of guest occupancy 78, *79*; maximum return 78, **79**; occupancy rate 76–78; under reduced capacity 78
Sizoo, E. 165
Škare, M. 12
SLTDA *see* Sri Lanka Tourism and Development Authority (SLTDA)
Small and Medium Enterprises (SMEs) 2, 11, 15
Small Island Developing States (SIDs) 11
small sized tourism enterprises (SMTEs) 252, 253, 255
small tourism enterprises (STEs): acceptability and perception 259; conceptual framework *254*; cultural values 261; data analysis techniques 257–258, **258**; data and sample collection 255–256; definition 252; development 258; entrepreneur's response 254–255; limitations 262; lockdown and social distance 260; pandemic distortion 253; personal characteristics 262; reassessing with smart strategies 255; response and systematic analysis 259; response measurement procedures 256–257; stakeholders 252, 253, 259
SmartPLS 150
social distance 14, 74
social media 2, 68
social messaging 93, 98
social protection 231
socio-cultural, tourists' ethical obligations 192
Solunoğlu, Ali 3
Sönmez, S. 181
Sousa, Bruno 3
South Carolina Dept. of Parks, Recreation & Tourism (SCPRT) 66
Spanish flu 9
Sri Lanka tourism 3; consumer trust and regional corporation 233; COVID-19 pandemic, global impact 228–230; DMCs 232; with employees 233–234; hospitality spaces 235–236; implications 226–228; qualitative methodology 226, 232; remedial measures 225; research significance 225; resilience 234–235; stakeholders 233–234; sustainable recovery planning 230–232; tourism operations 226
Sri Lanka Tourism and Development Authority (SLTDA) 226, 233
stakeholders 1, 12, 54, 95, 117; destination branding 111, 112; destination management organizations 112, 116; resilience 234; small tourism enterprises 252, 253, 259; tourism higher education 132–133
STEs *see* small tourism enterprises (STEs)
sustainability, events tourism: bio bubble events 244, 247; certifications and labels 245; debate 241; demarketing events 245–246; economic leakages 241; hybrid events 244; ICT, events planning and management 244; mutual aid events 245; post COVID-19 242–246, *246*; re-designing physical

spaces 243; virtual events 243; vulnerability 242
Sustainable Development Goals (SDGs) 116, 117, 231
sustainable recovery planning, Sri Lanka tourism 230–232
sustainable tourism 65, *66,* 117; definition 113; destination rebranding strategies 115–117; goal of 112–113; management and planning 114–115; quality-of-service needs 114; rebranding, after COVID-19 110; social media 114; travel trade industry 113–114

Taj Group 60
target markets destinations 55
TBCSA *see* Tourism Business Council of South Africa (TBCSA)
Technological Acceptance Model (TAM) 145, 146; educational tools 147; managerial implications 155; PUS 146–148; theoretical contributions 154–155; tourism education 146; VR Tour Creator tool 147, 148, 154–156
Tedmanson, Deirdre 216
THE *see* tourism higher education (THE)
thematic analysis method 2, 33, 194
Theory of Planned Behaviour 146
thermal hydrotherapy 38
Thomas, Anila 3
Timmermans, Frans 174
Tiwari, Pinaz 3
TMA test *see* Transcription-Mediated Amplification (TMA) test
Toader, V. 241
Tourism, E. 241
Tourism Business Council of South Africa (TBCSA) 14
tourism destination 11
tourism higher education (THE): academic/practitioner divide 132; axiology 133–135; conceptualisation 132; curriculum 132; data sources 132; destination 138; development 140; epistemological arguments 133; extrinsic values 135, 140; faculty 137, **137**; foundational philosophy 133; in future, students questions 142–143; HE institutions 130; hospitality 140; intrinsic values 135, 140; management 138; non-essential movement and services 141–142; Nordic, number and type 137, **137**; Nordic languages 138, **139**; recognition 132; reductionism 132; research context 129–130, **131**; research intensive institutions 138, **138**; research problem 128–129; research questions 129; research significance 129; rigour 132; service 140; stakeholders 132–133; students studying programs 141; systemic values 135; terminology 132; theory 132

tourist service facilities 48
Transcription-Mediated Amplification (TMA) test 214
Travel and Tourism Council 228
Tsaur, S. H. 181
Turkey statistics 22; activities 30, *31*; case distribution, by country 23, **24**; case distribution, by regions 23, **23**; code system 28, *29*; confidence 30, *31*; COVID-19 cases 24, *24*; COVID-19 complaints 27; deaths in 24, *25*; IMF 24; MAXQDA program 28; precautions 26–27, 30, *30,* 32, *32*; psychology dimension 29; qualitative research methods 28; tourism demand 25; tourist arrivals 26; training, hotel staff 27; vacation decision 28, *29*; WHO data 23, *23*
Tzeng, G. H. 181

Ultraviolet devices, sanitizing equipment 81
Unified Theory of Acceptance and Use of Technology (UTAUT) 146
United Nations Sustainable Tourism Development Goals (UN SDGs) 37
United Nations World Tourism Organization (UNWTO) 61, 62, 113, 182–183, 229
United States Environmental Protection Agency (US EPA) 80
UNWTO Global Guidelines to Restart Tourism 109
urban environments 8

Violaris, John 2
virtual events 243
virtual reality (VR) 236; data analysis process 150–151; data collection 149–150, **150**; hypotheses testing and results **153**, 153–154; limitations 156; managerial implications 155–156; measurement model 150,

151; model 148, *149*; reliability and validity evaluation 152, **152–153**; student engagement and satisfaction 148; TAM 145, 146 (*see also* Technological Acceptance Model (TAM)); theoretical contributions 154–155; tourism postgraduate students 145; *see also* VR Tour Creator tool
Visiting Friends and Relatives (VFR) packages 67
Voice Search 2, 93
VR Tour Creator tool 145, 147, 148, 154–156

Wang, K. C. 181
Wang, Yue 2
Wanjala, K. 22, 33
Wattret, Kenneth 24
wellness tourism: annual growth 39; ecotourism continuum 40–41, *41*; healing gardens concept 37–38 (*see also* healing gardens, wellness tourism); Indigenous-inspired spa tourism 40; nature-based and adventure tourists 41; revisit 39; situational analysis 38; traveller aspirations 39; UN SDGs 38
Wen, J. 268
Williamson, Chris 24
women rate business services and facilities 85
World Bank's International Finance Corporation (IFC) 14
World Economic Forum 167
World Health Organisation (WHO) 7, 8, 19, 92, 163, 168, 170–172, 179, 194, 204, 210, 236; Turkey data 23, *23*
World Tourism Organization (WTO) 19, 21, *21*, 25
World Travel and Tourism Council (WTTC) 10, 61, 62, 172
Wu, Bing 146, 147, 150, 155
Wudalianchi UNESCO Global Geopark 44, *45*, *46*

Yang, Y. 269
Yaşarsoy, Emrah 2
Yayla, Özgür 3

Zenker, S. 118
Ziakas, V. 247

Printed in the United States
by Baker & Taylor Publisher Services